D0412962

INDIGENOUS ORGANIZATIONS
AND DEVELOPMENT

INDIGENOUS ORGANIZATIONS AND DEVELOPMENT

Edited by
PETER BLUNT

and

D. MICHAEL WARREN

With a Preface by
NORMAN UPHOFF

INTERMEDIATE TECHNOLOGY PUBLICATIONS 1996

Intermediate Technology Publications Ltd,
103–105 Southampton Row, London WC1B 4HH, UK

A CIP catalogue record for this book is available from the British Library

ISBN: 1 85339 321 5

Typeset by J&L Composition, Filey, N. Yorks
Printed in UK by SRP Exeter

Contents

PART II   INDIAN SUB-CONTINENT

PART III   ASIA–PACIFIC

Preface

This book brings together two emergent subjects in the literature on development which have begun receiving increasing attention in the past fifteen years—indigenous knowledge systems, and local organizations. This convergence maps out a new area of concern—indigenous organizations—which leads us to consider what they can contribute to self-managed and, we hope, sustainable improvements in people's lives. Having worked myself on the subject of local organizations, I am glad to see Mike Warren, who has contributed to our understanding of indigenous knowledge systems, undertaking here with Peter Blunt, and colleagues from around the world, an exploration of this researchable territory.

A good many social scientists, particularly anthropologists, have documented the existence and functioning of indigenous organizations over a number of decades. Their potentials for accelerating and spreading development opportunities have, however, not been very much analysed. A legitimate concern has been whether working with and through indigenous organizations might compromise their existence and effectiveness (e.g., March and Taqqu, 1986). There are dangers as well as potentials when getting engaged with social networks and relationships that are part and parcel of people's lives rather than something which they chose to join, so the subject needs to be approached with due respect and caution.

This volume begins the task of mapping out the subject of indigenous organizations, which deserves both more attention and clearer delineation. The editors have started with a rather broad definition. The case studies presented here range from organizations that are clearly 'indigenous', even primordial, with their origins going back indistinctly but certainly many generations, to organizations that are quite contemporary in their inspiration and modes of operation. The latter blend into the broader and more generic category of local organizations that have been analysed in Esman and Uphoff (1984).

The Self-Employed Women's Association (SEWA) in India, for example, discussed by Srinivas in this volume, is in my view one of the most wonderful and most effective people's organizations anywhere in the world. But its purpose and functions are not what most persons would regard as 'indigenous', even though it has shaped itself creatively and compassionately to the circumstances of its members, some of the most oppressed and needy people to be found (Rose 1992). Its bank, for example, has adapted to poor women's schedules and constraints, but it functions as a bank rather than as a rotating credit association, a form of indigenous organization found among poor women (and men) around the world (Geertz, 1962, Ardener, 1964; Kurtz, 1973).

Since there is value in considering indigenous organizations as a subset of the larger category of local organizations, in my opinion, the latter kinds of case studies, however interesting they are in their own right, are for present purposes less instructive than the former. The first end of the continuum mentioned above is social territory less understood and less appreciated. It offers students and practitioners of development some very rich opportunities for thinking through new approaches to the multiple tasks of improving human welfare.

In between these two ends of a continuum, but tending toward the latter end, are organizations that are distinctly modern but which are composed of and serve the interests of indigenous peoples. These can be considered as 'indigenous organizations' by virtue of their membership if not because of their origins, but I would prefer to limit the category of indigenous organizations to those that have autonomous if not necessarily ancient origins. These constitute a universe of experience that could provide many valuable lessons for mobilizing and sustaining collective action for self-help and self-management in the modern world.

The contributors to this volume present no consensus on the question of how such capabilities could or should be capitalized upon for development. One possibility is to enlist (some would say co-opt) indigenous organizations into the development process, through discussions and negotiations or through some provision of material incentives. Readers will immediately perceive this as a contestable approach. Less controversial may be patterning contemporary forms of local organization according to indigenous norms, roles and responsibilities, so that development undertakings will be more familiar and acceptable to local or indigenous people. In either case, knowing how indigenous organizations function, how their members understand them, and what their capabilities and limitations are is important.

Economic and social development is seen by some people as antithetical to the interest of indigenous societies and cultures, which would seem to make either of the above approaches objectionable. We should defend the rights of indigenous peoples to determine for themselves the extent to which they wish to engage with various streams of world culture. At the same time, we should guard against paternalism which undertakes to decide for other people what kinds of lives they should lead. Preservationism can be motivated by concern for our sense of loss if cultures that differ from ours become more like ours. People having grown up in indigenous societies, or at least some of these persons, may wish to adopt and benefit from certain aspects of world culture. In this case, outsiders should recognize the right of self-determination also in this regard.

The cases in this volume convey a sense of great variety and inventiveness of people's solutions to the multiple problems of meeting material needs and maintaining personal and social identity and security. This wealth of experience provides a veritable seed-bed of practices and beliefs from which many contemporary efforts to solve such problems could be enriched. Indigenous peoples usually have many needs and wants in addition to preserving their social, linguistic and cultural heritages. They want better health, more agricultural production, convenient water supply, more pleasing housing and clothing—so one finds areas of activity where there is considerable willingness to make changes in material culture. But this is not unconditional or absolute. The processes of economic and social change will thus usually be eclectic, much as the adaptations of indigenous organization to 'modern' purposes are likely to be tentative and experimental, often more implicit than explicit.

In indigenous organization, as with indigenous knowledge, one confronts the reality that practices and beliefs are not things to be decided on independently and separately. There is a quality of connectedness and embeddedness which distinguishes 'indigenous' things from 'modern' things, the latter in the Western analytical tradition to be separated from each other and judged independently.

This is to say that process is often more important than product within indigenous culture spheres. How things are done is more important than what is done, with great emphasis placed upon social relationships and preserving the harmony and integrity of the community and culture, more than on individual recognition or advancement.

This observation should not be overdrawn. It does not mean that there is no instrumental calculation within indigenous cultures. Indeed, for survival purposes there have been and must be. But we should be cautioned against taking a purely instrumental view of indigenous organizations, assuming that outsiders can 'mix and match' according to their purposes. Adjustments and adaptations are possible, but according to the perceptions and suggestions of the people themselves. 'Tradition' is not and never has been static, but it has survived because of its close fit to the needs, values and interests of the people who uphold it. Changes which are consistent with these needs, values and interests can well be accepted and promoted within indigenous organizations, but not because outsiders desire this.

Outsiders need to approach indigenous organizations very circumspectly both for normative reasons and because of the limitations of their knowledge. Social and cognitive realities are often different from what they appear to be at first, and outsiders may never fully understand the operative situations. In many societies, for example, women quite evidently defer to men in public decision-making. Yet the Kenyan description of the Gabra by Linquist and Adolph suggests that the wife of the keeper of the sacred drum may be the most important person in the whole society, having responsibility for maintaining social cohesion and security.[1]

Westerners have become enamoured with the concept of 'lifestyle', but this is a pale approximation of what indigenous people and traditional societies understand as 'way of life', a more deep-rooted concept and value. 'Way of life' provides the foundation from which indigenous organizations grow. Thus, the case study by Linquist on introducing (desired) veterinary services to nomadic communities in Kenya shows how problems arose from establishing a drug store that was permanent in one location. While other aspects of the collaborative programme were acceptable to nomads, this particular innovation required further modification before it could become effective. It was not that 'Western' veterinary medicine was unacceptable but that the mode of delivery had to be made compatible with more important aspects of community way of life.

While indigenous organization is often ignored or misunderstood, one should not conversely assume that it is ubiquitous, and therefore always important and available. We discovered when working in the Gal Oya region of Sri Lanka, where Cornell and Sri Lankan colleagues were expected to improve irrigation management through farmer participation in a large USAID-supported project, that there were no operative organizations. This was a settlement scheme where people had lived and worked in a situation of relative anarchy for most of 30 years. What organizations existed were 'modern' ones, mostly ineffective, introduced by the government. Yet the quick and impressive success we had in establishing participatory farmer organizations was greatly facilitated by the existence of a traditional institution called *shramadana*, through which people donated labour for some public benefit. This custom was not being practised because of the lack of social coherence and solidarity in the settlement scheme, but it could be resurrected and was utilized to begin the process of knitting together social bonds for common interest and mutual advancement. (Uphoff,

1992). Our ability to activate more co-operative and altruistic behaviour was greatly assisted by the memories and positive valuation of this indigenous custom, which made our modern local organizations at least partly traditional.

Another way in which indigenous organizations are characterized is as informal. This means that they function according to shared understandings of common objectives, roles, expectations, responsibilities, sanctions, etc. rather than being determined by explicit, codified rules and regulations. Informal organization can be very contemporary, and thus it is not necessarily 'indigenous' but it is likely to have echoes of indigenous beliefs and values and will be the stronger for this. Formal modern organizations can thus be strengthened in their performance if supplemented by informal, more traditional structures of roles and behavioural patterns.

This is indicated in the case study from India by Narayan, of the Jal Samitis, which complemented the local government (*panchayat*) structure. This is similar to the success of a bridge-building program in Nepal documented by Pradhan (1980), where informal committees within five years constructed 62 bridges in one of the most mountainous parts of the country, some of them up to 300 feet in length, at a fraction of the cost and in much less time than the government's public works department could manage. Similarly, the self-water supply programme in Malawi, which has now brought clean water to over a million villagers at a very affordable monetary cost, benefited from the sanction and support of chiefs in mobilizing local labour and management responsibility to construct and maintain these impressive systems (Hill and Mtawali, 1989). As in Nepal and India, *ad hoc* committees supplemented the formal organizational structure, and these operated in ways more 'traditional' than their local government sponsors.

The study of indigenous organization is likely to lead not to a co-optation of traditional roles and relationships for 'modern' development purposes so much as to a greater sensitivity by development planners, managers and evaluators (national as well as expatriate) toward the many options that exist for evoking and sustaining collective action. They can draw on the repertoire of relationships and responsibilities that already exist in the shared memory of local people, rather than assume that introduced forms of organization are either necessary or necessarily superior.

Local people are often quite quick and adept at adopting 'Western' organizational forms, as seen with the burial societies in Botswana, documented by Brown (1982). This reflects in part their very flexible capacity to organize collective efforts for the attainment of a variety of ends according to traditional practices and beliefs. 'Organization' is not something uniquely 'Western'. This means that outside persons, whether officials, NGO representatives or scholars, should be prepared to defer to local ideas and initiatives in the organizational realm. This means also letting local residents determine what kinds of roles and relationships should be established or enlisted to achieve particular development goals. The result may well be a hybrid of introduced and indigenous practices, but as least it will enjoy consensual support rather than at best grudging acceptance.

Albert Hirschman in his brilliant analysis of a number of projects in Asia, Africa and Latin America (1994) has argued persuasively that we should unterstand development as a process of—and growing capacity for—problem-solving. This makes the role of indigenous organizations in development all the more significant. We should know about and utilize the full repertoire of organizational modalities which can be drawn upon, by development professionals and local people, for encouraging and supporting capacities for problem-solving and self-management. This means we appreciate and respect all the more the range of mechanisms and precedents that have already been evolved for problem-solving over many generations by people living in far-flung and diverse communities around the world.

Norman Uphoff
Cornell University
December 1995

Note

1. Some of our Cornell research on quasi-indigenous organizations in the Yemen Arab Republic in the 1980s, the local development associations (LDAs) (Cohen *et al.*, 1982), found that in this male-dominated society, although the organizations were composed entirely of men, important decisions were commonly deferred from one meeting to the next to enable men to discuss matters over with women within their households before a vote was taken. This became more important as many male heads of households migrated to the Persian Gulf for wage employment, leaving households represented in the LDAs by an eldest son or a wife's brother or uncle. [This process of consultation was discovered by the female anthropologist on the team.] Indigenous organizations have often managed to maintain their stability and effectiveness over time through various and intricate balances, not all of them evident to external view. So outsiders need to be wary of seizing on any one element as causal or determinant, when it is the complex of elements which guides collective behaviour.

References

Ardener, Shirley (1964). The Comparative Study of Rotating credit Associations. *The Journal of the Royal Anthropological Institute*, 94.

Brown, Chris (1982). Locally-Initiated Voluntary Organizations: The Burial Societies in Botswans. *Rural Development Participation Review*, 3:3.

Cohen, John M., Mary Hebert, David B. Lewis, and Jon C. Swanson (1981). Development from Below: Local Development Associations in the Yemen Arab Republic. *World Development*, 9:11–12.

Esman, Milton J. and Norman Uphoff (1984). *Local Organizations: Intermediaries in Rural Development*. Ithaca, NY: Cornell University Press.

Geertz, Clifford (1962). The Rotating Credit Association: A 'Middle Rung' in Development. *Economic Development and Cultural Change*, 10:3.

Hill, Catherine B. and Katundu B. Mtawali (1989). 'Malawi: Lessons from the Gravity-Fed Piped Water Scheme'. In R. Bheenick *et al.*, ed., *Successful Development in Africa: Case Studies of Projects, Programs and Policies*. EDF Development Policy Case Studies No. 1. Washington: World Bank.

Hirschman, Albert O. (1994). *Development Projects Observed*. Washington: Brookings Institution. Originally published in 1967.

Kurtz, Donald (1973). The Rotating Credit Association: An Adaptation to Poverty. *Human Organization*, 32:1.

March, Kathryn and Rachel Taqqu (1986). *Women's Informal Associations in Developing Countries: Catalysts for Change?* Boulder: Westview Press.

Pradhan, Prachanda P. (1980). *Local Institutions and People's Participation in Rural Public Works in Nepal*. Ithaca, NY: Rural Development Committee, Cornell University.

Rose, Kalima (1992). *Where Women Are Leaders: The SEWA Movement in India*. London: Zed Books.

Uphoff, Norman (1992). *Learning from Gal Oya: Possibilities for Participatory Development and Post-Newtonian Social Science*. Ithaca, NY: Cornell University Press.

Acknowledgement

Most of the considerable amount of administrative work associated with compiling this collection was shouldered by Hemali Seneviratne at the Northern Territory University. Her natural good humour, her efficiency, unflappability, reliability and sound judgement made everything we had to do so much easier than it would otherwise have been. We cannot speak highly enough of her contribution to this book.

Introduction

The embryo for this book began its formation three decades ago when each of us began, in addition to our regular university duties, a long series of short-term and long-term international development consultancies. Our consultancies have taken us to several continents, but the focus has been Africa where we have worked in rural development, public sector management, governance and training in development planning and management for local-level institutions—primarily local government. In the beginning of these experiences the development paradigm tended to be influenced by the top–down transfer-of-technology approach. It was during this period that the assumption prevailed that development planning and management were Euro-American concepts that needed to be transferred to clientele groups. It did not occur to any of us to attempt to discover whether counterpart concepts existed in the languages of the clientele groups.

In the 1980s a development paradigm shift began with emphases on the concepts of participation in development decision-making by the clientele group, building the capacity of individuals and institutions in the development process, and the sustainability of development activities after project funding ceased. This paradigm shift generated interest in the nature of indigenous or local-level, community-based knowledge and how it provided the basis for both individual and community-level decision-making. As more indigenous knowledge systems were recorded, it became abundantly clear that a major element in the new development paradigm had been overlooked. By taking the time and effort to record key indigenous knowledge systems, an important bridge to mutual understanding and communication became available between the local communities and the development practitioners.

Also in the early 1980s a number of scholar–development practitioners such as David Korten (1980), Milton Esman and Norman Uphoff (see Esman and Uphoff, 1984; Uphoff, 1986, 1992a, 1992b) stimulated further insights into the development process by exploring the nature of local-level institutions and the role these could play in development. Uphoff distinguished 10 levels of development decision-making, the top five ranging from the international level to the sub-district level. The lowest two levels were those of the individual and the household. In the middle were the three local-level institutions, the locality level which was multi-community, the community level, and the group level which included a self-identified set of persons with some common interest . . . like a neighbourhood, or an occupational, age, gender, ethnic or other grouping (Uphoff, 1992b: 5). Uphoff also distinguished between the institution and an organization, an institution being a complex of norms and behaviours that persists over time by serving some socially valued purpose, while an organization is a structure of recognized and accepted roles (Uphoff, 1986: 8–9). He noted that institutions can be organizations, and vice versa. Marriage, for example, is an institution that is not an organization, while a particular family is an organization (with roles) but not an institution (with longevity and legitimacy). The family, on the other hand, is both an institution and an organization. We will be concerned here with institutions that have an organizational basis (Uphoff, 1992b: 4).

Our use of the term indigenous organization refers to those local-level institutions with an organizational base that are endogenous as opposed to exogenous within the community. Exogenous organizations are those that were established through forces external to the community such as Islamic and Christian youth groups, Western-oriented credit unions, Boy Scouts and Girl Guides and the Rotary Club. These are the types of organizations that are familiar to the outsider serving in the role of technical assistant in a development project.

What tend to be more invisible to the outsider are the indigenous organizations established through endogenous forces. These range from community-wide development planning associations, hometown associations that provide opportunities for citizens living in other communities to establish branches and remain in contact with the hometown, and traditional councils to traditional credit unions, and occupational groups such as palm-oil producers and yam-sellers' unions. One can also find women's organizations, ethnic associations, traditional religious groups and a wide variety of other social groups. When one analyses the structures and functions of these groups, one discovers a surprisingly formalized set of organizational structures that include election of officers, regularly scheduled meetings, written records of meetings and fee structures for members with bank accounts. In terms of functions, one almost always finds development activities as one of them. Many of these indigenous organizations are most inclined to have and to use local knowledge, to respond quickly to changes, to handle conflict and to create climates of opinion influencing behaviour (Uphoff, 1992b: 8).

In recent efforts to conduct development planning and management workshops for community leaders of indigenous and exogenous organizations (see Warren *et al.*, this volume) several important lessons have been learned. One is that basic planning and management concepts long held to be generated out of the Euro-American experience also exist in the local languages. This should not have been surprising to us given the fact that every community has problems and must have mechanisms for identifying and dealing with them. That means there should be concepts of problem, resources, objectives and goals. Further comparative research in a wide variety of languages used in developing countries indicates that these concepts appear to be universal. Second, local-level participants in these planning workshops have the capacity to analyse their own organizations in terms of strengths and weaknesses, as well as a willingness to experiment with new organizational structures to see whether they might address some of the expressed weaknesses. This is definitely the basis for institutional capacity-building at the local level.

In addition to the pioneering work of Korten, Esman and Uphoff, there are now many scattered practical examples which illustrate how good a marriage development assistance and indigenous organizations can make. An excellent recent addition to the literature analyses the role of various forms of rotating savings and credit associations (ROSCAs) as local-level self-help associations, many with ancient roots (Ardener and Burman, 1995). As far as we are aware, there has been no published collection which describes a wide range of types of indigenous organizations. This book sets out to fill this gap in the development literature. It is expected to complement the recently published book entitled *The Cultural Dimension of Development: Indigenous Knowledge Systems* (Warren, Slikkerveer and Brokensha, eds, 1995).

The studies we have assembled differ greatly from one another in many respects. They refer to different facets of development, involving technologies of varying levels of complexity. They recount experiences related by both scholars and development professionals in many different countries. Some are concerned with macro-level initiatives. Three chapters emphasize the problems that emerge when new organizations are superimposed on an indigenous organization (Linquist with Adolph on Kenya; Cosway and Anankum on Ghana), and where national policy and central control override the capacity of local-level organizations (McAllister on South Africa). Three chapters explore the importance of Nigerian hometown associations in local-level development based on local resources complemented by financial remittances by migrants from the community (McNulty and Lawrence, Kolawole and Wahab). The contribution by Wolff and Wahab explores the Yoruba occupational association that has supported the production of traditional Nigerian cloth with evidence that shows that government interventions are doomed to fail when they ignore pre-existing indigenous organizations. Several contributions explore the rhetoric of empowerment, helping people help themselves, versus the reality of ignoring local decision-making and organizations (e.g. McAllister for South Africa; Wolfe-Keddie for the Australian Aboriginals). The collection cuts across many sectors, including case-studies on pastoralists in Kenya (Linquist with Adolph), indigenous financial institutions in India (Shah and Johnson), rural development in China (Li, Li and Zhou), water and sanitation in Ghana (Cosway and Anankum) and India (Kumar), health in South Africa (Green and Zokwe), wildlife conservation in Indonesia (Colfer, Wadley and Widjanarti), and agricultural extension in the Philippines (Armonia). Two contributions explore the role of training of local leaders in the development context for Nigeria (Warren, Adedokun and Omolaoye) and Ghana (Cosway and Anankum). Srinivas explores what is entailed in understanding the nature of indigenous organizations, while Pokhrel and Willet describe an indigenous organization in Nepal.

The chapters are organized into the following geographical areas: Africa, the Indian subcontinent, and the Asia–Pacific Rim. The Asia–Pacific section includes a number of excellent contributions which deal with indigenous organizations in Australia (Wolfe-Keddie; Hughes), Canada (Dana), and New Zealand (van Meijl), where indigenous populations are still seriously disadvantaged in social and economic terms.

We believe this to be a fascinating and important collection in a relatively new and sparse field. The book should appeal to development workers and to students and teachers of development studies and, particularly, development management.

Peter Blunt and D. Michael Warren
July 1995

References

Ardener, S. and Burman, S. (eds) (1995), *Money-Go-Rounds: The Importance of ROSCAs for Women*, Herndon: Berg Publishers.

Esman, M. J. and Uphoff, N. (1984), *Local Organisations: Intermediaries in Rural Development*, Ithaca: Cornell University Press.

Korten, D. (1980), 'Community Organisation and Rural Development: A learning process approach', *Public Administration Review* 40: 5.

Uphoff, N. (1986), *Local Institutional Development: An Analytical Sourcebook, with Cases*, West Hartford: Kumarian Press.

Uphoff, N. (1992a), *Learning from Gal Oya: Possibilities for Participatory Development and Post-Newtonian Social Science*, Ithaca: Cornell University Press.

Uphoff, N. (1992b), 'Local Institutions and Participation for Sustainable Development', *Gatekeeper Series*, No. 31. London: International Institute for Environment and Development.

1 The drum speaks—Are we listening? Experiences in development with a traditional Gabra institution—the Yaa Galbo

B.J. LINQUIST with DAVID ADOLPH*

IT IS DUSK on the Dida Galgalo and the early evening light is filled with a golden dust raised from the hooves of thousands of returning sheep and goats. The plaintive sound of the oryx horn rises over the hungry bleatings of the kids and lambs as they welcome their mothers back after a day's grazing separation. The faint sound of camel bells can now be heard and in the dim light it is just possible to see lines of camels streaming homeward single file. As the camels draw close and prepare to enter their gates the voice of the keeper of the firesticks is heard welcoming the camels back into their enclosures and praying for the peace and the welfare of all the animals and people. It is the New Moon and on this special night the horn must be blown, camel-welcoming prayers must be said and the sacred drum must be beaten after all animals are safely inside. The Intermediate Technology Development Group (ITDG) team has just arrived on a project visit to its partners, the Yaa Galbo. There are things to discuss, plans to make, animal health training to arrange and other issues to address but there will not be time for any of that in the next two days as the ritual celebrations must always take precedence.

On another occasion, a two-day workshop had been planned at the Yaa Galbo, the date and agenda were chosen by the Yaa and ITDG together. On the appointed day the ITDG staff bumped two hours over enormous lava rocks only to find the site deserted. The Yaa had moved! The rest of the day was spent not in the planned workshop with the invited government guests but looking for the Yaa. As Thursday was a propitious moving day the Yaa had decided suddenly to move 45km away to an area of better pasture.

ITDG in Kenya has been working in partnership with the Yaa Galbo, the mobile ritual, political and administrative centre of the Galbo section since 1990. We will begin with a brief overview of Gabra social structure and culture in general and the Yaa Galbo in particular and then detail equally briefly the history of the partnership and conclude with a discussion of challenges encountered, and lessons learned.

The Gabra

The Gabra live in the northernmost part of Marsabit district in northern Kenya on the border with Ethiopia (Robinson, 1985; Torry, 1973). They are closely related

* B.J. Linquist, DVM, MPVM, is Project Veterinary Officer and her husband David Adolph is Project Officer for Intermediate Technology Development Group, Marsabit Project, Marsabit, Kenya.

to the Oromo peoples of Ethiopia and speak the Borana dialect of the Oromo language. The great majority of the 30000 Gabra live as nomadic herders in one of the harshest environments in Kenya. Here they not only survive but thrive due to the organization of their society and to the highly sophisticated herding strategies of their camels, sheep, goats and cattle. Successful livestock management depends on a high degree of mobility as water and grazing are all extremely variable in space and time. Gabra live in small mobile villages called *olla* with houses made of poles, skins and sizal mats, which can be quickly dismantled and loaded on to a camel. Villages as a whole will often move and also at times individual species will be sent out to distant pastures to a *fora* camp with the young men to exploit a particular resource good for that particular species.

The generation age-set system called *luba* is the superstructure on which Gabra social life depends. In brief, all men travel in their lives through six basic classes (married women take their husband's grade). The first two of these are informal *luba* grades: *ijolle* or children, and *k'ero* or those circumcised and unmarried. Then there are four formal grades: *kommicha* are junior elders concerned with defence; *yuba* are political elders whose main task is the common welfare; *dabella* are the ritual elders who concern themselves with the proper celebration of rituals; and the final grade is *jarsa*. These *jarsa* are the retired elders who are supposed to be men of wisdom and counselling. It is through this *luba* system that disputes are settled, watering points and range properly managed, livestock redistributed, and tradition watched over and maintained (Stiles, 1991).

The Gabra are also divided into five sections or phratries called *gosa* or *dibbe* (drums). These are the Gara, Alganna, Galbo, Odolla and Sharbana. They will refer to themselves on formal occasions as the people of the 'Five Drums'. Each of the five sections has a supreme ruling council of elders and officers who live together permanently in a mobile village called the *olla* Yaa. The Yaa is the village as well as the assembly the council forms. Each Yaa represents the phratry itself and is responsible for the regular performance of rituals which ensure the blessing of God on the whole phratry. The sacred symbols of the phratry, the sacred drum, the firesticks and the horn, are kept in the Yaa under the guardianship of three selected elders. The Yaa also holds the highest judicial authority and decisions made by the Yaa are final. Although the Yaa has officers and an elected and inherited hierarchy the ruling body functions corporately as a unit and decisions are the result of collective consensus (Tablino, 1989). Each of the five Yaas has a core area that they move in and there are many rules and proscriptions as to where they can be and when. They are not allowed however at any time to move into the core area of another Yaa. The Yaa Galbo core area is south of the Ethiopian border, west of Torbi, east of the Hurri Hills.

History of the partnership

ITDG is interested in exploring a variety of methods of technology transfer in development work with communities. ITDG works in different ways in its various projects, from providing a bit of technical advice to an ongoing community development project, to direct project implementation. ITDG, in partnership with Oxfam, had developed an approach to working alongside of pastoral institutions among the Turkana. It was thought that this idea needed to be developed further with a truly indigenous pastoral institution. Ideally this approach would be one which would allow the institution to identify and articulate its own priorities and thus to manage its own development.

To this end, ITDG made contact with a number of traditional institutions in Kenya during an initial investigative trip and after several field visits to northern Kenya found what seemed to be a promising development partner in the Yaa Galbo. A self-help group with members of the Yaa and government officials was registered with the Ministry of Culture and Social Services and, over the following year, general discussions developed into setting the priorities for project work. The Yaa set the first priority as animal health, the second as water resources development, and the third as livestock marketing. The decision was made to begin the work together on the first priority. The ITDG veterinarian spent one week with the Yaa using participative techniques such as ranking, mapping and group discussion to get a general idea of the important diseases and commonly used traditional and modern treatments. This was followed by a three-month study by Linquist to take a closer look at the animal health situation (Linquist, 1992). A livestock survey was begun and ethno-veterinary interviews conducted both with ordinary herders and animal healer specialists. A small building was erected as a drug store in Torbi, the nearest trading post, and two storekeepers were chosen by the Yaa. Based on the priorities of the Yaa and greater community, and the results of the ethno-veterinary survey, training materials on ectoparasites were written and practical participative herder training begun on the use of safe insecticides for ticks and fleas.

ITDG has been particularly concerned not to introduce a modern, costly drug where there is an effective local remedy or method of prevention. It has also been concerned not to use environmentally harmful toxic insecticides and has emphasized Kenyan-grown, safe and effective pyrethrum products. The goal in the project as a whole and in the training in particular has been to support local knowledge and practice.

In the past, training sessions have been on individual topics with just one session per visit to a particular village. Yaa representatives felt that this training was not happening fast enough and suggested that it would be better to train people from all the mobile villages in the area on a number of different diseases and drugs over a period of several days. This was scheduled for a time after the long rains became fully established. In July 1994 the Yaa hosted this programme and ITDG provided the trainers and training materials.

Several Yaa elders have also requested assistance from ITDG in documenting some of their stories and experiences and views within the Yaa. ITDG is excited about this collaboration and feels that it could have far-reaching effects in local Gabra society. This has begun and there are plans to put their stories into a multilingual booklet.

Challenges encountered and lessons learned

Differing scheduling perceptions
As was demonstrated in the first two scenarios, the Yaa's agenda does not always co-ordinate nicely with a development organization timetable. We have had to remind ourselves that our priorities are their priorities and part of institutional support is to affirm those things which make the Yaa strong and that involves proper observation of the rituals even if that necessitates a second visit or an extended visit. In the second example, we pointed out to the disgruntled government functionaries that ITDG and the Yaa are working together on animal health and good grazing is fundamental to that. The Yaa too have learned that ITDG cannot always make previous commitments due to vehicle

breakdowns or accessibility of a site. In response to the Yaa's request for a longer, more thorough training workshop, ITDG has tried to schedule a time for that with them as a significant amount of preparation is involved. As mentioned above, this has not yet been possible as the Yaa feel it cannot even be discussed until the rains have begun in earnest. We have had to be flexible and relaxed on this matter.

All project topics require a large amount of discussion. These discussions will often go on over a course of days or weeks before a decision is made. All males involved must have a say and in the end must agree or be persuaded before a decision can be made. For example, the Yaa wished to plant a medicinal hedge around their small drug store and ITDG agreed to give a grant of about US$30 to assist in the endeavour. It took three months for them to decide and implement the project which involved hiring four young people for two weeks. Unfortunately the rains had come and gone by that time and they are now doubtful whether the hedge will survive.

Appropriateness of project activities

Early on, in project discussions the ITDG visitor suggested that since animal health was the first priority the Yaa should build a drug store. Stores have been a focal point for some of the ITDG/Oxfam development work among the Turkana and have been a means of confidence building among disenfranchised, impoverished, semi-sedentarized victims of the 1984 famine. Unfortunately in the case of the Yaa Galbo 'the store' became synonymous with the ITDG project. Any other discussions or ideas paled in comparison to the thought of building the store, a permanent structure in a trading post. The idea alternately alarmed, fascinated and distressed these highly mobile herders.

In the original discussions, it had been agreed that the store would be built jointly by ITDG and the Yaa. As time went by, however, we came to realize that although the store stood as a symbol of the partnership between ITDG and the Yaa, the Yaa were not going to contribute to the building itself. (They did raise money for the actual stock of drugs.)

The store continues to cause worry and a sense of helplessness to the elders among the Yaa. How can the Yaa oversee it when they are often far away and constantly moving? The latest request was for ITDG to build a permanent house for the storekeeper right next to the store. The storekeeper and his wife are also pastoralists. He often moves far away with the sheep and goats although his wife stays in their traditional house in Torbi town. For the first year of the store's existence the storekeeper moved the stock into a metal trunk in his own traditional doorless house for safety as it was thought that the drugs would not be safe behind the solid wooden locked door in the stone building. Recently he has moved his little three-house village up to the store site and divides the drugs between his house and the store.

The major lesson learned from this has been that project activities with nomadic institutions should remain within the scope of nomadism if at all possible or at least not conflict with them. Because the store idea was unfamiliar and somewhat frightening it deflected attention from the project aims.

To do or to be?

The elders with whom ITDG made initial contact were the ritual elders or *dabella*. They are primarily responsible for Gabra religious life. Their major responsibilities are to discuss matters, pass news, and to be a moral force in the society. Thus the individuals with whom ITDG discusses project matters are not the ones who actually implement the work. A *dabella*'s main function is 'to be'. The 'doers', the *yuba* and *kommicha*, are in fact very busy much of the time herding, watering and travelling around, and as such have not been involved in many of the discussions about the project. They are theoretically informed of discussions, but there may be some slippage in information flow, particularly in new topics where precedents for passing the news are not yet in place.

We have found it remarkably difficult to schedule workshops and training sessions at the Yaa due to the Yaa's tight and full schedule of ritual months, weeks and days. Recently we passed through several months which were not propitious and we thought this might be a good time to do some of the more secular aspects of the project. Unfortunately, however, it was in the middle of a long dry season and animals and people were widely dispersed. The Yaa did not want to discuss any project work until after the rains were established.

Self-help group
It was originally thought imprudent to register a traditional institution with the Ministry of Culture and Social Services. Thus a self-help group was formed which included some members of the Yaa (but not all) and some members from the settled townspeople. It was not very clear to the Yaa or the government officials whose project this really was and early attempts were made by some of the government officials to co-opt the project for its perceived benefits. ITDG now wonders if it made a mistake in encouraging the formation of a Western-style development self-help group superimposed on top of an already existing group. We have thought it wise to de-emphasize the self-help group model and instead emphasize the Yaa.

Are women part of the project? Are women part of the Yaa?
Early ITDG visitors to the Yaa were men and thus sat in men's resting places and even prayed inside the *nabo* with the elders. As such there was no precedent or history of women being part of the discussions. We have got to know many of the women personally. Individually they said they were interested in the project, planned to attend the formal meetings, and wanted to be trained in the use of modern drugs, but in fact they do not attend the meetings although some women are now being trained. In fact, we realize that we do not really know yet if women are considered to be part of the Yaa. This is something we must look at much more closely in the following months. We did learn rather accidentally that the wife of the guardian of the sacred drum is called the mother of the drum, from which she is seldom allowed to go far. She must care for it and protect it and it is she and not her husband who must be in the *olla* Yaa on Thursday evenings to beat the drum. It was suggested to us that in some ways she is the most important person in the Yaa!

Project ownership
Although we have gone into some detail on specific problems in the history of the project there have been many good things. The idea of a permanent structure has been an unfortunate distraction to project progress, yet the idea of ownership of a drug supply has been taken up enthusiastically. Some of the townspeople might feel that it is ITDG's drug store, but the Yaa do not. They know it belongs

to them and they raised the money for the initial drug stock. They chose the storekeeper and although semi-literate he has done an excellent job of keeping records in his head, and managing the drug stock. He and his wife are good salespeople and take their part-time job very seriously. He has done almost all of the restocking himself and established various contacts in a businesslike fashion. All this, and he is not even getting a salary. He still moves at times with his animals in far pastures and when he does he takes medicines with him and leaves some behind in the trading post for his wife to sell.

There has also been much positive learning for the ITDG staff as well. We have learned to listen more and to appreciate the methods of decision-making. We have been very impressed by the Yaa's superior camel management. Local educated Gabra staff have learned much about their own culture and traditions of which they were largely ignorant because they were sent to boarding school at an early age. The educational system ridicules and dismisses the nomadic lifestyle as primitive and irrelevant to modern life in Kenya, which often serves to alienate the students irrevocably from their parents and lifestyle. Thus, we hope that the Gabra staff are also learning to value and respect their traditions through their involvement with the project.

Summary

In summary, ITDG, a British charity, and the Yaa Galbo, an indigenous Gabra institution, have been working in partnership since 1990. During the first two years, ITDG visits were infrequent and thus that time was largely spent on general relationship building and priority setting. In 1992, we were contracted to provide part-time local input to the project. An animal health project has been set up, training has been initiated, and a drug store established in the area which is functioning as the first generally reliable sustainable drug supply in the Gabra area. The partnership has not always been smooth or without misunderstandings and while ITDG might wonder if the Yaa will ever talk about how they are going to pay their storekeeper and if there will ever be time among all the rituals to organize the training, the Yaa wonder why the ITDG vet cannot always take the time to treat all the camels that need to be treated and what really does ITDG do in its work. Still it is a working partnership and we hope that in the long run ITDG might be able to assist the Yaa with development initiatives which restore a sense of value in the time-honoured survival strategies that the Gabra have been abandoning. The Yaa in turn will assist ITDG to understand the process of development in a true partnership.

References

Linquist, B.J. with Adolph, D. (1992), *A Look at the ITDG Marsabit Project: A Short Sojourn with the Yaa Galbo*, Nairobi, Kenya: ITDG.

Robinson, P.W. (1985), *Gabbra Nomadic Pastoralism in Nineteenth and Twentieth Century Northern Kenya: Strategies for Survival in a Marginal Environment*, Evanston, Illinois: Northwestern University.

Stiles, D. (1991), 'The Gabbra Jilla', *Kenya: Past and Present* 23.

Tablino, P. (1989), *Time and Religion among the Gabra of Kenya*, Marsabit, Kenya: Marsabit Catholic Parish.

Torry, W.I. (1973), *Subsistence Ecology Among the Gabra: Nomads of the Kenya/ Ethiopia Frontier*, New York: Columbia University.

2 Traditional settlement, cultural identity and rural development in the Transkei

PATRICK A. McALLISITER*

Settlement patterns in the Transkei: 1800 to 1940

IN THE PRE-COLONIAL period, indigenous settlement in the Transkei was determined largely by the nature of the environment, which was characterized by 'small-scale repetitive configurations that contained a variety of natural resources' (Sansom, 1974: 140). Each small area within a tribal territory was similar, containing within it the resources needed for subsisitence according to the southern Bantu pattern—primarily arable land, grazing for livestock, perennial water, fuel, an area within which to hunt and gather, and access to resources such as thatching grass. Sansom has characterized this as the 'Eastern' (primarily Nguni) ecological adaptation, found right across southern Africa's eastern seaboard, between the escarpment of the Drakensberg and the sea, and he refers to the economy associated with it as one of 'contained investment' (ibid.: 135). Settlements were dispersed over the tribal territory (i.e. homesteads were widely scattered and not concentrated into villages) and subsistence activities were confined to the areas near the homesteads. The eastern 'unit of exploitation' was 'a small, concentrated area, containing the full range of natural resources that individuals wished to exploit' (ibid.: 139). Economic relationships were similarly concentrated. The inhabitants of each local area pursued their subsistence activities more or less independently of those in other areas.

This type of adaptation was associated with a decentralized political, judicial and administrative system, and with a high degree of local autonomy. Although each tribal area was under the overall authority of a chief (or paramount chief), ecological conditions were suited to local regulation of resources. The chiefdom was divided into economically self-sufficient districts, under sub-chiefs or headmen, the boundaries between districts being natural markers such as rivers. But even within a headman's area, further decentralization was possible, because 'repetitive configurations allowed definition of tiny areas associated with neighbourhood groups or kraals within a district' (ibid.: 140). Such groups often consisted of close kin, under the leadership of a senior agnatic kinsman. Rights to grazing, arable land and other resources were allocated on the basis of membership of the local group, though ratified by the headman and, ultimately, by the chief. In many parts of the Transkei, even today, this local group is called *ummango* (plural: *imimango*), literally a 'ridge', and consists of a group of homesteads occupying a small local area. Homesteads were usually located on hilltops or ridges, on land not particularly suited for cultivation, overlooking or near to their arable lands situated in the river valleys below, or on sheltered hill slopes (Kingon, 1915; Shaw and van Warmelo, 1972–81: 229–34). Typically, grazing was also found nearby, the cattle going out to graze each morning, and returning to the byres adjoining homesteads each evening.

---

* Patrick McAllister, a social anthropologist, is currently Research Professor and Director of the Institute of Social and Economic Research at Rhodes University, Grahamstown, South Africa.

Socially and economically, this produced a kind of 'inwardness' in terms of exploitation of basic resources (Sansom, 1974: 141). Homesteads near each other co-operated economically, especially with regard to grain production. Labour was offered on a reciprocal basis, though production was the business of an individual homestead. Livestock, too, were associated with a local group and herded collectively, though each homestead had its own particular animals. This helped to emphasize the unity and corporateness of the local group, which was often a kin group or based on a core of close kin. In some cases it may have consisted of a single extended family inhabiting a single, large polygynous homestead numbering between 10 and 40 huts.

The crops grown included sorghum and a variety of pumpkins and gourds. Milk was the staple, however, rather than grain, and the environment was able to support a relatively dense livestock population. This made possible differences in wealth, and also a complex network of social ties and obligations based on debts in livestock, since cattle were needed for bridewealth and for other purposes such as ritual, transport and food. Conflicts caused by incidents such as cattle trespassing into arable land were resolved at the local level, between neighbours (though recourse to the headman's, and ultimately the chief's, court was possible). Even the rituals associated with the seasons were celebrated locally and not synchronized at the tribal level, as with Sotho and Tswana speakers in the interior of the country.

In addition to the low-lying fields, many homesteads also had small, fenced gardens nearby, often on a fertile old kraal site, in which crops such as tobacco were grown. The fields, too, were fenced to keep out wild animals, but such fences were broken down at the end of the harvest, the lands effectively reverting to commonage, with cattle allowed to graze on the grain stubble in the winter months (Shaw and van Warmelo, op. cit.). Soils were relatively infertile, and old land was fallowed after a number of years and new fields established. This practice both maintained productivity at the desired level and prevented serious damage to the environment. From time to time homesteads split as sons moved out to establish their own homesteads nearby, sometimes on virgin territory. The political system as a whole was one 'geared towards expansion', and the sons of chiefs often broke away with their followers to establish a new chiefdom on new land (Peires, 1981: 53). People were able to cultivate as much land as available labour made possible, the right to such land being obtained simply by breaking the soil (Shaw and van Warmelo, op. cit.). Most of the agricultural work was done by women, men being involved primarily in clearing the bush off new lands.

The colonial period

During the colonial period a variety of significant changes took place in the Transkei, which affected both political and economic life, and necessitated certain ecological adaptations on the part of the people. As in other parts of Africa and Asia, colonial policies 'undermined traditional rural economies and forced African land users to maximize their use of land and skimp on conservation measures' (Blaikie and Brookfield, 1987, cited in Andrew, 1992). This process has been well documented for Xhosa-speaking people (e.g. Beinart, 1982; Peires, 1981; Craizi, 1992) and will thus be summarized only very briefly here. Restrictions on movement combined with pressure from white settlers and frontier wars limited the extent to which new land could be occupied from the late eighteenth century onwards. Much of the land occupied by Xhosa speakers was steadily taken from them which, together with increasing population, placed great pressure on available resources. From the mid-nineteenth century onwards, the demand for labour shaped a good deal of state policy, and various measures were designed to force peasants to leave their rural homes temporarily and to enter the labour market. Such measures were not altogether successful, partly because many peasants were able, in the period from about 1880 to 1910, to expand production to meet the demands of a growing economy. The introduction of iron hoes and of the plough made it possible to cultivate larger areas than previously, and production was increased to take advantage of favourable market prices. The plough was drawn by oxen, and this brought men into cultivation to a much larger extent than before, because women were not permitted to handle cattle. Women, however, still did the bulk of work such as hoeing and harvesting (Shaw and van Warmelo, op. cit.). Large increases in grain and livestock production took place in the Transkei right up to the 1930s, despite various setbacks such as rinderpest in the 1890s and East Coast fever in 1911, both of which decimated the herds and seriously affected production. Recovery was possible through temporary involvement in wage labour, with earnings invested back into cattle holdings and grain production.

The period of greater output lasted until the 1930s. It could not be sustained due to a number of interrelated factors: pressure on land due to growing population; restrictions on movement and other state policies (e.g. the Native Land Act of 1913, the removal of squatters from white Eastern Cape farms); land deterioration and overgrazing; increased pressure to enter the cash economy and dependence on migrant labour; competition from white farmers; lack of agricultural inputs and state support for agriculture in the reserves; droughts and other natural calamities. From about 1935 there was a marked increase in the number of migrants seeking work, and from about 1940 onwards agricultural production in the Transkei dropped (Andrew, 1992).

There were also important changes affecting homesteads and therefore the nature of settlements. From at least the late 1800s, if not before, the size and composition of Cape Nguni homesteads changed quite markedly (Hammond-Tooke, 1975: 82–3). Formerly, the large homesteads consisting of up to 40 huts and inhabited by an extended family were economically self-sufficient. Each homestead had enough stock and access to enough labour, and was managed by a male head, whose sons were dependent on him for their subsistence and for wives, since he controlled the cattle holdings (Hunter, 1936: 25; Beinart, 1982: 94ff; Hammond-Tooke, 1962: 35; Wilson *et al.*, 1952: 52–9; Wilson, 1981). A number of related factors led to a marked decline in homestead size. Land shortage and population pressure led to a general shortage of arable land. Since a man with his own homestead would have a greater claim to a field than one living in his father's homestead, it was to the advantage of a newly married couple to establish their own homestead as soon as possible. Homesteads may also have become smaller due to a decline in polygyny under Western and Christian influence, and because it was no longer necessary to concentrate for defensive purposes, which was itself related to the erosion of the power of chiefs by the colonial authorities. Finally, wage-earning opportunities and Western influence (e.g. notions such as individual property) may have fostered the growth of individualism. Wage labour enabled sons to become economically independent of their fathers and to establish their own homesteads earlier in life.

Coinciding with the above were changes in the nature and organization of rural production. The older, larger homesteads had a number of fields, at least one for each 'house' in polygynous homesteads (for a discussion of the 'house property complex' see Sansom, 1974), in which the main crop was sorghum. Each homestead also had cattle and other livestock, to provide milk and other products. The smaller homestead became associated with only one field, and the emphasis in agricultural production shifted from sorghum to maize. This suited the smaller homestead and allowed it to maintain its yields. Maize, unlike sorghum, allows for intercropping with subsidiary crops such as beans and pumpkins, and it is less labour intensive. Daily labour in the fields was not required, except for weeding and harvesting, which, along with the initial tilling, called for 'intensive inputs of labour at widely spaced intervals' (Beinart, 1982: 100). In many parts of the Transkei, maize production increased rapidly (see Hunter, 1936: 357).

The system that evolved depended, first, on access to oxen and ploughs, and thus on the wage earnings of migrant workers. Second, due to the smallness of most homesteads and the nature of the homestead development cycle, as well as growing shortages of livestock, the new system depended on collaboration between homesteads, both for access to oxen and ploughs, and for the 'intensive inputs of labour' mentioned above. Individual homesteads pooled their resources at critical periods of the agricultural cycle, through the formation of work parties and collaborative ploughing groups. In this the old relationships based on kinship and neighbourhood remained important, and it was the homesteads of a common locality, which had fields and grazing in the immediate vicinity, which co-operated (Shaw and van Warmelo, op. cit., 228–9). Dependence on neighbours was also necessitated by the absence of men as labour migrants. If a homestead head, in particular, was absent, someone had to be delegated to make production and other decisions in his place. Often this was a brother or other close agnatic kinsman living in a nearby homestead, but any good neighbour would do (McAllister, 1985). Even if the caretakers were kin, however, the point is that they were *neighbouring* kin. As Hunter (1936: 60) observed among the Mpondo of north-western Transkei, 'the more *imizi* [homesteads] subdivide the more kinship bonds tend to be replaced by ties binding neighbours'. Paradoxically, the principle of 'good neighbourliness', present from time immemorial, became even more important in the new adaptive mode, despite (and because of) the growth of individualism and the fragmentation of extended family homesteads. The ideology associated with a closely knit, economically independent extended family based in one homestead gave way to one of greater individualism, with smaller autonomous homesteads mutually dependent. Adjoining homesteads, now closer together than when homesteads were larger, because of land shortage, provided the basis of socio-economic interaction. These changes were reflected in corresponding changes in ritual and ceremonial life (McAllister, 1985).

During this period there was also a change in architectural style. When Xhosa speakers first encountered travellers and traders from Europe (in the sixteenth century) they lived in beehive-shaped huts consisting of saplings bent and bound together and covered in thatch (Shaw and van Warmelo, op. cit.). Similar huts can still be seen in parts of Zululand, and in the huts that Xhosa speakers build every year for the seclusion of male initiates. They were relatively impermanent, easy to dismantle and to reconstruct a distance away, in accordance with the nature of shifting cultivation and the semi-nomadic lifestyle of the era. As residential land became scarce and homestead structures more permanent, such huts gradually gave way to circular wattle and daub structures with low, thatched roofs, which in turn evolved into the more substantial mud-brick hut with a high-pitched, thatched roof, which is common today.

An important aspect of the maintenance of rural production, now in modified form, concerns state policy. Successive governments in South Africa, in both the nineteenth and twentieth centuries, were concerned to capture the labour power of the rural black population but at the same time to prevent large-scale black urbanization. The institution of a migratory labour system (through taxes and other coercive measures) and various restrictive policies designed to keep blacks in the rural areas, served to ensure, in some areas at least (large parts of Transkei among them), that a degree of rural production continued while blacks partici-pated in the cash economy as labour migrants. In time the two types of economic activity became intertwined, with rural production dependent on the cash inputs of labour migrants, and the migrant labour system being 'subsidized' by the fact that migrants had a rural base to fall back on for social security and in hard times. It has also been argued (Mayer, 1980; McAllister, 1991) that the terms under which they were forced to participate in the wider political economy fostered a conservative 'ideology of resistance' among rural Xhosa, characterized by a strong adherence to 'tradition' and a rural agricultural lifestyle. The relations of production based on local corporateness, as outlined above, were an important aspect of this ideology, since they made subsistence agriculture possible.

The political and administrative system, too, though used, distorted and adapted by the state for its own ends, did not lose its pre-colonial character completely. In terms of the Bantu Authorities Act of 1951, districts were divided into Tribal Authorities, usually under a chief, each consisting of a number of Administrative Areas or wards, under sub-chiefs or headmen. Headmen and chiefs were responsible to the district magistrate, and heads of Tribal Autho-rities were also members of a wider Regional Authority. Wards were informally divided into territorially based sub-wards, each under a sub-headman, and the various sub-headmen sat on the Tribal Authority, which performed both admin-istrative and judicial functions under the chairmanship of its chief. Sub-wards were essentially local groups, consisting of between 40 and 100 homesteads. Often, they were dominated by a particular clan, though they invariably included members of a variety of clans. In at least some Transkei districts, sub-wards were further sub-divided into named sections. These were neighbourhood groups of between 20 and 40 homesteads, often consisting largely of members of a single agnatic group and their wives and families. Larger sections were further sub-divided into even smaller neighbourhood groups, similar to the *imimango* mentioned above, the homesteads on a single ridge or small common residential area.

In this structure, the headman devolves authority over issues such as land to his sub-headmen, who rely, in turn, on the advice and opinion of senior men within their sub-wards. In effect, decisions concerning matters such as the allocation of arable land and homestead sites, and the control of grazing and other resources such as thatching grass, rests with these men. Since questions concerning land, grazing and other resources are the concerns of local groups (sub-ward sections), such groups have a good deal of say in these matters. The sub-headman consults with them, obtains the approval of the people of the sub-ward as a whole for decisions made, and the chief/headman often merely rubber stamps the decisions made at the lower level.

It is also at the level of sub-ward and sections of sub-wards that co-operative work such as the formation of ploughing groups and work parties is organized. The homesteads within a sub-ward section co-operate closely in their everyday economic activities, in which an ethic of mutual help and reciprocity plays an important part.

From fields to gardens

From about 1940 onwards, a further important adaptation started to take place in many parts of rural Transkei, due to the pressures on rural producers. Land shortage and population pressure started to take their toll on arable lands, situated in river valleys and the low-lying areas. It became impossible to leave some of these areas fallow while others were being worked, previously marginal land was brought under the plough (Andrew, 1992), and the same fields were used year in and year out. Fertility naturally declined. People responded to this situation by slowly ceasing to cultivate their fields and starting to develop the gardens next to their homesteads instead. The flexibility associated with traditional land tenure and the scattered settlement pattern facilitated this. The right to a homestead site included the automatic right to a garden, and there was no restriction on the size of this garden. Thus, as long as they did not infringe on the rights of their neighbours, homesteaders were free to develop gardens as large as their labour and other resources would allow. The fact that homesteads were spread out along ridges meant that there was usually enough space to facilitate this, and it also meant that the gardens so developed were usually on the slopes below the homesteads.

In an analysis of aerial photographs of the Shixini administrative area in Willowvale district, Transkei, Andrew (1992) has shown that the percentage of homesteads with adjoining gardens increased from 26 per cent in 1942 to 61 per cent in 1962 and 84 per cent in 1982. By 1990, the figure was 90 per cent. Mean garden size also increased, from 0.2088 hectare in 1942 to 0.4191 hectare in 1982. This represented an increase in the area under garden cultivation from 30 hectares in 1942 to 327 hectares in 1982. At the same time, the area being used as fields decreased from 1 327 hectares in 1942 to 650 hectares in 1982, although the area of fields being fallowed increased only slightly from 579 to 639 hectares over the same period.

Clearly, an attempt was being made to change cultivation practices and maintain production. Although the total area of arable land decreased and population increased, the number of homesteads rose from 501 in 1942 to 585 in 1962 and 836 in 1982. It is likely that per capita livestock holdings also fell over this period. From the 1940s onwards the number of livestock per capita fell in the Transkei, and Andrew's analysis reveals that the size of livestock byres became progressively smaller in Shixini between 1942 and 1982.

Apart from declining fertility and the lack of land on which to establish new fields, the decline in homestead size and the shortage of cattle probably made it difficult to keep using fields. Gardens were easier to work, being smaller than fields and next to the homesteads, making them easily accessible and requiring less labour. They were also easier to manure from an adjoining byre, and to protect, since they were fenced and fields were not (the practice of fencing fields probably ceased as the wildlife disappeared from the Transkei). The soils on which gardens were established were relatively fertile and loamier than the soil in fields, making for better moisture retention and less susceptibility to drought

(Andrew, 1992). Furthermore, intercropping was more feasible in gardens, and was practised extensively, which helped to minimize erosion and maintain soil fertility. Maize monocropping was common in fields. Finally, the boundaries of fields were fixed and immovable, while gardens could be extended or moved, often to incorporate a fertile old kraal site. In this way, garden cultivation was similar to the practice of shifting cultivation in the past.

Some people, invariably wealthier homesteaders, continued to use their fields as well as gardens, but to many the gardens became vital for production. Although generally smaller than fields, some homesteads developed gardens large enough (up to two hectares or more) to take the place of fields, and because of better soil fertility and other factors, even smallish gardens produced higher yields than did the overused fields (McAllister, 1979).

Betterment planning

From about 1945 onwards, the state started to make a direct impact on the nature of settlement and subsistence in rural Transkei. The most extensive form of intervention in rural areas was known as 'betterment planning' or 'rehabilitation'. It refers to successive attempts by various central and 'homeland' governments to, *inter alia*, combat the deterioration of natural resources and contribute towards the agricultural development of black rural areas. The following basic steps were usually involved:

○ Proclamation of a given area (usually a rural ward/Administrative Area) as a betterment area.
○ The development of a land use plan for the area, which included the division of the land into three types: residential, arable and grazing.
○ The relocation of people from their previous dispersed homesteads into the new, surveyed, villages.
○ Fencing of villages and grazing camps, and the introduction of measures such as contour ploughing and rotational grazing.

The plans sometimes also included provision for water supplies, agricultural extension services, livestock improvement, soil-erosion works, and so on. In later years such provisions were seldom implemented, and in the Transkei, at least, even basic materials such as fencing have been forthcoming with less and less frequency. Older plans made provision for development projects such as dairying schemes and small-scale irrigation works, but most of these, also, were never implemented. The original aims of 'rehabilitation' and agricultural development were soon abandoned due to shortages of funds and personnel, and after the National Party came to power in 1948 the policy shifted to one of 'stabilization', which aimed at the prevention of further deterioration rather than rehabilitation and development. With Transkei 'self-government' in 1964, betterment schemes became the responsibility of the Transkei administration, which continued with the policy of 'stabilization', though with less and less money. The result was that most betterment schemes in the Transkei involved the movement of people into villages, the excising of old lands and the demarcation of new fields, the establishment of grazing camps, and nothing more.

The results of betterment may be outlined as follows.

Residential relocation
People not living in the areas demarcated for villages had to relocate. This meant abandoning the old homestead site and reconstructing a new one in the new area.

This involved considerable cost. Compensation was inadequate or not forth-coming at all. Households which moved found themselves living next to relative strangers in the new areas. Groups of close kin who inhabited a common local area were broken up and well-established relationships based on occupation of a common locality were destroyed (O'Connell, 1981; Bigalke, 1969). This ser-iously affected local economic activity, which depended largely on an ethic of mutual help and co-operation, and in which reciprocal ties between kin and neighbours featured prominently. As illustrated above, this had evolved from the pre-colonial settlement system.

Spatial reorganization

The spatial reorganization associated with betterment usually meant that old territorial units based on common locality became irrelevant. The old sub-ward and sub-ward sections were merged in the new villages. The effects of this may be summarized as follows:

○ disruption of the existing political organization, which was based on territorial divisions and the relationships between these divisions (e.g. the sub-wards of the ward/Administrative Area, and the sub-ward sections);
○ coinciding with this were the loss of autonomy and control (e.g. over land) by local communities and the imposition of centralized, state control in its place;
○ destruction of economic relationships between sub-wards and sub-ward sec-tions.

Agriculture

Initially, betterment did involve fairly careful planning, but with the switch to 'stabilization' this soon deteriorated into a superficial exercise. Apart from problems such as excising land which was still productive and demarcating as new arable land areas which were totally unsuitable for agriculture (McAllister, 1989), the general effect of betterment in many areas was to reduce the total amount of arable land available (de Wet, 1989).

Furthermore, in areas where large gardens had been established to compensate for the declining fertility of fields, homesteads lost these gardens because they had to move to new, smaller 0.25-hectare sites in the villages, and existing householders in these areas had to reduce their garden size to conform to the new site boundaries. This was a serious setback to agricultural activity. Even for those who were allocated new arable land, turning such land from virgin grass-land into productive plots took time and money, and it has been recorded that betterment schemes, for reasons such as this, *discouraged* investment in agri-culture (O'Connell, 1981). Whisken (1991, cited in Andrew, 1992: 90) has shown that the implementation of a betterment scheme in Nqabarhana Admin-istrative Area in Willowvale district inhibited the switch to garden cultivation and slowed down the abandonment of fields, due to the allotment of new fields under the scheme. However, field cultivation continued to decline (without the corresponding development of gardens) probably due to factors such as the absence of labour and other resources required to use the new fields.

Ecology

Betterment was based on an assumption that rural people were ecologically naïve and did not exercise any control over their natural resources. In fact, as

Sansom (1974) showed, the pre-colonial settlement patterns of indigenous peoples in South Africa were well adapted to the nature of the environment and made ecological sense. It has also been shown that even today, where the residence pattern is still relatively undisturbed, rural people attempt to exercise control over resources such as land, wood, grass and water through the organizational structures based on territory and neighbourhood (Heron, 1990; McAllister, 1989). Betterment broke down these structures and thus the mechanisms through which at least a degree of environmental regulation took place.

In general, recent and existing betterment plans in the Transkei contain no provision for rehabilitation or conservation works and betterment has contributed towards environmental deterioration rather than towards conservation. There are a number of reasons for this apart from the ones already mentioned. The concentration of people into villages led to over-exploitation of nearby grazing, wood and water resources, and to the formation of erosion gullies along footpaths in and around the new homestead sites. The establishment of rotational grazing camps does not seem to have improved the supply of grazing either because the required extension work to institute and manage such schemes was not forthcoming, because fences were not maintained, or because the funding for fences was not made available in the first place. Another reason for lack of improvement to grazing was the establishment of the new villages on what were formerly grazing areas, and the unjustified assumption that areas excised as arable land would naturally resort to grazing in due course.

The Transkei Agricultural Development Study

The 'Transkei Agricultural Development Study', released in July 1991 as a Transkei government 'policy document', is a review of agricultural development in Transkei, and contains a variety of recommendations for a new agricultural development policy. These need to be evaluated both against the background of previous attempts at land use planning and rural development in the Transkei, and in terms of the adaptations made by Transkeians themselves prior to betterment.

In asking why agricultural development has failed and providing recommendations and strategies to facilitate such development in the future, an argument is presented that goes something like this. To promote agricultural development in Transkei the emergence of 'commercial' farmers is needed in the rural areas, to take the place of what is now 'subsistence' and 'sub-subsistence' agriculture. To do this, go-ahead farmers must be able to gain access to enough arable land to enable them to produce a surplus for the market. They are prevented from doing so by the system of communal tenure and the associated principle of 'one man, one lot', which allows land to be held by people who do not use it productively. Many of these landholders are away as migrant workers, others are incapable of or not interested in farming effectively. Nevertheless, they hold on to their land for security.

A related problem, it is argued in the study, is that of unlimited and free access to commonage grazing on the part of livestock owners. This practice means that only some people (the owners of livestock) benefit from this communal resource, and not others. Furthermore, it encourages livestock owners to accumulate as many animals as possible, irrespective of whether the veld can sustain them or not. This leads to problems of overgrazing and erosion, and inhibits the development of a viable livestock industry.

Four land reform measures are proposed to rectify these problems:

o 'The introduction of freehold title for residential land in selected, well-serviced, residential villages (preferably one in each Administrative Area) to provide security and decent facilities for the non-farmers.' The assumption is that people who are currently 'sub-subsistence' and 'token' farmers, when offered freehold title and other facilities designed to ensure their social security in such villages, will give up their arable land and take up residence in the villages.
o 'The promotion of rental agreements providing secure tenure on arable land.' Initially, such agreements would be between individuals who no longer want to use their arable land (e.g. those moving into villages) and those who wish to farm, but later the rental agreement would be between land users and the local authority which would eventually manage all land.
o 'The payment of economic grazing fees for all animals on the commonage grazing land.' This would, it is assumed, assist with the reduction of livestock numbers and the development of a more viable livestock industry (e.g. beef and dairying).
o 'The retention of all monies raised by rents or grazing fees for local use' (pp. 178–9).

Linked to this are certain other proposals designed to decentralize the administration and financing of rural development. It is suggested that existing taxes be replaced with a tax on earnings, as a condition for retaining rights to land and other resources, the right to social security (though what this means is not spelt out), and the right to membership of a local community with a say in local affairs. This money, together with the monies specified under the second and third proposals above, would be administered at the local level, by a revamped local government structure concerned specifically with development issues and which paralleled the Tribal Authority system. The latter would not deal with development issues. These 'Development Committees' (or whatever name is given to them) would liaise directly with the central government on development matters.

Before making some assessment of these recommendations, two further features of the study need to be pointed out. First, the study is emphatic that rural development of the 'top–down' variety will not work. Development should be a matter of 'helping people to help themselves' (p. 33) and not the imposition of new plans and programmes. What is needed is 'a strategy which accepts (the) principle of community based empowerment' (p. 291). Laudable as these sentiments may be, it would seem that they directly contradict the study's land-reform recommendations, which constitute a land-reform strategy for the Transkei as a whole, and make no allowance for local circumstances and differences.

Second, the study recognizes the failure of betterment (pp. 249–52, 262–3) and states that one of the priorities for immediate action is 'to officially terminate the Betterment Planning programme and replace it with proper land use planning and with a genuine soil conservation programme' (p. 34). But the question that comes to mind is whether these recommendations could lead to the same kinds of problems that betterment gave rise to? After all, the aims of betterment were not dissimilar to the aims of the study, and the study was motivated by the same kinds of concerns and based on the same kinds of assumptions that led to betterment planning, i.e. that:

○ The system of communal land tenure is incompatible with agricultural development, and land reform is required if development is to occur.
○ There is a distinction between productive and unproductive farmers; agricultural development requires that the latter give up their land to the former.
○ The Transkei is overstocked and overgrazed, and has a severe soil-erosion problem.
○ Those who own livestock benefit at the expense of those who do not.
○ Current animal husbandry practices are uneconomical.

There is considerable evidence to suggest that these assumptions are not justified. There is little evidence to show that indigenous (often glossed as 'communal') tenure is incompatible with agricultural development in Africa. De Wet (1991), in a comparison of two Ciskei villages—one with communal tenure and one with freehold—has shown that there was no significant difference in agricultural productivity between them. Instead, he argues, it is factors such as the availability of agricultural inputs, marketing facilities, credit, extension services and so on, that determine agricultural productivity, not land tenure. Security of individual tenure is quite possible and common under a communal system (see also Cross and Haines, 1988). The evidence of the switch from fields to gardens shows that indigenous tenure has provided rural Transkeians with a flexibility in the exercise of their individual rights that was very important in maintaining agricultural production from arable land. Such flexibility needs to be preserved.

What about the distinction between productive and unproductive landholders? It has been shown by anthropologists working in the Transkei and elsewhere (e.g. Spiegel, 1980) that household agricultural productivity is often *cyclical* in character, and fluctuates according to the stage that a household has reached in its developmental cycle. Furthermore, development through the cycle into an agriculturally productive household often depends on the household's membership of a local community, to which it contributes allegiance and labour. So it is not always easy to make a simple distinction between good and bad farmers, or those who use their land productively and those who do not. Today's productive farmer could be yesterday's 'token' farmer. And indigenous tenure is what makes this possible. Introducing rentals for arable land could simply push many would-be small-scale farmers off their land for good, and enable the existing élite to acquire large land-holdings, perhaps to sub-let, in turn, to the landless.

The study thus demonstrates considerable ignorance on the question of how people actually use their land, a failing it shares with those who conceived of betterment. This emerges also when questions of production are considered. Production is seen almost entirely in terms of amounts of maize per hectare. Beans are mentioned occasionally, but no attention is paid to the extreme difficulty of calculating harvests where intercropping is common and in a situation where people eat directly from the fields for two or three months prior to the 'harvest' (to mention but one of the many problems in estimating tonnage). Nor is attention given to the considerable quantity of other vegetable crops grown. Agricultural production is seemingly equated with *commercial* production. Subsistence and sub-subsistence production is seen as undesirable.

Cross (1988) and de Wet (1989) have pointed out that the aim of creating a sizeable class of commercial farmers in places like KwaZulu and Ciskei is unlikely to succeed given the location of these areas, the lack of infrastructure and facilities, the existence of more attractive and secure means of making a living, and the overall level of development. No amount of land tenure reform or other measures which do not take cognisance of the disadvantaged position of such areas will change this.

The same sorts of problems arise in considering overstocking and overgrazing. Here, too, the study has merely spelt out the conventional Western view that communal tenure disadvantages those who do not have much livestock, leads to unnecessarily large herds, poor quality animals, and overgrazing. There is very little sociological awareness of the role that livestock plays in rural communities, and no recognition of the benefits that non-livestock owners obtain from the herds of others (McAllister, 1992).

What about the recommendations themselves? Like betterment, the study proposes a villagization programme. Each Administrative Area should have a village with good facilities. Sites in the village will be held in freehold. Such conditions will supposedly be attractive to those who do not particularly want to farm. If they have land, they will rent it to a farmer and move into the village. Despite reservations, there is something to be said for this proposal, provided that it is established as an option that can be freely chosen. If successful, it could improve the lot of many rural residents, and foster agricultural development by making more land available for more productive farmers. But this alone will not lead to development, as the study recognizes. And in much of the Transkei— those 566 Administrative Areas already subjected to betterment—villages already exist. Choosing one village in each area and improving the facilities in it, in an attempt to attract people into it, should not be too difficult.

Improved facilities in villages, the provision of a variety of small-scale income-generating opportunities, and a restoration of local autonomy might well attract people, and would go at least some way to reversing the negative effects of betterment. Putting the control of land back into the hands of the local community could also allow for the flexibility that is so badly needed to make the best use of the land and to foster conservation of the environment. There is much to be said also for allowing those who want to farm to leave betterment villages and to settle near their arable lands, perhaps in small clusters or 'satellite' villages in clearly demarcated and mutually agreed upon areas. In some parts of the Transkei this is already happening (McAllister, 1991; de Wet, 1991).

A different strategy is required in the case of areas mercifully not yet subjected to betterment schemes. In these cases, some 450 Administrative Areas, it is vital to retain the land use flexibility associated with indigenous tenure and the scattered residential pattern, while at the same time making provision for non-farmers in some sort of 'village centre', along the lines suggested by the study. As we have seen, residential clustering in pre-betterment situations often makes sense in social, economic and ecological terms. Such clusters may be strategically related to available resources, and consist of close-knit groups of homesteads (sometimes groups of kin) which have developed a strong ethic of mutual assisitance and economic co-operation (McAllister, 1989; Heron, 1990). Development in such areas needs to build on such organization rather than to break it down.

Crucial to any attempt at rural development in the Transkei, as the study recognizes, is the effectiveness of local authority systems. The key question here, given the poor record of Tribal Authorities, is how to ensure that such Development Committees operate in a democratic, impartial and financially responsible manner. An effective local authority system could provide the potential to give people a real say in their own affairs, and to make local leaders accountable to their constituencies. This would go a long way towards restoring the sense of autonomy and local control that betterment took away, and to resolving the ill-feeling towards local leadership that exists in many areas. The existing Tribal Authority system was created in terms of the ideology of apartheid and separate development, and has proved to be little more than an extension of the control exercised by the state in the attempt to keep rural people under control. Betterment, as indicated above, was one of the ways in which this control was exercised and tightened. This kind of problem has to be avoided if any kind of rural development is to succeed. Attention thus has to be given to the question of how the proposed Development Committees would be structured and how they would operate, what sorts of measures would be needed to ensure their accountability, and that they do not become simply another means of control over the masses by local power élites. If Tribal Authorities are to be retained, their relationship with the Development Committees will need to be carefully structured in order to prevent such committees from being effectively run by the Tribal Authority, as happened in one development project in the Ciskei (de Wet and Bekker, 1985). The study is right in recommending local autonomy, but does not address the question of how this can be compatible with a national strategy and policy. It is right in pointing to the need for new forms of local authority, but it is clear that there is a good deal of work to be done before we know what these forms should be.

Conclusion

Many well-meant efforts at rural development have in the past brought more poverty than plenty, and more control rather than liberation. In the words of the American Anthropological Association's Task Force on Involuntary Resettlement, 'there is a tendency for outside assistance to undermine indigenous and dynamic coping practices and thereby diminish, rather than enhance, the ability of the displaced to establish a more independent and self-sufficient life' (AAA, 1991). Recognizing both the ecological adaptations made by rural Transkeians over the years and the problems associated with misconceived attempts at development, such as betterment planning, is an essential starting-point.

References

AAA (1991), 'White paper on involuntary resettlement by the AAA task force on involuntary resettlement, 3/24/91'. Unpublished mimeo, American Anthropological Association.

Andrew, M. (1992), 'A geographical study of agricultural change since the 1930s in Shixini location Gatyana district, Transkei', Unpublished MA thesis, Rhodes University, Grahamstown.

Beinart, W. (1982), *The Political Economy of Pondoland*, Cambridge University Press.

Bigalke, E. (1969), 'The religious system of the Ndlambe of East London', Unpublished MA thesis, Rhodes University.

Blaikie, P. and Brookfield, H. (1987), *Land Degradation and Society*, London: Methuen.

Craizi, C. (1992), *The Making of the Colonial Order*, Cambridge University Press/ Witwatersrand University Press.

Cross, C. (1988), 'Freehold in the "Homelands": what are the real constraints?' in C. Cross and R. Haines (eds) (1988), *Towards Freehold?* Capetown: Juta & Co.

Cross, C. and Haines, R. (eds) (1988), *Towards Freehold?* Capetown: Juta & Co.

de Wet, C.J. (1989), 'Betterment planning in a rural village in Keisikammahoek', *Journal of Southern African Studies* 15(2).

de Wet, C.J. (1991), 'The socio-economic consequences of villagization schemes in Africa', *Development Southern Africa*, 8, 1.

de Wet, C.J. and Bekker, S. (1985), *Rural Development in South Africa: a case study of the Amatola Basin in the Ciskei*, Occasional Paper No. 30, Institute of Social and Economic Research, Rhodes University, in association with Shuter and Shooter, Pietermaritzburg.

Hammond-Tooke, W.D. (1962), *Bhaca Society*, London: Oxford University Press.

Hammond-Tooke, W.D. (1975), *Command or Consensus*, Cape Town: David Philip.

Heron, G. (1990), 'Household production and the organization of cooperative labour in Shixini, Transkei'. Unpublished MA thesis, Rhodes University, Grahamstown.

Hunter, M. (1936), *Reaction to Conquest*, 2nd edn 1961, London: Oxford University Press.

Kingon, J.R.L. (1915), 'Native Agriculture', *Report of the South African Association for the Advancement of Science* 12.

McAllister, P.A. (1979), 'The rituals of labour migration among the Gcaleka', Unpublished MA thesis, Rhodes University, Grahamstown.

McAllister, P.A. (1985), 'Beasts to beer pots—migrant labour and ritual change in Willowvale district, Transkei'. *African Studies* 44, 2.

McAllister, P.A. (1989), 'Resistance to "betterment" in the Transkei: a case study from Willowvale district'. *Journal of Southern African Studies* 15(2).

McAllister, P.A. (1991), 'Reversing the effects of "betterment planning" in South Africa's black rural areas'. *Africa Insight* 21(2).

McAllister, P.A. (1992), 'Rural production, land use and development planning in Transkei: a critique of the Transkei Agricultural Development Study.' *Journal of Contemporary African Studies*, 11, 2.

Mayer, P. (1980), 'The rise and decline of two rural resistance ideologies', in P. Mayer, (ed.), *Black Villagers in an Industrial Society*. Cape Town: Oxford University Press.

O'Connell, M. (1981), 'Resettlement and development in Transkei', *Africa Insight* 11(1).

Peires, J. (1981), *The House of Phalo*, Johannesburg: Ravan Press.

Sansom, B. (ed.) (1974), 'Traditional economic systems', in W.D. Hammond-Tooke (ed.), *The Bantu Speaking Peoples of Southern Africa*, London: Routledge and Kegan Paul.

Shaw, E.M. and van Warmelo, N.J. (1972–81), 'The material culture of the Cape Nguni', *Annals of the South African Museum* 58, Parts 1–4.

Spiegel, A. (1980), 'Rural differentiation and the diffusion of migrant labour remittances in Lesotho', in P. Mayer, (ed.), *Black Villagers in an Industrial Society*, Cape Town: Oxford University Press.

Transkei Government (1991), 'Transkei Agricultural Development Study'.

Whisken, J. (1991), 'An assessment of the effectiveness of betterment planning in combating soil erosion', Unpublished B.A.(Hons) dissertation, Rhodes University, Grahamstown.

Wilson, M. (1981), 'Xhosa marriage in historical perspective', in E.J Krige and E. Preston-Whyte, (eds), *Essays on African Marriage in Southern Africa*, Cape Town: Juta & Co.

Wilson, M., Kaplan, S., Maki, T. and Walton, E.M. (1952), *Social Structure*, Keisikammahoek Rural Survey, Vol. 3, Pietermaritzburg: Shuter and Shooter.

3 Hometown associations: Balancing local and extralocal interests in Nigerian communities

MICHAEL L. McNULTY and MARK F. LAWRENCE*

Introduction[1]

HOMETOWN ASSOCIATIONS, ALSO known as progressive unions, improvement societies, ethnic unions and community development organizations, are a common feature of Nigerian communities. These institutions provide an especially useful lens through which to view the development of contemporary Nigerian communities and particularly to analyse the dynamic and still-unfolding relationship between local communities and extralocal entities including the state.

The nature of these institutions, their functions, membership, leadership, and their changing role in relation to local and extralocal interests and entities are examined in this chapter. The interpretation of these institutions is based on field research and interviews undertaken on four separate occasions between June 1989 and January 1993. Initial contacts in the communities of Fiditi, Aawe and Ara were greatly facilitated by professional colleagues at the University of Ibadan and the Nigerian Institute of Social and Economic Research who are respected citizens of the communities and active members of their hometown associations. Initial interviews were conducted with community leaders, officers of the hometown associations, past and present, as well as other local notables. Following the meetings with the community leadership, efforts were made to secure interviews with other members of the community, especially those not well represented in the leadership cadre; notably women, members of lower income and lower status groups.[2]

Why study hometown associations?

The choice of hometown associations as a point of reference for examining current social relations in Nigerian communities and for analysing the relationship between local communities and the Nigerian state should be explained. The selection of these organizations is based on the fact that they represent perhaps the most significant institution of civil society which is based upon ties to a specific locality of origin, although membership in the community and the association is not limited to local residents nor is the community defined exclusively in geographic terms. This last point is dealt with more fully below. Unlike many other institutions commonly referred to as constituting 'civil society', the hometown association seeks to speak for all members of the community, rather than representing the specific interests of particular trades, professions, religious groups or social classes. The extent to which they actually accomplish this is the subject of investigation below. What is certain is that these associations have sought to define their roles as speaking for the community and representing it in interaction with the Nigerian state. In

* Michael NcNulty is Professor of Geography and Associate Provost for International Affairs, and Mark Lawrence is a PHD candidate in the department of Geography, University of Iowa.

turn, the Nigerian state has at various times sought to promote the development of such associations and to involve them in numerous state initiatives in the name of local development and increased 'grassroots' participation. This relationship between local community organizations and the Nigerian state has been an ambiguous one and has undergone a number of important changes since the founding of the associations, dating back in most cases more than 60 years. The story of that changing relationship is valuable in understanding the evolution of local and national dimensions of social relations in Nigeria.

In focusing on the hometown associations we seek to understand the communities' efforts to find voice in the evolving relationship with first the colonial administration and later the succession of civilian and military Nigerian regimes. That is, to see the manner in which local communities sought to deal with external interests and to secure resources from the state. In addition, we seek to view the associations as an important arena within which various local interests compete and thus a useful vantage point from which to examine local social relations. Such general observations will be contextualized throughout the chapter by reference to a number of Yoruba communities, and in particular the community of Fiditi and its hometown association, the Fiditi Progressive Union (FPU).

Definition of hometown associations

The term community needs to be understood in the context of contemporary Nigeria. Berry notes:

> A Yoruba community in the middle of the twentieth century cannot be treated as a territorially based settlement whose inhabitants differ in their social identity and organize their interactions around the fact that they live and work in the same place. Rather, it is likely to comprise a group of people, scattered or moving across the map of the region and beyond, who maintain a tradition of descent from a common place and who often organize social actions and interpersonal relationships in terms of that tradition.[3]

Thus, it is common to find that Yoruba born and living in, say, Lagos, none the less refer to their place of origin, or that of their parents, as their 'hometown'. Moreover, traditional Yoruba gender relationships are such that children are raised to consider the patrilineal hometown as their own. Yoruba loyalty to a particular hometown is such that it may be shared avidly even by those who have never actually lived in the town. Moreover, some of a town's 'sons and daughters' (*omo ibile*) are born into families which have not been resident in their hometown for two or three generations. In fact, many of these distant citizens expend considerable effort to build or maintain close social and economic ties to the community. Many residents of Nigeria's largest urban centres have built houses or reclaimed family property in their hometowns with an eye towards retiring there. Many urban migrants sought out employment in the city only as a means of accumulating resources with which to strengthen their positions at home. Aronson reported the comment by an Ijebu migrant to Ibadan that 'the city is our farm'.[4]

That many people 'maintain a tradition of descent from a common place' is not accidental. This 'tradition' like most, is actively reproduced through a variety of formal and informal activities, rituals, obligations and reproduction of social norms. Hometown associations, progressive unions and improvement societies play a very important role in reaffirming and strengthening ties to particular places. In Fiditi, a town of just over 40000 inhabitants in south-western Nigeria, more than 50 social clubs and societies were identified.[5] In fact, most of Fiditi's clubs and societies have few members actually resident in the hometown; the secretary of the Fiditi Club, for example, lives in Lagos, and 75 per cent of Klub 55 lives in Oyo.[6] What distinguishes this myriad of societies, clubs, unions, and other formal and informal associations from the hometown associations (the focus of this study) is the role assumed by the hometown association as the 'apex' organization in the community. In that role it seeks to co-ordinate and direct the activities of other organizations as they pertain to local development. For example, the Fiditi Progressive Union is considering implementation of mandatory annual fees assessed from each registered associa-tion, above and beyond registration fees. Part of the reason for this move is that most associations claim as the majority of their membership people who are resident in places where they are more likely to have access to greater income than are those FPU members still living in Fiditi.

Hometown associations are made up of actors both local and extralocal who share a common goal of reaffirming ties to the locality and employing those ties for the purpose of marshalling resources in the name of the locality. The motives of those participating in the formation and maintenance of such organizations is subject to very different interpretations. Barkan, McNulty and Ayeni noted six different interpretations of such associations, including seeing them as: an expression of *civic virtue*; the establishment and operation of a *shadow state*; a local *bulwark* against the state; local *growth machines*; an intermediary *'broker'*; and as a manifestation of sentimental *attachment* to place. At different points in their histories, these associations have displayed characteristics of each of these interpretations and have played various roles at different times and in different localities. But, 'one function has remained important—their role as intermediary between the local community and each of the three levels of government that constitute the Nigerian state'.[7] This intermediary role is of particular interest in the present chapter and is discussed more fully below.

Intermediary institutions and the emergence of civil society

Hometown associations function as intermediary institutions between the local-ity and external constituencies—serving to mobilize financial and human resources to promote or protect common interests. The hometown associations serve as intermediary institutions in a number of ways. First in the sense that the association mediates the interests of the local community with the state and other national and international actors. Official delegations from local communities regularly approach government offices and ministries in efforts to put forward their case for resources and other matters of concern to the community. Associa-tions also serve as mechanisms for mediating local and extralocal interests in the community, that is, between those members of the community still based in the locality and those members of the community who reside elsewhere but maintain an active interest in local affairs. The association often becomes a contested arena, where local and national actors vie to influence and control the association and through it the collective actions of the community.[8]

The associations serve simultaneously as mechanisms for promoting localized social structures and wider, geographically dispersed networks to ensure the survival and reproduction of the locality. Both the local and the non-resident members of the community are interested in maintaining and controlling the associations, the local people in order to secure resources from the non-resident members of the community who provide not only resources directly through remittences and investment, but also access to state, national and international agencies and resources. The extralocal members of the community have a continuing interest in the well-being of the locality for a number of reasons. The locality represents their refuge in the event of civil strife and the breakdown of state security for life and property. In this regard, the experiences of the civil war have taught all segments of the population the importance of a secure homebase. This point was especially brought home to the Igbo population. Many of the Igbos who fled back to the east from the north and the west had no place to live when they crowded back into the region and vowed that it would never happen again. The massive investment in infrastructure and buildings in all areas of the former Eastern Region is testimony to that fact.[9]

Although initially viewed as essentially urban-based support organizations for rural migrants, these intermediary institutions are now recognized as important in creating and reaffirming links to home areas, in reproducing ties to localities of origin, representing local interests at the national level, and infusing national concerns and interests into local social structures. Through an extensive network of social and economic relations, hometown associations serve as effective mechanisms for reinforcing a sense of community in those resident outside the locality and as a channel for mobilizing and focusing the community's resources for local development projects.

What becomes important, therefore, is analysis of the forces which shape what Bellah calls 'communities of memory' and especially how those forces have changed character over time.[10] Stretching across the disciplinary lines of geography, sociology, planning and political science, there is a vast literature on the 'politics of place' which is of assistance in making a conceptual approach to these types of questions.[11] Harvey employed the concept of 'structured coherences' to refer to the outcome of the process of production and reproduction of places which reflects dominant social relations.[12] More recently, he has added that new means of facilitating capital accumulation have led to an acceleration in creation and re-creation of structured coherences, among other things provoking new innovations in promotion and reinforcement of distinctive local identities.[13]

By one name or another, 'sentiment' has long played a role in analyses of what constitutes a distinctive local identity and why people struggle to maintain it.[14] Many earlier studies assumed that sentimental attachment to place would inevitably be eroded by demographic expansion and the social transformations accompanying urbanization.[15] But numerous studies have shown that population size and density have less to do with the strength or weakness of sentimental attachment to place than such factors as length of residence, income and age.[16] Fischer and others have even enabled us to dispense with any presumption of less attachment to urban as opposed to rural places.[17] Evidence suggests that attachment to place not only is capable of withstanding demographic expansion, in many cases it even appears to be strengthened in response to it.[18] Gugler's research in eastern Nigeria indicates that, contrary to predictions, hometown ties among migrants in Enugu are as strong or stronger than they were 30 years ago, even among members of the second generation who have never lived in their ancestral homes.[19] Why such strong ties persist, and why non-resident members of the community continue to maintain close contact with their communities of origin have been the subject of considerable speculation and research. Most of the literature can be characterized as representing one of two interpretations. The first explains the persistence of such links as an expression of 'primordial ties' involving blood, kinship and ethnic relationships which bind people together, and provide 'cultural maps' for locating oneself in relation to others.[20] Although they exist all over the world, such ties are seen to be especially strong in contemporary African societies. The second interpretation locates the reason for the ties in the economic logic of self-interest and personal security. The impact of generational and spatial separation have not led to a significant loosening of ties to the hometown because most migrants feel that the hometown is still the final refuge in the event of economic disasters or political crises. Thus the reaffirmation of 'sentimental' ties through the use of tradition, ritual and regular home visits actually hides the underlying economic motives behind a socio-cultural mask. Laitin argues that despite the erosive effects of increasing geographic and social mobility among the Yoruba since the turn of the century,

> the ancestral city remains today the central basis for political identification and mobilization within the Yoruba states of the Nigerian Federation. In each city, the myth of common descent is sustained by regularly scheduled rituals honouring the gods of special importance to that city. The festivals associated with those rituals bring back many emigrants and their families. During the festivals, successful members of the city's diaspora are showered with status rewards, especially if they performed services in support of their 'home' cities. Yorubas who live in the anomic cosmopolitan centres like Ibadan or Lagos derive great pleasure on returning to their ancestral city from seeing people bow to them at every encounter and having 'praise singers' follow them through the town, immortalising their origins and their worldly successes.[21]

Logan and Molotch emphasize that sentiment plays a role in shaping and reshaping locally structured coherences only insofar as it is organized.[22] Similarly, Hoben and Hefner emphasized that: 'Far from being static, primordial ties are renewed, modified and remade in each generation.'[23] Indeed, a central point of the analysis presented here is that it is important to identify organizations and individuals within them which at any given moment have the wherewithal to redefine the local discourse on what is acceptable and what is unacceptable for the community.

The history of hometown associations: an attempt at periodization

The emergence of hometown associations as formal entities complete with constitutions, officers, and regular meetings began at the turn of the century. Their emergence signalled a significant change in the local political scene in Nigeria. These newly formed hometown associations represented a serious challenge to the political and social hegemony represented by traditional authority. Their early success in spearheading and successfully completing local development projects assured their leadership a legitimate place in the local political scene. Drawing on membership from both residents and those who had left the community, the associations created a forum in which local and extralocal interests had to be considered, if not balanced. Many hometown associations were established more than 60 years ago, and the degree of local or extralocal influence in the associations has waxed and waned as local and national contexts have changed. From their inception, however, hometown associations have served as significant links between the local community, the 'sons and daughters of the soil' resident elsewhere, the state, and other important national or international actors. Since both local and extralocal members of the community have shown interest in maintaining influence and control, associations have served on a number of occasions as contested arenas, where these actors vie to influence and control the leadership of the association and through it the collective actions of the community. Thus, the associations serve as mechanisms for simultaneously promoting the growth of localized social structures and wider geographically dispersed networks to ensure the survival and reproduction of the locality.

The periodization of these relationships which follows is a generalization of the experiences of several hometown associations including those which were part of our fieldwork as well as others whose histories have been reported elsewhere in the literature.

Pre-colonial social institutions

Nigerian communities have always had indigenous forms of associations which functioned to serve community collective needs. Each Yoruba community had an authority structure dominated by an *oba* or king, with each of the quarters within the town led in turn by its *baale* or lineage elder. Groups of households associated with one another as *idile* or lineage groups. Neither colonial rule nor independence has erased this culture. Fadipe links the development of ethnic or community associations to this social organization of Yoruba towns into compounds. Members of the community, often organized along the lines of age sets, performed specific functions for the compound or community including provision of roads, security, and sanitation. The older forms of such institutional ties were based on religion, age, lineage and occupation. Such earlier types of associations include *esusu* or rotating-credit groups, *aro* or agricultural mutual help associations, and *Egbe Iyalode* or traders' associations working to secure favourable market conditions.[24]

In the first half of this century, the institutions traditionally responsible for reinforcing attachment to place and organizing the community for collective action were weakened and gradually replaced in large part by other types of associations. Prefiguring this history was the era of protracted civil war among the Yoruba in which different city-states vied for control of powerful imperial offices. There had of course been wars among the Yoruba in earlier times, but the conflicts taking place at the close of the nineteenth century were remarkable for being characterized by the practice of 'total' war involving the destruction of whole communities. This transformation of traditional conflict was in large part facilitated by access to European firearms. Due to massive refugee migrations, many communities developed considerably heterogeneous populations during this period as a result, and in many cases refugees maintained their separate identities even after resettlement. This further diluted the authority of traditional rulers—Phillips pointed out, for example, that in 1853 no less than four thousand people were engaged in the administration of Abeokuta.[25]

Early colonial period (1893–1925)

The British consolidated their control of almost all of Yorubaland after 1893, and continued to alter what had been the traditional form of political society. In seeking to establish effective administration of the new colony with as little cost as possible, London sought to employ certain traditional authorities in a system of indirect rule. The British succeeded in further altering the Yoruba authority structure, already greatly affected by the rise of military leaders during the period of the Yoruba wars, by giving their chosen *obas* considerably more autonomy of action than traditional rulers had hitherto enjoyed.

Importantly, the history of Fiditi reflects the intrusion of this alien vision of what was to constitute an appropriate authority structure. The town's founding in the 1840s had much to do with the migration of refugees and exiles from the nearby city of Ijaye during a period of civil war (inspired in large measure by the collapse of an economy originally encouraged by European interests in obtaining large supplies of slaves). Descendants of those refugees call themselves the Asu and live in the eastern half of the town. Another people already living in the area at the time of Fiditi's founding now dominate the western half of the town; these are the Modeni or Omodeni. For more than seventy years, each side of the town was content to have its own *baale*. But during Captain Ross' tenure as the British Colonial Office Resident in Oyo (1914–31), Fiditi was ordered to have only one *baale*. The Resident set up a system of baaleship which would alternate between the two sides of the town. But the Asu side very quickly came to dominate Fiditi's baaleship. In June 1981, Chief Alayeluwa Ezekiel Oyegbenle Akande 1 became *baale*. He created 12 honorary chieftaincies in June of 1982, and died in 1988. He was from the Asu population of Fiditi, and many in the town believed that he had been too free and partisan with the creation of new chieftaincies. These and other tensions led the Modeni to press their neglected claims in the courts. Although this process has dragged on for many years, a decision was considered imminent in mid–1990. In the meantime, the town has no *baale*, providing political elbow-room for the FPU and other parties interested in trying to redefine discourse about local development.

Importantly, the colonial revision of power roles and relationships was significantly connected to the growth of a money economy. Traditional authority gave way gradually to waged authority; thus, even though the *baale* of Ibadan had gathered greater prestige and military power than the *alafin* of Oyo before the advent of colonial rule, the latter's traditionally superior rank among Yoruba regions was reasserted by a higher salary. In fact: 'Some chiefs were paid for acting as judges in the local courts: titles which offered neither a salary nor a place on the bench tended to be left vacant.'[26] Even after the British began to reassess and rehabilitate the roles of lesser chiefs, traditional authority positions suffered decreasing income and were increasingly less attractive to the new educated élite. During this period Christian missionaries were active in Yorubaland and in Fiditi churches were established by the Methodists, the Baptists and Catholics in 1902, 1910 and 1914, respectively.[27] The churches recruited and trained a new generation of leaders who were to change profoundly the discourse on community matters in the decades which followed.

A new set of aspiring community leaders was emerging and a new form of institution, based on hometown affiliations, was being promoted by the migrants to Lagos, Ibadan and other colonial administrative centres. Control of these new hometown associations was often in the hands of non-resident urban migrants or their fellow educated and Christian brethren who were returning home as schoolteachers, ministers, or businessmen. The stage was set for this new leadership to offer an alternative to the traditional authority and leadership of the chiefs and *obas*. These self-styled 'progressive' movements set out to transform rural Nigeria, bringing to it the infrastructure, values and accoutrements of Western, urban society.

Later colonial period (1925–50)

As a consequence of the degradation of the institutions of traditional authority, the institutions of colonial civil society became increasingly more influential. Beginning in the 1920s, Yoruba communities began to develop a new form of *egbe*, the *parapo* or 'progressive union'. Generally speaking, social status was becoming less dependent on contacts with traditional authorities and more dependent on links to the churches, participation in the exchange economy and access to those commodities which served as hallmarks of the dominant, European society. The progressive unions were generally organized by migrants resident in Lagos or other major metropolitan areas.[28] Frequently the list of founding members and progressive union leaders was dominated by Christian men employed in the colonial civil service or the colonial economy. These men were determined to bring to their home communities some of the benefits of the urban and European environments they were witnessing. Since the colonial government showed little interest in or willingness to provide even minimal infrastructure and services to areas outside of the administrative centres, these 'sons of the soil' organized the communities to undertake a series of self-help efforts. Initially these efforts focused on securing educational and health facilities. Officers of the hometown associations, often working in alliance with the churches operating in Nigeria at the time, succeeded in establishing schools and clinics in town after town. The efforts of those who eventually founded the Fiditi Progressive Union contributed to the establishment of primary schools and post-primary institutions, including a government technical college for graduates of secondary institutions. These community leaders were also instrumental in securing a dispensary (opened in 1932) and a postal agency which was formally and officially opened in 1941. Although the relations between this new cadre of educated leaders and traditional authorities were not always smooth, in most instances the co-operation of the *obas* and *baales* was secured. By bestowing their blessings on community improvement projects traditional leaders helped to legitimize efforts of the Progressive Union to raise funds and to encourage the co-operation of the general public who were often asked to contribute in cash or kind to the projects.

In this way, communities often pulled together to secure important infrastructure and services which they might otherwise not have enjoyed. Internal differences within the community were often muted in order to present a united front to the colonial administration. The success of the hometown associations during this period in securing resources and implementing projects meant that they enjoyed a good reputation and the leaders were considered respectable men of high integrity.

The First Republic period (1950–65)

Beginning in some cases in the 1930s many *parapo* engaged in local political reform movements and later established links with the emerging nationalist parties, but with the approach of independence, the political parties overshadowed the progressive unions in terms of negotiating with the government for local and regional development. The emergence of party politics also quickly undermined the sense of community and unity of purpose with which the hometown associations had sought to operate, at least ideally, until now. The existing schisms within the community were exacerbated as they were imbued with greater ideological meaning and linked to the promise of greatly increased access to the state's resources to be acquired through political victory. The stakes were raised significantly, the external force of the colonial state, often used as a rallying point for community efforts, was replaced by the idea of a national treasury as prize, well worth competing for. In some areas the existence of these hometown associations greatly facilitated political organization and recruitment.[29] In other areas of the country, the impact of party politics was to politicize local issues and the ensuing quarrels wrecked what had been at least a facade of community unity and pulling together in the face of the colonial administrations unwillingness or inability to provide services to the community. The political struggle between Chief Obafemi Awolowo and Chief Samuel Akintola over control of the Action Group in 1962 split many Yoruba communities.[30] The effect on community organizations was often devastating. In Fiditi, the Awolowo–Akintola feud split the community and although the town remained loyal to Awolowo the conflict 'almost crippled the Progressive Union' and rendered it 'practically ineffective', in the words of one of the past officers. The importance of the associations during the First Republic was further affected by policies of the Nigerian government which were marked by inconsistency and indecisiveness. As Adejumobi has noted, 'For a long time, community development was tossed from one ministry to the other because there was no consensus on which ministry should manage it'.[31]

The military/civilian regimes: 1965–present
In the succession of military and civilian regimes following the first coup in 1965, efforts to encourage, support and promote community action were launched periodically, but never really seriously got underway until after the local government reforms of 1976. However, none of the previous efforts approached the ambitious programme promulgated by the Babangida regime beginning in the mid-1980s. The formation of the Directorate for Food, Roads and Rural Infrastructures (DFRRI) and the Directorate for Social Mobilization (MAMSER) marked an effort to identify and register community organizations where they existed and to encourage the formation of them where they did not already exist.[32] Hometown associations, Community Development Associations as they were termed, were encouraged to register with DFRRI and to turn their attention and resources to economic development projects. Whereas earlier community development projects were focused largely on the provision of public goods and services, now the government was urging communities to promote investment in directly productive activities. To add weight to the argument, the Federal Military Government proposed to support the creation of community banks throughout the country, but only in those communities in which Community Development Associations had been established and which could meet a number of financial and other criteria requiring community action. Although it is still too soon to gauge the impact that this recent interest on the part of the state ultimately will have on the activities of the hometown associations, the immediate effect has been to increase competition among communities and reinforce the position of the associations' leadership in seeking to speak on behalf of the community. This raises an important question as to the extent to which the hometown associations actually reflect the interests of the community. In short, who speaks for Fiditi and the other communities?

In the case-study which follows, the legacy of the (still ongoing) competition of local and extralocal interests will be explored by looking at how transformations of class relations, gender relations and culture in Fiditi are reflected by and reflect upon the character of the Fiditi Progressive Union's history, membership and agenda for the town's development.

Fiditi: a case-study

Fiditi and its immediate environs cover an area roughly 8x10 miles, jurisdiction-ally known at the time this research was conducted as the Afijio Local Govern-ment Area.[33] There is little manufacturing (two furniture shops, a bakery and a civil-engineering firm with few local projects), and village industries such as the cloth-weaving centre use only small labour forces. Housing construction has been at a standstill since 1986.[34] A sketch of the town in 1982 identified eight primary schools, the First Baptist primary school being the oldest, founded in 1910. In addition, there were four post-primary institutions, including a govern-ment technical college for graduates of secondary institutions. There is one post office (opened in 1939), a government health centre (opened in 1932), a local police station (opened in 1959), and a national police station on Iware Road (opened in 1968). Piped water came to the town in 1962, electricity in 1973 and a town planning office opened in 1980.[35] Politically, the town produced a First Republic minister and a Second Republic Deputy-Speaker for the national House of Assembly. In addition, by 1982, a Fiditian (Chief (Deacon) S.I. Ojelabi) held the first full-time member post of the Central Schools Board.

At present, Fiditi has a population of about 42000. Most of this population lives on farmland surrounding the town, and agricultural technology in the area is still chiefly reliant on hoes and cutlasses. Some aspects of the agricultural economy in Fiditi are worth noting here. In the late 1960s, tobacco had been introduced into the area, but production never amounted to much. Fruit farming in the district became commercially viable after the local cocoa economy collapsed. Cocoa had been dominant before 1950, generally grown on farms of 0.5–5.0 acres in size, but then pest problems, a prolonged drought, and a severe *harmattan* in 1956 destroyed the local cocoa economy. By 1970, 85 per cent of district farmers had become fruit cultivators.

As elsewhere in Nigeria, associational life in Fiditi is quite diverse. As of mid-1990, there were more than 50 clubs and societies in the community co-ordinating activities with the FPU. Operated on a day-to-day basis by a 10-member executive, the FPU acts as an umbrella organization, co-ordinating certain activities among the multitude of clubs and societies in or connected to the town and gleaning financial support from them for its own projects.

The current FPU president has called the organization 'a government at the grassroots level', noting that the Local Government Areas (LGAs) are simply too large to adequately represent local interests. The organization's general secretary likewise calls the FPU the 'main organ of development for the town'. The president emphasizes the role of democratic process in the FPU internal activ-ities, but also admits that constitutional review and rewriting is ongoing. Among other changes, the FPU is trying to formalize triennial meetings with the heads of all registered clubs and societies to integrate better these member associations in the FPU's decision-making process. In 1990, the following external chapters of the FPU were listed: Ibadan, Lagos, Ile-Ife, Osogbo, Kano, Sokoto, Kaduna, Iseyin, Shaki and Oyo/Aawe. In addition, Fiditi has its own chapter. Some groups of Fiditi expatriates are so large that there is more than one chapter in the FPU branches of some cities—for example, Lagos has four, Ibadan three and

Oyo/Aawe two.[36] When interviewed, the current FPU vice-president emphasized the role of the Lagos chapters in the creation of a health centre in Fiditi in 1984, suggesting that the Lagos branch can raise more naira in a single luncheon than the executive can raise on Fiditi Day, the FPU's major annual fundraising event at home.[37]

The executive charges registration fees for any association seeking to become affiliated with the FPU, and levies annual dues from each individual member and member association. Additionally, each chapter levies its members at each monthly meeting to raise funds for the town. An informal competitive spirit between the chapters helps motivate members to donate, especially as the executive uses Fiditi Day as a forum for announcing how well each chapter has done. For instance, the Oyo chapter, with more than 100 members, levies its members a minimum of 30 naira annually. The executive dictates minimum naira amounts to branches, and called for more money when the national economy was faring better. According to the current treasurer, 80 per cent of the operating budget of the FPU is raised among its branches, although the executive sometimes levies the entire membership N10 each.[38]

Class relations and the FPU
Logan and Molotch have noticed the inclination of the social élite to organize on behalf of community, and both Domhoff and Galaskiewicz have explored the character of the social ties and class culture of élites and how these intersect with the politics of place.[39] Though Fiditi is a poor community, one may readily distinguish those who enjoy élite status. For some, their status is related to traditional titled roles; for others, status is more importantly connected to income level and educational achievement. In recent years, there has been a convergence of these two roles as communities select men to fill traditional positions in the community from among the better-educated and wealthier members of the royal families. The members of the hometown associations have also begun to play a much more influential role in selecting new chiefs.

According to the FPU constitution: 'Membership shall be open to all sons and daughters of Fiditi not less than 18 years of age irrespective of their religious, political or ideological beliefs and convictions.'[40] Interestingly, although the FPU is not a government agency, its constitution expects that the *baale* of the town will belong to the Union, although it hastens to add that the *baale* 'shall not have any right to vote or engage in any debate or table a motion'.[41] The only other formal restrictions on membership are that the president and vice-president must each be no less than 40 years old.

The researchers were frequently told that participation in leadership roles is not confined to the economic or educational élite. The most influential criterion for leadership is the respectability, intelligence and dedication of an individual to his community, regardless of social class. However, the FPU executive has always been solidly controlled by men, and mostly staffed by university-educated men.[42] The current president is the registrar of a teacher's college; his vice-president is principal of a grammar school in Aawe; the general secretary is principal of Fiditi Grammar School, as was his predecessor; and a former treasurer received a Ph.D. from the University of Iowa. Officers who have not completed higher education have none the less been important businessmen in the community. A former treasurer is the town's only contractor, with construction projects across the state and federal contracts elsewhere. Officers need not reside in the town—for example, both the current FPU president and vice-president live in Oyo.

Class distinctions in Fiditi are also facilitated by the effects of the FPU agenda. Certain FPU projects have particularly benefited certain executive members, while other populations in the town have felt economically threatened by the organization. For example, the union was able to establish telephone service in Fiditi, but of the 52 lines that were connected, only three can be used to make calls outside of town: one of these is in the offices of the Nigeria–Arab Bank, and the other two are in the office of the businessman who was FPU treasurer when the project was undertaken.[43] Studying the town of Iree, Berry provides a similar illustration, noting that the progressive union there in the 1970s was led by individuals who built houses 'fitted with plumbing and electric wires in anticipation of the arrival of the requisite amenities in the town'.[44]

The FPU does not only facilitate class relations within the town; it also becomes a means for expressing class relations between the town and its *omo ibile* who live and work abroad. The group relies primarily on donations from its branches in the urban centres, and in at least one case this has led to a conflict in terms of who gets to set the agenda for the further development of the town. From March through mid-June of 1990, Fiditi was without electrical power. When it was discovered that the restoration of electrical power was going to cost as much as N70 000, the executive decided to redirect funds from other projects in order to facilitate the necessary repairs. In particular, the Business and Development Committee's town hall project was stalled when N8 000 earmarked for it had to be diverted. Meanwhile, prices for materials used in the town hall project rose; the executive has tried to recoup the lost funds, but other projects have since received higher priority. Consequently, the important Ibadan branch refused to deliver some money it had raised until construction of the hall was begun again.[45]

In fact, it may be possible to view the intersection of FPU activities and class relations in Fiditi in terms of the formation of a *rentier* class. That is, to the degree that a *rentier* class does not seek to improve the productive capacity of places, but rather to maximize the rate of return on investment in existing capacity, FPU concerns for infrastructure instead of income, as well as factional concerns for symbolic investment, do not speak of a focus on improved productive capacity. Boone develops the notion of West African rentierism further by suggesting that 'rentier activities are *politically mediated* opportunities' for nonproductive accumulation.[46] But it is important to suggest that access to and use of resources in a rentierist way may be 'politically mediated' not only in the sense of resources being controlled by the state, but also in the sense of the state neither having significant resources on hand to be distributed nor being motivated to promote an entrepreneurial class which might be able to challenge an already fragile political order. Gathering these thoughts together should underscore the need to assess more carefully the ways in which class relations are involved with the development of hometown associations. What is missing from the present research in this area is explication of the household histories of those individuals who founded and have maintained the FPU.

Gender relations and the FPU

But class relations mask deeper divisions within the community. Much of the daily reproduction of the community relies on a particular gender division of labour and its concomitant ideology of gender roles (which, in turn, has significant material consequences). The history of gender relations in Fiditi, like the history of class relations, has been strongly influenced by the legacy of the nineteenth-century Yoruba wars and subsequent struggles, with the fusion of Yoruba and alien cultures into a 'Nigerian' identity.

Regarding the relationship of gender to the character of FPU membership, of key interest is that the current version of the group's constitution is the first to mention ex-officio positions, informally created six years ago. The FPU has an elected executive made up of seven officio members and two ex-officio members; there is also a tenth, non-elected executive post (the registrar of associations affiliated with the FPU). There are five subcommittees within the organizational hierarchy of the union for more local attention to issues dealing respectively with education, social-economic planning, health, security and development, and welfare. While other executive members are elected, the ex-officio members are currently still appointed by the union's president; as with the other executive positions, ex-officio terms run for three years. It is surely quite significant that one of these two positions is to be specifically reserved for a woman. In fact, both positions are presently occupied by women. One was a secondary school teacher of the current FPU president, while the other is the Afijio LGA secretary for the newly created Social Democratic Party. Both women have been highly visible in the community, the former by attending every meeting of the FPU and the latter especially by attempting to provide day-care services for the children of some of the town's poorest families.[47]

When asked why female participation has not appeared sooner, male respondents have gently dismissed women as 'the weaker vessel', while female respondents have privately complained about the strictures of 'tradition'. Likewise, according to the principal of the Methodist schools and primary organizer of Fiditi Day (a woman), 'domestic duties keep women from attending every FPU meeting'. No females have ever been nominated (let alone elected) to the FPU executive, and the current ex-officio members are the first women to hold any executive-level positions in the organization. However, they are adamantly optimistic about the emerging possibilities of women gaining top positions in organizations such as the FPU, suggesting for instance that women may be 'more sociable' than men and therefore better able to serve as the FPU's top officers.

The women of Fiditi are active in the FPU's subcommittees. Three of these subcommittees have five members; the other two have seven members. Of a total 29 subcommittee members, 10 are women. One of the ex-officios is a member of the Welfare Subcommittee. On the other hand, none of the five subcommittees is chaired by a woman, and women are outnumbered on each subcommittee (in fact, there are only two women on each subcommittee).[48]

The FPU executive indicated that when the FPU first began town-wide levies for projects, it asked for three naira from each person; in 1950, the levy rose to six naira. Now, each man is levied 10 naira and each woman five. These amounts may not remain constant but depend on the condition of the general economy and the amount needed to be raised directly from the town for a given project, but in general, women are levied half as much as men. Presumably, the women of Fiditi do indeed have less income to levy, but interviews with past and present FPU leadership figures suggest that the group does not seem conscious of or at least comfortable with confronting such gender-based economic distinctions.

Gender relations in Fiditi also appear to be echoed inside the FPU in terms of decision-making and agenda-setting for the town's development. There is some difficulty distinguishing the executive from the FPU's subcommittees and some of the organization's member associations, and in each case the overlapping leadership positions are occupied by men. The vice-president heads the Education Subcommittee, and former treasurers have seats on the Social–Economic Planning Subcommittee. The vice-president belongs to the Fiditi Club, the Trinity Society of the Methodist Church in Fiditi, and is presently organizing a new society called The Catalyst. The general secretary is a member of Fiditi Club, and before Executive Council days served on the FPU's water and town hall project committees. A former FPU treasurer is a member of the Fiditi Christian Society, and also served as treasurer of the Fiditi Club from 1973–89 (and helped to establish the club in 1973). He donated the land for the Nigeria–Arab Bank, where the FPU keeps its treasury.

Two other points are worth noting here. First, there has been a strong history of lineage-building within the executive, and this history seems to be reserved for men. A former FPU general secretary, for example, was principal of Fiditi Grammar School (FGS) while in office. Importantly, FGS was the FPU's first project for the town, and in the years immediately before and after independence, the organization made considerable efforts to provide scholarships for the education of Fiditians who were expected to return to the town to teach at FGS. As FGS principal, the former general secretary sponsored one of his pupils as a candidate for an FPU scholarship to attend university. The pupil took an English degree at the University of Ife, and upon completing his education, returned to teach at FGS, where he now serves as the principal while acting as general secretary of the FPU. Whether or not this lineage-building is consciously undertaken is less important at the moment than the implications of its established history.

But the crux of the issue about the relationship between gender relations in the community and the FPU's agenda deals with the ambivalence the organization feels about deciding whether or not to invest time, money and effort in income-generating projects. This obliges certain interests in the town to absorb such risks alone and without the financial and material support network which the union enjoys. Many of the women in the town, for example, have for many years hoped for the establishment of a fruit cannery in Fiditi. Approximately 100 women, organized as the Adi Co-operative Society (ACS), are presently arranging to collectivize palm-oil production efforts. In a dramatic undertaking, the ACS is clearing a piece of land by hand in order to set up a co-operative site. The women are unable, despite their collective financial efforts, to afford the rental costs of a bulldozer or even a tractor. The group also plans to purchase an engine to facilitate increased productivity of cooking oil, laundry and bath soap, and animal feed, even though its site is two miles from the centre of town, is not reached by any paved road, and has yet to be hooked up to Fiditi's electrical supply. The group admits that it may have to ask the FPU for help, but it is neither enthusiastic nor hopeful about the possibilities of such an alliance.[49]

The SDP secretary who occupies one of the ex-officio seats within the FPU executive also has strong opinions about what kinds of development Fiditi needs right now—installation of industries, not infrastructural fine-tuning, is her greatest priority. This of course contrasts sharply with opinions gleaned from interviews with the FPU's male-dominated leadership, who seem more inclined to take a wait-and-see approach to income-generating projects at best, hoping for private investors to lead the way. In fact, there are some male *omo ibile* (particularly a Fiditian living in Lagos) who are setting aside some land for small-scale industry, but the economy has proved too severely constrained so far: a yam-flour enterprise had been set up but failed in 1988.[50] The ex-officio, on the other hand, sees economic development coming to Fiditi in the form of organizational effort, not individual initiative. She wants more attention from an agricultural development think-tank based in Ibadan in establishing *gari* factories and fruit canneries in the area, for example.[51]

Local culture and the FPU

Cultural change has been essential to the rise of the progressive unions. In this regard, the arrival and adoption of Christianity had profound effects on Yoruba society. The principal effect of conversion was to emphasize the process of individuation of households, which had begun because, among other reasons, of the growth of an exchange economy and a monetary taxation system. The colonial state formalized this alienation of the individual from the household and the household from the compound at the level of political society,[52] but the spread of Christian ideology strongly assisted its legitimation at the level of civil society. Christian Yoruba had better opportunities in the colonial society and the colonial government interceded in local disputes more often than not on behalf of Christians.[53] But the Westernized state bureaucratically rewards the individual for merit instead of culturally rewarding the group to which that individual belongs—the new forms of political titles and awards are not systemically subject, as were the old forms, to dynastic control.[54]

Indeed, changing patterns of inheritance are also helpful in revealing much of how agenda-setting for local development has come to rest with the leadership of a particular form of civil society. In the past, the children of a Yoruba estate were alienated from it in favour of the deceased's full siblings who, given the common practice of polygyny, might have been numerous.[55] In effect, this was a system which, 'in its harsh operation towards the children of deceased persons . . . provide[d] no incentive for accumulation of fortune'.[56] But conversion to Christianity has led to increased incidence of monogamy and thereby further pressure for articulation of exclusive, agnatic forms of kinship solidarity. Together with the import of a European model of the state, inheritance patterns have now shifted towards recognition of primogeniture, and thereby the concentration of wealth instead of its dispersal.[57]

The rise of Christianity among the Yoruba also led to isolation of converted households through the churches' ability to produce literates who could deal more profitably with the colonial state.[58] Christian Yoruba have exhibited higher rates of educational achievement than their Muslim or animist counterparts. It is the educated members of the community, moreover, who tend to fulfil family obligations not by maintaining physical contact as much as financial contact.[59]

In general, the kinship principle in the Yoruba community has been redefined; there is now an incentive for accumulation at the household level, which in turn provides certain individuals in the community with greater bargaining power than others in terms of making and implementing decisions about the community's development. Kinship, or more broadly speaking 'belonging', is now defined by those who stand on one side or the other of that bargaining process and its outcomes. Social control in the locality is no longer based solely on a hierarchy of culturally defined roles of fixed status, but instead on a shifting coalition of interests graded by the sophistication and success of individual accumulation strategies.[60] Wealth is still used within the corporate boundaries of the *idile*, but individual households within that lineage group are now better positioned financially to struggle for leadership roles within the group. Generally speaking, kinship ties became increasingly challenged by loyalty to the state, while at the same time the state became more dispersed among rival localities.[61]

In line with these general observations, in Fiditi culture change has been reflected in an absolute monopoly of Christian control of the executive since the inception of the FPU, despite the fact that Fiditi has a sizeable Muslim population. In a similar vein, Berry describes some of the tensions between Muslims and Christians in the town of Iree, where Muslim contributions to supposedly 'community' projects led to the building, for example, of the Baptist Welfare Centre and the Iree Baptist High School. In the latter case, *omo* Iree sent abroad for training as future teachers at the school were all Baptists.[62]

Implications for future work

Several matters remain disturbingly unclear in this project so far:

o First, the constraints facing the research presented here denied even initial attention to the macro-structures which lie outside the locality. One of these macro-structures is the international economy, another is the political reality of the country.

o A second issue, therefore, has at least to do with the as yet imperfect sense of the role of the Nigerian state in promoting hometown association-driven development. Following Boone, it is important to realize that the state has multiple roles to play in shaping accumulation; at the very least, the state is used to *create* wealth, but at the same time operates more autonomously to condition the *deployment* of wealth.[63] Helpful here is use of notions about 'clientelism', which can be thought of as a strategy employed by the state in structuring predispositions for this deployment.[64] Although the present chapter has not focused on issues of this type, it is none the less possible to make the suggestion that hometown associations can be thought of as clients of the Nigerian state, especially now that the state has begun implementing a brace of policies meant to foster closer contact with the voluntary associations. In this regard, Boone believes that: 'By particularizing demands on the state, clientelism pre-empts the mobilization of broad-based political demands and collective political consciousness.'[65] What remains to be seen, of course, is the degree to which this may be true in the Nigerian case—what are the conditions for co-ordination or competition among the hometown associations now being more attentively recognized by the state?

o Third, it remains to be seen whether or not a *rentier* class is actually in formation in places such as Fiditi. It may be that the lack of productive investment by *omo ibile* does not reflect a tendency towards *rentierism*, but simply hypersensitivity to the volatile economic conditions prevailing in Nigeria today, as well as to the rapidly shifting political strategies of those with control over the economic powers of the state. In any case, Berry reminds us that the Yoruba are highly mobile regarding economic opportunity, making it 'thoroughly misleading . . . to assume that location can be used as a proxy for patterns of . . . social organization'.[66] The development of *rentierism* would be likely to present conceptual challenges to the use of any hypothesis which assumes a certain territoriality to definitions of non-productive investment.

○ Fourth, further studies need to emphasize differences in economic and institutional resources among hometown associations and among their member societies and clubs, as much as similarities, before any general picture can be developed.

○ Fifth, there has been a significant tendency in some of the literature on locality and social movements to view them as 'benign, historically consistent, and utterly autonomous'.[67] Alinsky and others have described social movements which are as reactionary as progressive, and Dunleavy has emphasized both the ability of the state to suppress or deflect hostile political developments and the consequent necessity of studying political inactivity in addition to overt political action.[68] The FPU has tried to maintain a balanced relationship with the authorities.[69]

○ Sixth, part of what needs to be explored further is the role played by tradition in the continuing development of places like Fiditi. While it is necessary to support the reinforcement of indigenous knowledge systems and forms of social welfare, it also becomes clear that the directions in which the progressive unions often pursue their rendezvous with tradition are those which lead away, not towards, the most helpful use of limited time, effort and resources. The current executive recognizes, for example, that there is a strong undercurrent of desire for greater involvement in the FPU's decision-making process among the ranks of its youth element (aged 18–40). This group wants, among other things, formally to quantify the criteria for honorary chieftaincies. Prevailing opinion has it that this is because the late *baale* gave away honorary chieftaincies without respecting traditional criteria; in the past, the FPU has advised the *baale* about the conferment of such titles. One has to wonder, however, at how much of a different dialogue about the development of the town is silenced (or simply never initiated) in light of the union's efforts in this area.[70]

○ Seventh, we may need to be careful in accepting Barkan's assumption that identification and clarification of processes and institutions which link state and society will both increase the responsiveness of government and its legitimacy in the eyes of the governed.[71] Such a project might, in fact, accomplish the latter but not the former; that is, by so altering the governed's sense of what 'legitimacy' means, it will be society, not the state, which will be subject to more accountability.

Notes

1. The research reported herein is part of a larger project supported in part by the Centre for International and Comparative Studies at the University of Iowa. Earlier research, published in an article by Joel D. Barkan, Michael L. McNulty, and M.O.A. Ayeni, 'Hometown Voluntary Associations, Local Development and the Emergence of Civil Society in Western Nigeria', *The Journal of Modern African Studies* 29 3, (1991), 457–80, was supported in part by the Center for Advanced Studies at the University of Iowa. Field research by Mark Lawrence in the summer of 1990 was supported in part by a Stanley–UI Support Organization grant for International Graduate Research. The continuing collaboration between scholars in Nigeria and Iowa has been facilitated by a USIA Institutional Development Link (1989–92) between the University of Iowa and the University of Ibadan.

Indigenous Organizations and Development

2. See Lawrence, M. (1993), 'Local Development, Progressive Unions, and the Transformation of Civil Society in western Nigeria', Department of Geography Research
   Paper, Iowa City, Iowa.
3. Berry, S. (1985), *Fathers Work For Their Sons: Accumulation, Mobility, and Class
   Formation in an Extended Yoruba Community*, Berkeley: University of California
   Press.
4. Ibid.: 43. See also Aronson, D. (1978), *The City is Our Farm*, Cambridge,
   Schenkman.
5. A partial listing of the names of these clubs and societies in Fiditi reflects the wide
   variety and nature of groups involved in maintaining ties to the community and
   promoting activities within the town. As of 1990, the list included the Alliance Club
   of Fiditi, the Alpha Club of Fiditi, the Asu Aspirants Club (whose members are
   Fiditians resident in Lagos and Ibadan), the Asu Christian Society, Club 8 of Fiditi,
   the Comrade Club of Fiditi, the Egbe Omolere, the Egbe Oni Lemu (a fruit sellers
   association), the Ero Mimo Women Society, the Esquire Club of Fiditi, the Fiditi
   Christian Society, the Fiditi Club, the Fiditi Dynamic Social Club of Nigeria, the
   Fiditi Movement Club, the Fiditi New Life Club, the Fiditi Prestige Circle, the Fiditi
   Solidarity Brothers, the Fuji Natural Group, the Great Noble Club of Fiditi, the
   Ibukun Olu Women Society, the Ife Loju Omo Fiditi (Ibadan based), the Iludun Ora
   Star Brothers, the Irawo Asu of Fiditi, the Irawo Ntan Social Club, Klub 10 of Fiditi,
   Club 55 (mostly resident of Oyo), Klub 84, the Oredegbe Society, the Pathfinders
   Club of Fiditi, the Patriotic Club of Fiditi, the Peacock Club, the Pioneer's Club of
   Fiditi, the Reformers Club, the Tepamose Society and the Unity and Peace Club of
   Fiditi.
6. Information supplied by the FPU Executive. It should be noted that this situation of
   executive non-residence is not unique to Fiditi but common among Yoruba communities.
7. See Barkan, McNulty and Michael, note 1.
8. See Lawrence, note 2.
9. Gugler, J. (1991), 'Life in a Dual System Revisited; urban-rural ties in Enugu,
   Nigeria, 1961–87', *World Development* 19(5), 399–409.
10. Bellah, R.N. (1985), *Habits of the heart: Individualism and commitment in American
    life*, Berkeley: University of California Press, 172.
11. See Reynolds, D.R. and Knight, D.B. (1989), 'Political geography', in G.L. Gaile
    and C.J. Willmott, eds, *Geography in America*, Columbus: Merrill, 582–618.
12. See Harvey D. (1985b), *The Urbanization of Capital*, Baltimore: Johns Hopkins
    University Press.
13. See Harvey D. (1989), *The Condition of Postmodernity*, Oxford: Basil Blackwell.
14. See examples: Geertz, C. (1963), 'The integrative revolution: Primordial sentiments
    and civil politics in new states', in C. Geertz (ed.) *Old Societies and New States: The
    Quest for Modernity in Asia and Africa*, New York: Free Press, 105–57; Hunter, A.
    (1974), *Symbolic Communities: The persistence and change of Chicago's local
    communities*, Chicago: The University of Chicago Press; Hunter, A. (1978), 'Per-
    sistence of local sentiments in mass society', in D. Street, and Associates, eds,
    Handbook of Contemporary Urban Life, San Francisco: Jossey-Bass, 133–62; Lof-
    land, L.H. (1973), *A World of Strangers: Order and action in urban public space*,
    New York: Basic Books; Suttles, G.(1968), *The Social Order of the Slum: ethnicity
    and territory in the inner city*, Chicago: University of Chicago Press.
15. Kasarda and Janowitz labelled this the 'linear–development' model of community
    attachment, tracing its origins to the writings of Toennies, Durkheim, Simmel,
    Summer and Wirth (Kasarda, J.D. and Janowitz, M. (1974) 'Community attachment
    in mass society', *American Sociological Review* 39(3): 328–39).
16. See, for example, Goudy, W.J. (1990), 'Community attachment in a rural region',
    Rural Sociology 55(2): 178–98.
17. See Fischer, C. (1982) *To Dwell Among Friends: Personal networks in town and city*,
    Chicago: University of Chicago Press. See also for example Foley, D.L. (1952),

Neighbours or Urbanities? Rochester: University of Rochester; Hunter, op. cit.; Wellman, B. (1979a), 'The community question: the intimate networks of East Yorkers', *AJS* 84(5): 1201–31; and Wellman, B. and Leighton, B. (1978b), 'Networks, neighbourhoods, and communities; Approaches to the study of the community question', *Urban Affairs Quarterly* 14(3): 363–90.

18. Castells provides us with the story of the creation of distinctive local identities in Madrid in the midst of tremendous and rapid population growth (Castells, M. (1983) *The City and the Grassroots*, Berkeley: University of California Press, 213–88).

19. See Gugler n. 7.

20. Hoben, A. and Hefner, R. (1991) 'The integrative revolution revisited', *World Development* 19(18).

21. Laitin, D.D. (1985), 'Hegemony and Religious Conflict: British Imperial Control and Political Cleavages in Yorubaland', in P. Evans, D. Rueschemeyer and T. Skocpol (eds), *Bringing the State Back In*, London: Cambridge University Press.

22. Logan, J.R. and Molotch, H.L. (1987) *Urban Fortunes: The political economy of place*, Berkeley: University of California Press, 122.

23. Hoben, A. and Hefner, R. (1991), 'The integrative revolution revisited', *World Development*.

24. Fadipe, N.A. (1970) *The Sociology of the Yoruba*, Ibadan: Ibadan University Press, 243–60. See also Awe, B. (1977), 'The Iyalode in the traditional Yoruba political system', in A. Schlegel, ed., *Sexual Stratification: A cross-culture view*, New York: Columbia University Press.

25. Phillips, E. (1969), 'The Egba at Abeokuta: Acculturation and political change, 1830–1870', *Journal of African History* 10(1), 118.

26. Eades, J.S. (1980) *The Yoruba Today*, Cambridge: Cambridge University Press, 103. See also Oluwasegun, T.D. (1984), *Political Change in Yorubaland: A case study of the Alafin's office*, University of Ibadan, Department of Political Science, B.Sc. (Hons) thesis.

27. Lawale, J.L. (1983), *A Short Revised History of Fiditi Town*, Fiditi: Ola Apeena Printing Works.

28. Ibid.: 61–3; Asiwaju. A.I. (1967), *Western Yorubaland under European Rule 1889–1945*, Atlantic Highlands New Jersey: Humanities Press, 243–4. See also Enya, G.I. (1988), 'Voluntary Associations and Community Development in Afikpo Local Government Area, Imo State', University of Ibadan, Department of Adult Education, MA thesis.

29. Smock, Audrey C. (1971), *Ibo Politics: The Role of Ethnic Unions in Eastern Nigeria*, Cambridge, Mass: Harvard University Press.

30. Dudley, B.J. (1973), *Instability and Political Order: Politics and Crisis in Nigeria*, Ibadan: Ibadan University Press.

31. Adejumobi, A. (1991), *Processes and Problems of Community Organization for Self-Reliance*, Ibadan: Nigerian Institute of Social and Economic Research, Monograph Series No. 1.

32. See, Babangida, Major-General Ibrahim (1986), *Mobilising Popular Participation for Rural Development*, Lagos: Federal Government Printers, and a pamphlet by the DFRRI Chairman Larry D. Koinyan. 'Why You Need to Form Your Community Development Association'.

33. It is not within the scope of the present study to detail the process and rationale of state creation in Nigeria. But it would be noted that at the time the fieldwork for this chapter was undertaken, there were 22 states in the country; as of this writing (April, 1993) there are 30 states. Fiditi was and remains located in Oyo State, even though that state has now been divided.

34. Barkan *et al.*, 28. See also Boboye, J.O. (1970), 'The Diffusion of Innovation: The Case of Fruit Farming in Fiditi District', University of Ibadan, Department of Geography, B.Sc. (Hons) thesis.

35. The planning office was closed in 1990.

36. The terminology used here is not necessarily formalized by the FPU, but for purposes

of these notes, a branch is the main FPU group organized in a particular place, while each branch may have more than one chapter. Of course, it is also possible for a branch to have just one chapter.

37. The naira is the Nigerian basic currency unit.
38. Information supplied by Deacon Oyedele, FPU treasurer.
39. Logan and Molotch, 135. Also see Domhoff, G.W. (1983), *Who Rules America Now? A view for the 80s*, Englewood Cliffs: Prentice Hall; and Galaskiewicz, J. (1985), *The Social Organization of an Urban Grants Economy*, New York: Academic Press.
40. We would like to thank Rev Femi Oladela and Dr S.A. Agunbiade for their gift of a draft copy of the latest FPU constitution, dated June 1990.
41. A note on idiom: whereas 'to table a motion' in the US means to postpone discussion of an issue, in Nigeria this phrase has exactly the opposite meaning.
42. It is important in this regard to recall that the 'early dominance of men in founding these organizations is a reflection of their educational and other opportunities in colonial society' (Barkan *et al.*, 463(fn19). See also Afonja, S. (1981), 'Changing modes of production and the sexual division of labour among the Yoruba', *Signs* 7(2); Johnson, C. (1982), 'Grass roots organising: women in anticolonial activity in south western Nigeria', *African Studies Review* 25(2/3); Little, K. (1972) 'Voluntary associations and social mobility among West African women', *Canadian Journal of African Studies* 6(2); Parpart, J.L. (1988) 'Women and the State in Africa,' in D. Rothchild, and N. Chazan, eds, *The Precarious Balance: State and Society in Africa*, Boulder: Westview Press, 208–30; Stichter, S.B. and J.L. Parpart, eds (1988) *Patriarchy and Class: African women in the household and workplace*, Boulder: Westview press; Trager, L. (1990), 'Women's economic organizations in south western Nigeria: Local basis and regional linkages', Paper presented at the 33rd Annual Meeting of the African Studies Association, Baltimore, 1–4 November, 1990; and Trager, L. and Osinulu, C. (1991), 'New Women's Organizations in Nigeria; One response to structural adjustment', in, C.H Gladwin., ed., *Structural Adjustment and African Women Farmers*, Gainesville: University of Florida Press.
43. Information supplied by a former FPU treasurer.
44. Berry (1985), 166–91.
45. Information supplied by the FPU Executive.
46. Boone, C. (1990), 'The making of a rentier class: wealth accumulation and political control in Senegal', *The Journal of Development Studies* 427.
47. The SDP Secretary's role has caused some problems for the FPU, which has historically sought to avoid the appearance of becoming involved with partisan politics. During the time this research was conducted, she was admonished for flying the SDP flag over the compound; she removed the flag on condition that the National Republican Convention Party not be allowed to fly its flag inside the town.
48. Information on the membership of the subcommittees provided by the FPU General Secretary.
49. We would like to thank members of the Adi Co-operative Society for their assistance in providing us with the information presented here, and a teacher of the Methodist Secondary School and the Better Life for Rural Women programme for her kindness in acting as translator. This lady is also a member of the FPU's Education Sub-committee.
50. Information supplied by a former FPU General Secretary.
51. The group in question is the International Institute of Tropical Agriculture.
52. Asiwaju, 211.
53. Berry (1985), 167–8.
54. See Laitin. See also Ajayia, J.F.A. (1965), *Christian Missions in Nigeria 1841–1891: The making of a new elite*, Evanston: Northwestern University Press; and Gbadamosi, T.G.O. (1978), *The Growth of Islam Among the Yoruba, 1841–1908*, Atlantic Highlands, New Jersey: Humanities Press.
55. Fadipe, 140–46.
56. Ibid.: 145.

57. Eades, 55.
58. Asiwaju, 240.
59. Fadipe, 315–16
60. Harvey, D. (1985a), *Consciousness and the Urban Experience*, Oxford: Oxford University Press, 1–35, where the principal argument is that a money economy 'radically transforms and fixes the meanings of space and time in social life and defines limits and imposes necessities upon the shape and form of urbanization'.
61. See Lloyd, P.C. (1965), 'The Political Structure of African Kingdoms', in M. Banton, ed., *Political Systems and the Distribution of Power*, London: Tavistock; and Lloyd, P.C. (1968), 'Conflict theory and Yoruba kingdoms', in I.M. Lewis, ed., *History and Social Anthropology*, London: Tavistock.
62. Berry (1985), 172–3.
63. Boone, 428.
64. See Flynn, P. (1974) 'Class, clientalism, and dependency: Some mechanisms of internal dependency and control', *Journal of Commonwealth and Comparative Politics* 12(2): 133–56.
65. Boone, 429.
66. Berry (1985), 43. See also Berry, S. (1983), 'Work, Migration and Class in Western Nigeria: A reinterpretation', in F. Cooper, ed., *Struggle for the City*, Beverly Hills: Sage.
67. Molotch, H.L. and Logan, J.R. (1990), 'The space for urban action: Urban Fortunes, a rejoinder', *Political Geography Quarterly* 9(1), 90. See also Castells.
68. See Alinsky, S. (1969), *Reveille for Radicals*, New York: Vintage; and Dunleavy, P. (1977), 'Protest and quiescence in urban politics: a critique of some pluralist and structuralist myths', *International Journal of Urban and Regional Research* 1:193–218.
69. For instance, the organization found land to set aside for a stadium after the local government suggested that Fiditi would be an appropriate location for such a facility, even though land is scarce in the area. Still, the local government is not always ready to reciprocate. Water quality and water-pressure problems were taken to the council, only to be shifted to the Water Corporation, which has been slow in rectifying the situation. Around 1982, the FPU tried to establish a technical college in the town, but the state government blocked the project's implementation. In fact, much more work needs to be done in the area of uncovering the details of the progressive union's relationship to the state.
70. Indeed, part of the need to penetrate the relationships which obtain between progressive unions and traditional authorities has to do with the changing history of the latter. Thus, although the FPU constitution specifies as one of its aims the raising of 'the status and prestige of our paramount chief', it is important to understand this objective as involving an attempt by the organization to formalize the privileges and powers of the *baale*, to be associated with their validation.
71. Barkan *et al.*, 457.

4 Indigenous organizations and development: the case of Ara, Nigeria

D. MICHAEL WARREN, REMI ADEDOKUN
AND AKINTOLA OMOLAOYE*

OVER THE PAST several decades international and national development agencies have discussed ways to improve the capacity of individuals and organizations to carry out development activities, to provide the basis for participatory decision-making involving both the agents of change and the client groups, and to ensure that the approach to development leads to sustainability of the efforts. Within the last decade several components that facilitate capacity building, participatory decision-making, and sustainable approaches to development have been identified. These are the indigenous knowledge and decision-making systems, the indigenous organizations, and the indigenous approaches to experimentation and innovation leading to the solution of community problems. It is now abundantly clear that these indigenous structures present in every community have been invisible to many agents of change.

Indigenous knowledge, the local knowledge unique to a particular community or ethnic group, has been ignored or marginalized by Western-oriented change agents. Yet it is the indigenous knowledge of any given community that provides the basis for community-based decision-making as the community attempts to identify the changing set of problems and constraints it faces at any given point in time. Equally invisible to outsiders are the numerous formal and informal associations that exist in even the smallest towns. Many of these associations have development functions and have existed for long periods of time. Community-level associations provide fora for citizens of the community to identify, discuss, and prioritize problems and to seek means to solve them. This frequently leads to local-level experimentation and innovation with community-level evaluation of the results.

By taking the time and effort to record the indigenous knowledge and decision-making processes and to identify and understand the structures and functions of the indigenous organizations that exist within the community, the agent of change can work with citizens to understand the relative strengths and weaknesses of the existing systems. This leads to greater understanding of the local situation and provides the basis for improved communications between change agents and members of the clientele.

This case-study involves the community of Ara, an ancient Yoruba town of about 10000 inhabitants located 15 miles from Oshogbo, the capital of Osun State in Nigeria. All three of the co-authors have a special relationship to Ara. D.M. Warren, an American married to an Ara citizen since 1967, was installed in

* D. Michael Warren is Professor of Anthropology and Director of the Center for Indigenous Knowledge for Agriculture and Rural Development (CIKARD) at Iowa State University. Remi Adedokun is a Lecturer in the Department of Theatre, University of Ibadan. Akintola Omolaoye is a graduate student in the Department of Geography, University of Ibadan.

June 1990 as the *Atunluse* of Ara, the chief in charge of development in the community. Remi Adedokun, a lecturer of theatre at the University of Ibadan, is a native of Ara, as is Akintola Omolaoye, a son of the *Alara* of Ara and a graduate student in geography at the University of Ibadan. All three have been deeply involved in community development in Ara during the past several years. The case-study is an excellent one to depict the indigenous knowledge and indigenous organizations that exist within a community but remain invisible even to knowledgeable 'outsiders' such as Warren.

Warren has visited Ara since 1968 an average of twice a year for periods of a few days to several months. Moreover, he has been involved in development projects in Ghana and Zambia designed to improve the capacity of district councils in the areas of management and development planning. It was, however, only after being installed as the *Atunluse* that the inadequacy of his understanding of the community became obvious. During a sabbatical year (1991–2) spent at the Nigerian Institute of Social and Economic Research, it was decided by Warren and community leaders of Ara that a one-week development planning workshop would be conducted to improve the management and planning skills in the community. This was the first time that Warren was to facilitate such a workshop in the local language, in this case Yoruba with the able assistance of Akintola Omolaoye. In preparation for the workshop Warren discovered that the major management and development planning concepts that he and many other development practitioners had assumed were the domain of Euro-America already existed in the Yoruba language (see box, p. 49). During the one-week workshop it also became clear that the community had dozens of associations and organizations that had development functions, the majority of these totally unknown to Warren despite the numerous visits to Ara over a 25-year period.

What has transpired in Ara since the one-week workshop in August 1991 provides important lessons for both community leaders and development practitioners. In many development ventures, it is far more cost-effective to work with and through existing organizations in ways that strengthen their capacity to carry out development activities that reflect priority problems identified within the community itself than to establish a new organization.

The community of Ara is the political seat of the *Alara*, the *oba* or traditional leader of the citizens of Ara as well as 40 smaller towns and villages located in the Egbedore Local Government area of Osun State. The *Alara* is the head of the Ara Traditional Council which comprises 23 chiefs including several who are women. One of the 40 towns is headed by an *oba*, seven others are headed by *baales*, chiefs lower in status than *obas*, and the remaining farming villages are led by headmen. The total population of the entire traditional state is about 40000.

Ara traces its origin to Orira who migrated from Ile-Ife as early as the tenth century. Orira was a son of Aranfe, one of the sons of Olofin Oduduwa, the forefather of the Yoruba. Ara is located in the tropical rain forest. The vast majority of the inhabitants are engaged in full-time and part-time farming. Two farming systems characterize this part of Nigeria. The older, more dominant one, is a perennial mixed plantation system of trees bearing cash-crops. The most important trees are kola, cocoa, oil palm, coffee, citrus, rubber and mango. The second farming system that has rapidly grown in importance involves biennial and annual mixed cropping of arable crops. These include yam, cocoyam, cassava, plantains and bananas, maize, sweet potato, beans, groundnuts, and numerous vegetables such as okra, leafy greens, tomatoes, *egusi* melon and peppers.

Many inhabitants are also involved in the processing of agricultural produce. Women control the production of palm oil and other products from the oil palm, as well as *gari* flour from cassava and *elubo* flour from yams. Others are engaged in commerce and trade, tailoring, craft production of baskets and pottery, and various trades such as masonry, carpentry and plumbing.

The oldest and most prominent indigenous organization in Ara is the Ara Traditional Council which includes the *Alara* and his chiefs. The council has executive, legislative and judicial functions. It is the governing council of the town, and settles disputes, receives visitors, enacts and enforces laws guiding the security and well-being of its citizens, discusses and either endorses or rejects all proposed development projects, ensures that the market is well managed, represents the interests of the citizens of Ara at the local, state and federal levels of government, removes chiefs who do not fulfil their responsibilities, and endorses the installation of new chiefs. The *Alara*'s chiefs comprise the advisory organ for the king; they deliberate daily with the *oba* on issues affecting the progress of the town, and serve as the kingmakers should the *oba* pass away. The *Alara* himself is responsible for crowning and installing any new *oba* or *baale* for towns under his suzerainty, presides over the Customary Court in Ara, has the responsibility for the allocation of land, and has the power to give honorary titles. The *Alara* and his chiefs have used the indigenous kinship system as a primary means for mobilizing the citizens for community-wide efforts. This indigenous organization is particularly invisible to outsiders as it has no officers as such. Called the *Egbe Olomo Ile*, literally the 'Children of a Household', this ancient management system is very effective in supporting development projects through donations of materials, financial resources and communal labour.

In addition to the Ara Traditional Council, there are two other broad-based development-oriented community associations, the Ara Descendants' Union (ADU) and the Ara Development Council (ADC). The ADU, a hometown association founded in 1947, has 19 branches in cities in Nigeria and Ivory Coast. The largest branch, with headquarters in Abidjan, serves as an Ara hometown association uniting the 500 Ara citizens who live and work in the Ivory Coast. The ADU branch in Abidjan and several Nigerian branches such as Oshogbo play important roles in the planning and financing of Ara's self-reliant development projects. The ADU also serves as a parent umbrella organization for the numerous social clubs in Ara, helps to mobilize the community for the implementation of development projects, and serves as a useful forum for the settlement of disputes. The Action Committee of the ADU was founded in 1989 to provide a mechanism for concentrated mobilization of community efforts through a limited number of highly committed citizens.

The Ara Development Council, founded in 1949, had several community development association predecessors that can be traced by oral history to well over a hundred years ago. At the turn of the twentieth century two community development associations existed in Ara, the *Kila* Association and the *Oba n'Basiri*. Some of the achievements of these associations early in the twentieth century, still remembered with pride, were the construction by communal labour of the first roads and bridges linking Ara with other towns. During World War II these two associations were replaced by the *Egbe Ibile* which continued efforts directed at extending the road system as well as initiating an improved local tax-collection system. During the post-World War II period, it became fashionable in Ara for development-oriented groups to be registered with the local government for legal status and government recognition. During this period, one of the important development associations in the Ara was the Arapeju Atunluse Brothers. This association had the function of a community mobilizing caucus, membership was by subscription and consisted of prominent citizens. The first chairperson was Pa Atanda and the first secretary was Reverend Adegoke. In Ara, this development association merged into the Ara Development Council. Other major development projects planned and implemented through these community development associations include the construction of primary schools (the first established in 1933), a secondary school (1960), customary court (1950), town hall (1951), postal agency (1951), Farmers Co-operative Union (1950), maternity hospital (1954), dispensary (1956), police station (1981), co-operative credit union (1986), pipe-borne water (1988) and electricity (1990). Most of these projects were based entirely on self-reliant community efforts that involved problem identification, development planning, acquisition of capital and implementation through communal labour.

The community leaders decided to open the August 1991 workshop to any leader of an Ara association who could devote the full week. The result was 110 participants representing a wide range of interests and backgrounds. This proved to be especially important when participants were asked to work in teams using brainstorming and nominal group techniques to identify and prioritize problems and constraints hindering development efforts in the community. This was one of the first opportunities for many women and youth leaders to present their views in such a broad forum. The workshop goal was to improve the quality of life of Ara citizens through the sharing of experiences and viewpoints on community development. The objectives were to provide an opportunity for community leaders to experience a variety of management and development planning skills that leaders in other communities had found useful, to design an Ara development plan and development handbook, and to design a strategic plan to raise the resources required to implement the plan.

Many development practitioners have been involved in improving organizational effectiveness for several decades. Experiential approaches to training have been found the most effective for adult participants in workshops designed to improve management and development skills. Experiential approaches emphasize team-building, the use of team exercises to draw out development lessons during the group processing of the exercises, little emphasis on traditional lecture presentations, and the practice of new skills by workshop teams in the workshop environment where mistakes can be made without jeopardizing any actual project. Evaluation has shown that participants retain more knowledge and skills through this approach. Although these types of workshops have been common for government officials, far less emphasis has been placed on the strengthening of development planning capacity of indigenous organizations that exist at the community level.

The authors found that experiential approaches work very well with participants ranging from the non-literate to those literate in Yoruba and those literate in both Yoruba and English. Team-building exercises known to be effective in workshops with government officials proved to be equally effective with non-literate and semi-literate participants. Most of the exercises worked as well with the Ara leaders as they had with government officials. The training modules were used to introduce teams to problem situations specific to the community of Ara. Teams analysed the history of their own development associations and activities.

One of the most exciting parts of the workshop was the careful analyses of organizational constraints within the community that impede local development efforts.

The primary constraints to Ara's development as identified by participants working in teams were ineffective communications and inadequate representation of all of Ara's interest groups in the development decision-making process. Considerable time and effort in the workshop was expended in the analysis of relative strengths and weaknesses of community-wide development associations. Yoruba culture is patrilineal and patriarchal in nature. The Ara Development Council, established in 1949 but tracing its roots to predecessor organizations to well over a hundred years ago, was comprised of male representatives of the major extended family households of Ara.

Workshop participants decided to experiment with a new organizational structure based on representatives of the various types of associations within the community. These would include the social clubs, the women's associations, the Muslim and Christian communities, the occupational associations, the commercial associations, the Ara Descendants' Union, the Ara Traditional Council, the PTAs, the farmers' co-operative societies, the eight towns with an *oba* or *baale,* the 28 farming villages led by headmen, as well as the elected councillors representing Ara on the Egbedore Local Government. It was also decided to elect officers for two-year terms. Monthly meetings would be open to all citizens of Ara who were not elected representatives on a non-voting basis. To facilitate liaison and communications between the ADC, the ADU, and the Ara Traditional Council it was decided to appoint an Ara Development Liaison Officer. Akintola Omolaoye was the first one chosen.

The functions of the new Ara Development Liaison Officer are to provide liaison and communications links among the ADC, ADU and its Action Committee, and the Traditional Council (TC); to help monitor development efforts; to assist the editor of the *Ara Development Newsletter;* to help organize communal labour to support community development projects; to organize joint quarterly meetings of the ADC and TC, and monthly meetings of the ADC and the ADU and its Action Committee; to monitor and assist the various development committees; and to improve civic pride and action among the Ara youth through talks in the Ara schools. The liaison officer was also in charge of organizing the annual two-day evaluation workshops to be held every December during which time the community would discuss progress made during the current year and design a realistic plan for the upcoming year. The workshop participants identified the key development functions of the Ara Traditional Council to be the monitoring of progress on development projects; those of the Ara Development Council to be the design and evaluation of projects; and those of the Ara Descendants' Union and its Action Committee to be the facilitation of the implementation of projects.

Communication was also expected to be enhanced through the publication of the *Ara Development Handbook* and the *Ara Development Newsletter* edited by Remi Adedokun. Considerable effort went into the production of the handbook, which includes maps showing the location of Ara and its surrounding towns and villages, history of Ara and its towns, descriptions of numerous associations and names of members of various development project committees.

For long-term planning purposes it was decided to hire professional geographers from the University of Ibadan to produce maps showing the accurate layout of the lands under the suzerainty of the Ara. These provide the basis for future planning to extend amenities to the outlying communities. These maps are now displayed in the new Ara Community Development Planning Office that was opened in 1993.

Among the numerous problems identified and prioritized were limitations for short-term credit, difficulties in adequate child-care facilities for working mothers, inadequacy of the technologies used by women to produce palm oil and *gari* flour, lack of training opportunities for disabled citizens, the very difficult road linking Ara with major urban centres, the need for a new town hall and a renovated palace, the need to complete several partially constructed churches and mosques, the need to extend the electrical and pipe-borne water grid to households in Ara without these amenities and to make plans for effective extension of these to surrounding communities, and the need to bring into the community improved tree-crop species such as hybrid oil-palm seedlings.

By the end of December 1993, when the second annual evaluation workshop was held at the *Alara*'s palace, it was apparent that considerable progress had been made on development objectives set in the 1991 workshop and in the first annual evaluation workshop in December 1992. The community had opened the Ara Community Day Care Centre; the Ara Community Library; the Ara Community Development Planning Office; had the new Ara Community Bank constructed up to the roofing stage; inaugurated the new Ara Women's Co-operative Food Products Enterprise with a new facility to hold appropriate technology machines that will greatly reduce the time and effort of women in the production of palm oil and *gari* and provide the means to produce for the first time in Ara both palm kernel oil and cake. In addition the Holy Cross Centre is partially constructed and being organized to provide training opportunities for disabled citizens; the contract has been signed by the Osun State Government for the new highway that will link Ara with Ejigbo and Ede in 1995; new hybrid oil-palm seedlings are being grown; electrical and pipe-borne water-lines have been extended to many more households in Ara; concerted efforts are continuing to complete partially constructed mosques and churches; and initial plans have been made for the construction of a new town hall and the renovation of the *Alara*'s palace.

Lessons for development practitioners include the following:

○ Experiential approaches to training work exceptionally well with non-literate and semi-literate participants.
○ Management and development planning concepts often exist in local language.
○ Grassroots participants comprehend the content of training exercises and training modules as well as government officials.
○ These exercises and modules can be translated into local languages without difficulty.
○ Local leaders and citizens have a comprehensive understanding of weaknesses and strengths in their own indigenous organizations and are very open to experimenting with new management approaches.
○ Citizens of Ara were very open to providing a wider array of leadership opportunities for women.
○ It was also apparent that outsiders to the community are excited about development innovations and willing to support these efforts in various ways. Numerous Nigerians from other communities as well as people from

the USA, Canada and Japan have been interested sufficiently to contribute resources and to visit Ara personally.

Yoruba terms for management and development planning concepts

Abayori tabi iyanju	Solution
Agbarijo eniyan	Team
Ajosepo	Teamwork
Alumoni adanida	Natural resources
Alumoni afojuri	Physical resources
Alumoni eniyan	Human resources
Alumoni owo	Financial resources
Amojuto	Management
Anfani	Opportunity
Ayewo	Evaluation/assessment
Egbe tabi ibasepo	Association
Eto lesese/ikojo	Organization
Idagbasoke	Development
Idagbasoke ilu	Community development
Idasile	Creativity
Idi	Objective
Idiwo	Constraint
Ifilole ohun titun	Innovation
Ifinufindo tabi idanwo	Experiment
Ilana	Designing/creating the path towards an objective
Ilosiwaju	Progress
Imo ako tabi abo yato	Gender
Ipinnu	Decision
Ipo isiwaju	Priority
Iseto	Organizing or planning
Isoro	Problem
Nilo tabi aini	Need
Opin	Goal (endpoint)

---

5 The Ogbomoso *Parapo*:
A case-study of an indigenous development association in Nigeria

G.O. KOLAWOLE*

ORAL HISTORY RELATES the establishment of Ogbomoso by a group of hunters possibly as early as AD 1600. These Yoruba hunters came in search of wild animals whose meat and skins they could sell. Among the hunters was a particularly brave one called Ogunlola. He noticed smoke from a site near where Ogbomoso is now located. Ogunlola and his hunter colleagues took the initiative and met other hunters in the area. He invited them to form an association which they named the Alongo Society around 1677 AD.

This was the first hometown association in this new settlement. Based on oral history, the objectives of the society were common defence against raids by Sunmoni slavers, group hunting of wild animals and other forms of mutual assistance. Every evening, the hunters met at Ogunlola's settlement and he was made the first head of the Alongo Society. They would discuss such things as current affairs and protection strategies from slave raiders and wild animals. The news of the Alongo Society spread and other hunters moved their settlements closer to that of Ogunlola. Ogbomoso began to grow in size and population from this period.

The hunters and warriors who originally settled in Ogbomoso played an important part in the active defence of the old Oyo Empire (1600–1836) and later the new empire (1836–1890).

Some Ogbomoso local people such as Toyeje were installed as the *Are-Ona Kakanfo* (the Chief of the Warriors) of the old Oyo Empire because they helped to prevent the Fulani invasion spreading further south from what is now the area of Ilorin. Later descendants of these hunters have assumed the title of *Are-Ona Kakanfo*, such as the late Chief Samuel Akintola, Premier of the old Western Nigeria (1961–66).

Although few contemporary citizens of Ogbomoso know much about the Alongo Society, many of them are active participants in the associations based on this society such as the Ogbomoso *Parapo* (Parapo in Yoruba means 'to join together' or 'to unite'). Other development-oriented contemporary societies include the Ogbomoso Progressive Union, Egbe Itesiwaju Ogbomoso, Ogbomoso Ajilete Group, Ogbomoso Development Association, Ogbomoso Descendants' Union, Ogbomoso Women's League and the Ogbomoso Students' Union. Like similar associations in other Yoruba communities, these Ogbomoso associations provide the mechanisms for citizens to participate in the social and economic development of their city.

The Ogbomoso *Parapo* and other associations have been responsible for self-reliant efforts to improve roads, water, electricity, schools and colleges in the area. They have also worked closely with government to provide resources for priority social and economic projects. A recent development is the selection of

* Mr. G.O. Kolawole is Head of The Department of Business and Public Administration, The Polytechnic, Ibadan, Nigeria.

an annual day for Ogbomoso when citizens come home to socialize and decide on the development plans for the coming year. Ogbomoso celebrated its first Ogbomoso Day on November 19, 1993.

The population of Ogbomoso was about 140000 people according to the 1963 census, placing it in the third position after Lagos and Ibadan.

The Ogbomoso *Parapo*

The purpose of this case-study is to give a descriptive account of the Ogbomoso *Parapo*. The organizational structure and functions of this indigenous organization will be discussed, particularly how development activities are managed. Suggestions will be made regarding how this indigenous organization could be strengthened for development activities.

The Ogbomoso *Parapo* was established at the end of World War II when many Ogbomoso citizens began to move to many other localities both within Nigeria as well as other places in West Africa, especially the Gold Coast (now Ghana).

The idea of the Ogbomoso *Parapo* grew from citizens of Ogbomoso living in other localities who wanted a mechanism to link all of them into a network tied to the home base. The primary efforts came from the numerous citizens who went to trade and farm in Kumasi, Accra, Tamale, Sekondi and other localities in the Gold Coast. Other Ogbomoso citizens living in Nigerian towns supported the idea of joining together through branches of the proposed Ogbomoso *Parapo*.

Once the branches were established, a movement among the Ogbomoso youth emerged in the late 1950s. For each branch of the Ogbomoso *Parapo*, one soon found student sub-branches representing the students attending secondary schools, polytechnics, colleges of education and universities located in metropolitan areas.

My first experience with the Ogbomoso *Parapo* was at the Baptist College in Iwo (1962–64). The name we used then was the Ogbomoso Students' Union. Our objectives were set in line with the Ogbomoso *Parapo* for the adults even though we had little money and influence with which to embark on serious development activities.

Structure of the Ogbomoso *Parapo*

The organizational structure of the Ogbomoso *Parapo* is simple. The Ogbomoso *Parapo* Federal Council has officers elected when many citizens return home for Christmas and New Year. All citizens are welcome to attend the annual December 16 meeting when the Grand Patron, the custodian of the Ogbomoso culture and custom, the *Shoun* of Ogbomoso (*Oba* or king) gives a short address and answers questions. When the *Shoun* departs, the Federal Council meeting is continued by the elected and nominated officers. People in attendance include both home-based citizens and representatives of branches of the Ogbomoso *Parapo* from other localities. Members present ideas for possible development activities and discuss ways to secure the resources required to pursue them. Committees are set up to monitor each approved project. The Federal Council reports periodically on the progress of each project to all of the branches of the Ogbomoso *Parapo*.

Localities with large numbers of Ogbomoso citizens may have several branches of the Ogbomoso *Parapo*. Each branch is free to draw up its own constitution and set its own objectives, although most of these are similar and directed towards the development of Ogbomoso.

Each branch of the Ogbomoso *Parapo* chooses its own patron, vice-patrons and elects its own officers, typically a chairperson, vice-chairperson, financial secretary and treasurer. The officers of a branch comprise the executive board. The executive discusses matters before the general meeting, which is scheduled once or twice a month. The executive can also initiate actions which are later discussed and approved at the general meeting. The patrons are not required to attend every meeting, but they may be called upon to provide advice or give financial support for an approved developmental activity that the branch *Parapo* wants to pursue for Ogbomoso.

Development activities for Ogbomoso are pursued from two approaches. The Federal Council pursues the larger-scale development activities by raising financial support from the branches of the *Parapo*. Individual branches can also pursue independent smaller-scale projects for the city. For example, when the Osogbo branch undertook to build covered shelters at bus-stops, the Akure and Ondo branches co-ordinated to do the same at different locations in the town.

In addition to the Ogbomoso *Parapo* Federal Council engaging in large-scale development projects, and the branch *Parapo* in other towns pursuing smaller development objectives, a third approach was initiated in 1984. The Ogbomoso *Parapo* Southern Council was established to co-ordinate branch activities in the five states in southern Nigeria. The Southern Council still recognizes the leadership role of the Federal Council and at times passes development plans to it for execution. This third approach was designed by one of the High Chiefs of Ogbomoso. Chief S.T. Ojo, the *Otun Shoun* of Ogbomoso (second in rank to the king or *Oba*), felt that many developmental projects could be achieved by a stronger union of *Parapo* in cities of southern Nigeria which had large numbers of Ogbomoso citizens. The Southern Council that he proposed would be able to perform better and more formidably than the individual branches on their own. He called all the chairpersons of different branches in southern Nigeria to form the Ogbomoso *Parapo* Southern Council. The members of the Southern Council are the branch *Parapo* in southern Nigeria. Each branch is represented by its chairperson or secretary or any other member nominated during its general meeting. The Ogbomoso *Parapo* Southern Council was established on 31 November 1984 with membership from branches in Oyo, Ondo, Ogun and Lagos states, and more recently from the newly-created Osun state. Now there are 15 member branches. The branch in Togo sent a representative to one meeting.

The Southern Council has a constitution similar to those of the branches. The executive officers are zoned. The Ibadan branches provide the chairperson and general secretary; Oyo the assistant general secretary; Osogbo the financial secretary; Lagos the treasurer and public relations officer; towns north of Ibadan the auditor; and Mefoworade, Ife and Ondo zone the vice-chairperson.

Ogbomoso *Parapo* Southern Council has met quarterly every year since 1985. The venue of the general meeting is shifted from town to town and from state to state. The branch members originally contributed a membership fee of N20 at each meeting. The fee was later increased to reflect the financial capability of each branch. Lagos now contributes N600 a year, Ibadan N450 a year, while Osogbo, Oyo and other branches contribute N150 each, annually.

The Executive Council sets out the agenda for the general meeting a week in advance. Prominent citizens are invited as guests of honour to the general meeting. These men and women donate money for the development activities that the Ogbomoso *Parapo* Southern Council proposes on the day of the general meeting. An examination of the constitution of Ogbomoso in the USA and Ogbomoso *Parapo* Southern Council indicates a strong concern with development activities. Among the numerous objectives set in the constitutions are the following which the Ogbomoso *Parapo* pursues:

o Fostering of unity, understanding and co-operation among sons and daughters of Ogbomoso wherever they may be located on the face of the earth;
o Seeking and promoting social, cultural, educational and economic development of Ogbomoso;
o Assisting deserving sons and daughters in all legitimate matters;
o Serving as watchdogs and advisers in all matters of administration in Ogbomoso;
o Safeguarding and protecting the customs and traditions of Ogbomoso; and
o Co-operation with other organizations with similar objectives and raising funds for economic and social development of Ogbomoso.

Ogbomoso *Parapo* has completed many developmental projects, both large-scale and small-scale in the city and its satellite towns. An *ad hoc* committee set up by the United Nations Organization in 1963 published a monograph on Community Development and Nation Building in which community development was described as 'a means for reducing rural isolation by new knowledge, better communications, and improved local organizations. The contribution of local organizations need not wait for highly developed educational and technical services. Important advances can be made within a short time by the application of simple skills and the wise use of available resources aided by the impetus that comes from greater confidence and unity of purpose.' The notable achievement of the Ogbomoso *Parapo* and the management systems in all their development activities validate the United Nations statement.

There was no secondary school in Ogbomoso until 1952. Sons and daughters of Ogbomoso citizens had to go to distant places like Abeokuta, Iwo and Lagos for it. This type of problem was discussed in one of the *Parapo* meetings. Committees were set up. One committee worked with the Ministry of Education to seek approval for the establishment of a secondary school. Another one sought to attract a principal who was a university graduate. A third committee worked on the acquisition of a site and a timetable.

A graduate teacher was attracted by the provision of a house and a car. An existing primary school was converted into a temporary secondary school in 1952 with admission of a few male students. Ogbomoso was no longer disadvantaged in educational development, and the Ogbomoso *Parapo* then began to provide scholarships to send young peole to study overseas who would return and teach in the new school. A retired principal, an Ogbomoso resident, remarked at a meeting in 1988 that he was committed to the ideal of the Ogbomoso *Parapo* because of the scholarship given to him to study geography in the United Kingdom.

Successful execution of this project and the expansion of collective activities gave the Ogbomoso community the confidence to undertake even larger development projects. The *Parapo* continued sending outstanding youth to study overseas. Ogbomoso *Parapo* also then began initiatives to educate women.

Based on their 1952 experience in establishing a boys' secondary school, the *Parapo* was able to establish the Ogbomoso Girls' High School in 1957.

Another notable achievement of the Ogbomoso *Parapo* was the completion of the *Shoun*'s Palace which was commissioned in early 1978. This idea was first suggested in the 1950s and took more than 25 years to achieve. The palace became a thing of beauty to the town and it encouraged the Ogbomoso *Parapo* to build a comparable town hall. Near this town hall, a large office complex was also built to accommodate local government employees. It is in this hall that the December 26 General Meeting of the Ogbomoso *Parapo* is usually held. It can accommodate about 2 000 delegates.

All these are large-scale development projects achieved by the Ogbomoso *Parapo* Federal Council and the money to do them with came from branch *Parapos* and individual citizens. Another large-scale project for which some money has been contributed but has not been used is the technical college project. The *Parapo* wants this technical college to be one of the best in the country. The Federal Council also engages in numerous other small projects like provision of accommodation for resident doctors in the general hospital, lobbying for any development project to be sited in Ogbomoso and its satellite towns.

The individual branches of the Ogbomoso *Parapo* are often called upon to give financial assistance to the Federal Council when there is a shortfall for any development project. Notwithstanding this financial assistance, the individual branches also give scholarships to children from Ogbomoso, they repair roads and underwrite business ventures such as an agro-allied industry initiated by Ogbomoso Development Association. These branches of *Parapo* are very aggressive, dynamic and bold, and can knock at government doors seeking social and economic improvements for the town. Branches work on improved water supply and electricity and better communication between the townspeople and government. The Ogbomoso Women's League has provided materials and a baby incubator to the general hospital in the city. The Ogbomoso *Parapo* Southern Council which has just been established has bought a large amount of land which it wishes to give to a development project. There are also small-scale projects it has given assistance to. An example is the library worth a million naira that the Lagos branch of the Ogbomoso *Parapo* is building near the university in the town. Though it is the Lagos branch of the *Parapo* that is building the library, the Southern Council gave a cash donation. Book donations are being sought from the New York branch.

The Ogbomoso *Parapo* believes that community-based development can be enhanced by better communication between government and people. The communities can become effective partners in achieving national objectives.

In 1990, the Oyo state government decided to establish a new state university. They sought individuals and groups to participate in the contribution of resources to fund it. All communities in Oyo State were requested to contribute as much as they could. As a result, each town in the different local governments of Oyo State donated money or promised materials and money. A large amount was gathered to complement what the government had. Ogbomoso contributed handsomely. Ogbomoso mobilized different *Parapos* to donate to the university fund and the town was able to raise nearly seven million naira, far more than any other town.

The Oyo state government later chose Ogbomoso as the site for the new

University of Technology, now named after Chief S.L. Akintola, former *Are-Ona Kakanfo* of Yorubaland and the last Premier of Western Nigeria.

Other notable achievements of the Ogbomoso *Parapo* include the following:

○ Constant assistance to the technical college located in the city;
○ Settling disputes among prominent citizens;
○ Award of scholarships to promising students;
○ Money and material assistance to an orphanage and government hospital;
○ Building of covered shelters at bus-stops to protect people from sun and heavy rain by Osogbo and Ondo branches of the Ogbomoso *Parapo*;
○ Provision of infrastructure such as building of culverts and bridges;
○ Cash donation to build a modern library by Ogbomoso *Parapo*/Lagos branch;
○ Proposal to give Ladoke Akintola University of Technology a sum of N50 000 by Ogbomoso *Parapo* Southern Council.

Ogbomoso *Parapo* in different towns have financial reserves which can be donated for a specific developmental activity when there is a call for assistance. For example, the Ogbomoso *Parapo* Southern Council has bought two parcels of land which it is willing to donate for a deserving development project free of charge. It is also working on the improvement of the town's water supply, improved open-air day-market, and a more dependable supply of electricity for Ogbomoso.

Conclusion

Ogbomoso *Parapo* has its own management problems. The Federal Council, for example, does not meet regularly without the support from the branch Ogbomoso *Parapo* and often lacks financial means to execute development plans. Citizens and branches within the city of Ogbomoso are unlikely to assist the Federal Council and are even less interested in undertaking projects with the name of Ogbomoso *Parapo*.

Another problem facing the *Parapo* relates to identification and prioritization of development activities. Selecting the most promising development projects often results in hot debates at the general meeting. For example, there was a great argument over whether the priority activity would be the extension of the water supply or the provision of a large day-market.

One way to resolve these problems and strengthen the hometown associations for development is to elect retired educated men and women who may take some remuneration for their services. All executives currently perform their jobs free of charge. They only receive transport and food allowances. If some sort of remuneration was allowed for officers, they would be able to travel to lobby for development programmes with government and other *Parapos*.

6 Community development associations and self-reliance: The case of Isalu Community Development Union, Iseyin, Nigeria

BOLANLE W. WAHAB*

Introduction

INDIGENOUS ORGANIZATIONS ARE grassroot associations built on the principles of co-operation and organized group work. These purely traditional organizations, which include community development associations or unions, have existed for many centuries in different forms, especially among peasant societies, and have been responsible for much of the socio-economic and physical development of their respective communities.

Warren (1992: 5) observes that indigenous organizations and associations play very vital roles in community-level efforts to identify and prioritize their problems and seek solutions. In the past few years, considerable work has been done by various scholars around the world on the invaluable roles being played by these indigenous organizations (IOs) in the development process (Warren *et al.* 1989; Warren, 1991, 1992; Warren *et al.* 1995; Adejumobi, 1991). Many of the studies confirmed the important self-reliant development functions being carried out by the IOs in their various communities for many generations.

In most developing countries, citizens, especially those in the urban areas, look to their governments to provide for their needs. In the last two decades, however, governments, especially in Africa, have found it extremely difficult to meet people's socio-economic and welfare needs. The hallmarks of the crisis in Africa are its dwindling resources, growing external debts, declining economic performance reflecting very poor earnings, environmental degradation, insufficient food production and political instability. These and other factors have forced governments to explore the contributions community-based organizations can make towards self-reliant development.

Narrowing public-sector activities and commitments and the increased capacity of the private sector to engage in socio-economic activities have reinforced this dramatic shift to community-based organizations as providers for the needs of their communities. Development planners and policymakers have also realized that it is cost-effective to work with and through indigenous organizations on any development programme. The scope of development has also expanded to include what Brown and Korten (1989: 6) called a process by which members of a society develop themselves and their institutions in ways that enhance their ability to mobilize and manage resources to produce sustainable and justly distributed improvements in their quality of life.

Every community in Nigeria has always had a variety of indigenous organizations and associations which play important roles. Fortunately, all three levels of government in Nigeria have recognized the need for concerted community self-help efforts in order to realize the needs and aspirations of all Nigerians. Governments now appeal to and encourage communities to organize themselves

---

* Senior Lecturer, Department of Town Planning, The Polytechnic, Ibadan, Nigeria.

into Community Development Councils (CDCs) in order to achieve self-reliance and self-sustaining development. Community development was incorporated into development planning in Nigeria in the 1975–80 Third National Development Plan as a means of promoting meaningful physical developments in villages and towns.

There are 315 indigenous organizations in Iseyin, the activities of which reach into the social, political, occupational, cultural and religious spheres of life. Some of them are gender-specific associations. Unfortunately, the existence and activities of most of them are not known to people in larger communities. Isalu Community Development Union (ICDU) is one such community-based voluntary association in Iseyin which has successfully undertaken several developmental projects for the benefit of its members within the town and in the hinterland but whose activities are not known to some sections of the town and almost certainly not to outsiders. The task of this chapter is to expose the 'magic of success' of the ICDU by providing a documentary of its establishment and activities in all their ramifications. ICDU is an indigenous organization which evolved from the indigenous knowledge systems (IKS) and is the underlying secret of its success.

Aim and objectives

This chapter examines the past and present activities, potential and capacity of the ICDU to undertake self-initiated and self-financed community projects towards achieving self-sufficiency and self-reliance. The objectives are:

○ to disseminate information about the functions, characteristics and organizational structure of ICDU;
○ to appraise the process of decision-making, project selection and execution;
○ to examine sources of money and mode of spending;
○ to highlight its achievements and constraints/weaknesses;
○ to identify means of strengthening the capacity of ICDU for self-reliance and to enable it to contribute further to the socio-economic and physical development of Isalu, in particular, and Iseyin town, in general.

Methodology

The methodology used in this chapter is what Goode and Hatt (1952) termed the '*in situ* participant' approach. The author has been an active member of ICDU since 1964 and has been involved in every activity. Minutes of meetings, correspondences, project files and other relevant documents were consulted. Discussions with past and current officers of the union especially Mr Onatunji and Chief Siji Oke (the current chairperson) enhanced the accuracy of the information contained in the chapter.

Conceptual framework

In discussing the concept of community development association it is considered necessary to look at the underlying concepts.

The term 'community' has been defined by different authors from varied perspectives (Akorede, 1986; Abiodun and Aguda, 1986; Nottridge, 1972; Omuta, 1986; Kolajo, 1960; Abram, 1971; Wey, 1988). While some see community as people who have a common interest (Webster's *Dictionary*) or a specified geographical entity that can be identified in space, such as a town, others see it as houses and people located in a given area.

The concept of community has been further defined in terms of the more common trait of members having a sense of identity and developing common interests, experiences and roots, which help them to recognize and outline the attributes of their environments as resources, as well as a social wholeness in which each member has a stake and in which life is regulated by co-operation rather than by competition and conflict (Kolajo, 1960; Abram, 1971).

The concept of development is a complicated one having technical, socio-cultural and emotional connotations and one which can be defined from spatial and environmental points of view. Fisher (1984), De Blij (1993) and Friedmann (1981) have all written on the subject. Development is a term used to describe the process of overcoming poverty and diseases as well as the provision of infrastructural facilities such as bridges, hospitals, schools, electricity and water in areas where these are lacking (Olayiwola, 1990).

Development in relation to community development involves the stimulation of self-help and citizens' active participation in community affairs (Ekong, 1988). It implies improvement in the quality of life of a given people (Elaigwu, 1988).

Community development (CD) is the physical transformation of backward habitats in stages represented by the symbolic presence of such structures as modern buildings or town halls, schools, hospitals, roads and bridges, pipe-borne water and electricity (Takaya, 1988). The XIth International Conference of Social Work held in 1962 in Rio de Janerio gave a definition which fits appropriately to the objective of this chapter. It defined CD as 'a conscious and deliberate effort aimed at helping communities recognize their needs and to assume increasing responsibilities for solving their problems thereby increasing their capacities to participate fully in the life of the nation' (Ekong, 1988: 368).

Community Development Association (CDA)

Hicks and Gullett (1982) observed that an organization is formed by the coming together of individuals trying to achieve their personal objectives. In this way, the survival instinct of an individual, as Adedokun (1993) puts it, becomes a collective survival instinct. An association is simply a special-purpose group (Broom and Selznick, 1973: 206). Following from the above definition, a community development association can be defined as a voluntary association or interest group made up of people with mutual interests, common purposes, traits and peculiarities, coming together with the sole aim of collectively tackling a common problem or meeting a need (which is often socio-economic) while still retaining a degree of self-independence.

The main objective of most community-based organizations is the social and economic development of their various communities. Through their untiring efforts, such grassroot associations have undertaken communal construction of roads and bridges, police stations (e.g. Oje Owode via Saki), schools and banks (e.g. Ara Community Bank, Ara Community Day-care Centre and the commu-nity library), markets, health centres, post offices, town halls, mosques, churches, dams, and palaces (Warren, 1992; Agbola, 1988; Olowu et al., 1991;CASSAD, 1992; Togunde, 1994). Other achievements are the granting of soft loans and other financial assistance to members as with the Weavers' Association in Iseyin

(Wolff and Wahab, 1995). Women's associations have been equally effective not only in the dissemination of information on family planning, immunization, and Oral Rehydration Therapy (ORT), but also in the establishment of agro-based industries. The Ara Women's Co-operative Society established a palm-oil and food processing industry in Ara Town (Warren, 1992; Adedokun, 1993).

Self-reliance is the expression of human faith in people's own abilities (Nweze, 1988: 4). It is a conception of development in which peoples of a given society are mobilized to transform their physical, technological, political, administrative, economic and social environments for their own well-being (Nwosu and Nwankwo, 1988: 64).

The Isalu Community Development Union

Iseyin, the headquarters of the Iseyin Local Government Area of Oyo State, Nigeria, is located 96 kilometres north of Ibadan and 43 kilometres north-west of Oyo town. Iseyin is widely reputed for the weaving of narrow-strip cloth. A great number of its citizens are employed in this craft. They produce very fine quality native cloth, *Aso Oke*, hence the popular saying, 'Iseyin—the home of *Aso Oke*'.

There are hundreds of indigenous associations in Iseyin, each with its own name, constitution and times of meeting, modes of operation, management styles and level of achievement. There is, however, one basic objective that is common to all of them which is to enhance the socio-economic status and living standards of individual members to enable them in turn to contribute positively to the physical and socio-economic growth and development of Iseyin.

Iseyin is made up of eight wards. Of all the wards, Isalu ward has an enviable record of social and physical development through collective self-help efforts. Since the 1940s members of the Isalu community have been living and working together as a team with the motto 'Strength in Unity'. Every indigenous member of the community belongs to the ICDU automatically.

In pursuance of the latest efforts of the Nigerian government to encourage the formation and proper functioning of Community Development Associations (CDAs), the Oyo State Government launched the Oyo State Chapter of the Community Development Council (CDC) in early 1989 at Ibadan. The Iseyin local government version of the CDC is the CDC Committee which is supposed to oversee the affairs of all CDAs within the local government area. At the time of writing there are 301 registered CDAs within the local government, eight of which are in Isalu. The ICDU is larger in scope and greater in membership, functions and activities than any of the present CDAs. An appraisal of the activities of the other CDAs is the subject of another chapter.

Founding of the ICDU

Isalu Community Development Union is a very dynamic, progressive and well organized indigenous association. It evolved over the years because of the realization of its members that development would not happen if they relied on government to provide the essential services needed in the community. Of the eight wards in Iseyin, it is in Isalu that the government developmental effort is least felt.

In the early 1940s the elders of Isalu community came together to establish a society called 'Majeobaje Society, Isalu'. Every adult in Isalu, irrespective of religious faith, political leaning and socio-economic status, was a member of the society. Although the majority of the members were illiterate, they were people who knew much about every aspect of life in the community and the town as a whole. The chairperson of the society was the late Mustafa Dogo who ran the affairs of the society for almost 20 years. One reason for this was the fact that the society was a non-political organization set up mainly to promote the physical and economic development of Isalu. There was no cut-throat competition for a position in the society and, in any case, holding an office called for considerable dedication and sacrifice.

Members of the Majeobaje Society met regularly at the Catholic Mission in Bode Isalu and contributed a small amount each. At such meetings various issues were discussed, but the focus was always on the inadequate socio-physical infrastructure in the community.

The Majeobaje Society has the credit for initiating and opening up the 38km (24 miles) Isalu–Ikere road in the early 1940s. This is the road that leads from Bode Isalu to the site of the Ikere Gorge Dam (presently under construction). This road links together the villages where the people of Isalu have their farmlands: Elebiiri, Igboro, Alayin, Olobo, Agbede, Abugaga, Onitoto, Elekuku, Eleera, Onisaho, Ikodu, and Balelayo among others.

In 1954, the Majeobaje Society was granted permission by the Western Regional Development Board based in Ibadan to undertake the construction of a 4.4km road through the board's Upper Ogun Livestock Estate to Alayin village from where a link road was later constructed by the society to Ipapo town. Furthermore, in March 1955, the society commissioned the Owode market built in Ikere where buying and selling of farm products took place.

It is unfortunate that most of the developmental activities of the Majeobaje Society were not publicized. In 1961, the educated members of the Isalu community came together and launched the Isalu Literates' Union (ILU). The union's objectives were to bring into the limelight the laudable programmes and activities of the Majeobaje Society, to promote the educational advancement of members, to educate members of the community on the importance of self-help community projects, and to promote social interaction between members and other people in the town.

For many years the ILU functioned independently of the Majeobaje Society while complementing its activities. A point was reached, however, when the separate existence of the two associations was viewed as unhealthy. In order to remove this notion, and, more importantly, to ensure the participation of all citizens in community activities, the ILU was changed to the Isalu Progressive Union (IPU) in December, 1982. The nomenclature of the association was changed again in 1990 to the Isalu Community Development Union (ICDU) with the motto: 'Progress in Togetherness'. The new name was adopted to emphasize the community development orientation of the union.

Aims and objectives of ICDU

The ICDU is the only recognized body that brings together every citizen of Isalu and the one through which the common goal and aspirations of the ward could be achieved. The objectives of the ICDU as contained in its constitution are the same objectives stated earlier for the ILU. One difference is that the ICDU has an unlimited scope. Religion and politics are perhaps the only two areas that the union does not concern itself with, though it tackles such political problems as asking for representation in the local government administration.

Organizational structure
As stated earlier, membership of ICDU is free and open to every male and female citizens of Isalu. There are three branches of the Union—the Home Branch and the Ibadan and Lagos branches. The membership strength of each branch varies but the Home Branch has the highest number. There is one parent body to which every branch is responsible.

Each branch is organized in the same way. Officers include a chairperson, vice-chairperson, general secretary, assistant secretary, financial secretary, treasurer, internal auditor and a social secretary. The difference in the organizational structure of the branches and that of the parent body is that the parent body has a president and a vice-president as opposed to the chairperson and vice-chairperson for the branches.

Officers are elected in the same way, usually at the end-of-year general meeting. As for the parent body, the end-of-year general meeting comes up on every Boxing Day, 26 December. Any member from any of the branches is eligible for election into any office except the post of the general secretary which, by convention, is usually restricted to the home branch, for ease of co-ordination of activities.

Elections are peacefully and democratically conducted. Every nominated member reserves the right to accept or reject his/her nomination based on personal conviction.

Meeting schedule
Meetings are held in all branches once a month. The Ibadan Branch, for example, holds its meeting on the first Sunday of every month at three locations in Ibadan on rotation—Beere, Bodija and Ojoo. This is to encourage the attendance of members who are scattered all over the city. The parent body holds two quarterly meetings and one end-of-year general meeting, all in Iseyin.

The language of the meeting in all the branches is Yoruba. This is to encourage the full participation of all members, especially the elders, the majority of whom do not speak English.

Decisions are usually taken on matters after a thorough discussion where everyone who has an opinion is allowed to express it. Voting then takes place and the majority's wish is upheld. Projects for execution are selected by the same process.

Characteristic features
Some of the characteristics of the ICDU which have sustained it over a time are that: it is a grassroots (community-based) association; it is independent and autonomous; it is built on truth and a sense of purpose; though membership is (by birth) compulsory, there is no coercion; it pursues the needs of members to enjoy a meaningful existence; though guided by a constitution which every member tries to observe, it employs indigenous knowledge in its operations.

Funding
ICDU, like any other development-oriented organization, requires funds to operate. The union's usual sources of funding are annual subscriptions, occasional levies, launchings, donations, gate-takings and sales of almanacs/calendars.

Initially, each member contributed a five-naira subscription per year through the relevant branch. This has since been raised to 20 naira per year and is sent to the parent body to fund any project in hand. Each branch is run through small additional contributions by members. For example, the Home Branch has what it calls a 'secret bag' in which members who attend its monthly meetings would drop into it any amount he/she could afford. Money from this source has never been adequate because, small as it is, some members still find it difficult to pay. For example, the Ibadan Branch raised only 1 000 naira as annual subscriptions in 1993. Other sources of funding have therefore been introduced.

There are occasional levies on members, especially whenever there is an urgent problem to solve or a project to finance. A flat rate would be levied on members. Each branch would collect the levy from its members and remit it to the parent body. The collection of subscriptions and levies from members of the Home Branch is the most difficult. The branch officers usually enlist the support of compound heads to collect money from people in the respective compounds. Announcements on such matters are usually made in mosques and churches during congregational prayers.

In addition, funding is sought from well-to-do members of the union in the form of donations towards a particular project. Such affluent members have always responded enthusiastically. Until a few years ago, the ICDU also organized friendly football matches between it and other clubs within and outside Iseyin. Proceeds from the gate usually went to the purse of the union. In 1969, the ICDU produced its first almanac/calendar which was sold to members of the public. The proceeds were put into the union's account. This went on until 1990.

In 1989, the ICDU launched its 50 deep-wells project with a view to raising additional funds to complete the first phase of the project in addition to publicizing the activities of the union. This launching was the first of its kind for a community-based organization in Iseyin.

The ICDU is lucky to have members who belong to various professions: town planning, architecture, pharmacy, medicine, law, bricklaying, carpentry and auto mechanics. Apart from cash contributions, some members contribute in kind, especially their expertise towards group projects. For instance, the town planner in the union assisted in the location and distribution of the deep wells and the acquisition of a 0.8-hectare site for the proposed Isalu Community Centre. Member bricklayers and private contractors have supervised the construction of the deep wells free of charge.

As a way of reducing the cost of projects, the ICDU used the direct labour approach to a large extent, especially in its formative years and up until the early 1980s. All the roads opened up and culverts built were through direct communal labour. Compound heads would lead their members (which include males and females, children and adults) to construction sites armed with their hoes, cutlasses, axes and calabashes. Maintenance of the roads is carried out through the same process. At the time of writing, this age-old practice of road maintenance by members of the community still goes on, especially of the local access and farm roads. This practice is what Adedokun (1993) termed 'Volunteer Workers League' in his study of the Ara community in Osun State, Nigeria.

Achievements

The ICDU has achieved a lot within the short period of its existence and, given the resource constraints (especially financial) of its members, it is now considered one of the few educationally advanced wards in Iseyin with its members spread widely throughout the society, including politics. The table below shows some of its achievements.

Table 6.1: List of community development projects undertaken by the Isalu community, Iseyin

Project	Year	Cost
35km Bode Isalu–Ikere road	1940s	Direct labour
4.4km Olobo–Alayin road	1954	Direct labour
Owode market at Ikere	1954/55	*Not available*
1½km Ita Molosin–Isoko–Oluwole road	1967	Direct labour
1km Bode Isalu–Oke Igere–Oke Alafia road	1970	Direct labour
1½km Bode Isalu–Our Lady Hospital–Saki road	1972	Direct labour
1km Bode-Isalu–Olokooyo–Itan road including 3 culverts	*Not available*	*Not available*
10 deepwells (already commissioned)	1988/89	30000* naira
5 deepwells (almost completed)	1992/93	20000 naira
1.0 hectare land to build Isalu Community Centre at Elera, Isalu	1993	25000 naira
Purchase and perimeter survey of 1 128m² of land at Ogunbado, Isalu	1993	5000 naira

* plus free service

The 10 deep wells first constructed are evenly distributed within Isalu ward. One each is located at Isoko, Oke Adeta, Irawote, Ojudo Ogunbado, Ojude Akala/Otugbede, Idi Iyalode, Ojude Awe, Ojude Afuku, Ojude Gbodo, and Ojude Aworan. The wells have improved the quality of life of members of the community, especially during the dry season when the various compound wells (usually very shallow) and most streams dry up.

The ICDU also succeeded in convincing the Directorate of Foods, Roads and Rural Infrastructure (DFRRI) of the need to build a road from Ikere to link Iseyin with Igbeti, a town in the Irepo Local Government Area. Work has already begun on the project.

Factors responsible for the ICDU success
It is useful here to highlight the factors that made it possible for members of the ICDU (from the time of the Majeobaje Society to date) to achieve its objectives. The ICDU adopts a combination of three approaches in its operation: the community, self-help, and special purpose or problem-solving approaches which are three of the six approaches in the development processes as identified by Long *et al.* (1973). Within ICDU, there is broad-based participation, adherence to democratic procedures, application of indigenous leadership and a holistic approach to community problems. The union usually lists things considered as problems facing the community and attempts to set one or two (e.g. road, water, farmland, school buildings, schoolteachers) as targets for immediate attention. The union takes advantage of its educated members who are highly placed in government or in the society in its approach to issues.

In over half a decade of its existence, the union has not experienced any factions or divisions among its members. Although people of similar ages exchange more pleasantries and relate more with one another, such rapport has been used positively to make union work more effective.

There is an absence of leadership fights as officers are democratically elected as provided for by the constitution of the ICDU. The traditional community leaders in Isalu (Omkosa, Ogboye, Aaba, and Baale Ikere) usually give their full moral support to and permit all the activities of ICDU including the election of officers. There is no coercion of members.

The ICDU does not operate very rigid rules; rather there is flexibility in the way issues are handled and problems tackled. Accountability is taken seriously. To date, no officer of the union has ever been accused of corruption of any sort, including embezzlement of union funds. Statements of accounts are rendered punctually.

Politics are de-emphasized within the union. Although members of the Isalu community have always individually belonged to different political parties existing in the country, such feelings are usually put aside when it comes to matters affecting the community. Members act in unison.

Constraints

The Isalu Community Development Union is faced with some problems ranging from inadequate finances to low levels of commitment. As stated earlier, the sources of finance for the union activities are limited and a bit unreliable as many members do not pay either the subscription or the occasional levy. This affects the number and time of project completion.

The present subscription of 20 naira per member per year is grossly inadequate and should be raised in line with the current rate of inflation in the country. In addition, raffles, films, and other fund-raising events should be organized regularly. There is ignorance on the part of some members of the benefits of community development activities. Awareness talks should be organized from time to time for members. The level of commitment and personal ability varies greatly among members, especially among students and apprentices who do not contribute financially to any project.

The Home Branch is found not to be as effective as either the Lagos or Ibadan branches. This may be explained by the simple fact that most of the members of the Lagos and Ibadan branches are much more enlightened and accustomed to the self-help projects of communities in which they work or live.

There is a gender problem, as the ICDU is almost 90 per cent male. The reason is that very few women of Isalu community marry within the community. Women from outside the community who married members of the union do not belong to the ICDU. It is suspected that there would be greater participation and better funding if membership of the ICDU were to be based not only on the birthplace but also on marriage.

Conclusion

The ICDU has come a long way. With very limited resources at its disposal, it has been able to achieve most of the objectives for which it was established, especially the attainment of self-reliance through group action or community development.

The ICDU has, from its inception, engaged in a process of mobilizing and creating awareness among its members on the need for group action and/or collective efforts to develop themselves and their community. It is now seen by most observers as a movement towards the social, economic, cultural and political emancipation of members of the Isalu community. ICDU is a movement designed to promote better living for the whole community. It has successfully done this through the communal construction as well as maintenance of roads and culverts, markets, and, recently, a block of four classrooms (donated to the Teachers' College in Iseyin) and provision of water. Construction work on the Isalu Community Centre, which will have a hall, library, postal agency, nursery school and recreational facilities, is to commence in January, 1995.

The union has constantly been used as a tool to redress imbalance in the distribution of amenities or services and even representations in the local government's affairs. It has, on a few occasions, initiated court actions against certain individuals who trespassed on its communal land, against cattle rearers who invaded farms with their cattle thereby destroying mature crops, and also against a larger community for pocketing the Isalu community's share of the royalties being paid on the land which belongs entirely to the Isalu community.

ICDU has become a method and, interestingly, a model being copied by the other communities in Iseyin, for achieving group goals and objectives, especially for addressing the basic needs in the community which government is unable to provide.

Members of Isalu community have not only developed a spirit of self-reliance, they have demonstrated it. The ICDU has great capacity and potential to attain an enviable level of self-reliance in all endeavours. It is endowed with a group of highly educated members who are arousing greater consciousness in the uninformed members and mobilizing the women for greater community development programmes. Unity, co-operation and mutual interest, which are basic to successful community development, are openly exhibited by members. Once their individual economic ventures and earnings improve and, if the union can get some assistance from any international donor agency, it would conveniently expand its community development activities and become more self-reliant.

References

Abiodun, J. and Aguda, A. (1986), 'Spatial Organization of Urban Communities'. Paper presented at the Conference of the Nigerian Geographical Association, ABU, Zaira.

Abram, C. (1971), *The Language of Cities*. New York: The Viking Press.

Adedokun, R.A. (1993). 'Lessons From Self-Reliant Development: The Case of Ara'. Paper presented at ARCIK Organized Workshop held at NISER, Ibadan, December 15–17.

Adejumobi, A. (1991), 'Process and Problems of Community Organization for Self-Reliance', *NISER Monograph Series*, No. 1, Ibadan.

Agbola, T. (1988). 'The Private Sector and Physical Planning in Nigeria', *NITP Journal*, Vol. X.

Akorede, V.E.A. (1986), 'A Geographical Analysis of the Pattern of Integration Between the Discrete Communities in Ile-Ife', Unpublished Ph.D. thesis, Department of Geography, University of Ife, Ile-Ife.

Broom, L. and Selznick, P. (1973), *Sociology—A Text With Adapted Reading*. New York: Harper & Row.

Brown, L.D. and Korten, D.C. (1989), 'The Role of Voluntary Organizations in Development: A Concept Paper', Boston Institute for Development Research.

Centre for African Settlement Studies and Development (CASSAD) (1992), 'Community-based Organizations as Vehicles for Socio-Economic Development in Nigeria: Policy Options', *CASSAD Monograph Series 2*, Ibadan.

De Blij, H.J. (1993), *Human Geography—Culture, Society and Space*, New York: John Wiley & Sons.

Ekong, E.E. (1988), *An Introduction to Rural Sociology*. Ibadan: Jumak Publishers Ltd.

Elaigwu, J.I. (1988), 'Governments and Community Development Programmes', in A.

Nweze, (ed.), *Perspective on Community and Rural Development in Nigeria*, Jos: Centre for Development Studies Publications, University of Jos.

Fisher, J.S. (ed.) (1984), *Geography and Development: A World Regional Approach*. Columbus: Merrill Publishing Co.

Friedmann, J. (1981), 'Regional Planning for Rural Mobilization in Africa', *Rural Africana*, Nos. 312–13.

Goode, W.J. and Hatt, P.K. (1952), *Methods in Social Relations*. New York: McGraw-Hill.

Hicks, G.H. and Gullett, R.C. (1982), *Organizations: Theory and Behaviour*. New York: McGraw-Hill.

Kolajo, J. (1960), 'The Concept of Community', *Rural Sociology*, 25.

Long, H.B., Anderson, R.C. and Blubaugh, J.A. (eds) (1973), *Approaches to Community Development, Iowa City*, Iowa: National University Extension Association and the American College Testing Programme.

Nottridge, H.B. (1972), *The Sociology of Urban Living*. London: Routledge and Kegan Paul Ltd.

Nweze, A. (ed.). (1988), *Perspective on Community and Rural Development in Nigeria*, Jos: CDS Publications, University of Jos.

Nwosu, H.N. and Nwankwo, G.O. (1988), 'Self-Reliance as a Strategy for National Development in Nigeria', in A. Nweze, (ed.), *Perspectives on Community and Rural Development in Nigeria*. Jos: CDS Publications, University of Jos.

Olayiwola, L.M. (1990), 'A Study of the Adequacy of Infrastructural Facilities in Rural Areas of Oranmiyan Local Government', unpublished Ph. D. thesis, Obafemi Awolowo University, Ile-Ife.

Olowu, D., Bamidele, S.A. and Akande, B. (eds.) (1991), *Local Institutions and National Development in Nigeria*. Ile-Ife: Obafemi Awolowo University Press.

Omuta, G.E.D. (1986), 'The Urban Informal Sector and Environmental Sanitation in Nigeria: Needless conflict', *Habitat International* 10(3).

Takaya, B.J. (1988), 'Structural Imperatives for Virile Community Development Movement in Nigeria', in A. Nweze, (ed.), *Perspectives on Community and Rural Development in Nigeria*. Jos: CDS Publications, University of Jos.

Togunde, O.O. (1994), 'A Review of Self-Help Efforts in Oke-Ogun, Oyo State, Nigeria'. Paper presented at the National Conference on Regional Underdevelopment at the Conference Centre, University of Ibadan, Ibadan.

Warren, D.M., Slikkerveer, L.J. and Titilola, S.O. (eds) (1989). 'Indigenous Knowledge Systems: Implications for Agriculture and International Development', *Studies in Technology and Social Change* 11, Ames: Iowa State University, Technology and Social Change Programme.

Warren, D.M. (1991), 'Using Indigenous Knowledge in Agricultural Development', *World Bank Discussion Paper* No. 127, Washington: The World Bank.

Warren, D.M. (1992), 'Strengthening Indigenous Nigerian Organizations and Associations for Rural Development: The Case of Ara Community', NISER Occasional Paper No. 1, Ibadan.

Warren, D.M., Slikkerveer, L.J. and Brokensha, D. (eds) (1995) *The Cultural Dimension of Development*. London: Intermediate Technology Publications.

Webster's Dictionary of the English Language (1987), New York: Lexicon Publications.

Wey, S.O. (1988), 'Community Development and the Process of Economic Development.' in A. Nweze, (ed.) *op. cit*.

Wolff, N. and Wahab, B. (1995), 'The Importance of Indigenous Organizations to the Sustainability of Contemporary Yoruba Strip-weaving Industries in Iseyin, Nigeria', in P. Blunt, and D.M. Warren, (eds.), *Indigenous Organizations and Development* (this volume).

7 The importance of indigenous organizations to the sustainability of contemporary Yoruba strip-weaving industries in Iseyin, Nigeria

NORMA H. WOLFF AND BOLANLE W. WAHAB

Introduction

'*ASO-OKE*', THE HAND-WOVEN strip cloth of the Yoruba[1], has retained its economic and cultural importance in south-western Nigeria for well over two centuries. A number of towns in the northern Yoruba area, such as Iseyin, Shaki, Igboho, Igbeti, Oyo and Ilorin are indigenous centers of strip-woven cloth production and are still homes to large numbers of weavers. Other more southern towns such as Ibadan and Ondo have gained recent prominence as weaving centres of strip-woven cloth catering to the urban élite.

The resilience of Yoruba strip-weaving industries has been proven repeatedly as forces of cultural change emerging inside and outside Yorubaland have tested the craftspeople's ability to adapt to ever-changing shifts in taste, competition from outside markets, dwindling local supplies of raw materials, unstable weather that periodically affects production, changing technologies, inflation, intrusive government development policies and projects, and the lure of modern sector occupations drawing away the work-force.

Indigenous organizations in Yorubaland that shape production and marketing of crafts continue to play an important role in assuring the continuing vitality of the *aso-oke* industry. The importance of such organizations to the continuity of hand-woven cloth production is particularly evident in the town of Iseyin, an historically important Yoruba weaving centre. This chapter focuses upon the weaving industry of Iseyin[2] and the key role that indigenous production and marketing organizations have played in adapting the weaving industry to changing conditions and how such organizations have contributed to keeping the *aso-oke* industry alive and flourishing. The degree to which attempts by the government to 'modernize' the weaving industry have succeeded will also be described.

The importance of Yoruba strip-weaving

Cloth production has been important to the Yoruba for almost three centuries. The Yoruba use both the West African narrow-strip double-heddle horizontal loom and the vertical loom. The vertical loom is an older technology; the horizontal loom came from the north with Islam. Historically, weaving narrow-strip cloth became an economically important male occupation, while cloth production on the vertical loom remained a female vocation.

Scholars generally agree that the wide distribution of the horizontal loom in West Africa is tied to the movement of Muslim scholars and traders in Western

* Norma H. Wolff is an Assistant Professor in the Department of Anthropology at Iowa State University, Ames, Iowa, USA. Bolanle W. Wahab is a Senior Lecturer in the Department of Town Planning in the Polytechnic, Ibadan, Nigeria.

and Central Sudan. The textile arts of weaving and embroidery are common occupations for Muslim scholars even today. In Iseyin, for example, over 88 per cent of weavers were Muslims in 1980 (Wahab 1980). Based on the indirect evidence of the spread of Islam, the horizontal loom and the production of narrow-strip cloth reached the northern edges of the Oyo Yoruba Empire area by the seventeenth century, spreading southwards from the Hausa and Nupe (Kriger 1990: 39). By the end of the seventeenth century the high quality of Yoruba cloth, produced on both the horizontal and vertical loom, was noted by European traders who purchased it to sell for higher prices elsewhere (Captain [John] Phillips 1693–4, quoted by Thornton 1990: 10). In 1823 a trader, J. Adams, who cruised the west coast of Africa as far south as the Congo, stated:

> The cloth manufactured in Hio [Oyo] is superior, both for variety of pattern, colour, and dimensions, to any made in the neighbouring countries
>
> (Law 1977: 204).

William H. Clarke, a Baptist missionary, who travelled through most of Yoruba-land between 1854 and 1858, noted that the quality of both men and women's weaving was excellent.

> As good an article of cloth can be woven by the Yoruba weavers as by any people, and for durability far excels the prints and homespuns of Manchester. Hence the native cloths are by far the more costly
>
> (Clarke 1972: 273).

Narrow strip-woven cloth, in particular, became important to the internal and external trade of the Oyo Empire over the next century. Oyo Ile, the capital city of the Oyo Empire (c.1600–c.1836), was a major production centre for the craft, and cotton and indigo were raised in quantity in the vicinity to meet the needs of the craft (Law 1977: 204–5). By the late eighteenth century, the products of Oyo Yoruba weavers entered the long-distance trade networks of the Sokoto Caliphate to the north (Kriger 1990: 41; Perani 1992: 102).

In the early nineteenth century, the Oyo Empire began to disintegrate, due to political unrest and disruption of the trade routes, and the Oyo Yoruba suffered a 'severe commercial depression' (Law 1977: 281). A series of wars followed, and the evacuation of Oyo Ile in 1836/37 marked the end of the Empire (Law 1977: 245–99). There was a disruption of cloth production as weavers fled the doomed city, but weavers quickly returned to their looms in their new homes. Iseyin, the focus of this study, was a refuge for many Muslim weavers who fled Oyo Ile during the period of final conflict (Bray 1968: 271). The town quickly became a recognized centre for *aso-oke* production, and it has a worldwide reputation as a producer of quality hand-woven cloth today.

Yoruba cloth was competitive with imported European cloth throughout the nineteenth century despite British efforts to dominate the market. *Aso-oke* continued to be an important Yoruba regional export, particularly to the north where it was highly prized by the Nupe and Hausa (Kriger 1990). In the 1900s, however, export of strip-woven cloth to other parts of West Africa, especially the areas of Benin Republic, Togo and Ghana began to diminish as imported textiles became increasingly important for clothing. Nevertheless, local demand for strip-woven cloth remained high, so that the initial impact of colonialism on indigenous cloth production was relatively slight. Colonial influence was most strongly felt in the introduction of machine-spun weaving thread to the Nigerian market. The indigenous weavers quickly perceived the advantages of using the imported thread which was easier and faster to weave than handspun thread and increased production. However, the adoption of machine-spun thread created unforeseen problems for the weavers. The colonial policy of discouraging modern spinning (and weaving) mills inside the British West African colonies[3] made the weavers dependent upon imported thread. Thus the *aso-oke* industries faced a crisis during the Second World War when the colonial government not only banned cloth exports to the Gold Coast but also banned thread imports. This led to a decline in production that continued until the 1950s when higher incomes, a surge of nationalist sentiment, reopened markets, and the resumption of thread importation, invigorated the industry again (O'Hear 1987: 512).

Ultimately, the fate of Yoruba *aso-oke* industries in the twentieth century has been closely tied to in-group patronage, that is, Yoruba demand. *Aso-oke* is used for clothing and is thus greatly influenced by the vagaries of fashion. The Westernization of Nigerian culture since the turn of the century, with the adoption of European-style dress and the flooding of the Nigerian market with cheap imported cloth, has been cited as a death threat to the *aso-oke* industry (e.g. Robinson 1982: 45–51). This has not been the case. European-style clothing never dominated Yoruba fashions, although tastes for imported cloth have periodically affected indigenous hand-woven cloth production since European contact. From 1900, when British influence strengthened, a small but influential group of Westernized Yoruba élites tied to a newly emerging urban society adopted European fabrics and dress. In Lagos, where the population was more than 80 per cent Yoruba, Western style of dress was common among those people who had attained the highest level of European formal education, including repatriates from Sierra Leone, missionaries, businessmen and educators (Wass 1979: 334–5). While Yorubas in the more provincial towns and cities and the rural populations were not as apt to adopt European-style of clothing, the availability of cheap and luxury European imported cloth in every market influenced textile purchasing patterns. Spreading from the Yoruba educated élite populations of Yorubaland's large cities, such as Lagos, Abeokuta and Ibadan, fashion vogues in imported damasks, brocades, velvets and 'laces' influenced the market for indigenous strip-woven cloth.

Politics and a rising demand for self-determination in Nigeria following the Second World War gave *aso-oke* a boost as the cloth of choice. Among the Yoruba élite who had adopted Western dress as a visible social indicator of the educated, urbanized Christian, a return to the wearing of indigenous styles signified identity with the independence movement and a renewed pride of ethnic heritage (Wass 1979: 339). Indigenous dress began to be worn more often, particularly by men, in the decade preceding independence (1950–59) (Wass 1979: 341). The demand for *aso-oke* grew and weaving industries such as those of Iseyin and Ilorin flourished (O'Hear 1987:511). Since that time, Yoruba indigenous dress has continued to be worn along with Western and pan-African fashions, and *aso-oke*, despite fluctuations in tastes for imported cloth, has never totally lost its appeal. It remains important as a status symbol, especially for expressing 'Yorubaness', and is worn particularly for those important ceremonies that mark life transitions such as naming ceremonies, graduation ceremonies, weddings, funerals and chieftaincy installations (Wolff 1991).

This does not mean the product has not changed. Strip-woven *aso-oke* cloth has remained competitive because of the weavers' willingness to adapt to changing taste. Materials and patterns have changed continually. For example, when shiny imported rayon and damask cloth became popular, glossy synthetic threads were incorporated into the cotton strip-woven *aso-oke*, usually in an overlaid weft-float pattern (O'Hear 1990). In the 1990s, a contemporary taste for lightweight cloth is being met by the adoption of lighter weight cotton and lurex threads. The gleaming '*shain-shain*' cloth woven with a mix of cotton and metallic-like lurex thread is considered to be cool and light-weight, and success-fully competes with imported options.

Having determined that a demand for narrow-strip cloth has never completely disappeared, we now turn to how indigenous organizations have contributed to keeping the *aso-oke* weaving industry lively despite market fluctuations.

The nature of Yoruba craft organization

To understand the importance of indigenous organizations to weaving, it is necessary to look at the way Yoruba people organize themselves for craft production, both within the basic kinship group and in additional groups that transcend family and kinship ties.

Among the Yoruba, certain patrilineages specialize in the production of specific crafts, so that the organization of the craft group is inseparable from the lineage structure (Lloyd 1953: 31). Weaving is such a craft. Weaving skills are taught in the context of the family compounds by related specialists who trace common ancestry to a male founder. The linkage of occupation and kinship lowers the opportunity costs for learning the craft, because apprenticeship takes place in the context of family enculturation. With the looms located in the compounds, opportunities to observe and experiment with weaving are available to children from an early age. When the child gains the skills needed, the family usually helps with the cost of start-up (i.e. the loom and its parts).

The lineage or extended family compound residents make up a production unit, although it is not compulsory that all take part in the lineage craft. Due to the simplicity of the technology involved in Yoruba crafts, little co-operative labour is needed. Each craftsperson can carry out the full production process with occasional help solicited from siblings or children (Lloyd, 1953: 32). Independence in production is also encouraged by the fact that the costs of production tend to be minimal. Tools are simple in design, made locally and cheap to obtain. In most indigenous crafts, the capital outlay for raw materials is also low.

In weaving, the thread is the most expensive production cost. With the contemporary dependence on machine-spun bought thread, weavers must often call on the help of prosperous entrepreneurial weavers, both from within and from outside the family, to obtain the essential raw materials. Once the thread is obtained, however, the weavers work individually at their own looms. The economic individualism that characterizes the kin-based production of indigen-ous Yoruba crafts, such as weaving, contrasts with the more recent guild organizations that distinguish the modern Yoruba crafts such as tailoring, auto-mobile repair, tinkering, gold and silver smithing, as well as many of the contemporary co-operatives which produce crafts inspired by indigenous forms (Lloyd 1953: 36; Koll 1969).

Family-based weaving, either as a full- or part-time occupation, within the family compound allows the craftsperson economic flexibility and cuts the costs of production. For the weaver, the costs of food and shelter that have to be factored into the selling price of products are lower when working at home.

Family support in times of economic stress is available, and farming on lineage land is always an option to provide subsistence needs. In addition, the compound-based group has a broad labour base. For example, in the past when handspun thread was commonly used, the cotton was spun by the family women so that thread did not have to be purchased from traders. Today, the labour of women and children frees the weavers from time-consuming tasks such as winding bobbins and preparing warp bundles. A final economic advantage of basing production inside the lineage compound involves marketing directly to end-use consumers who come to order cloth for special ceremonies and events. This is seen as an advantage to both buyer and seller. Through direct contact, the consumer is able to explain exactly what is wanted and negotiate the price with the producer. The master weaver, with whom they deal, avoids either the commission which must be paid to a middleman or the costs of carrying cloth to market.

The bonds of kinship, tradition and economic advantages explain in part why weavers continue to site production in lineage compounds. In addition, a final reason that most *aso-oke* weaving remains compound-based is the social comfort that such an arrangement provides. The simple technology of the horizontal strip-cloth loom does not require a factory set-up for weaving.[4] In 1993, Iseyin weavers consistently stated their preference for working at home where loom benches and racks are set up on verandas and in the open spaces between houses and compounds. The weavers prefer being near family, where property and children can be supervised. A weaver can easily take a short rest when tired or be served a meal when hungry without leaving the weaving spot. It was also felt that the home compound offers open airy places to weave, in contrast to central weaving buildings such as were advocated in some government-sponsored programmes.

While economic individualism is practised in production, an overall hierarchical organization in the lineage compound affects the craft. The importance of a craft makes matters of production a concern for all compound residents. In craft lineages, the business of the craft is the business of the family. The *bale*, or eldest resident male in a compound, is not only the head of the kin group, but is also the final authority on all matters related to the family craft. He acts as an intermediary between the craftspeople and important clients in the marketing of products, and presides over periodic family meetings in which matters concerning production, prices and disputes are settled by consensus (Lloyd 1953: 34). In the past, if the same craft was practised by several lineages in a town, a larger overreaching organization made up of the heads of craft compounds was common. The *bale* of the most important or senior lineage was given jurisdiction over similar craft lineages, and only he dealt directly with the local *oba* (king) or chief. Inter-lineage meetings of practising craftsmen were held so that he could be aware of the needs of all who practised the craft (Lloyd 1953: 34–5). Today, with the decline of many of the indigenous crafts and the breakdown of traditional authority, these kinship-based organizations for the promotion of the crafts beyond the lineage have largely disappeared.

Beyond kinship, the Yoruba organize themselves in other ways that have relevance for craft production. Membership in associations (*egbe*) which criss-cross lineage lines is very important to Yoruba men and women. An *egbe* is basically a common interest group. Age sets, title associations, religious cults and occupational groups are organized to promote and protect common interests in politics, economics and religion; other *egbe* are formed on the basis of friendship for recreation and enjoyment (Fadipe 1970: 243). Today town improvement associations and hometown associations formed by enclaves of Yorubas living outside their birthplaces are also common (Eades 1980: 61–2). *Egbe* membership enters every aspect of life, because 'a person who had no *egbe* [is] not a properly adjusted and socialized being' (Fadipe 1970: 257); such a person is regarded as an introvert and a bit of a social misfit. In all *egbe*, even those formed on the basis of common occupation, a sense of friendship, mutual aid and support binds members together and involves them in participation in each others' projects, celebrations and life-cycle ceremonies. The ubiquity of the Yoruba *egbe* is reflected in the saying: 'Put two Yorubas together and they will form an *egbe*.'[5] The cultural tendency to formalize group relationships is commented upon by the Yoruba anthropologist, N.A. Fadipe, as follows.

> One interesting result of this tradition of associations is that wherever there is an appreciable community of Yoruba, either outside Yorubaland or even only outside their own particular communities, an organization will spring up complete with officers. This organization will certainly have judicial functions, and will have its convivial and mutual help features strongly developed. It has been said that even in the New World, during the time of the slave trade, the genius of the Yoruba for organizing associations found expression in ways that were not always welcome to their masters.
>
> (Fadipe, 1970: 243)

Two types of *egbe* are particularly relevant to understanding indigenous craft organizations: the *esusu* and the occupational *egbe*.[6] The *esusu* functions as a kind of credit association in which a group of people pool their money. Set contributions of cash are collected from members periodically, and the total is given to one member as a lump sum in rotation. Members receive their share in sequence (Fadipe 1970: 256–7; Eades 1980: 77; Bascom 1952). The *esusu* is still an important financial institution in Yorubaland, and it is common for friends and co-workers in the formal sector to organize *esusu*. They are also a feature of the informal sector, particularly among craftspeople and traders who need to invest money periodically in their businesses (Eades 1980: 77). The *esusu* allows the craftsperson to buy raw materials or tools and the trader to expand stock with relative ease.

Occupational *egbe* emerge when the products of a craft industry gain importance as a commodity, such as in the case of strip-woven cloth. Occupational *egbe* are formal organizations that are established to protect the economic status and interests of a craft, to regulate production and trade, and to provide mutual aid to members (Fadipe 1970: 254–55; Eades 1980: 160). They differ from *esusu* in that they do not pool money to lend to members. They basically fill the gap left by the disappearance of the older kin-based organizations made up of lineage heads, but the membership is less restricted. Most weavers, for example, belong to one or more occupational *egbe* in which members are bound to each other not only economically but also socially. Members support each other not only in the interests of their craft, but also in their life events—weddings, naming ceremonies and funerals.

In the past, it was often the case that only members of the appropriate *egbe* could practise a trade in a particular town (Fadipe 1970: 254–5). These occupational groups resembled the craft guilds of the European renaissance in that membership was a prerequisite to producing and selling a craft. Apprenticeship took place within the context of the group, the group provided financial help in times of need, and acted as a 'power block' in dealing with the local government (Cole 1983: 20–1). However, one must question the uncritical use of the term 'guild' to describe these Yoruba *egbe* that linked kin-groups, that is, lineages, together for common action. The membership of European guilds was not based on kinship, and the guild was more of a mechanism through which the political and religious élite controlled the production of the arts than an organization formed for the common good of the membership (Cole 1983: 20–1).

In the case of cloth weaving, the indigenous occupational *egbe* has played an important role in organizing production, and particularly in marketing. In addition, the importance of cloth as commodity has encouraged external efforts to control and shape production and marketing. Attempts have been made by the British colonial and Nigerian national governments to establish craft centres and co-operatives. However, as we shall show, it is the indigenous forms of organizing production and marketing—lineage-based production groups and *egbe* marketing associations—that have prevailed and are responsible for the continuing vitality of the *aso-oke* industry. Iseyin provides an example.

Iseyin: a case-study

Iseyin, the present headquarters of the Iseyin Local Government Area of Oyo State, Nigeria, has been a centre for the production of *aso-oke* strip-woven cloth since the town was established in the early nineteenth century during the period of the Yoruba wars that marked the decline of the Oyo Empire. In the 1820s, the population of Iseyin swelled with the influx of refugees from Oyo Ile and Ogbomosho, including a vigorous Muslim community that brought the weaving techniques of the horizontal loom to the town (Bray 1974: 143). Iseyin lay at the junction of two established nineteenth-century long-distance trade routes, one running west to the region of present-day Ghana and the other linking the northern Hausa-dominated trans-Saharan trade routes to the southern Yoruba population centres, such as Abeokuta and Lagos (Dodwell 1955; Falola 1991: 125). Once peace came to the area, the *aso-oke* industry in Iseyin was energized by these trade opportunities. However, with the twentieth-century development of major arterial roads and the railway system, Iseyin was bypassed. The town lost importance as a market centre. It retained its trade links for *aso-oke* largely through the efforts of indigenous long-distance traders and trading organizations (*egbe*), so that it continued to be a major production centre for *aso-oke*. To this day, the marketing of the bulk of Iseyin cloth is in the hands of weaver–traders who carry *aso-oke* to regional cloth markets (such as Oje market in Ibadan, Jankara market in Lagos, the Ede market, and, of late, Araromi market in Oyo), which attract traders who buy goods to carry to secondary markets in Nigeria and other areas of West Africa.

In the mid–1950s. shortly before Nigerian independence, the Iseyin stripweaving industry was described as 'flourishing' (Dodwell 1955). C. B. Dodwell, who studied Iseyin in 1952–3, described a town where one in five adult men were weavers who produced about one million square yards of *aso-oke* a year (Dodwell, 1955: 118).[7] Dodwell linked the vitality of the industry to a general increase in textile purchases throughout British West Africa in the prosperous period following World War II (Dodwell 1955) Once the wartime ban on imported thread was lifted, production in Iseyin expanded to meet these new demands. In the decade following the war, the value of thread imports to Nigeria rose from L450000 in 1945 to L1734000 in 1953 (Dodwell 1955: 124).

Iseyin consumed 20 per cent of these imports (Dodwell 1955). In a more thorough study done in 1965–6, Jennifer Bray described an Iseyin strip-woven cloth industry that had grown in the twelve years since Dodwell made his observations. Drawing upon the 1966 Iseyin tax rolls, she estimated that 27 per cent of the total male population was engaged in full-or part-time weaving, with 1540 full-time weavers drawn from 188 of the 670 compounds of the town (Bray 1974: 144). Eighty per cent of the full-time weavers were concentrated into six of the 17 town quarters while most part-time weavers were scattered through the non-specialist quarters (Bray 1969: 540). The annual production of *aso-oke* by Iseyin weavers at that time was estimated at a minimum of 1031800 square yards by full-time weavers and an additional 1333330 square yards by part-time weavers. 'It is probably no great exaggeration, therefore,' Bray claims, 'to suggest that the annual production of cloth in Iseyin is approximately 2.5 million square yards' (Bray 1969: 548). Bray concluded that:

> Iseyin is by far the most important center of men's weaving in Nigeria, and the combined production of other towns, such as Ilorin and Oyo, is unlikely to be higher than that of Iseyin itself.
>
> (Bray 1969: 548)

At the same time, however, Bray voiced a concern about the future of the Iseyin industry, pointing out that it was 'stagnant' with little or no recruitment to the craft taking place (Bray 1969: 551).

Despite Bray's doubts, Iseyin has remained an important centre for weaving, despite the competition from newly emerging weaving workshops in Ibadan, Ondo, Ilesha, etc. There are a number of reasons why the Iseyin weaving industry has remained vital despite the competition it faced. Most important are the ways in which Iseyin weavers organize themselves for production and for marketing.

Organizing for production and marketing

Indigenous organization
When Dodwell visited Iseyin 40 years ago (Dodwell 1955), he observed three categories of economic and social groupings that organized *aso-oke* production. These were the extended family or lineage production group, production units within the lineage controlled by entrepreneurial weavers, and, finally, independent weavers who broke away from the other types of groupings to work alone. All were indigenous developments and are still evident in Iseyin today.

The kin-based group made up of a core of related weavers who weave in their lineage or extended family compounds is still conspicuous. Such a group can be as small as a father and his unmarried sons working together or may involve a larger residential group made up of the married and unmarried members of a patrilineage living and working in a large residential compound. As we have already seen, this type of kin-based co-operating production group has a number of advantages. It is in this context that a boy usually receives his initial training as a weaver and at the same time contributes to the production and economic gain of the family. Beginning with simple tasks such as winding thread on to spools and preparing warp bundles, by the mid-teens a child is capable of unsupervised work and is set up by the family with the equipment and working capital needed to weave independently. The elder male compound head normally gives up weaving to supervise the family work. He determines patterns and quantity of cloth to be produced, buys and distributes the thread needed for production, sells the finished cloth, and distributes the profits between the family weavers (Dodwell 1955). This type of craft organization with its roots in the indigenous social organization of Yoruba patrilineal society is still the norm in Iseyin today. The greatest change has been the role of women in the *aso-oke* industry. In the past, wives and daughters played a vital role in spinning and dyeing thread. Today little handspun thread is used and machine-spun thread is most often bought already dyed. However, an important change has occurred in the gender restrictions of craft production in weaving. Strip-weaving, which in the past was restricted to males, is now also done by young women. This is in part due to the lack of opportunities for female school-leavers in their natal hometowns, government encouragement of open apprenticeship, and the vitality of the weaving industry which can incorporate an ever-growing work force.

The second type of grouping for weaving production involves the organizing abilities of entrepreneurial master weavers who supervise production and market the products. Entrepreneurial weavers who have accumulated sufficient capital to support other younger weavers take on young people as apprentices or hire those who are already trained in the basics of weaving but lack the capital needed for independence. Young weavers can turn to these master weavers, usually relatives,[8] who supply them with thread, the principal expenditure in weaving. The master then sells the finished cloth, takes a commission, and returns the remaining profit to the producer or pays him or her an agreed-upon fee for the job done. At the time Bray did her study in the early 1960s, this arrangement usually involved a family group in which an older successful member carried out his entrepreneurial activities in the context of family. Today, entrepreneurial weavers practise a more open recruitment policy in building up a production unit. Apprentices are accepted from outside family groups and even outside Iseyin itself. In field observations in 1993, we discovered that apprentices, especially students, came from other towns such as Shaki, Okeho, Oyo, Ogbomosho, Ado-Awaye and even Ibadan.

The final category of production organization involves younger independent weavers, who, through their own efforts, raise the capital to break away from a dependency relationship with an entrepreneurial master weaver. They own their equipment and buy their own thread or get it on credit and sell their cloth for themselves. With time, many of these independent weavers raise the capital to become entrepreneurs themselves. Dodwell noted that the majority of dependent weavers were able to achieve independence by the age of 35. By age 40 most were fathers training their sons and were themselves often extended family heads, so that production reverted to the family-based indigenous pattern (Dodwell 1955). Individual weavers often work in the context of all three types of organization in their life careers (Dodwell 1955: 132–4).

Whether weavers are part of a family, entrepreneurial, or independent production unit, the family compound still remains the preferred production site in Iseyin. Attempts to introduce weaving centres or villages have failed because individual weavers perceive the advantages mentioned previously to working in family compounds.

Marketing, like production, is organized using indigenous guidelines in Iseyin. The *aso-oke* traders are also weavers, assuring that there is a close linkage between market demands and cloth production quantity and quality. The weaver-traders are organized into occupational *egbe* that have the primary function of linking weavers into regional trading networks that broaden the market-base for Iseyin cloth. Local marketing is still primarily in the hands of individual weavers who sell their own cloth or that of their apprentices in the compounds. In Iseyin, weavers can sell directly to the terminal consumers, either to patrons who come to their compounds to commission cloth or who buy stockpiled goods in the Iseyin night market which has been in operation for over one hundred years. However, most Iseyin *aso-oke* is sold outside the town. This trade has been dominated for many years by members of *egbe* trading organizations who carry the cloth to regional markets, particularly those that specialize in cloth in Ibadan and Lagos.

According to Alhaji Gbeko Shittu, the Baba Alaari of Iseyin,[9] who was in his eighties when interviewed in 1993, the cloth traders first organized into *egbe* trading organizations about 50 years ago to increase their marketing opportunities outside of Iseyin. Up to that time, Shittu stated, each weaver sold his own products in Iseyin. The organization of the first *egbe* may very well have been due to factors associated with World War II when petrol shortages affected travel and transport within the country at the same time as it created an increased demand for locally produced goods, such as cloth.

In 1955, Dodwell noted that the *aso-oke* industry in Iseyin was 'dominated by the cloth traders, the most interesting and important figures in it' (Dodwell 1955). At that time, these traders were formed into two organizations. One group carried cloth to Ibadan for resale, the other to Lagos (Dodwell 1955). As reported by Bray almost a decade later (1963), all trade in Iseyin cloth to the important cloth markets of Ibadan and Lagos was controlled by these two large Iseyin *egbe*: *Egbe Ero Ibadan* and *Egbe Ero Eko* (Lagos).[10] Members were full- or part-time affluent weavers from large compounds; no non-weavers were allowed to join. Weavers from smaller compounds and part-time weavers, who were less likely to have accumulated the capital needed for trade, called upon members of the organizations to represent them in the markets to the south (Bray 1968: 276). *Egbe Ero Ibadan* had 311 members and *Egbe Ero Eko* had 335. Their combined membership incorporated over 40 per cent of the full-time weavers in Iseyin (Bray 1968: 276). The primary function of the two trading organizations was to transport and sell cloth. Money collected as entrance fees and dues was used to rent lorries so that traders could carry cloth to the markets for a minimal charge (Bray 1968: 276). The associations left the problems of capital accumulation to initiate weaving to compound and extended family production units; individual weavers could apply to their local *esusu*. However, the trader–members often bought the imported thread where it was cheaper for the use of the weavers in their own compounds to promote production. The traders who attended the periodic cloth markets also played an important role in keeping the weavers informed about fashions in cloth. Although individual patrons played some part by bringing fashionable *aso-oke* samples to be copied, the weaver–traders who attended the markets introduced popular new designs into the repertoires of their hometowns (Okuwa 1989: 34).[11]

In the 1990s, the *Egbe Alaso-oke Iseyin* (The Association of Iseyin *Aso-oke* Cloth Sellers), dominated by members of the *Egbe Ero Ibadan*, was the organization most mentioned by master weavers as controlling cloth production and marketing. However, the dominance of the association was challenged in 1993 when a third trading *egbe* emerged. A group of trader–weavers formed a new association with the goal of establishing a major cloth market for Iseyin products at Araromi market in Oyo, a large city a few miles away on a major north–south road. At that time petrol shortages were the norm, and travel expenses were on the rise. The idea was to increase profits by reducing the expenses of long-distance transport, as well as reduce travel risks. A further advantage was that cloth unsold at the end of a market day could easily be carried back to Iseyin, rather than being sold at a reduced price in Ibadan or Lagos. The new market was established at Oyo, but it had limited success. A division among the sponsoring weaver–traders quickly emerged, and some traders renewed their affiliation with the *Egbe Alaso-oke Iseyin* and returned to trading in Ibadan.

The continuing strength and long life of the *Egbe Alaso-oke Iseyin* is largely due to its links with the largest and most dominant cloth market in the region: Oje market in Ibadan. Founded at the end of the nineteenth century, the Oje cloth market is a specialized periodic market for cloth that meets every 16 days and attracts thousands of traders from the region. Cloth sold at Oje is carried to secondary markets throughout Nigeria and many parts of West Africa. While the *Egbe Alaso-oke Iseyin* is an indigenous organization which arose to meet local needs, its links with Oje market assures the Iseyin weavers a place in the wider regional trade network.

Recent research done at Oje market (Ogunsanwo 1985; Okuwa 1989) reveals that the *Egbe Alaso-oke Iseyin* is part of a much larger indigenous marketing organization. An *Egbe Alaso-oke*, founded in Ibadan in the late 1890s, meets regularly with representatives of 'sister associations' from 26 towns that take part in the Oje cloth market (Ogunsanwo 1985: 41–3). Iseyin is one of these. The 27 local *egbe* make up a larger association, *Egbe Awon Alaso-oke* (The Association of Aso-Oke Sellers), with representatives weavers–traders from the major *aso-oke* weaving towns including Iseyin, Shaki, Ilorin, Ogbomosho, Ede and Oyo (Okuwa 1989: 52). Okuwa estimated there were over 5000 members of this association in the late 1980s. The *Egbe Awon Alaso-oke* as an organization has little formal structure, no entrance fees or dues, no appointed officers, and no regular meetings. If group decisions need to be made, the officials of the local *egbe* co-operate to instigate action (Okuwa 1989: 53). Despite the lack of organization, each individual member of the *Egbe Awon Alaso-oke* is issued a membership card that acts as an entrance ticket to sell in Oje market and is said to help 'to sustain a friendly, peaceful and co-operative atmosphere among weavers, especially when they come to trade in Oje market' (Okuwa 1989: 53). While the *Egbe Awon Alaso-oke* appears rather benign, it has the potential of being mobilized for action when needed. For example, in the 1970s, when inflated prices for the thread used in weaving meant that indigenous strip-cloth could not compete with the prices of imported cloth, the *Egbe* stepped in and acted as an agent to get thread in bulk for members at a lower rate. At that time most cotton thread being used in the manufacture of *aso-oke* was being imported from India. The weaving associations of all the 27 towns of the *Egbe Awon Alaso-oke* joined in contributing money to send representatives to India to purchase thread directly for the joint association, thereby bypassing the middlemen who had kept the price of thread high. In 1977, they dealt with another crisis. In that year, the importation of thread was banned by the government. The association was able to redirect their bulk purchasing to newly established Nigerian thread factories in Ilorin and Kano (Ogunsanwo 1985: 44). Much of the thread used today is still purchased and resold through the sister associations of the *Egbe Awon Alaso-oke*.

In recent times a number of different associations has emerged alongside the older *egbe*. Such organizations have been less focused on marketing, and have concentrated instead on the needs of the producing weavers and their financial and technological requirements. Most have taken the form of co-operatives organized with the aid of the government. They have failed largely because of their lack of indigenous organization.

Government-sponsored organizations
The broader background. Craft production has been a focus of government intervention programmes in Nigeria beginning in the colonial period and extending to the present. Early attempts to organize indigenous craft production occurred in the period between world wars I and II. This period between 1920 and 1940 was a time of economic stagnation in European countries and in their dependencies (Crowder 1962: 235). In Nigeria, the colonial government focused its efforts on increasing agricultural development for export, and to achieve this set up co-operatives. The British attitude towards Nigerians' ability to organize themselves for production is expressed in its most extreme form in a speech made by Lord Leverhulme, the head of Lever Brothers, at a dinner held for Sir Hugh Clifford, then Governor of Nigeria, in 1924. Leverhulme, who was hoping to set up plantations in Southern Nigeria, made the following statement:

> I am certain that the West African race have to be treated very much as one would treat children when they are immature and underdeveloped. We have excellent materials. I don't know better materials anywhere for labour in the tropics than the natives of West Africa, but they are not organized . . . Now the organizing ability is the particular trait and characteristic of the white man . . . I say this with my little experience, that the African native will be happier, produce the best, and live under the larger conditions of prosperity when his labour is directed and organized by his white brother who has all the million years' start ahead of him!
>
> (Crowder 1962: 236)

The plantation system proposed by Leverhulme was never imposed upon Nigeria, but a certain amount of paternalistic policy was evident in the programmes implemented to increase the efficiency of agriculture and craft production.

In 1933, the British colonial government commissioned an expert on co-operatives in India, C.F. Strickland, to examine the possibilities of establishing such organizations in Nigeria (Koll 1969: 60). While Strickland was primarily concerned with agricultural co-operatives, he called attention to preserving and expanding handcraft production (Koll 1969: 60). Noting that craftsmen were no longer training their children and apprentices in the skills of their trades because of the declining market for indigenous arts, he recommended the following. Not only should craft co-operatives be organized, but, in addition, local technical industrial schools should be established 'to teach a genuinely African art, while improving technical methods and multiplying African designs' (Strickland 1934 quoted by Koll 1969: 61). School-leavers, trained in advanced forms of a craft, would become core members of co-operatives. Local co-operatives were to promote sales of their craft products by building sales shops on main roads, appointing representatives in major cities such as Lagos to publicize and sell their products, and distribute illustrated catalogues with price lists. This would all be done with financial aid from the Native Authority (Strickland 1934 in Koll 1969: 61). Such a programme would, he argued, make the products of the co-operative societies competitive with foreign imports. For the success of such projects, Strickland recommended:

The task of the co-operative organizer is to discover what improvements of any description the more reflective of the people theoretically desire, and then to organize them in a joint effort to secure the improvement
(Strickland 1934: 3–4 quoted in Koll 1969: 61)

The Co-operative Societies Law, passed as a result of Strickland's recommendations, took a paternalistic stance. State-controlled co-operative societies were to be supervised closely so as not to make mistakes and should not be exposed to 'the risks of independence' (Koll 1969: 69). Strickland's perception of co-operatives was a European concept to be transplanted to the Nigerian context which was seen as 'an empty bowl waiting to be filled' (Koll 1969: 68).[12] Strict regulations regarding the by-laws and structure of the new co-operatives did not take into account pre-existing indigenous societies (Koll 1969: 69). 'A co-operative understanding and spirit will need time to grow' (Strickland 1934: 3, quoted by Koll 1969: 69). In 1935, a national Co-operative Department was set up following Strickland's advice (Koll 1969: 62). A government-appointed registrar was given authority to direct the development of co-operative organizations and see that they conformed to the regulations stipulated by law. In colonial Nigeria of the 1930s, this meant that the registrar had to satisfy the needs of an export economy by concentrating on the production of raw materials for European markets. The focus, from the beginning, was on agricultural co-operatives. Almost no action was taken on craft co-operatives until 1938/39 when the first survey of native crafts was carried out. K.C. Murray and A. Hunt-Coke, working in the Yoruba area, suggested that already existing indigenous craft societies should be encouraged to:

eliminate the inefficient and redundant worker, to regulate prices and prevent cut-throat competition, and to guarantee to the public some measure of quality.
(Murray and Hunt-Coke quoted by Koll 1969: 62–3)

Murray further suggested the need for additional exclusive 'Guilds of High-Grade Workmen' to set the standards for a craft (Murray 1938: 13–114 quoted by Koll 1969: 63). These recommendations were 'filed and forgotten' (Koll 1969:63).

The first officially sanctioned craft co-operatives to emerge—the Ikot-Ekpene Co-operative Raffia Marketing Society in eastern Nigeria and the Benin Co-operative Woodworkers' Society in south-central Nigeria were reported in the 1944 Report of the Co-operative Department. They were oriented towards public service and the production of utilitarian materials—raffia for export and European-style furniture (Koll 1969: 63). The government's lack of interest in craft organizations continued, so that between 1945 and 1951 only eight craft societies were registered with the Co-operative Department (Koll 1969: 64). Only four additional co-operatives for crafts were registered in 1952, seven in 1953–4 and 14 in 1960–61.[13]

Government-sponsored organizations in Iseyin. Government efforts during the colonial era to organize hand-loomed textile production focused on introducing new technologies. In 1937, Murray and Hunt-Cooke, who had described Iseyin as 'the chief stronghold' of men's narrow-strip weaving in their survey of indigenous craft industries in southwestern Nigeria, proposed that European broad-loom weaving be introduced through the Iseyin Native Administration school. The immediate goal was to provide cloth for uniforms for Native

Administration employees. Through instructing the sons of weavers, Murray proposed, the Iseyin weavers would be encouraged 'to develop their craft and keep in step with the general progress of Nigeria by taking up some improvements on their present methods.' He further added, 'The co-operation of the local weavers would be essential to the success of the scheme.' Despite several attempts over the next 25 years (the latest in 1963) broad-loom weaving never replaced the indigenous technology.[14]

Government attempts to organize the Iseyin strip-weaving industry also met with indifferent success. In Iseyin, the first co-operative society for weavers was founded around 1958 with headquarters at Oke-Oja, one of the busiest quarters for weaving and marketing of *aso-oke*. It was called the 'Co-operative Weavers' Thrift and Credit Society' (Wahab 1980:23). The commercial importance of cloth production was reflected in the fact that the society was registered as a 'Thrift and Credit' co-operative rather than an 'Arts and Crafts' society.[15] The society's major function was similar to that of the indigenous *esusu*. Members contributed fixed amounts of money out of which loans were given to members who had investment needs and who paid the money back with a fixed interest (Wahab 1980: 23). The society also attempted to increase members' profits by acting as a marketing organization, selling cloth woven by members in bulk outside Iseyin. An additional money-raising strategy involved giving contracts to non-member weavers to weave *aso-oke* which was marketed for the profit of the society (Wahab 1980: 23). Unfortunately, the contractors to whom they loaned money did not always produce the promised cloth. The society collapsed in 1966, when they went bankrupt as the result of 'bad loans'. In retrospect, it was felt that 'the society failed also because of the uncooperative attitude of some members who showed no sense of direction and dedication' (Wahab 1980: 23).

In 1966, Bray observed four weaving co-operative societies in Iseyin that had been registered with the government since September 1963 (Bray 1968: 277). Although Bray remarks that 'weavers' co-operative societies are now a conspicuous feature in the production and marketing of traditional cloth in Iseyin', only 126 weavers were members of the four societies (Bray 1968: 277). Membership was tied to lineage membership and residence so that three of the societies drew their weavers from single quarters and group of families related through kinship, while the fourth larger co-operative catered to a wider range of weavers (Bray 1968: 277). Like the earlier Thrift and Credit Society, these organizations played roles similar to the indigenous *esusu* societies, but with government-monitored funds. Membership entrance fees and regular dues were deposited in the Co-operative Bank in Ibadan and members were issued shares in the co-operative. Loans were made to members for weaving purposes only, particularly to buy thread. Loan applications were discussed by meetings of the full membership. Each co-operative functioned as an independent organization although representatives had to report progress at monthly joint meetings of all such trade co-operatives in Iseyin (Bray 1968: 278). In addition to acting as a loaning agency, three of the four co-operative societies functioned as buying and selling organizations for their members. Two societies had accounts with expatriate trading companies and were able to buy and sell thread cheaply. One society, in fact, set up a shop on the main street of Iseyin where it sold thread, charging slightly lower prices to its own members (Bray 1968: 278). Three or four members of each of these co-operatives belonged to older well-established *Egbe Ero Ibadan* and *Egbe Ero Eko* in order to have access to the major cloth markets to the south (Bray 1968: 278).

In 1993 the co-operatives described by Bray were defunct. Interviews with master weavers revealed that co-operatives had low visibility and seemed of little concern. Only one new co-operative, the 'Weavers' Association', was mentioned. It was organized to aid weavers in Koso Quarter where weaving had only recently challenged farming as a major economic activity.

Other government-sponsored weaving organizations have emerged in Iseyin as new needs arise. For example, the 'Nigerian Native Clothes Weavers' Association', was observed in Iseyin in 1980 (Wahab 1980: 24). The main goal of the association was to re-establish cotton growing in the region, so that the raw materials needed for thread could be produced more cheaply. Established in 1974, the association was regional in scope with branches in 20 other towns cutting across Oyo, Ogun, Ondo and Kwara states. There were 52 members in Iseyin. Members contributed money to the accounts of the association as well as sold cloth in bulk and diverted the profits to the society (Wahab 1980: 24). This association was not mentioned by weavers in 1993. This is not to say that there is a dearth of weaving organizations in Iseyin at this time.

Master weavers interviewed in 1993 mentioned a number of weaving-related groups. The 'Weavers' Brothers and Weavers' Sisters', which recognizes the growing number of women who have turned to strip-weaving in the last decade, is said to be challenging the older *Egbe Alaso Oke*. Two other associations, with weavers as members, seem to be akin to *esusu* societies. The 'Amuludun Society' and the 'Ifesowapo Society' were organized 'just to help each other in the business'. A 'Junior Weavers' Club', established in 1986, is very active. The goals of this organization seem very similar to indigenous age-grade *egbe* associations. The club assists members 'having misfortune', protects the interests of members from outside interference and provides representation to the government. Members assist the local authority in the case of provision of local amenities, and 'rally round each other during ceremonies' and in times of trouble or difficulties.

Iseyin weaving organizations seem to be most successful when they emerge spontaneously to band together for mutual aid at times of perceived need. The *egbe* that incorporates indigenous leadership structures and administrative arrangements and is built on the bonds of friendship as well as shared occupation is as successful today as it was in the past. Government intervention programmes that ignore such pre-existing indigenous organizations seem doomed to failure. An example of government intervention in craft production provides us with a cautionary tale. This is a story of a well-meaning government-sponsored weaving project in Iseyin that failed because of the lack of indigenous input.

In 1963, the Ministry of Agriculture and the Ministry of Trade and Industry (without the Co-operative Department) launched an Integrated Rural Development Scheme. A White Paper on Integrated Rural Development was issued by the Western Nigerian government, presenting a scheme to provide employment for school-leavers which would keep them in the small towns of their birth through establishing farm settlements and rural industries. Weaving was a focus for a co-ordinated programme involving several ministries.[16] Locally grown cotton, obtained through the Ministry of Agriculture and Natural Resources, would be spun into thread in small factories set up by the Ministry of Trade and Industry and sold to Training Centres for Weavers and Co-operative Weavers' Production Units, also organized by the Ministry of Trade and Industry. The final link in the chain was to make it compulsory for local schools to buy the cloth for their school uniforms from the weaving co-operatives and patronize Co-operative Tailors' Production Units. It was calculated that this scheme would provide approximately 20000 new jobs in the region (Koll 1969: 86). The scheme failed.

The Iseyin Weaving Centre, established in 1963[17] and closed two and a half years later, provides an example of the experience. The Western Region government built the Weaving Centre at Iseyin with the aim of modernizing the narrow-loom weaving industry. It provided 50 'modern' looms and equipment and the capital to cover the cost of initial expenses. The Iseyin District Council chose 50 students (46 males, four females) who were sent to train at the Oyo Weaving Centre which had been established earlier. After six months of training, they returned to Iseyin to form the Co-operative Textile Weavers' Society which was registered with the government and was eligible for government monetary incentives.

The Iseyin Weaving Centre was not a true co-operative. The young newly-trained and inexperienced weavers were under the control of salaried administrators appointed and paid by the ministries. There was one Higher Textile Officer, one Textile Officer, two Demonstrators and a Supervisor. The officers went to the schools in the area and collected the patterns to be woven for the school uniforms. The weavers at the centre, who were given a monthly stipend, were allocated these patterns to produce. On completion, the officers would collect the cloth, sell it to the schools and deposit the money into the co-operative's account. The monthly stipends paid to the weavers were based on the total amount of cloth each produced.

At its height, the Iseyin Weaving Centre produced school uniforms for four primary schools and two secondary schools, along with napkins, towels and women's wrappers, as major products. However, the centre and co-operative society collapsed in less than three years. A number of reasons can be mentioned.

o The quality of the product was poor. The schools complained that the uniforms, now compulsory for students, lasted only a few months.

o The new technology introduced, that is, the new loom types, was perceived as having no advantage over the indigenous narrow-strip looms in use in Iseyin. The technology was not considered appropriate by the local weavers, and the weavers complained that weaving on the new looms was more strenuous than using the older-style looms.

o The income of the centre weavers was low. While the new looms provided wider cloth for 'modern' uses, the weavers produced fewer yards per day than was possible on the narrow-strip horizontal looms used in the town. The weavers, paid by the yard, complained that they did not make the equivalent of independent weavers.

o The government offered no further financial aid beyond the initial start-up costs for the centre. Once the start-up fund was finished, the centre got into financial difficulties. Customers were often slow to pay for goods, and in some cases defaulted. In addition, stockpiled goods sold slowly. With a lack of available capital, the centre had difficulty purchasing thread and other materials needed for the production of further orders.

o The lack of funds also meant that often the weavers were not paid promptly for their work. For example, at one point, the weavers did not receive their stipends for four months and were unable to meet their domestic and social responsibilities.

o The government's focus upon organizing co-operatives and training opportunities primarily as a measure to provide employment for school-leavers was inappropriate. The youth and inexperience of the weavers was a factor in an area where weaving was well established and value was placed upon age, seniority and experience.

o Finally, the government policy of keeping government ministry employees in the position of decision-makers for the co-operative prevented involvement and acceptance by the larger weaving community of Iseyin.

Thirty years later, the basic distrust of those in control of this experiment in co-operative production was voiced by weavers who remembered the centre. Reasons mentioned for the failure of the centre included: 'financial mismanagement and politics', 'bad administration, financial inefficiency', and 'lack of incentives by the government'. Further statements sum up the local attitude— 'It failed because people lacked co-operation. Some people went against the idea while some supported the idea.' 'Failure was due to the fact that the weavers believed that to run their business independently is better than being under government.'

It is, perhaps, this final reason that gets at the heart of the problems that beset the Iseyin Weaving Centre and prevented its success. The government planners ignored the fact that in Iseyin weaving production and marketing were already organized and regulated by functioning organizations that were accepted by the people and that had been in place for a long time. It has been said that to be successful co-operatives must be self-supporting grassroots developments generated through local efforts and profitable to members. Members must also be self-governing and self-policing so that ethical standards and product quality are maintained. The indigenous lineage-based production groups and *egbe* weaving organizations of Iseyin fulfilled these criteria. Rather than build upon these roots, the government planners chose to introduce new technology and products, change the structure of the work force and take almost total control of production and marketing. This is why the Iseyin Weaving Centre failed.

In contrast, it is possible to blend the indigenous organization with the government-registered co-operative. The *Egbe Alaso-oke Iseyin* was registered as a co-operative with the Department of Co-operatives in 1967. Already well organized as an indigenous *egbe*, it merely expanded its functions when it became a co-operative. Its major goals, today as in the past, are primarily concerned with the marketing of Iseyin *aso-oke*, to keep production prices low, and to regulate market prices and competition. Besides controlling cloth trade, the *Egbe Alaso-oke Iseyin* as a co-operative has added the further functions of educating weavers by advising them on production, materials and prices; giving technological and financial assistance to members; and advising them on how to relate to the government.

Conclusions

Aso-oke, the popular Yoruba textile, has stood the test of time and has retained its value as a status symbol and an expression of Yorubaness in the face of stiff competition from modern fabrics and technologies, as well as unfavourable government policies. The Iseyin *aso-oke* industry has not only survived but grown in the modern era. This is in large part due to the strength of the indigenous organizations that regulate production and marketing through both kinship structures and *egbe* organizations that cross-cut kinship ties. The economic character of the industry in which production remains in the context of the lineage and marketing in the hands of local trading organizations has guaranteed that price and quality of products remain competitive in the modern market.

Marion Johnson, the economic historian, in a discussion of the competition that local hand-woven textile industries had to face as textile imports from Europe and Asia flowed into West Africa, attempts to explain why local hand-woven cloth industries survived and successfully met that competition (Johnson, 1978). The West African market for cloth is huge. While textiles can be considered a luxury because they are not essential for survival, they have become 'conventional necessities' (Johnson 1978: 266). Throughout West Africa, with the rise of cash incomes and the new 'middle-class' élite that accompanied colonialism, consumption of cloth, once the prerogative of the indigenous leadership élites, began to rise. To this day, increases in population and living standards continue to widen the market for all types of cloth (Johnson 1978: 267–8). Clothing from hand-woven indigenous types of cloth, in particular, has been adopted by the contemporary élites as a visible symbol of prosperity, status and pride in ethnic heritage.

The *aso-oke* weaving industry of Iseyin, along with Ghanaian *kente* weaving industries, are mentioned by Johnson as examples of 'the most successful of the modern industries' that have expanded as a result of the patronage of these new élites and 'the loosening of many old restrictions' surrounding textile use (Johnson 1978: 267). Ultimately, according to Johnson, they are successful because they can price their products to be competitive with other prestige textiles.

An élite demand depends partly on fashion, partly on political and religious attitudes, and very little on price; indeed, any attempt to reduce prices might prove self-defeating, since part of the demand depends on the expensiveness of the product. For all but the wealthiest consumers, however, price is important. Only if the local weaver can produce cloth whose price, in terms of attractiveness and durability, can compete with imported cottons, can he hope to stay in business (Johnson 1978: 267).

For Johnson, indigenous textiles such as *aso-oke* can successfully compete in the market-place with machine-loomed cloth because the price is right. She attributes this to the fact that the costs of production are low because the average weaver works in the context of the family residence, often farming and relying on the labour of other family members. 'Under such a system the marginal costs of production are virtually nil' (Johnson 1978: 267). This is true, as we have shown. The strength of the Iseyin weaving industry—and that of other weaving towns—is that production is located in the context of kinship group compounds. The compound provides a safety-net for members. Weaving and related craft skills are learned by most children in the context of family. It is an occupation that can be picked up as a full-time adult occupation or something to fall back upon if other professional opportunities do not emerge, or terminate.

Johnson's argument that home production keeps the cost of producing cloth down is sound, but cost of production alone does not explain how Iseyin has gained its fame as 'The Home of *Aso-oke*'. Despite the individual weaver's supposed freedom in the production and sale of *aso-oke*, indigenous organizations and the leadership and support they provide continue to exert tremendous influence on every aspect of the weaving industry. Without the localized trading *egbe* that collaborate in the marketing of Iseyin cloth throughout the region, the industry could not support the level of production it now attains.

In Iseyin, *Egbe Alaso Oke*, in particular, is very active in regulating every aspect of production and distribution of *aso-oke*. Various smaller *egbe* complement the role of *Egbe Alaso Oke* by assisting members in acquiring start-up and production costs, but also link members together in networks of friendship and meaningful communal activities. These indigenous organizations have operated successfully, have demonstrated their ability to adapt to changing social and economic conditions, and are still growing stronger. Government attempts to supersede this arrangement and introduce new forms of weaving production and marketing have failed, because they did not take into consideration the existing indigenous organizations and administrative structure. The indigenous *egbe* remain strong because membership forges strong social and economic links, and members recognize and have confidence in their leaders who are usually appointed on the basis of age and experience.

Outside agencies must recognize that there is little to be gained by replacing a functioning system of indigenous organizations that has proven its ability to succeed in the competitive arena of textile marketing such as we see in Iseyin. In terms of future development, it is clear that the value of working with existing indigenous weavers' organizations must be recognized. Such indigenous organizations not only provide local leadership acceptable to the producers and consumers of an important cultural commodity, but also provide opportunities for individual members to participate in the development process. Efforts should be made to encourage every weaver in Iseyin town to be an active member of these important organizations which are pivotal to the continued vitality of the indigenous textile industry. Government at all levels (especially the state and local governments) are implored to pay attention to and support the weavers' organizations. Easy access to grants or loans by the weavers' organizations as a body would be worthwhile, because these organizations are unlikely to have all the financial resources required for effective operation and to offer incentives to their members. With government financial support added to the 'know-how' of the indigenous weaving and marketing *egbe*, the textile industry of Iseyin can grow even stronger.

Despite a few ups and downs of demand and the effects of inflation, the *aso-oke* industry has survived and has come to stay. For a very long time to come the strip-woven cloth weaving industry of Iseyin, which has demonstrated that it operates best using indigenous technology and marketing techniques, will remain unbeatable as a major supplier of *aso-oke*. As long as there are Yorubas, *aso-oke* will remain a symbol of prestige, affluence and cultural pride, and Iseyin will remain 'The Home of *Aso-oke*'.

Notes

1. Strip cloth is woven on the 'West African narrow-strip loom', defined by John Picton as a horizontal double-heddle loom in which the warp is attached to a wooden sledge weighed down by a heavy stone (Picton 1992: 20). The strips in the Yoruba area are usually about four inches wide with a warp length of 15 yards.
2. Interviews with weavers and traders were carried out in Iseyin in 1980 and 1992 (Wahab). Iseyin as a focus also offers the advantage that a series of field studies over the past 40 years provide us with basic data on the history of indigenous and external influences on the weaving industry (Dodwell 1955; Bray 1968, 1969, 1974; Lamb and Holmes 1980; Wahab 1980, 1992; Robinson 1982; Sanni 1989).
3. It was feared that such factories would drain away the cotton resources of the area

that were essential to the textile industries in England, as well as compete for the markets in West Africa (Bashir 1986: 90).

4. The exceptions are the new workshops which have been set up in towns such as Ibadan by entrepreneurial weavers who practise open apprenticeship under government-sponsored programmes (NISER 1990).

5. Thanks to LaRay Denzer of the Department of History, University of Ibadan, for calling this to our attention.

6. '*Egbe*,' according to Lloyd, is used to refer to craft guild organizations among the Yoruba. In this chapter we are avoiding the term 'guild', which has been used in a number of ways. Nadel (1942) uses guild to refer to craft organizations based on kinship ties of extended family or lineage among the Nupe. Lloyd (1953: 36) equates guilds with Yoruba craft organizations where the apprentice–journeyman relationship is typical. Ben-Amos (1980: 10), describing the craftsmen who work for the *Oba* of Benin, uses the term for craft groups under the control of a ruler.

7. In this same decade it was estimated that 59 million square yards of imported cloth were sold in a single year (1950/1) in the Western Region of Nigeria which encompasses Yorubaland. In that same period, about 150 million square yards total of cloth were imported into Nigeria as a whole (Galletti *et.al* 1956: 246–52).

8. Bray observed that 76 per cent of the entrepreneurial weavers at that time supplied cotton yarn to members of their own compound group alone (Bray 1968: 273).

9. Alhaji Shittu is referred to as the *Aloga (Alaga) Aso Oke* by Lamb and Holmes who interviewed him in 1978. *Alaga Aso Oke* is the title given to the head weaver who presides over a council of master weavers who have gained their position on the council on the basis of seniority (Lamb and Holmes, 1980: 29).

10. Bray identified these organizations as '*Egbe Ibadan*' and '*Egbe Eko*' (Bray, 1968: 276). The addition of *ero* (which translates as 'passenger' or 'traveller') underscores their commitment to long-distance trade.

11. Unlike many Western artists, Yoruba weavers are 'often eager to share' their innovation and designs with other weavers (Okuwa, 1989: 24).

12. The 'empty bowl' concept was proposed by early critics of colonial and Western development agencies.

13. For an extended discussion of the early development of government-sponsored co-operatives into the first decade of independence, consult Koll (1969).

14. Documents on early attempts to establish broadloom weaving education in Iseyin are found in 'File 372, v.1, Weaving—Oyo Province' at the Nigerian National Archives, Ibadan.

15. See Koll (1969: 71) for a summary of co-operative types recognized by the Department of Co-operatives.

16. The Co-operative Department concentrated on initiating craft co-operatives which built on indigenous crafts, but not weaving. It focused its efforts on leather workers, goldsmiths, and calabash carvers with the goal of providing art and crafts for customers interested in the local culture (Koll, 1969: 78).

17. Additional weaving centres were established in the same year in Ikire, Ayedade, Oyo and Ogbomosho (Wahab, 1980: 22).

References

Ben-Amos, P. (1980), *The Art of Benin*, London: Thames & Hudson.

Bray, J.M. (1968), 'The Organization of Traditional Weaving in Iseyin, Nigeria', *Africa* 38: 270–79.

Bray, J.M. (1969), 'The Economics of Traditional Cloth Production in Iseyin, Nigeria', *Economic Development & Cultural Change* 17: 540–51.

Bray, J.M. (1974), 'The Craft Structure of a Traditional Yoruba Town', in *The City in the Third World*, D.J. Dwyer (editor)., Macmillan, 142–58.

Clarke, W.H. (1972), *Travels and Explorations in Yorubaland 1854–1858*, Ibadan: Ibadan University Press.

Cole, B. (1983), *The Renaissance Artist at Work*. New York: Harper & Row, Publishers.

Crowder, M. (1962), *A Short History of Nigeria*, New York: Frederick A. Praeger.

Dodwell, C.B. (1955), 'Iseyin, the Town of Weavers', *Nigeria* No. 46: 118–39.

Eades, J.S. (1980), *The Yoruba Today*, Cambridge: Cambridge University Press.

Fadipe, N.A. (1970), *The Sociology of the Yoruba*, Ibadan: Ibadan University Press.

Falola, T. (1991), 'The Yoruba Caravan System of the Nineteenth Century', *International Journal of African Historical Studies* 24(1): 111–32.

Galletti, R., Baldwin, K.D.S. and Dina, I.O. (1956), *Nigerian Cocoa Farmers*, Oxford: Oxford University Press.

Johnson, M. (1978), 'Technology, Competition and African Crafts', in *The Imperial Impact: Studies in the Economic History of Africa and India*. Athlone Press.

Koll, M. (1969), *Crafts and Cooperation in Western Nigeria*, Bielefeld: Bertelsmann Universitatsverlag.

Kriger, C. (1990), 'Textile Production in the Lower Niger Basin: New Evidence from the 1841 Niger Expedition Collection', *Textile History* 21(1): 31–56.

Lamb, V. and Holmes, J. (1980), *Nigerian Weaving*, Lagos: Shell Petroleum Development Company of Nigeria.

Law, R. (1977), *The Old Oyo Empire c.1600–c.1836*. Oxford: Oxford University Press.

Lloyd, P. (1953), 'Craft Organization in Yoruba Towns', *Africa* 23: 30–40.

Nadel, S.F. (1942), *A Black Byzantium: The Kingdom of Nupe in Nigeria*, London: Oxford University Press.

Nigerian Institute of Social and Economic Research (NISER) (1990), *Report of World Bank/Niser Project on Education and Training for Skills and Income in the Urban Informal Sector in Sub-Saharan Africa: The Case of Urban Informal Sector of Ibadan City, Nigeria*, Ibadan: NISER.

Ogunsanwo, A.T. (1985), *A Traditional Market in Modern Ibadan: A Case Study of Oje Market, 1960–84*, University of Ibadan, Unpublished BA essay.

O'Hear, A. (1987), 'Craft Industries in Ilorin: Dependency or Independence?' *African Affairs*, 505–21.

O'Hear, A. (1990). 'The Introduction of Weft Float Motifs to Strip Weaving in Ilorin', in *West African Economic and Social History*, D. Henige and T.C. McCaskie (eds). Madison: African Studies Program, University of Wisconsin, 175–88.

Okuwa, A.I. (1989), 'The Socio-economic Organization of Aso-oke Trade in Oje Market', BA Final Year Project, Anthropology, University of Ibadan.

Perani, Judith (1992), 'The Cloth Connection: Patrons and Producers of Hausa and Nupe Prestige Strip-weave', *History, Design, and Craft in West African Strip-woven Cloth*, Washington: National Museum of African Art, 95–112.

Picton, J. (1992), 'Tradition, Technology, and Lurex: Some Comments on Textile History and Design in West Africa', *History, Design, and Craft in West African Strip-woven Cloth*, Washington: National Museum of African Art, 95–112.

Robinson, G.A. (1982), 'Cloth-weaving Technology in Yorubaland: Iseyin as a Case Study', University of Ibadan, BA essay.

Sanni, S.O. (1989), 'The 'Aso-oke' Weaving Industry in Iseyin: A Comprehensive Appraisal', The Polytechnic, Ibadan, thesis for Higher National Diploma in Business Administration.

Thornton, J. (1990), 'Precolonial African Industry and the Atlantic Trade, 1500–1800', *African Economic History* 19: 1–19.

Wahab, W.B. (1980), 'Economic-base/growth of Iseyin—'The Home of "Aso-oke"'. The Polytechnic, Ibadan, Higher National Diploma.

Wass, B.M. (1979), 'Yoruba Dress in Five Generations of a Lagos Family', *The Fabrics of Culture*, J.M. Cordwell and R.A. Schwarz, (eds), The Hague: Mouton.

Wolff, N.H. (1991), 'A Yoruba Woman's Search for Identity in Nigerian Contemporary Society: An Anthropological Approach', *Symposium on Africa and African Identity*, African Studies Program, Kent State University, Kent, Ohio.

8 Traditional leadership and community management in Northern Ghana

NANCY COSWAY AND STEVE A. ANANKUM*

Introduction

THERE HAVE BEEN numerous water and sanitation projects initiated during the Water Decade of the 1980s in Asia, Latin America and Africa. Government and non-government agencies have been involved, with varying degrees of help from the local recipients. Some projects have been conceived, planned and organized without input from the recipients. The donors viewed the people as recipients and beneficiaries of these projects, not as key players in the design, implementation and evaluation of the projects. Donors often did not involve the beneficiaries as they may have thought that it was more efficient to plan outside the community; it was imagined that local people did not understand and they did not have the technical knowledge or skill required; it took too long to reach agreement on approaches to the project; and donors knew what had worked in other places. In the 1970s development tended to involve the transfer of technology and the belief that if the South had access to technology, whether it was tractors, grinding mills, or water-pumping equipment, development and an increased standard of living would follow. There was little if any involvement of the beneficiaries of the technology; they were 'recipients', almost like empty vessels to be filled.

The people of Asia, Latin America and Africa do have much to contribute to their own development planning: what they want; how they will use it; what benefits are most appropriate; and particularly how it will be managed in the context of their community. Community activities like managing the local market, planning and co-ordinating festival activities, co-operative farming, marketing of produce, building and maintaining health clinics and many other activities have been successfully implemented and managed for generations. Successful management confirms that people have knowledge and capabilities for the development and sustainability of projects to benefit their community.

> Communities are structured to provide leadership, conduct social and religious activities, and attend to legal, property and economic matters affecting their members. The control of traditional water supply sources is part of this structure . . . Physical environment dictates the need for a certain level of management as well as the character of the society.[1]

* Nancy Cosway, a Canadian, has worked in the community development field, involving research, programme planning, design and implementation. She has been deeply involved in health education and community participation in the water and sanitation sector. Steve A. Anankum is a Ghanaian community development specialist and has worked in his native area of northern Ghana for a number of years for the Department of Community Development in the water and sanitation sector.

Fortunately, the thinking of donors changed during the 1980s and the recipients of development projects are now involved in the planning, implementation and evaluation of projects. Information from community members is needed at all stages of a project: before starting the project; during design and formulation of the project; and for the successful implementation and sustainability of the project. Project planners need to recognize that the recipients have information and knowledge that will contribute to the success of all stages of a project. It is acknowledged that it may be time consuming to plan with the local people who will benefit from the project. Collecting information or searching for the appropriate knowledge is not an easy task if you are an outsider looking in.

This chapter describes a rural water project in the Upper West and Upper East regions of Ghana and examines the development of a community management strategy for the water resource. The strategy was developed following investigation of self-help community projects and the documentation and analysis of indigenous knowledge and traditional leadership practices.

Historical overview

The Water Utilization Project (WUP) in the Upper East and West regions of Ghana has evolved with a growing recognition of indigenous knowledge and the role of traditional leadership. This knowledge and leadership structure assisted communities in determining a management strategy for their water resource. The Water Utilization Project was a water and sanitation scheme funded by the Canadian International Development Agency (CIDA) and implemented between 1984 and 1992 by Wardrop Engineering Inc. The overall goal of the project was to help villagers maximize the potential health benefits of potable water from 2600 boreholes constructed and fitted with handpumps by the Upper Region Water Supply Project (URWSP) in partnership with Ghana Water and Sewerage Corporation (GWSC). The project had three components: health education, pump site development and community development.[2]

Health education
The health education component of the project attempted to acknowledge and build on the understanding and beliefs of people regarding specific water-related diseases. This required the investigation and study of local beliefs and practices by the educators through developing an open and trusting relationship with the local people. The purpose of the health education component was to change behaviour towards healthier practices concerning the storage and use of water and to prevent water-related illness. Traditional ways of learning and sharing information among people were examined and incorporated into the education programme. New information which could influence behaviour was shared with village members, particularly women, in traditional ways like story-telling, drama and songs.

The health education component was based on adult education principles which recognized that adults have a wealth of knowledge and skill and, as educators, we must build upon it. The training sessions were three days long and held in a catchment area of a number of villages. Attendance by all was crucial. The training programme used traditional ways of learning throughout; story-telling, drama, songs and group discussion. Government workers in partner agencies provided the community educators with feedback, support and encouragement to continue the work in their own community.

Many of the women who attended training sessions were older and had been selected because they were respected in the community by the younger women. Elderly women were looked to for their knowledge of child-rearing and health matters. It was difficult for a younger woman to contradict an older women about these practices. If behaviour change was to be achieved, the people responsible for passing on the traditional health knowledge had to be integrated into the training programme. There was also a cultural bias towards sending older women on training as there was resistance to sending younger women away from their homes.

Community members were able to compose songs that talked about the use of oral rehydration therapy for diarrhoea, storage of water for drinking in covered containers, and collection of water for drinking from the handpumps. Dramas were staged by community members to illustrate hygienic water practices and there was often spontaneous participation by the audience. The experience, knowledge and skill of the learners were an integral part of the learning process and formed the base for all health messages.

The village women educators accepted the responsibility to take information back to their own community, and participants were actively involved in the education of their fellow community members and educated their fellow villagers. The problems and issues that the health messages addressed were encountered in everyday life: diarrhoea, dehydration, safe collection and storage of drinking-water and other water-related concerns.

Community development

The community development component evolved over time as the WUP workers, GWSC and the funding agency recognized that local people could best organize and manage development activities in their own community. One of the project's first tasks was to set up Water Users' Committees (WUCs) in the communities to discuss and address issues related to the handpump. Frequently, it was requested that a new committee be formed rather than using an existing village development committee. The expectation placed on the WUC was that some problems could be solved locally or a solution suggested and agreed by the villagers and implemented by GWSC. Selecting the committee members was left to the community, although there were some guidelines. These included that women should be represented, and the handpump caretaker should be a member. The role of women was recognized as managers of water and as a significant voice in the management and utilization of water within the household. There has been considerable progress and increase in women's participation but we still need to respect and possibly observe the barriers that may exist in some societies.

Pump site development

Much of the activity of the Water Users' Committees involved organization of communal labour for construction of pads and animal troughs at the pump sites, backfilling of the pump pad with sand and stones to prevent erosion, cleaning of the pump site and maintenance of an access road for GWSC handpump mechanics to come to maintain and repair the pump. Within communities, there already existed a system for assigning responsibility to different sections to meet the workload demands. Women were traditionally responsible for cleaning and sweeping at the pump site. Carrying sand and stones for construction was also the role of women and they continued to perform this task for the Water Users' Committees.

As the project continued and evolved many of the Water Users' Committees took on the task of collecting the tariff for the handpump. This tariff was levied by GWSC and was partially to fund the cost of maintaining the pumps. Different ways of collecting the money were tried within communities. Whether payment was by individual, family or clan varied from one community to another. GWSC was only concerned with the collection of the tariff and did not get involved in deciding the method of collection within the community.

Strategy for community management

In June, 1990 a Community Animation unit was formed within the WUP to develop a strategy by which people in the villages could successfully manage their water resource. The strategy was to be developed from data collected on the incidence and management of self-help community development projects in communities, and an analysis of the reasons for their success or failure.

The Community Animation Unit undertook the following research in order to develop a strategy for community-based management of their water resource (i.e. hand-pumps):[3]

o The frequency of village-based self-help development projects was evaluated;
o The reasons for successful and unsuccessful experiences were analysed; and
o Case-studies were conducted in a few villages to develop an understanding of the decision-making processes and other factors contributing to success.

The focus here will be to discuss the findings concerning community leadership, structure, and decision-making processes regarding self-help projects. Examples will be cited from the survey and case-studies illustrating the traditional leadership structure and decision-making processes.

Methodology
The survey and case-studies were conducted by Ghanaians attached to the project who had knowledge and skill in community development, handpump maintenance and health education. They also could speak the local languages and were from the Upper East and Upper West regions. Survey instruments, training programmes and field supervision were designed and implemented with the assistance of a Canadian adviser.

The survey was conducted in 100 randomly selected villages in the Upper East (55) and Upper West (45) regions. The purpose of the survey was to examine the methods of management and maintenance of self-help projects and to identify any common components in the villages that contributed to their success. The researchers wanted to confirm, as they believed, that within the village there were traditional leaders and indigenous knowledge that contributed to the success of community development activities. The researchers trained interviewers who spoke the local dialect and knew local protocol when collecting information from villagers. A number of individuals were interviewed and one group meeting was held in each community. There was co-operation in all 100 villages. People seemed pleased to talk about their successes and elaborate on their community management abilities. Identification of a project that was unsuccessful was more difficult but was accomplished in a number of villages. Only nine out of the 100 villages had never had a successful self-help development project. This low failure rate was very encouraging and indicated there must exist some community leadership and structure which contributed to the success of projects.

The case-studies were conducted in six villages with a view to documenting how formal and informal organizational structures operated within the community with respect to community development and self-help projects. Important aspects of community life that were examined included: decision-making processes; role of women, youth and the elderly; interaction of traditional and modern political structures; and identification of components necessary for success. Researchers worked with local residents to collect the data and lived with the people in the village for a short time to observe informal interactions within the village.

A third source of information on community structures and management was a nearby project, a UNDP-funded project, which operated in 50 communities with handpumps in Bolgatanga District (Upper East Region). In this project the handpumps had been replaced with village-level operation and maintenance (VLOM) models and Community Water and Sanitation Management Committees established in each community. These committees had been closely monitored and supported by the UNDP staff who had transferred to the Community Animation Unit of WUP.

There were thorough community investigations, with a variety of opinions sought and a wide range of views, to obtain a clearer understanding of how the community functioned. Investigators wanted to define clearly the responsibilities the community assumed for itself in self-help projects.

Findings

Most of the findings described in this section are a result of the survey and case-studies conducted by the WUP Community Animation Unit staff. Other findings were a result of conversations and debriefing sessions with Ghanaian staff working on the WUP project, partner agency staff and UNDP staff.

It is interesting to note that in the survey of 100 villages, all of which had at least one handpump, no one community identified the handpump as a self-help development project. Possible reasons for this could have been: GWSC initiated the installation of handpumps in villages rather than acting on requests from the community; communities paid a tariff to GWSC and perceived GWSC as the owner of the pump; pumps were repaired by GWSC mechanics, not locally trained people; involvement of villagers during construction was minimal; researchers were linked to GWSC and village people may have assumed they wanted to know about projects other than the pump; and division within the community over using a specific pump did not necessarily follow traditional lines of division in the village. From the research, the following understanding of project implementation and management emerged.

Implementation of projects

Usually the chiefs and elders, who formed the traditional leadership structure, introduced a self-help project to the community. The idea may have been presented to the chief and elders by an individual or specific interest group but the traditional leadership presented the idea to the community as a whole at a general meeting. This community meeting would be held after the chief and elders had sufficient time to discuss the idea and agree that it would be beneficial to the community.

Traditionally, the meeting would be attended by men and women but the men would do most of the discussing and the women answer questions only when specifically asked. The decision would be made at the meeting to accept or reject the project. Decisions were made by consensus rather than formal voting with majority rule. The discussion sometimes took more than one meeting and all views needed to be expressed. At times the meeting could get quite heated but people would discuss and listen until a consensus was reached.

Elders were respected and recognized as having an understanding of the history and value system of their community. Their opinion was often sought by the chief when making a decision. Others that may have been involved with the chief and elders were representatives of external political structures like the District Assembly and Committees for the Defence of the Revolution.

Most frequently, the people of the village accepted the decision of the chief and elders as they respected and trusted their leaders to have the knowledge and authority to make decisions that would benefit the community. The degree of community cohesion influenced the quality of leadership. The more cohesive the community was, the more respected was the leadership and the more influential in village decision-making. Community projects were also much more success-fully managed and implemented. There were a few cases where the traditional leadership was not respected and held little power in the village. In these situations an alternative leader, youth leader, *Tindana*, or other respected villager spoke out and gained support for the proposed project.

It appeared that in all the survey, case-study and UNDP villages, the tradi-tional leadership of chief and elders, with occasional input from external political structures, brought forth ideas to the community and usually the decision of the chief and elders was accepted by the community.

Management of projects

Many communities had a Village Development Committee (VDC) which was responsible for all its development activity. The Village Development Commit-tee was seen as a modern structure outside the traditional leadership, but one that did recognize the importance of the traditional leadership, as local government law stated that the chief was the chairperson of the VDC. Most people in the community saw the VDC as having responsibility for the management of village development projects, although in a number of situations it was stated that everyone was responsible, not only the VDC. Widespread responsibility was a feature of villages which were small and well organized.

Decisions about the project, once accepted by the community, were left to the VDC. Many of the committees had managed a number of projects within the community. There did not seem to be a need or desire to set up a new committee for each and every project. Many of the committees were well organized, functioned successfully and had been given responsibility by the community to manage the project.

In all successful projects the community members had identified a structure that existed within their community and was accepted as having direct respon-sibility for managing and directing the project. To outsiders this structure or organization may not be obvious as they may not understand the organization and lines of authority. Enhancing an already functioning and successful decision-making and management structure or hierarchy is more beneficial to a project than creating new and unfamiliar structures. The Village Development Committee is a good example of an effective structure within the community.

In villages with successful self-help projects and the potential to manage the pump successfully, there was a strong history of co-operative practices. These were implemented by a variety of interest groups including women farmers, *pito* brewers, local artisans, dance groups, bakers, and so on. The interest groups often gave support to the local leadership by taking the lead role in decision-making with the community. These various groups within the community commanded respect and action from fellow members.

There were several management skills necessary to manage successfully the handpumps, which were well documented in the 50 UNDP handpump communities. Financial management was the most critical. Most communities were familiar with the process of collecting money for a communal activity or project, but saving of money for future activities or expenses was not a common practice. Thus, banking was new to many of the communities and the skills and knowledge of banking procedures had to be learned.

Women, most frequently, were seen as the most trustworthy and honest to collect and ensure that money was put to the purpose it was intended. Men were seen as untrustworthy as in the past they had collected money for communal activities and had spent it on themselves or misused it in other ways. Illiterate women had methods of keeping track of the money collected and from whom. A literate person, usually a man, would help keep the ledger and deposit the funds in the bank account. However, it appeared that whenever money was needed to replace a broken part, it was collected on the spot rather than the savings, previously deposited, being used. One person likened this to buying meat in the market even though he had several goats and sheep which were insurance so that when he did not have money to buy meat this reserve could be used.

Lessons learned

Project staff need to recognize that there is a structure in communities for decision-making and that it is suitable and sustainable. There needs to be attention given to the formal and informal leadership based on interest groups as all have recognized leadership and decision-making processes.[4] This was supported by the findings in the WUP case-studies and survey data. The chief and elders, as well as VDCs, have a major role to play in management.

The *Tindana* needed to be involved in the Water Users' Committees because in many communities in the north of Ghana the *Tindana* was the landowner and since water comes from the earth, he was seen as responsible. This person was highly respected in the community and his role was clear to all community members. This traditional leadership and respect for the *Tindana* needed to be acknowledged and incorporated into the management structure.

It is important that enough time be allowed for discussion of a project within the community to ensure that traditional decision-making processes are engaged and that there is complete agreement and acceptance. The community, from the chiefs and elders to the individual members, needs time for discussion and refinement of the proposal. A feeling of 'ownership' of the project will better ensure commitment and success. Decisions by consensus take longer but can assure the support of all involved.

External project staff should be aware of traditional divisions within the community. Some villages may be divided by clan, by language group, by family, or by religion, into separate sections. Each section has its own leadership which then has a relationship with and accountability to the overall chief and elders. These divisions are the basis for much activity in the village, and project staff need to be aware of them and use them when appropriate. These divisions were not necessarily considered when installing boreholes and handpumps as there were other determining factors as to where these should go. It was possible that one side of the village had two handpumps and another side none. This may have caused some problems with payment of the tariff and accessibility of water for all on the side of town without the handpump. In order to be the least disruptive and have the greatest possibility for success, external project staff need to enhance the already established and accepted leadership. Project staff must have knowledge of the village structure and divisions.

The method and assignment of collection of the tariff is a community decision. GWSC did not dictate how the tariff was to be collected, or the contributions to be made by individuals or families. This non-interference with the community collection process acknowledged that communities did have skill and abilities to collect money for a communal purpose. If a new and unfamiliar system had been imposed, it is unlikely that it would have been successful. A system imposed from the outside may have created some animosity towards GWSC, caused friction or confusion within the community, and the authority of the traditional leadership may have been undermined.

An external agency attempting to have the community assume management of a project can only move as quickly as the village members are willing to allow. Sustainability and success will only be achieved when the community is allowed the time to understand and participate in project development and to utilize traditional community management structures and priorities.

John Pickford, in his publication *The Worth of Water*,[5] states there are five conditions for success in self-management:

o The community must be involved at all stages of the project.
o Roles and responsibilities of community and government agencies must be clearly defined and obligations fulfilled.
o Government and agencies act as supporter of the community, not as owner or manager of the resource.
o Contact between community and agency is through staff whose primary skills are organizing and motivating the community.
o Government agencies fulfil their limited but vital tasks of motivation, training and technical assistance.

In the publication by G.F. White, *Drawers of Water* (1972), the author suggested that local people need to be included in a significant way in the planning and implementation of rural water-supply projects. Twenty-two years later it is still a challenge to the planners, development agencies and implementing agencies to fulfil this vision.

Notes

1. WASH Technical Report No. 71, February 1993, 'Models of Management Systems for the Operation and Maintenance of Rural Water Supply and Sanitation Facilities', P. Roark, J. Hodgkin and A. Wyatt, p.14.

2. 'End of Project Report', Water Utilization Project, CIDA Project 400/10971, August 1992, 1.
3. Field Paper No. 49, 'Community Management Strategy', Water Utilization Project, CIDA Project 400/10971, July 1992, 1.
4. WASH Field Report No. 217, 'CARE/Sierra Leone Community Participation Assessment', Dec. 1987, by M. Yacoob, K. Tilford, H. Bell, T. Kanah, 33.
5. Pickford, John, (1991) *The Worth of Water*, London Intermediate Technology Publications.

Additional reading

CIDA (1990), 'The Water Utilization Project, A Case Study on a Water and Health Education Project in Northern Ghana'.
Donnelly-Roark, P. (1987), WASH Technical Report No. 52, PROWWESS Report No. 50, 'New Participatory Frameworks for the Design and Management of Sustainable Water Supply and Sanitation Projects'.
Isely, R.B. (1981), WASH Technical Report No. 7, 'Facilitation of Community Organization: An approach to water and sanitation programs in developing countries'.
Narayan-Parker, D. (1989), 'Indonesia: Evaluating Community Management', PROWWESS/UNDP Technical Series: 'Involving Women in Water and Sanitation: Lessons, Strategies, Tools'.
Roark, P. (1990), WASH Technical Report No. 64, 'Evaluation Guidelines for Community-based Water and Sanitation Projects'.
Roark, P., Hodgkin, J. and Wyatt, A. (1993), WASH Technical Report No. 71, 'Models of Management Systems for the Operation and Maintenance of Rural Water Supply and Sanitation Facilities'.
Wardrop Engineering Inc. (1992), Field Paper No. 40, 'Survey of Community Development Activities in 100 Villages', Water Utilization Project, CIDA Project 400/10971.
Wardrop Engineering Inc. (1992), Field Paper No. 41, 'Evaluation of Community Water and Sanitation Management Committees', Water Utilization Project, CIDA Project 400/10971.
Wardrop Engineering Inc. (1992), Field Paper No. 49, 'Community Management Strategy', Water Utilization Project, CIDA Project 400/10971.
Wardrop Engineering Inc. (1992), 'End of Project Report' (Draft), Water Utilization Project, CIDA Project 400/10971.
White, G.F. (1972), *Drawers of Water*, Chicago: University of Chicago Press.
Yacoob, M., Tilford, K., Bell, H. and Kenah, T. (1987), WASH Field Report No. 217, 'CARE/Sierra Leone Community Participation Assessment'.

9 Indigenous healer associations and a South African AIDS-prevention project

EDWARD C. GREEN AND BONGIE ZOKWE*

Indigenous knowledge and international development

INDIGENOUS KNOWLEDGE SYSTEMS (IKS) refer to that body of accumulated wisdom that has ' . . . evolved from years of experience and trial-and-error problem solving by groups of people working to meet the challenges they face in their local environments, drawing upon the resources they have at hand' (McClure, 1989: 1). That the abbreviation IKS as now used in some international development circles suggests there is recognition—however belated—of the value of people's existing or traditional ways of understanding their own world. It is also becoming recognized increasingly that an understanding of indigenous organizations is invaluable to the planners and implementers of development programmes.

Development assistance programmes typically introduce a 'modern' or 'scientific' technology based on a knowledge system deemed superior to a pre-existing knowledge system that will, it is hoped, be supplanted. In this way, development assistance resembles colonialism and imperialism. The implicit or explicit assumption is that the traditional or indigenous knowledge system is irrational and dysfunctional, that it is based on myths or superstitions, and that in any case it remains an obstacle in the way of realizing the benefits of the new technologies of the donor group (Warren, Slikkerveer and Titilola, 1989; Compton, 1989). What this view fails to recognize is that traditional systems may be well suited to the social, psychological and other needs of participants in these systems. They tend to be a great source of comfort to Africans undergoing rapid cultural change, providing security and continuity in an unpredictable, changing world; and tend to be genuine functioning systems whereas the same cannot as yet be said of the modern, urban alternative (Green 1988: 1128).

Furthermore while it may be true that nations in a position to provide development assistance are in general technologically superior to recipient nations, it does not follow that all forms of the recipient country's indigenous knowledge are inferior. That country may not have developed sophisticated weapons systems but it may have developed a way of growing maize under conditions of uncertain rainfall that are well-suited to local conditions. Or it may have discovered natural medicines that relieve the symptoms of high blood pressure or diabetes. In any case, a society's creativity and genius is embodied in its IKS. IKS forms the basis for local decision-making in health as in other domains. An understanding of health-related indigenous knowledge is also

---

* Edward C. Green is an independent consultant who has done applied medical anthropological research in Swaziland, South Africa, Mozambique, Nigeria, Liberia, Bangladesh, the Dominican Republic and elsewhere. Most recently he worked in the Mozambique Ministry of Health. Bongie Zokwe is former Deputy Program Officer of the AIDSCOM/AIDSCAP programme in South Africa. Since returning to South Africa from living as an ANC exile in various countries in Southern Africa, she has devoted most of her time and energy to AIDS prevention.

essential for health planners and programme implementers, if plans and programmes are to be culturally appropriate and therefore effective. And such
knowledge is accessible to planners, implementers and others through
approaches that involve the co-operation of traditional healers, if only through
research.

This chapter summarizes an attempt of an AIDS- and STD-prevention effort in
South Africa to profit from the IKS as well as the role and prestige of indigenous
or traditional healers. Like many such collaborative public health programmes
involving traditional healers and supported by outside donors, the initial
approach was to work through national, or at least formal, professional associations of traditional healers (see Warren, 1982, 1986 for Ghana; Green, 1989a,
Tahzib, 1988 for Nigeria; Green, 1994, Nhlengethwa and Perez, 1991, Hoff and
Maseko, 1986 for Swaziland; Green, Jurg and Dgedge, 1993 for Mozambique;
Hogle *et al.*, 1991 for Uganda.) The South African AIDS/STD project, aspects of
which are described here, suggests that there may be significant advantages to
working collaboratively with *traditional* indigenous organizations of healers
rather than with *formal*, national organizations modelled after urban, Western
professional associations. If true, such a finding has policy and programme
significance for donor organizations, NGOs and local government agencies
that seek to implement public health or other development programmes in
collaboration with traditional healers and perhaps with other indigenous leaders
as well.

National associations of healers

Before turning to the programme in South Africa it is useful to summarize a
forum-type discussion published some 15 years ago in response to a paper by
D.D.O. Oyebola (1981), thought to be the first attempt to describe the aims and
functions of indigenous African healer professional associations, in this case
among the Yoruba of Nigeria. The points raised by Oyebola and a panel of
experts responding to the paper provide a framework for understanding the
findings and policy issues from South Africa, presented in the next section.
Oyebola (1981: 92) argued that the co-operation and support of professional
healer associations 'will be needed if proposals to utilize traditional healers for
health care delivery in the developing countries are to be successful'. He also
notes the usefulness of associations in facilitating 'research ventures into traditional medical systems'.

Bannerman (Bannerman *et al.*, 1981: 93), former head of the WHO's Department of Traditional Medicine, was upbeat on the future of professional healer
associations, believing that they would encourage the enactment of appropriate
legislation for the licensing and registration of healers, assist inter-sectoral
collaboration and protect the patient through quality control of healers'
practice. For his part, Bibeau rejected the widely held view that traditional
healers are secretive and uncooperative. 'Priest–healers' and 'ritualists' in
particular have always been organized in formal associations characterized by
regular meetings and 'control over individual practice by elders in the initiation'.
National associations, however, are new and Bibeau believed 'they cannot exist
for the time being'. He advocated efforts aimed at developing 'strong local,
regional, limited associations' noting that the national associations with which
he was familiar were 'purely legal empty forms without any power of mobilization'. The 'sociological traits' of 'efficient healers' associations' are that: first,

they are rooted in a geographical area or in a particular form of therapy; and second, 'they are highly personalized, in the sense that leadership is assumed by a healer of great fame in the area' (Bannerman *et al.*, 1981: 94).

Dunn held the notion that 'some form of healers' association, however local and small in scale, can be found in any society that supports traditional healers . . . past or present' (Bannerman *et al.*, 1981: 95). Fosu (Bannerman *et al.*, 1981: 96) also found evidence for the antiquity of associations 'organized at the community level' characterized by 'networks of communication channels . . . through which they gathered information to help them in their practice'. He went on to say:

> attempts to organize them at the national level are recent. Such efforts have not always been successful for several reasons, notably internal strife for leadership positions and difficulties in legitimization and integration into the national health care system.
>
> (Bannerman *et al.*, 1981: 96)

Nevertheless Fosu thought local government support could help overcome some of these problems and that 'the advantages of having accredited traditional healer associations are many'.

Heggenhougan (Bannerman *et al.*, 1981: 97–8) felt that collaboration with healer associations on the part of national study groups can 'serve to overcome the information gap'. He noted that reluctance on the part of many healers to join national associations is not necessarily due to their own competencies or wish to be secretive, rather it is because: 'Healers are aware that initiators of such associations are sometimes motivated by special interest, political or self-serving considerations rather than by the potential benefit to the healers and their parents.'

Background to project

In South Africa, two USAID-funded projects, AIDSCOM (AIDS Communication) and AIDSCAP (AIDS Control and Prevention) collaborated as a joint programme between 1991–3. The USAID programme in South Africa operated under anti-apartheid legislation from the US Congress, which meant that assistance must be through non-governmental channels, specifically through 'progressive', anti-apartheid organizations. The joint programme's experience in AIDS prevention during the first year convinced AIDSCOM/AIDSCAP of the importance of traditional healers in HIV/AIDS and STD control in South Africa. The first author was asked to assist in designing a pilot project for traditional healers, conducting baseline and formative research, facilitating a preliminary workshop for healers, and evaluating the overall effort.

One decision had been made before his arrival in South Africa, namely to turn over most of the responsibility for selecting workshop participants to five formal traditional healer associations that claimed national membership: the Traditional Doctors AIDS Project (TRADAP) with headquarters near Johannesburg; the Traditional Healers' Organization of South Africa (THOSA) with headquarters in KwaXuma; the Professional Herbal Preparations Association of Inyangas (PHPAI), with offices in Johannesburg, Qwa-Qwa and Bergville; the Traditional Healers' Organization of Africa (THOA), headquartered in Siteki, Swaziland, but said to have two branch offices in South Africa; and the African Natural Healers' Organization (ANHO) with offices in Johannesburg. AIDSCOM/AIDS-CAP provided some selection criteria in order to ensure gender and geographic balance, but the five healer associations did the actual selection. Virtually every major region of South Africa was represented in the final roster of participants.

The original and ideal plan of this project was to train 30 healers as trainers-of-trainers skilled in HIV/AIDS and STD prevention during the first workshop. These 30 were to train 30 additional healers within six months of the workshop, in addition to incorporating this training into his/her healing practice with patients. The former group of healers was referred to as the first generation, and the latter, the second generation. It was anticipated that the second generation would be trained in special workshops although it was recognized that informal or non-workshop sharing of AIDS knowledge would also occur, for example, between trained healers and their initiates or apprentices. AIDSCOM/AIDSCAP would help defray the costs of workshops held by first-generation healers, although it was hoped that healer associations would also make in-kind contributions to defray costs. In addition, the project would provide material and technical assistance for those workshops.

After six months, the original group of 30 healers would be reconvened by AIDSCOM/AIDSCAP for an assessment. It was hoped that by then 900 healers would have been exposed to AIDS/HIV training. There would be an evaluation of the second generation of healers and plans for training a third generation would be developed based on lessons learned to date. If the 900 healers of the second generation would each train 30 more healers in AIDS prevention within the same time-frame, some 27000 traditional healers a year could be trained from programme start-up. Such was the ideal plan.

The number of healers' clients that could be reached potentially was even more impressive. Our baseline survey of healers participating in the first workshop suggested these healers saw an average of 2000 clients per year. Even allowing for half that number to be repeat (as distinct from new) clients, that is still 1000 clients or patients per year. That means that 27000 healers potentially could reach 1000 clients each with HIV/AIDS/STD preventive education, or some 27000000 South Africans. Of course, second- and third-generation healer–trainees might not see as many clients as the group in the first workshop, and not all clients (some of whom are children) would be exposed to AIDS education. Furthermore there may have been some exaggeration of numbers on the part of first-generation healers. But still the potential seemed there for South African healers quickly to reach large numbers of people with AIDS- and STD-related information.

The preliminary workshop for South African healers was held 22–27 November 1992, south of Port Elizabeth. Due to last-minute changes and confusion over the stipulation that all participants had to be traditional healers—not just members of healer associations—28 rather than 30 healers actually attended. Workshop facilitators were from AIDSCOM/AIDSCAP, SABSWA (South African Black Social Workers Association), PPHC (Progressive Primary Health Care) and the ANC Health Department. Plenary sessions were conducted in English, while smaller group work was conducted in the Xhosa, Zulu, Pedi, Sotho, Tswana, Venda and Tsonga languages.

Based on an immediate assessment of participant opinion, the workshop appeared to be successful (Green, Zokwe and Dupree, 1992). Far more important measures of success were that within seven months of the initial workshop, some 630 second-generation healers had been trained by other healers in 12 workshops held in diverse parts of South Africa. (Well over 700 had been trained by the ninth month.) In addition to these 630 direct beneficiaries of training, up to 229320 patients or clients of these healers may have benefited from AIDS education within six months of the second-generation training (calculated as 26 weeks times an average of 14 patients a week per healer[1] times 630 healers trained). Of course not all these healers specialize in STDs or AIDS, but most of them see a great number of STD patients. Finally, an impossible-to-estimate number of friends, family members, and others in the local community (local associations, sports teams, youth groups) benefited from informal AIDS education.

The total direct cost of training these 600 was R79.28 (US$23.30) per healer, or R19.82 ($5.90) per day per healer.[2]

Evaluation of training

During July and August, 1993, the authors evaluated the impact of HIV/AIDS prevention training on the second generation of traditional healers. Data were gathered during site visits to seven representative areas throughout South Africa where training occurred. A sample of 70 second-generation healers was interviewed; information was also gathered through informal methods such as open-ended, key-informant interviews and group discussions. According to survey findings, there was clear evidence of a significant increase of healers' knowledge about HIV, AIDS and STDs. High percentages of those interviewed were able to define and describe HIV accurately; describe three or more correct AIDS symptoms (and not give incorrect symptoms); and accurately describe three or more means of HIV transmission and prevention.

There was also evidence of positive results on healers' practices. Almost all healers reported providing correct preventive advice regarding AIDS and STDs not only to clients but to family members, friends, and to a variety of individuals and groups in the local community. The same was true for condom demonstrations. Condom provision occurred but was constrained by lack of condom availability. There was evidence of other positive training results, such as referrals of patients to hospitals, including for HIV testing; improved relations with local health personnel including a marginal increase in referrals from hospitals to trained healers; improvements in healers' reputation and business locally; reports of healers trying to influence the sexual behaviour of their patients by counselling them or providing sex education; and reported use of only one razor blade per patient or asking each patient to bring a fresh blade. All rated their workshop 'very useful', the most favourable category.

One might expect that the training provided to the first generation of healers would become somewhat diluted in the second generation. Yet the second generation was found to be at least as well-trained as the first, as measured by a 'post-test' type of quick survey of the knowledge and practices of the first generation (Green, Zokwe and Dupree, 1993).

Problems dealing with national organizations

In the course of evaluating the impact of training on the second generation, we asked what organizations of traditional healers (national, regional or local) the healer had belonged to, beginning with any present organization and going backwards in time. What stood out in the answers was the number of healers who had switched association membership recently or who had dropped out of associations altogether. In one informal group discussion, a group of urban healers estimated that only about 20 per cent of all healers in the Johannesburg area were affiliated with formal healer organizations. They believed a greater number may have belonged to an organization at one time and then dropped out.

National and regional organizations appear to be unstable due to power struggles, politics, and rank-and-file healers resenting leaders who 'start acting superior to us'. One widely respected healer commented: 'As soon as a leader starts talking about "my people" he or she is going to cause a lot of resentment and that leader is on the way out.' Another commented, 'Formal associations breed jealousy among healers. No one is treated with respect in them.' In the course of group and individual discussions during site visits, we compiled the following complaints made by healers trained in AIDS against healer associations that claim national membership. Many of the complaints have to do with the nature and behaviour of association presidents. Keep in mind that most healers interviewed—and trained in AIDS—were women:

o Association membership is not truly national. Membership lists may include false addresses for some members to make it appear that membership is national.

o Presidents collect money to pay for legal services, funerals and financial support upon the death of a spouse as well as other things of interest to healers, yet such funds are often not available for members when they are in need—in fact the funds often disappear.

o There are no traditional or agreed-upon mechanisms for conflict resolution within associations.

o Association presidents tend to be men, and they 'boss' members around, women in particular. They do not treat members with the respect they deserve.

o Presidents of major associations may be non-South African in origin. Some healers accused presidents of being 'mainly interested in collecting money from healers in South Africa'.

o Presidents break the very moral behavioural codes they pretend their association upholds. Some have forced themselves sexually upon their female *amatwasa* (initiate-apprentices). Some have seduced patients.

o Some presidents have dubious credentials as *sangomas* (diviner–mediums), at least according to locally-recognized criteria such as membership in a known *impande* (see below). If presidents did not undergo the formal process of *sangoma* initiation,[3] 'their behaviour is not acceptable to the traditions and cultural beliefs of *sangomas*'.

o Many healers may be reluctant to join formal healer associations because they cannot read and write, or because they cannot speak English or African languages other than their own. Such healers may also be gullible and vulnerable and easy prey for a smooth-talking, would-be president.

o Some presidents have tried to make paid membership in their associations a prerequisite for attending AIDSCAP-supported workshops, or specifically for receiving a training certificate. Others have tried to enlist first-generation healers to recruit local second-generation healers for their own association, collecting fees on their behalf. Loud complaints were voiced over this at a group meeting of second-generation healers.

A columnist in the (Johannesburg) *Star* (8/5/93) could have been speaking about national healer associations when he wrote, 'Presidentialism has been the curse of Africa precisely because it concentrates so much power in one person.'

South African healers are strongly egalitarian; they are deeply suspicious of any peer who claims superior status and tries to exercise authority over the rank-and-file. Although there is a traditional hierarchy of statuses, status differences are either between types of healers or they relate to seniority, meaning that today's trainee will become tomorrow's senior *gobela* (trainer). It is also true that formal associations are an historically recent attempt on the part of healers to exercise power in the larger state polity (Last, 1986; McCormack, 1986). As such they are still in an inchoate and unstable developmental stage; they have not yet evolved structures that ensure stability and continuity. Most seem bedevilled by problems of financial management.

Because of the foregoing, we decided to explore the possibility of AIDSCAP/ AIDSCOM *not* formally dealing with national associations but instead with indigenous, existing associations of healers that seem to have existed in South Africa for many generations, namely *impandes*. This term is used or at least understood by virtually all black groups in South Africa, although ethno-linguistic variants may be used.[4] Ngubane (1981) describes these associations among the Zulu as *sangoma* networks, yet without providing a Zulu or other Bantu name for them (cf. also Ngubane 1977).

Based on our admittedly very limited period of research in South Africa, we offer this definition: an *impande* is a named network or association of *sangomas* that trace what might be called spiritual kinship ties through association with a *gobela* (initiator or trainer of diviner–mediums), a *gobela*'s initiator *(koko)* or a *gobela*'s initiator's initiator *(kokogasi* for females or *kokokhulu* for males). The term *impande* refers not only to people but to the medicines and distinctive rituals and ceremonies used by all who 'descend' from the same *gobela*. Initiates (a term preferable to members) in the same *impande* refer to one another as sister or brother if they have been *sangomas* for roughly the same period of time. Those who are two or more 'generations' of initiates above a *sangoma* are both addressed and referred to as *gogo* (grandmother) or *koko* (great-grandparent).

Like lineages, *impandes* may be subdivided or segmented into smaller groupings consisting of more restricted membership, depending on need or purpose. As *impandes* become too large and dispersed, new *impande* groupings or segments develop, yet a sense of belonging together remains between members of the larger, older *impande*. Members of an *impande* are known by special insignia, such as beads of a certain colour or other decorative items that are worn.[5] Names used to designate *impandes* may refer to a recent *gobela*, although a full name might actually consist of a succession of names of senior *gobelas*— one's lineage of initiators—as well as the places where initiation took place. An *impande* name may also refer to a class of spirits, such as *emandau* or *emanzawe* (believed to be the spirits of people from ethnic groups other than one's own who were slain during the period of tribal warfare). The insignia of diviner–mediums possessed by *emandau* consist of a necklace of white and red beads from which is suspended a beaded object.

No one knows the exact size of an *impande* since written records are not kept and since new *impandes* or *impande* segments develop at a perhaps indefinable point of growth. Certainly they grow exponentially: a *gobela* may train or initiate as many as 100–200 healers in her lifetime. Her *amatwasa* may in turn train 100– 200 others in their lifetimes, as may their *amatwasa*. Even if some *amatwasa*, upon becoming *gobelas* themselves, initiate far fewer numbers, an *impande* of several thousand members may easily develop within a generation.

The question arises: how feasible would it be for AIDSCAP/AIDSCOM or other donors to work with *impandes* rather than national healer associations in AIDS prevention? Others things being equal, it might seem preferable to build upon an existing structure rather than upon a newly emerging one fraught with controversy. We discovered several additional characteristics of *impandes* that would seem to recommend them further over national—and perhaps any formal—associations.

One is their multi-ethnic membership. It can be observed that *sangomas* often apprentice under a *gobela* from a different ethnic group. *Sangomas* are emphatic in insisting that it is one's ancestors and not oneself who chooses the *gobela*, but it can be observed that ancestors often guide would-be initiates to a *gobela* from a different ethnic group. We might refer to the mechanism that ensures *impande* multi-ethnicity as ethnic discordance in the initiation process, and it would doubtless be interesting to speculate as to why it developed in southern Africa. One result of the practice is that *sangomas* have some intimate familiarity with another culture. This might be a factor of how a healer practising in a plural society can attract clients from diverse ethnic groups, although a *sangoma* would never explain this feature of the initiation process in such terms. Nevertheless we saw that urban-based healers attract clients from diverse groups. At a deeper functionalist analytic level, ethnic discordance in the initiation process might be seen as a functional mechanism that has developed to mitigate and reconcile ethnic divisiveness and strife in the broader society as it moves toward greater socio-cultural integration. In any case the structure and function of *impandes* seem to make it unnecessary for AIDSCAP/AIDSCOM or other donors to issue criteria designed to ensure equal access by 'tribe' to donor resources; South African healers are already adept practitioners of cultural pluralism.

Impande membership is also geographically dispersed. As noted, healers may train and be initiated in a different area of South Africa—even a neighbouring country—and then return to practise at home. Moreover healers seem to be geographically mobile. Initiates of an *impande* quickly spread all over the country and beyond. A *sangoma* can travel anywhere in the region and expect to see another *sangoma* wearing the beads characteristic of her *impande*. When this happens, the two greet each other joyfully and there is said to be an immediate sense of kinship and intimacy.

Another characteristic of *impandes* is that members are bound to each other by spiritual ties; they are forbidden by custom to squabble with each other but if this occurs, mechanisms exist for conflict resolution. A dispute is brought to the common *gobela* (or *gogo*, or *koko*) who with the ancestors serves as a kind of court of appeals that provides a spiritually sanctioned resolution for any conflict. *Impandes* are described as apolitical or above political concerns. Again the explanation lies with the ancestors: they are said to care nothing about politics. In the words of one *sangoma*: 'The ancestors don't know who the ANC or Inkatha Freedom Party are; they have never heard of them.'

Impande initiates meet regularly, such as during ceremonies when newly initiated *sangomas* demonstrate their spiritual qualifications. Initiates are also expected to share healing information with one another and with their *gobela*, and to refer clients to one another. There is said to be mutual respect.

As already noted, second-generation training in the Northeast Transvaal (Gazankulu) appears to have been especially successful. Here healers were recruited and trained through the Northeast Transvaal Tinyanga and Herbalists

Association (NETTHA), a local as distinct from national association. We found that about 95 per cent of NETTHA's membership belonged to the same *impande*. Most members formerly belonged to a larger formal association based in the Tsonga self-governing area of Gazankulu, but they became disillusioned with it for most of the reasons already cited as problems with national organizations. At the time of the evaluation NETTHA was trying to build upwards, joining with local organizations in Venda, Lebowa, and elsewhere to form a truly regional, multi-ethnic organization for the Northeast Transvaal. The passage of time might show if it is better to build from regional associations up than from Johannesburg down. In fact it may prove useful to work with or through regional as distinct from national healer associations, if that is what healers in areas such as the Northeast Transvaal wish to do. However, paid membership in any association should not be a pre-condition for benefiting from AIDSCAP-supported training.

It should be emphasized that our research into the nature of *impandes* must be considered very preliminary. Certainly more extensive and detailed research would be desirable before reaching any policy or programme decisions. However on the basis of our preliminary findings, we recommend that at the very least, AIDSCOM/AIDSCAP (and other foreign donors by implication) not even give the appearance of making paid membership in national healer associations a prerequisite for benefiting from training in AIDS prevention. We recognize that donors might well be more comfortable dealing with formal, 'national' associations than with informal networks of healers the nature of which remains obscure even to most Black South Africans. Furthermore donor organizations (and now, a Black-dominated South African government) need to communicate with traditional healers with the benefit of some organizational structure. However, coerced membership in Western-modelled organizations could undermine the functioning of indigenous networks of healers, with unforseen consequences. For example, we have already noted that *impandes* are characterized by multi-ethnic membership and that this appears to have a salutary effect on one of the most dangerous and destabilizing forces in broader South African society today, namely 'tribalism' or ethnic divisiveness. It should be a tenet of those promoting recognition of the value of indigenous knowledge and organizations that unless there are compelling reasons to the contrary, it is best to build on existing knowledge, beliefs and social organization in all development or efforts at social change.

Notes

1. This figure was derived from the evaluation of second-generation healers.
2. The costs in dollars were calculated based on rand exchange rates in August 1993.
3. For a description of this process, see Green (1989b).
4. For example, the Xhosa may use the term *ingcambu*.
5. The red ochre and braided hair characteristic of many *sangomas* is apparently not an identifier of *impande*. Hairstyle is said to be something one decides on after consultation with one's ancestor spirits. The observant outsider might note that this may change within a lifetime and might relate to urbanization as well as to urban or occupational identity.

References

Bannerman, R.H., Bibeau, G., Dunn, F., Fosu, G., Heggenhougen, K., Maclean, U. and Zempleni, A. (1981), 'Discussion' of D.D.O. Oyebola's 'Professional Associations,

Ethics and Discipline Among Yoruba Traditional Healers of Nigeria', *Social Science and Medicine* 15b, 93–102.

Compton, J.L. (1989), 'Strategies and Methods for the Access, Integration, and Utilization of Indigenous Knowledge in Agriculture and Rural Development', In D.M. Warren, L.J. Slikkerveer and S.O. Titilola, *Indigenous Knowledge Systems: Implications for Agriculture and International Development*. Ames: Technology and Social Change Program, Iowa State University.

Green, E.C. (1988), 'Can Collaborative Programs Between Biomedical and Indigenous Health Practitioners Succeed?' *Social Science and Medicine* 27(11), 1125–30.

Green, E.C. (1989a), *A Survey of Health, Fertility and Human Reproductive Knowledge and Attitudes among Nigerian Traditional Healers*, Washington: The Futures Group, 22 February.

Green, E.C. (1989b), 'Mystical black power: the calling to diviner-mediumship in Southern Africa', in C.S. McClain (ed.), *Women as Healers: Cross Cultural Perspectives*, NJ: Rutgers University Press, 186–200.

Green, E.C. (1994), *AIDS and Sexually Transmitted Disease in Africa: Bridging the Gap between Traditional Healing and Modern Medicine*, Boulder, Colorado, and Oxford: Westview Press.

Green, E.C., Jurg, A. and Dgedge, A. (1993), 'Sexually Transmitted Diseases, AIDS and Traditional Healers in Mozambique', *Medical Anthropology* 15(3), Spring, 261–81.

Green, E.C., Zokwe, B. and Dupree, J.D. (1992), 'The Role of South African Traditional Healers in HIV/AIDS Prevention and Management', Arlington: Family Health International, AIDSCAP Project, December.

Green, E.C., Zokwe, B. and Dupree, J.D. (1993), 'Report of the Second AIDSCAP Workshop for Traditional Healers, Emaweni, South Africa', Arlington: Family Health International, July.

Green, E.C., Zokwe, B. and Dupree, J.D. (1995) 'The experience of an AIDS prevention program focused on South African traditional healers.' *Social Science and Medicine* Vol. 40, No. 4, 503–15.

Hoff, W. and Maseko, D.N. (1986), 'Nurses and Traditional Healers Join Hands', *World Health Forum* 7, 412–16.

Hogle, J., Lwanga, J.S., Kisamba-Mugerwa, C. and Musonge, D.L. (1991), 'Indigenous Knowledge and Management of Childhood Diarrhoeal Diseases' (*Ugandan Traditional Healers Initiative—Phase One: Research*), Arlington: Management Sciences for Health (PRITECH Project).

Last, M. (1986), 'The Professionalization of African Medicine: Ambiguities and Definitions', in M. Last and G.L. Chavunduka (eds), *The Professionalization of African Medicine*, Manchester: Manchester University Press, 1–19.

McClure, G. (1989), 'Introduction', in D.M. Warren, L.J. Slikkerveer and S.O. Titilola, *Indigenous Knowledge Systems: Implications for Agriculture and International Development*, Ames: Technology and Social Change Program, Iowa State University.

McCormack, C. (1986), 'The Articulation of Western and Traditional Systems of Health Care', in M. Last and G.L. Chavunduka (eds), *The Professionalization of African Medicine*, Manchester: Manchester University Press, 151–62.

Ngubane, H. (1977), *Body and Mind in Zulu Medicine*, London: Academic Press.

Ngubane, H. (1981), 'Aspects of Clinical Practice and Traditional Organization of Indigenous Healers in South Africa', *Social Science and Medicine* 15b, 361–5.

Nhlengethwa, T. and Perez, L. (1991), 'Report of the Training of Trainers Course for the Traditional Healers Organization in HIV/AIDS Prevention', Mbabane, Swaziland: Project HOPE/FLAS HIV/AIDS Prevention project, May.

Oyebola, D.D.O. (1981), 'Professional Associations, Ethics and Discipline Among Yoruba Traditional Healers of Nigeria', *Social Science and Medicine* 15b, 87–92.

Tahzib, F. (1988), 'Sokoto Traditional Medical Practitioners' Project', Second Progress Report, Nigeria: University of Sokoto.

Warren, D.M. (1982), 'The Techiman-Bono Ethnomedical System', in P.S. Yoder (ed.),

African Health and Healing Systems: Proceedings of a Symposium, Los Angeles: Crossroads Press, 39, 85–106.

Warren, D.M. (1986), 'The Expanding Role of Indigenous Healers in Ghana's National Health Delivery System', in C. Fyfe, and U. Maclean, *African Medicine in the Modern World*, University of Edinburgh: Centre of African Studies, Seminar Proceedings No. 27, December, 73–86.

Warren, D.M., Slikkerveer, L.J. and Titilola, S.O. (1989), *Indigenous Knowledge Systems: Implications for Agriculture and International Development*, Ames: Technology and Social Change Program, Iowa State University.

Acknowledgement
Part of this material has been published in Green, E.C., Zokwe, B. and Dupree, J.D. (1994), 'The Experience of an AIDS-Prevention Program Focused on South African Traditional Healers', *Social Science and Medicine* Vol. 40, No. 4, 503–15.

10 History of an indigenous community management organization in Nepal

DURGA POKHREL and ANTHONY B. J. WILLET*

OVER THE LAST decade or so, development practitioners and academics have shown a resurgence of interest in indigenous knowledge and indigenous organizations, and in the potential this knowledge and these institutions hold for development. The purpose of this chapter is to take a closer look not only at some of the functions performed by an indigenous community organization, but at the broader political, socio-cultural, and spiritual context, and the nature of local leadership, for that functioning. The point to be made is that indigenous organizations in the Hindu Kingdom of Nepal functioned traditionally within an holistic cosmological context which was universally understood and respected, and provided a framework for activity. In particular, the elders who provided leadership embodied that traditional cosmology and, emanating from it, the wisdom to manage that great variety of roles and harmonize local social and natural relationships. Therefore, this chapter focuses on two aspects of a local indigenous organization in Nepal:

o Community management/development and collective authority; and
o Characteristics of main leaders and their personal authority.

In Nepal, until 1960 when the king introduced authoritarian rule outlawing a 10-year-old democratic government, local indigenous organizations (LIOs) were responsible for managing almost the entire spectrum of social, legal and developmental activity in their communities. Two primary factors explain the pre-eminence of LIOs in community management and development work until that time. First, the tradition of local self-government was established in the Indian subcontinent, including Nepal, from at least the Vedic era four to six thousand years ago, and Vedic texts lay down categorically 'multi-sectoral' community management roles and responsibilities of five well-respected elders of a local area, along with the procedures for their selection. Such organizations headed by five elders were called *Panchayat* (*pancha*, five, plus *ayat*, house), which means simply 'a house of five' or an organization composed of five. The tradition of *panchayat*, and the indigenous knowledge of their

* Durga Pokhrel was a lecturer, journalist, and active member of the social democratic Nepali Congress Party which was banned between 1960 and 1990. Since 1990, she has concentrated on writing books about her experience as a dissident in Nepal, and about human-rights abuse, particularly of women, in Nepal. Anthony Willet has 15 years' field experience as a programme/project manager, adviser and consultant in international rural development in several African countries, India and Nepal, including work for governments, international development agencies, and private voluntary/non-governmental organizations. Currently he is Senior Conservation Analyst, World Wildlife Fund, Washington DC.

functioning, has been handed down from generation to generation, and some periods in Nepal's history are regarded as 'golden eras' during which great social and cultural harmony, economic prosperity, and all-round development prevailed in the state, with LIOs forming the local units of governance and the backbone of the larger system.

A second explanation for the significance of such LIOs until 1960 was the experience at various times of oligarchy and other undemocratic political systems at the central level in Nepal which left local government and development in a condition of benign neglect. This permitted LIOs to continue their community management roles largely undisturbed.

Between 1960 and 1990, the environment for LIOs changed drastically as the authoritarian government introduced by the king actively obstructed the LIOs of five elders from carrying out their traditional roles. A motto of the regime of this period was 'no organization', and in 1969 the government promulgated an 'Organization Control Act' which effectively killed all organizations in Nepali society other than those sponsored by the ruling system. Individuals wishing to continue community service could do their work under the auspices of a centralized government-created organization, the National Social Service Coordination Council, chaired by the Nepal Queen. A law was introduced requiring that any nongovernmental social/economic development organization had to be first registered by a local office of the government and then by this council.[1] For local registration, clearance from the local police was necessary to confirm that an individual's political beliefs were not inconsistent with the prevailing political system. Inevitably, a person with a police record of pro-democracy activity in opposition to the king's authoritarian system would be denied any role in local community management and development which had been an effortless tradition of Nepali social culture.

Since multi-party democracy was reinstated in the kingdom in 1990, a multitude of nongovernmental, social and private-sector organizations has been born as people exercise their restored freedoms of expression and rights of association. Among this multitude are a few organizations which are labelled as 'indigenous'. The question that interests us is whether these newly emerging, or re-emerging, organizations embrace ideals similar to those of their historical forebears. To stimulate reflection on this question, we introduce in this chapter a local indigenous organization which was thriving until the government rendered it void after 1960, substituting for it another local organization in the new hierarchy of the king's authoritarian system.

Ironically, the king named his totalitarian system *Panchayat*, stealing the name of the local indigenous organization of the ancient past, and distorting what had been a simple and effective system of local governance prescribed in the Hindu texts by applying it as the 'partyless *Panchayat* system', a centralized, four-tier legislature—village, district, zonal and national—with an organization inspired by communist China. Thus, Nepal's indigenous *panchayat* organizations were replaced by the king's *panchayats*, and the respected local elders steeped in indigenous spirituality, culture and knowledge were substituted by cadres of people screened by a central politburo for their loyalty to the 'palace clique'.

Unlike new *panchayat* cadres, the leaders of indigenous *panchayat* organizations were chosen through a process of public consensus in each village. From among the village elders, these leaders possessed a quality of special knowledge, or wisdom, to share with others and to guide their communities as they resolved all manner of day-to-day problems. Local people still refer to such elders as

'*Janne*', a Nepali word which means 'knower'. In actually addressing an elder, the more polite term '*JanneBa*' is used, meaning 'Knower Father' and conveying a deep level of confidence and respect.

These *JanneBa* father figures who headed local community management organizations could be from any caste or of any ethnicity depending partly on the majority caste or ethnicity of a village, but mainly on respect for the quality of the person and their traditional wisdom upon which members of the community would depend for guidance, protection, and advocacy. Formal education, even in the traditional Sanskrit system, was also not necessarily a requirement. A *JanneBa* could be illiterate.

Although the LIO leader was selected, usually for the term of his entire life, by the people through general consensus, other members could be selected on an *ad hoc* basis in response to particular cases, problems, or the nature of a task. For example, if there was a case of an *illicit relationship*, particular members might be selected from among the village elders. Again, a 'subcommittee' or 'user group' of other elders would be selected for managing a community development effort such as mobilizing local contributions towards a drinking-water supply project. Such groups would continue to function until their tasks were accomplished.

The organization whose biography is described here was based in the Dhankuta District village of Kachiday in Nepal's eastern Koshi Zone hills. Dhankuta has remained the district and regional headquarters through all the vicissitudes of Nepal's political development. Kachiday itself consisted of some 21 households with an average family size of between seven and eight members. Together, the households of Kachiday functioned as one large extended family, with everyone knowing everybody and accepting one another as close relations. The four other villages whose common property and social affairs were also managed by the Kachiday-based LIO also knew one another intimately.

Source of data

Primarily the data recorded in this chapter are drawn from the observations of the principal author, Durga Pokhrel, who lived in Kachiday village for 20 years in the house of the leader of the Kachiday LIO. Other methods of acquiring the data recorded here involve what the Vedic indigenous knowledge system terms *sruti*, the heard, and *smriti*, the remembered. Based on what was observed, heard and remembered, we feel we have sufficient and valid material and experience to share with other like-minded people. In addition to the above methods, we have referred to a few written documents. One was the autobiography of the LIO leader, and another was one of his handwritten manuscripts.

Community management and collective authority

Collective tasks and activities were those for which all members of the community had an equal share and responsibility, and whose management any member of the LIO, or any villager informing one of the elders, could assume. By-laws governing collective activities were developed and enforced by the LIO always through a consensual process. In the rare cases when enforcement was required, an elder would present the case to a general gathering of the five villages which would have to reach consensus on the violation and any sanction to be imposed on the violator. The indigenous *panchayat* judicial process implemented the

Vedic concept of *danda*, whose principal purpose was to restore collective consciousness as well as realization of *dharma* (right duty in relation to universal or natural law) by the wrongdoer. Therefore, in matters of enforcing collective sanctions, even the violator had to be included in the consensus.

Community forest and grazing-land management

There were two major forest areas surrounding Kachiday village to which the other four villages by tradition also had access. Much of one of the forests had been planted by villagers, and contained many species of sacred and other precious trees, medicinal shrubs and edible wild berries. The other forest might have been more natural in composition, with large timber-yielding trees, other fuel and fodder species, and thatch and tall forage grasses. Every year, just before the outbreak of the main monsoon, a socio-religious ritual would be observed, the replanting celebration, *Brikshya ropan*, to enhance the viability of young tree seedlings.

In neither forest could anyone cut trees, thatch or fodder without LIO permission. Permission to cut fuelwood was granted depending on household size, and gathering of thatching grass was allowed in proportion to roof area of a house. Similarly, tall forage grass and fodder gathering was rationed according to a household's livestock holding. There was no restriction on harvesting of wild berries, collecting dead branches from the ground for fuel, or cutting of short grasses. Neither was there any limit imposed on the number of *saal* tree leaves which could be picked for making fresh green leaf plates used for serving food in religious and social festivals. People knew that they should not harm the branches in the process. Cowherds could take their animals into the forests for grazing during the day on condition that they prevented their cows destroying the young medicinal shrubs. Villagers living near the forest boundaries would keep an eye open for violators of forest by-laws, and had the authority to warn suspects on the spot or report them to the LIO.

The outskirts of the forests were common grazing lands, also for daytime use. People were prohibited from leaving their cattle to graze overnight unless an animal had strayed and could not be traced before nightfall, an event which had to be reported in a timely fashion. In the middle of each grazing area, people had worked together to dig a catchment tank, or *aahal*, where rainwater collected and was used for watering the cattle and buffalo. The *aahals* were oval in shape, and about 10 by two metres in size. In the event of drought, people would sometimes dig a long *kulo*, or irrigation-type channel, to redirect water from the nearest available source. Altogether, there were three *aahals* in the Kachiday grazing lands, and another one was located in the middle of Kachiday village itself a little below the public drinking-water stand-pipe where villagers would bathe and wash clothes. Overflow from this stand-pipe accumulated in the *aahal* and was particularly enjoyed by the water buffalo which bathed in it, making it very murky. Overflow from this *aahal* was distributed via a *kulo* for watering household vegetable gardens. Cowherds were given preference to water their cattle first, as far as it was feasible, in the grazing-land *aahals* whose water, being rainwater, was in any case purer. The village *aahal* was further polluted by the drainage from the stand-pipe where women would wash their personal pads, along with soiled baby clothes. Recognizing this, the LIO leader built a concrete drinking-water trough for the cattle adjacent to the public stand-pipe. A bamboo pipe took water from the stand-pipe to the trough, and whoever was the last to use the stand-pipe at any time had the duty of reconnecting the bamboo pipe so that the trough was filled. The LIO would ensure that someone was always on duty at the trough around 10 a.m. and at dusk each day when the village cattle came to drink on their way to and from grazing. At these times, cattle had priority at the stand-pipe, and the bamboo pipe would be in place ensuring that the trough remained full. People would wait until the cattle had finished drinking before taking their turn to use the stand-pipe water. Water was a scarce resource in the village. Besides the one stand-pipe, there were three small well-springs in the village which gave out in the dry season.

Community development

The main community development tasks carried out by the Kachiday LIO were management of irrigation water, drinking-water supply, trail construction and education. Most of the residents of the five villages had their paddy fields 2000–3000 feet lower down the hillside and in the valley floor below Dhankuta. They would plant paddy, with pulses on the terrace edges, twice a year, with the first crop largely dependent on irrigation water, and the second more rainfed. Maintenance of the *kulo* channels and rotational distribution of the irrigation water were managed by a users' group. Users would contribute in cash, kind or labour for repair or improvement of the *kulos*, with shares depending on irrigated land size.

Until the end of the 1950s, Kachiday had only the three hand-dug wells to supply its drinking water. Later, the LIO co-ordinated the request for the stand-pipe from the local government. This involved a mile-long iron pipeline to bring water from the main pipe supplying the Dhankuta bazaar and government quarters. Although the Kachiday LIO succeeded in brokering the supply from Dhankuta, the water flow was controlled by the local government and came only for two to three hours each morning and evening. Given this rationing, the LIO played an important role in stemming and resolving conflicts over use of the water arriving in Kachiday.

Trail construction and maintenance was an annual event in Kachiday. As there was no main road even to the government headquarters and bazaar of Dhankuta until 1983, trail construction refers to the building and repair of footpaths for pedestrian traffic within the village area and between the village, other villages and Dhankuta bazaar. The annual work began about two months before the main Hindu festival of *Dasain* (known as *dashera* in northern India). The villagers would assemble in the courtyard of the LIO leader's house, and decide, by general consensus, as always, on any new trails that needed to be built and on repairs to existing ones. Contributions to the trail work were in the form of labour according to household size. The LIO leader sometimes donated additional building materials.

As elsewhere in Nepal, perception of the need for modern education came later, and it was only in the 1950s that the LIO formed an educational subcommittee and opened a local primary school. The school eventually received government accreditation and still opens today. Kachiday LIO led the nation in campaigning for girls' access to education to the extent that, by the late 1960s, people in surrounding villages used to comment that 'in Kachiday maybe even a dog is a graduate'. Although older-generation Kachiday men had received mostly Sanskrit education, the LIO leader and other villagers were instrumental in starting an English-language high school serving the whole district, and also founded the first college offering BAs outside the Kathmandu Valley. In addition, the LIO actively advocated adult and female literacy.

Community co-operation

The extended-family atmosphere of Kachiday village reflected not only the co-operative minds of the village people acting themselves, but the role of the LIO in creating an environment of harmony. When a family needed help from others, this would be sought through the LIO or its leader. But often the LIO or LIO leader needed not to be involved, so co-operation was arranged informally, the potential role of the LIO in helping arrange inter-family co-operation being implicit in the background as long as controversies or disputes did not arise. In such cases, LIO intervention was always available. Labour exchanges between families were arranged according to such an understanding. One family might help weed another family's field in exchange for the second family's help with harvesting. If the second family did not reciprocate, then the LIO would intervene to ensure that the first family received either the promised exchange of labour, or equivalent compensation in cash or kind. Some co-operative community efforts were organized directly by the LIO, such as borrowing of seed in exchange for grain at harvest. Such loan arrangements would be witnessed by the LIO, and should the borrower fail to pay back at harvest, the LIO would resolve the dispute.

There were many other forms of community co-operation. If a long illness affected a member of a family, neighbours would take turns to relieve others in the family from the exhaustion of caring for the sick member. If an affected family did not receive such assistance, the LIO would reinforce the custom and mandate relief services by neighbours. Similarly, the LIO would arrange for necessary help in taking a sick person to hospital and in maintaining a rotating watch over the patient at the hospital.

When somebody died in the village, at least one person from each household would attend the cremation. In case a household failed to follow the spiritual tradition of mourning, the LIO would summon a general village meeting to discuss how to penalize the family in question. The customary length of the initial mourning period varies with ethnicity, but is generally 13 days for a close relative. However, the LIO would not impose the dominant ethnic tradition on another ethnic group. In cases where a family was uncertain how many days of mourning should be observed, for example in the case of a more distant relative, the LIO leader would consult the Hindu texts himself, as well as a priest, before making a ruling.

Certain religious festivals were organized collectively as well. During the great *Dasain* festival of *Durga puja*, everybody in the village would gather at the LIO leader's house to receive the *tika* blessing on their foreheads and to eat *prasad*, prepared blessed food. Besides this ritual, those assembled would reminisce about all the pleasant events in the community over the past year, and also discuss informally outstanding problems, such as the need for building another *aahal*. *Dasain* was a festival that united all castes of the community, including the so-called untouchables who would receive their *tika* blessing in a small leaf bowl and apply it to their foreheads themselves. In addition to *Dasain*, there was another important religious and social ritual performed by the village priest at the LIO's initiative each year. This was celebrated just before preparing the land for planting in the expectation that the lord of rain would provide sufficient rain for the farmers' crops and the mother goddess would play her role in ensuring a bountiful harvest. On this day, each of the five villages performed their own separate rituals, although the location was down in the paddy lands where all the villages had their paddy fields. No mandatory contribution was levied for these rituals, and families would contribute whatever they could afford. Whether or not a family had given a donation, or even attended the ritual, the priest would make sure that every household in the village received the *prasad* in the evening. Volunteers would distribute the *prasad* to each and every house.

Economic management

Although the LIO could not act to redistribute land equally, complete landlessness was unknown in the village. The LIO ensured that all families had enough land to cultivate, and sufficient to build their houses. Over time, needs arose for individuals to acquire more land, or build a new house, such as when a son separated his livelihood from his parents, or a newcomer arrived in the village. In these instances, the LIO would mandate that every household in the village contributed according to their capacity either in labour, cash or kind. In the event of a drought, more affluent households were required to donate grain to poorer households, sometimes, although not necessarily, in return for labour services. The LIO would also arrange that a poorer household be granted land to cultivate if areas of 'nobody's land' were available. The LIO leader maintained the land records for the village area. He also collected land revenues and forwarded them to the government's revenue department, obviating the need for every household to deal with the revenue office directly. The LIO leader received no payment for this service; the villagers expected the leader, the *JanneBa*, to deal in their name with the outside world of government offices and the like, and to perform such brokering roles correctly. Underlying their reliance on the LIO leader was a desire to avoid external influence or intrusion which was inherent in the self-reliant and self-sufficient tradition of indigenous *panchayat* self-government.

Legal management

Hindu norms operated as the guiding principles for Kachiday society, and everyone in the village believed in his or her responsibility to maintain social *dharma*. As a result, crime was an insignificant problem in the village. If a crime did occur, it would be reported first to the LIO, and the leader of the organization would call an assembly of all villagers who wished to be present, including the suspect. The entire process was carried out orally. The *danda* concept guided the conduct of the proceedings. If the suspect really had committed the crime, inevitably he or she would confess: 'Maybe I was misguided by some negative force and became blind, causing this to happen. Punish me as befits my misdeed.' Any compensation involved for the injured party would be resolved by the assembly on the spot, as in the case when one person's cows had destroyed another's crops.

A number of examples may illustrate the way the LIO was able to conduct justice in the community. On one occasion, a widow of untouchable caste became pregnant, a condition carrying extreme social stigma in Hindu society. The woman was called by the LIO to the leader's house, where, in the presence of other villagers, she revealed the name of the man who had made her pregnant—her late husband's younger brother. According to Hindu laws governing their caste, the relationship was acceptable, and the LIO declared them husband and wife, averting further social harassment. If a Brahmin widow had entered into such a relationship, the couple would have been demoted to an inferior caste status and, suffering such humiliation, might have chosen to leave the village. After the king's *Panchayat* system usurped the customary procedures of the indigenous *panchayats*, such cases were dealt with most unjustly. Many cases were reported in which a high-caste widow was deliberately made pregnant by a close male relative for the purpose of inheriting her property to which a widow lost all rights if she failed to maintain her widow *dharma* of refraining from involvement with another man. Usually, the male culprits either belonged to, or were loyalists of, the king's *Panchayat* system, and were able to claim all the support of the police and the new legal system. In such cases, the man who had raped the widow would himself report the widow's undesirable social condition to the police, or, in other cases, even assist the widow to perform an illegal abortion and then manipulate her arrest and appearance in court. After the woman was jailed for life, the sentence for abortion, which is treated as a murder charge in Nepal, the man would inherit her confiscated property. Some cases of this type are described in detail in our forthcoming books, *Shadow Over Shangri-La* and *Rape of Dharma.*[2]

Another case dealt with by the Kachiday LIO involved an illicit relationship between a boy and a girl. Although the boy's maternal great-grandfather and the girl's paternal great-grandfather had been brothers, the young couple declared themselves as married. Following Hindu law for their caste, the village assembly called by the LIO pronounced them guilty of illicit relations, blackened their faces, signifying their social disgrace, and ordered them to move to another village. Under the king's *Panchayat* system, the customary notion of illicit relations became very vague. The king and his own sons married their cousins for political reasons. Under state, i.e. Hindu, law sexuality within such a blood relationship is regarded as illicit. However, there were women in jail of more humble backgrounds caught for such illicit relationships and punished with property confiscation and four years' imprisonment.

A third example of indigenous *panchayat* legal management is in relation to theft. A man was reported to have stolen 100 oranges from another person's garden in the village. In the village assembly called by the LIO, the man confessed. His punishment was to labour in the garden from where he had stolen the oranges an equivalent length of time to the value of the stolen oranges. Under the authoritarian *Panchayat* legal system, no matter how little a culprit had stolen, the punishment became four years' imprisonment.

The examples given here show how the indigenous legal system of the LIO implemented consistently, impartially and appropriately the customary values of Hindu law. However, justice was arrived at by a subtle and humane process through which all parties would gain realization of some kind, and the culprit would face the penalty voluntarily. Force was never invoked, or a punishment imposed without consent. In Kachiday, there were no major crimes during the jurisdiction of the LIO leader described below. In the neighbouring villages major crimes did occur, including one case of murder. This happened during a brawl between two drunk men, when one of the men stabbed the other with a traditional Nepali *khukri* knife. Before the LIO/village assembly, the killer, who had regained sobriety, cried and begged for mercy. His punishment became to pay compensation to the murdered man's family. Both families belonged to an ethnic group which called themselves a 'drunkard caste', being in the regular habit of having too much homemade alcohol, especially during their festivals, which was when such crimes tended to occur. Many times LIO elders attempted to convince this group about the negative aspect of their drinking, and although the group was unable to control this habit, it did become more careful not to carry *khukris* during its drinking sprees.

Under *Panchayat* rule, the practice of drinking alcohol spread well beyond the 'drunkard castes'. Even powerful personalities of high caste opened liquor businesses in the capital, which, in terms of quick profit, became second only to smuggling cultural antiquities, such as valuable idols stolen from temples, to foreign countries, and foreign goods into Nepal. The new legal system never caught such 'big shots' except in the cases of a couple of top military and police officers shortly before the final collapse of the *Panchayat* system.

Kaviraj Narapati Pokhrel

Biography
The name of the main leader of the Kachiday LIO was Kaviraj Narapati Pokhrel. *Kaviraj* was his title—the form of address for an *Ayurvedic* doctor. In fact, he was one of the first four physicians in Nepal trained to the doctoral level in *Ayurveda* (the holistic indigenous system of medicine, or 'science of life') at Banaras Hindu University. He spent his entire professional career in public service at His Majesty's Government's Ayurvedic Hospital at Dhankuta. As a physician, he worked under three government regimes: under autocratic Rana rule until 1950, under democratic government from 1950 until 1960, and, between 1960 and 1971, under the king's authoritarian rule. However, as the leader of the LIO, his formal role ended with the introduction of the king's *Panchayat* system. Nonetheless, people continued to consult him constantly on the full range of their affairs. After retiring, he moved down to Dharan which, in the lap of the foothills, was warmer than Dhankuta. There, he worked partly in a community *Ayurvedic* clinic established by a Hindu seer, and partly in his own clinic which he managed from his home, until a week before he died in 1983.

Until the age of nine, his father, who was a Vedic pandit and later became renowned as a seer, taught him Sanskrit and the Vedic tradition at home. At the age of nine, his marriage was arranged with a girl of seven. After his marriage, with his child-wife remaining behind with his parents, he was sent to study under a spiritual *guru* in the mountains four days' walk north of Dhankuta. According to Hindu custom, his *guru* remained *brahmachari* (celibate) for his whole life. There, Narapati Pokhrel learned the foundations of Vedic knowledge. Instilled in his deepening consciousness were these basic principles:

○ *Bashudaiva kutumbakam:* the whole universe is one family.
○ *Janani janmabhumi scha swargaadapi gariyasi:* mother and motherland are greater than heaven.
○ *Satyam bada:* speak truth.
○ *Dharmam chara:* perform *dharma* (right conduct).
○ *Matridevo bhava:* mother is as God.
○ *Pitridevo bhava:* father is as God.
○ *Acharyadevo bhava: guru* is as God.

After living with his spiritual *guru* for several years, he was sent to Kathmandu to receive formal Sanskrit education in the Vedic tradition. With the equivalent of a high-school leaving certificate, he proceeded to Banaras for his *Ayurvedic* medical studies. Throughout all his higher education, Vedic knowledge formed the strong integrating framework for his learning. Completing the degree in *Ayurveda*, the science of life, he returned to Dhankuta to begin his life's work.

Dhankuta had been the eastern capital of Nepal until 1950, and so had the only medical facility for the whole eastern region. Every year, Kaviraj Pokhrel would conduct cholera and smallpox immunization camps in the outlying villages. He was deeply concerned about public health, and believed in preventive methods and in teaching people about the intimate relationship between diet, health and hygiene, concerning which knowledge is highly evolved in *Ayurveda*. His house was open to any visitor 24 hours a day for consultation on any problem, whether or not health-related. To help him in the hospital, he trained several local people who would provide care in his absence. He also trained his wife and children to assist him in running the home clinic.

Although he was a medical practitioner, he preferred to think of himself as a farmer. He acquired sizeable lands and, during any spare time, would be found working with his own hands in the fields. He planted many varieties of medicinal herbs in the land nearer the house, and tended his plants according to Vedic techniques with loving care as though they were his children. He would plant only pure, *sattvik* (with the quality of truth, or goodness), health-giving varieties of fruits, vegetables and grains. For example, he would not grow jakfruit, onion or chillies. He used to say that such dullness or passion-intensifying foods would not cause significant harm to the physiology if eaten only once or twice a year, but were inadvisable as part of a regular diet. Similarly, he would advise that finger millet was suitable only for those engaged in heavy manual work. Constantly, he would give lectures to the village people, advising them on the kinds of food they should consume according to their body type and the type of work in which they were engaged, in order to bring the physiology into balance, harmony and well-being.

His motto in life was 'to waste time without doing something productive is sin'. Accordingly, he kept himself busy always and encouraged others to follow the same principle. He was liberal in dealing with social issues such as child marriage and women's education, and set an example by educating his own daughters and instructing his wife in literacy. Even his maids and servants became literate, and, in turn, kept themselves productively busy.

He was the community's 'opinion leader'. His word counted the most in the community, partly because he was the eldest among four sons and three daughters, and, later on, the most senior citizen in the village. More importantly, he was a pious man of good conduct who unceasingly advocated justice and *Rta* (the Vedic concept of harmony, embracing social, natural and cosmic harmony) for the community. Community development and social service were his pastimes. Although village activities were generally decided collectively, the LIO leader exercised discretion in relation to many issues.

Personal authority

There were two ways in which the leader exercised his personal authority. First, there were certain fields of activity over which he exercised community-sanctioned discretionary authority. Authorizing the cutting of a tree from the community forest for house-building timber, or the cutting of thatching grass for roof repair, were two examples. Villagers would disturb him at any time of the day or night in order to obtain his permission, sometimes waking him at 2 a.m. so that they could proceed with their work at dawn. When absent, he would leave clear instructions and guidelines with his family members who would take over his authority. Deciding the rate of land tax, according to land category and area, was also an area of his jurisdiction. In addition, he would be the one to mobilize the people in trail construction and repair work.

A second way in which he exercised his authority was in cases where the LIO or assembly was unable to reach a clear conclusion, and an on-the-spot decision was called for. Occasionally, a case would arise when a man failed to follow an established local or national custom, such as shaving his head upon his father's death. Sometimes, in such cases, the LIO or assembly might be unable to reach a decision, for example, as to whether the social offender in this case should have his head forcibly shaved, or be otherwise punished and would leave the ultimate decision for the leader to make.

This deference to the leader might have reflected the community's dependence on his greater education. However, in many LIOs the leaders were uneducated and of other ethnicity, yet they performed a similar role, exercised the same quality of influence, and their authority was accepted in the absence of any trace of imposition of force. This raises the question of the source of this personal authority. More than on formal education, community acceptance would appear to have been founded on trust in these elders' character and grasp of traditional knowledge which, being the prime criterion for their selection, embodied the Hindu–Buddhist cosmology and, emanating from that, the social, cultural, moral and spiritual values which Nepalis respect.

LIOs: past and future

How local indigenous organizations eroded

Three issues are of particular interest in relation to indigenous *panchayat* organizations in Nepal as exemplified by the Kachiday LIO: the process of erosion of LIOs in Nepal; promoting their revival; and the challenge of identifying authentic leaders.

As explained briefly above, the main erosive influence on local indigenous organizations in Nepal was the imposition of an authoritarian political system from national to village level. The indigenous five male elders, or *panchas*, were replaced by new *'panchas'* picked up by the local government administration and the state's intelligence system. These new *panchas* were generally no more than young thugs selected for their aptitude in performing any immoral action or repression against the banned democratic opposition to the king's authoritarian system. Within five years of the 1960 palace coup, a chain of such neo-*panchas* had been created, from the village level, through the districts and zones, to the level of the national *Panchayat* legislature. Although the main trend of politics, planning, and administration was centralized and top–down, the new *pancha* cadre was given complete autonomy for the purpose of local repression. Thus, the *Panchayats* of the modern state apparatus became political in character, whereas the LIOs, the indigenous *panchayats* of ancient Nepali heritage, had been dedicated to fostering social, economic, cultural and spiritual welfare and harmony in their communities. After 1960, the crime rate in the kingdom multiplied as criminals were spawned in almost every village and crimes were dealt with by a corrupt local administration, police and court system. As the new *panchas* took political, legal, and executive power at every level, and the police presence became pervasive, the harmony and peace which had been the custom in the villages disappeared. Rules were made by the new *panchas* for others which they themselves violated, and a pattern of creating scapegoats to cover their crimes developed. During times of food shortage, the new *panchas* would extend loans to the poor which, if not repaid in time, would be 'recovered' through confiscation of property, creating homelessness. Victims would flee the village and join the underground democratic and communist movements. Community forests were nationalized under the '*Panchayat*' system, and trees were cut to provide timber for the new *panchas* dwellings or for their business purposes. The community forests of old were renamed '*Panchayat* forests'. The *Panchayat* government attracted huge quantities of foreign assistance funds for implementing its centrally planned development programme through the *Panchayat* hierarchy. It was common knowledge that the achievement of 'targets' was more on paper than in reality. Funds were spent, but buildings and roads would be substandard, and irrigation channels built by local offices of state agencies might slope the wrong way, or remain incomplete. *Panchas* and their local cronies were the contractors.

As, one after another, state agencies took over functions previously performed effectively by LIOs, for several years there was great confusion among the villagers over who were the real *panchas* to look after their interests. The king would tour around each of his development regions once every four years. In his royal lectures, he would always address and praise the local leaders as his 'dear *panchas*', which created a gap between the new *panchas* and the rest of the people of Nepal. Slowly, the villagers and the old *JanneBa*s gave up. If any individual opposed the government regime, that person would be branded as 'anti' the system, and construed as being anti-monarch—the only crime in the kingdom bearing the death penalty. Thus, the death of local indigenous organizations in Nepal was caused directly by the pervasive spread of the king's authoritarian system.

How to revive local indigenous organizations?

Within a 30-year period, 1960–90, the Partyless *Panchayat* system all but extinguished Nepal's heritage of indigenous local organizations through the constitutionally backed, systematic repression of people organizing other than for the purpose of affiliating with the government system. The indigenous reaction, the response of the disenchanted Nepali people, was to join the pro-democracy movement. Underground until 1976, this movement by 1990 ultimately forced the king to abolish his *Panchayat* system and restore multi-party democracy. Now, under democracy, one of the main rights restored is the right to organize, and many Nepalis, particularly in urban areas, have exercised this right by starting all kinds of organizations. From the democratic government's point of view, what is most vital in sustaining democracy is successful decentralization and the emergence of flourishing village-level organizations of local people. These do not need to be 'facilitated' by outsiders. Until not so long ago, the local people were already 'empowered'. The destruction of local indigenous organizations occurred through their disempowerment by a misguided state. Therefore, the first step in decentralization should logically be re-empowerment to recreate as near as possible the conditions that existed until recently. Natural resources such as forests should be handed back to communities to manage, as in the past. After 30 years of mismanagement, it will take a long time to restore them to their former state, but it could happen. Now, with the kingdom enjoying the spirit of democracy, the people might wish to vote for their LIO leader. As experience is gained in democratic processes, communities will learn to recognize the qualities a local leader needs. If the government plays an important role in promoting indigenous knowledge and reviving indigenous wisdom and values, specialists in those fields of knowledge may again be identified and trained. To promote LIOs once again as the basic unit of decentralized development policy, the government can adopt specific guidelines. For example, in a Sherpa village, the government should assist the people to protect and promote their culture of being the best mountain guides, and perhaps reinforce the customary *Dhikur* revolving credit association system which protects needy families.

In a Brahmin village, an LIO should be encouraged in its performance of priestly activities, and specifically in the revival of Sanskrit education, *Ayurveda*, *Jyotish* (astrology), *Sthapatyaveda* (Vedic architecture and spatial planning) and other Vedic sciences. Nepali pandits, priests and other Vedic specialists show great concern over the destructive impact of Western education and culture on indigenous Vedic knowledge and institutions in Nepal.[3] In the absence of their revival, there is a chance of spiritual collapse in the kingdom, even though the democratic constitution has kept Nepal as a Hindu state. To sustain this constitutional vision, indigenous organizations embedded in Hindu values must be protected and promoted.

In a mixed-caste and -ethnic village like Kachiday, the people can elect a *JanneBa* as in the past who will act neutrally with respect to religion and culture, and protect all in the community by nurturing local wisdom, practising traditional systems of health, guiding the management of natural resources and the production of medicinal herbs of value to their health and well-being, and advising on the production of healthy food.

How to identify an indigenous leader

In every Nepali village there are still pious, knowledgeable, impartial, old *JanneBa*s. It is vital that new LIOs select these elders as their initial leaders or advisers. Such an approach will provide the opportunity for the traditional elders to hand down their knowledge to the next generation of leaders. The essential point to note is that setting up local organizations in Nepal does not involve creating new traditions. The shadow of indigenous organizations and knowledge was always there, even during the darkest times of the authoritarian period. The task is to revive a socio-cultural and spiritual tradition which was eclipsed for a time by political repression. The *JanneBa*s have already recorded their anxiety over the erosion of their indigenous knowledge in Nepal. They have also indicated the urgency of its revival, ways in which indigenous specialists can be incorporated in the national development effort, and their eagerness to be appointed to such positions.[4] If, under the new democracy, their involvement and advice is sought, and they are encouraged to share their knowledge with the new generation, it is clear that they will be more than happy to do so.

Members of the older generation, i.e. the traditional elders and indigenous specialists, are the main source of new LIO leadership who have the capacity to help create future generations of LIO leaders. They should be encouraged and assisted by the democratic government, and by Indigenous Knowledge activists in Nepal, to continue their role as in the past, following the eternal principles of their tradition.

Conclusion

From this analysis of the experience of local indigenous organizations in Nepal, it seems that the proper functioning of indigenous organizations is intimately associated with the political climate of the state. However, no matter how autocratic the state might be in a larger political sense, LIOs can sustain their customary roles provided they are not actively repressed or obstructed. If, however, the political climate is repressive at the local level, then LIOs can quite quickly—within a generation—become displaced, weakened, and even destroyed. LIOs in Nepal performed a diverse, holistic role in community management and development which was made possible by the leader being a traditional elder and/or indigenous specialist who embodied the totality of the sacred cosmology held by the community. Even after a period of disturbance in the political climate for the functioning of indigenous organizations, provided such elders and specialists can still be found, the opportunity for reviving LIOs and, thereby, sustaining democracy through culturally meaningful decentralization, still exists.

Notes

1. This raises an important area of IK research, i.e. the legal constraints on indigenous organizations imposed by authoritarian rule and modern development.
2. Durga Pokhrel and Anthony B.J. Willet, *Shadow Over Shangri-La: A Woman's Quest for Freedom in Nepal,* and *Rape of Dharma: Stories from Women in Prison in Nepal,* Brasseys: London and Washington, July 1996.
3. Willet, Anthony B.J. (1993), 'Indigenous Knowledge and its implications for development and agricultural education: a case study of the Vedic tradition in Nepal', Ph.D. dissertation, Iowa State University.
4. Ibid.

11 Building on the *Panchayat*: using *Jal Samitis* in Uttar Pradesh

YOGESH KUMAR*

Rationale

THE POST-INDEPENDENCE development process in India, as elsewhere in the world, has experienced mixed results. Examples of successes and failures in these development programmes are numerous. Various differences in programmes are an outcome of complexities of planning, implementation and social realities. As a result, various of India's states have achieved different levels of development and it builds up a case for investigation of planning processes, delivery mechanisms and involvement of indigenous organizations.

Aspirations for rapid development as well as wider coverage have predominated with technology-driven or bureaucratic solutions ignoring the crucial role of indigenous institutions for attaining gradual but sustainable development. Technology-driven programmes have created facilities. Their acceptance and effective use, however, have posed major problems. Many of the development programmes, which are administered in a bureaucratic and centralized manner, have ended up as glorified examples of achievement of targets. Community-oriented projects, implemented by voluntary agencies, though more successful in terms of generating local support, suffer from the limitations of narrow coverage and doubtful replicability.

It may be argued that the nature of any programme whether technology driven, bureaucratic or community oriented will depend primarily on the objectives and nature of intervention of the programme. Yet there is a clear need for identifying an ideal mix of the three approaches in the context of attaining the goal of self-reliance and sustainability.

In any social development programme, the role of indigenous organizations becomes pertinent in order to relate effectively community needs and programme goals as well as to create issue-based participatory structures within the socio-cultural settings of the community for promoting community management (Warren, 1991). In this perspective of development, this chapter aims primarily at presenting the experiences of utilizing indigenous organizations in a rural water-supply programme in Uttar Pradesh.

The scenario in Uttar Pradesh

Uttar Pradesh (UP), in the northern part of the country, is the most populated state of India. One hundred and thirty-nine million people live in the state which means that every sixth Indian is the resident of UP. For planning purposes, the state has been divided into five economic regions: Western, Eastern, Central, Bundelkhand and the Hill. Uttar Pradesh is a state of villages as about 80 per cent of the population live in its 112 600 villages. There are 74 000 village

* The author is a development economist and rural development specialist with Development Associates, Lucknow, India.

councils called *Gram Sabhas*, the grassroots-level democratic institutions, and 8000 *Nyay Panchayats*, the grassroots-level judicial institutions.

Uttar Pradesh is among the most underdeveloped states of India. It was penultimate in terms of its human development index among the other 22 states of the country as reported in the UNDP's Human Development Report 1993. Additionally, in UP the sex ratio is unfavourable for women as there are 879 females per 1000 males according to the 1991 Census. The state average for literacy in 1991 was recorded at 41 per cent whereas in rural areas it is 33 per cent. The female literacy rate is less than half the male rate. In 1988, the state recorded the highest infant mortality rate (154 per 1000) which is primarily due to neo-natal tetanus, premature births, malnutrition, unsafe water and lack of sanitation.

The economy of the state is based on the agricultural sector, which employs 70 per cent of the working population. Per capita income in the state was Rs26998, 30 per cent lower than the national average, at 1988 prices. About 45 per cent of people were living below the poverty line at the time of the 1984 official records.

Provision of safe drinking-water facilities is a daunting task for the state: 105180 villages of UP were identified as 'problem villages' in 1987 by the criteria laid down by the government. By the completion of the Seventh Plan,[1] 88274 of these problem villages had been supplied with water. In 6884 non-problem villages, additional water facilities were created. A number of selected villages have been provided either with a sufficient number of handpumps or piped water. Of the total villages covered, 350000 handpumps have been installed in three-fourths of the villages and the remaining have received a piped water supply.

Water and people: vital link

Safe potable water is a basic human need. Therefore, the state is committed to providing this facility under the Minimum Need Programmes by installing two deep-bore handpumps in every village. Though the handpump is a convenient source of drinking-water, it is often seen that the community does not accept it as its own asset unless its involvement is ensured from as early as the stage of identification of the waterpoint location. Provision of water cannot be seen as a mere technical solution. Installation of a handpump will not itself attract people to use and maintain it. It is commonly observed in the villages of Uttar Pradesh that people take their cattle to the handpump, make them drink and bathe them properly for mere convenience. They prefer to take water from the wells or other traditional sources for drinking and cooking purposes, with the notion that it is tastier and better for their health. Such indifference prevails due to lack of health education and their non-participation in the programme.

The Indo-Dutch Programme in Uttar Pradesh was started more than a decade ago as a technical programme to meet massive targets of handpump installation. The communities were treated as the passive recipients of the facilities. Therefore handpumps were installed in front of the houses of influential people who have a high position in the village due to their social, economic or political status. Village headmen often determine the location of pumps without fairness or need, taking only the proximity of the élite and their own personal political gains into account. Handpumps are a status symbol as well as an issue of conflict, therefore economically and politically powerful people try to influence selection of water locations in their favour.

Gradually, it was increasingly realized that this technical programme should be complemented with social action. Thus in 1988, a Programme Support Unit[2] was added to the Indo-Dutch Programme primarily to involve the community in the scheme as well as fostering alternative models of community management. In the district Allabad, in one of the pilot project villages a handpump was installed at an inconspicuous place, very close to the house of a big landowner, who was politically well connected and a cousin of the village *Pradhan*. It was installed with the clear intention to be used only by one economically and politically powerful family. There were several poor families who were never allowed to use the handpump. The potential users of that handpump protested against this private use of the facility and, after sufficient confrontation, a new more acceptable and accessible site for the handpump was identified with the help of the village *Panchayat*. There are many other cases where handpumps are located in front of the houses of powerful, mostly unsocial or antisocial people, thus negating the benefit of safe water for socially weaker people. Women are hesitant to use such handpumps. A sizeable number of handpumps are not in use due to improper construction of drains or the lack of a platform around the handpump. Such facilities are likely to create more health hazards than they solve.

A review[3] of about 2785 handpumps installed under a bilateral programme revealed that 5.3 per cent of pumps were installed at socially unacceptable locations; 25 per cent lacked platforms; 42 per cent of the handpumps had no proper drainage; and about 3.9 per cent were found to be out of order. It has been observed that both cases of social unacceptability of handpumps and improper drainage can be minimized with the involvement of the community. Local people offer innovative and appropriate solutions for the installation of hand-pumps and wastewater disposal. Local masons can solve the problem of drainage by constructing an underground drain, using pipes or local materials to cross the roads for example. Such solutions are cost-effective and minimize the possibility of disputes. In order to maintain cleanliness around the handpumps, plants which are considered sacred to the people, have medicinal value or other social uses have been promoted near the handpumps: sacred plants called *Tulsi* have been planted by the users. Planting popular trees also enhances the acceptability of this new technology.

The most widely used handpump in India, called India Mark II, is based on simple technology. It can therefore be maintained by village members themselves. A centralized system of maintenance is normally found to be inefficient as the time taken during breakdown and repair depends on communication between the community and the maintenance agency, identification of the fault by the repair team, and arrangement of spares and tools for repairs by the agency.

Solutions have been attempted by forming *Jal Samitis*, or water committees, and identifying a caretaker. Selected users, especially women, have been trained for handpump repairs and provided with tools and spares. These women have added to their traditional roles and boldly accepted new challenges as handpump mechanics. The trained mechanics identified by the villages are important human resources for developing a decentralized system of handpump maintenance.

These well-intentioned interventions are a few examples reflecting the potential of local communities to make the programme sustainable. However, they highlight the need for identifying indigenous organizations operating at the grassroots for wider coverage and replicability of such examples. In a state like Uttar Pradesh, where more than 139 million people are to be provided with safe water, the involvement of universally available and acceptable indigenous organizations is essential. Village *Panchayats*, the lowest level of self-government, have emerged as a crucial institution enjoying sufficient legitimacy from the state and functioning in the village system over a long time. The need for creating issue-based organizations below the village level has also emerged as an effective solution for the management of resources like water by the direct users. Such structures are called *Jal Samitis*. The case of village *Panchayats* and water committees in sustainable water-supply programmes is being discussed here, with their strengths and weaknesses as indigenous organizations identified.

Village *Panchayats*: age-old indigenous organizations

Within the given conditions of massive targets for the provision of water facilities under diverse socio-economic conditions, the need for identifying the most universally present and acceptable indigenous organization became apparent. The search was necessarily for a village-based organization, which is rooted in the socio-economic milieu and cultural ethos of the village. In India, the 'village *Panchayat*' or a village-level democratic system of self-government, has a long history. Considerably before the enactment of the Local Self Government Act of 1919, the *Panchayat* as an indigenous institution existed in villages and enjoyed empowerment and legitimacy from the community (Jain *et al*, 1985).

It would be difficult to trace the genesis of these indigenous *Panchayats*; however, one finds mention of the power of *Panchayats* in ancient scriptures, fables and epics. *Panchayat* literally means an assembly or committee of five men. *Panchayat* is a symbol of togetherness of five persons generally acknowledged as wise, knowledgeable and respected (most often elderly) people who were unanimously identified with the primary objective of resolving civil and criminal disputes within the village. The *Panchayat*'s decisions enjoyed strong social support. The commitment of the members of *Panchayats* to fairness and objectivity helped in institutionalizing *Panchayats* (Srinivas, 1987: 34–5).

Respect to the *Panchayat* as an institution was so great that members of the *Panchayats* were equated with divinity. The institution has evolved within the community system and survived as an indigenous organization for centuries. The village council was represented by dominant caste members; however, 'the council observed certain rules and principles which operated universally, such as respect for the custom of each caste, respect for the principle of hereditary succession . . .' (Srinivas, 1987: 34).

Panchayats as an institution survived until the Mughal period. They underwent a significant change during the British period as the colonial administration perceived village *Panchayats* as the lowest level in the pyramid of administration. As a result village *Panchayats* were reduced to being the lowest subordinate agents of the government. The strength of *Panchayats* as indigenous organizations suffered a serious setback, during the struggle for independence, when Gandhi categorically denied this position of the people's institution at the bottom of the government's pyramid. Instead he visualized *Panchayats* in a collaborative and supportive relationship with the government and people. The Gandhian vision of village *Panchayat* was not limited to it being an extension of existing social systems but a dynamic institution helping usher in a new society.

Panchayats in development dynamics

With the growing complexities of caste, class and power relationships in rural areas, village *Panchayats* changed in terms of status, social respect and leadership in post-independence development dynamics (Beteille, 1991: 343). In *Panchayat* councils dominant caste members are no longer important but politically and economically sound persons have assumed powerful positions in village councils. In most of the villages, *Pradhans* are landowners, educated and possess sufficient muscle and money.

Besides the socio-economic transformations at the village level which can undermine the genuine characteristics of *Panchayats* as indigenous organizations, political will was also unsupportive of the *Panchayat* institutions. Around 1966, the newly emerged central and state leadership was a weak supporter of Gandhi's philosophy and had a fragile ideological commitment to the *Panchayat* system. The decline in the position of village *Panchayats* happened as the state leadership considered *Panchayat* leadership as its competitor and rival, therefore posing a threat to its position and standing. The political system was getting more and more centralized and the pace of centralization accelerated considerably during the mid-1970s. The technological innovations of the 1960s, for example the Green Revolution for agricultural development as promoted through centralist forces, relegated *Panchayats* to a lower and even unimportant position. Planned integrated rural development programmes (IRDP) also systematically bypassed the role of *Panchayats* and used bureaucratic procedures for the transfer of technology in rural development (Jain *et al.*, 1985: 197). Such cumulative centralist forces and weak political will considerably hampered the position and status of this indigenous organization in promoting local leadership, and expediting the rural development process.

It was in this overall context in late 1977, that a Committee on *Panchayati Raj* institutions suggested measures to strengthen these institutions. The most momentous recommendation of the committee was the creation of a two-tier district system as the first point of decentralization. The second level was created by grouping villages into populations of 15000–20000. Hence, in the scheme of reorganization, village *Panchayats* did not appear as an important elective participative organization.

Village *Panchayats* as democratic institutions ceased to exist over the last three decades. By an executive order of the government in 1991, the village *Panchayats* were revived, first, by providing them with funds directly from the centre, and second, making it mandatory to hold elections of village *Panchayats* every five years. Participation of women and socially weaker villagers was also made mandatory. District development administration was perceived to be functioning as a facilitator for the disbursement of funds, monitoring the democratic functioning of village *Panchayats* and regulating proper use of funds.

Socio-economic heterogeneity is increasing in rural society due to sharpened caste and religious identities and the changing economic position of farmers as a result of the Green Revolution. It questions true and democratic representation of the community in the village *Panchayats*. Villages are now more divided. The only binding factor of the village community is the common cultural base which has not significantly changed with the transformation of the economy and power structure.

As the villages are becoming more family- and cluster-oriented, the form, structure, function and representation of the village as a community are also

Table: 11.1. Strengths and weaknesses of village *Panchayats*

Strengths	Weaknesses
1. Enjoys legitimacy from the constitution of India.	1. Unhealthy dependence on the government and district development administration.
2. As an institution emerged from the grassroots.	2. Inadequate representation of women and socially deprived sections; they remain in a state of subordination.
3. Historically existed in India over a long period of time.	3. Indiscriminate distribution of funds for development as 'dole' has distorted its organic nature as a grassroots-level institution. These powers are being used to promote personal gains also.
4. Provides a platform to promote village-based leadership.	4. With increasing power and authority, leadership rests in the hands of economically sound and politically well-connected people.
5. Uses local wisdom and identifies indigenous local solutions for development.	5. Growing technological complexities have undermined the importance of *Panchayats* when development is rapid.
6. Has potential to survive as an effective unit of decentralization.	6. With the disappearance of the concept of village as an homogeneous unit, the strength of *Panchayats* as a powerful indigenous organization has deteriorated.

changing. The indigenous organizations need to be reorganized in line with changing development and village dynamics.

With the rise in population, villages are growing in size. Poorer people usually settle in hamlets segregated from the village, spread over a large area. The village *Panchayats*, if dominated by the upper-caste members, pay little attention to the interests of socially weaker sections, who live at the periphery of the village. Involvement of *Panchayats* in the whole gamut of development activities also decreases the importance of the upkeep and maintenance of water resources.

It has been observed that the interest of the direct users in the programme cannot be maintained unless their reservations, preferences and solutions are taken into account. Women also participate actively at the hamlet or handpump level as their daily routine revolves around the use of water and must be included. Hence, an effective participatory structure of management should emerge directly from the heaviest users of the facilities. Integration of such social systems within the institutional framework of *Panchayat* as a support organization for effective management of the water programme has been experimented with by forming water committees.

Emerging issue-based supportive indigenous organizations

Diversification of the functions of *Panchayats* and integrated efforts to help the development process through inter-sectoral links have resulted in the identification of issue-based participatory organizations supporting the village *Panchayat*. The *Panchayat* will delegate some of its functions to these organizations for effective participation of actual target groups, encouraging them to identify more innovative solutions to the local problems.

Formation of *Jal Samitis*, or water committees, in the rural water-supply programmes in Uttar Pradesh is an example of the creation of such issue-based participatory indigenous organizations. *Jal Samiti* is a handpump-based body of the users where members are nominated by the users. *Pradhan*, the headman of the village *Panchayat*, is an ex-officio chair of the water committee.

As *Jal Samiti* is a very local unit of participation, a large number of women as well as the socially deprived are nominated as *Jal Samiti* members. One of them assumes responsibilities as a caretaker.

The name of the water committee has been deliberately kept as *Jal Samiti* not as *Pani Panchayat*[4] in order to promote these issue-based participatory organizations as supportive to the existing village *Panchayat*, not as an alternative, nor as an independent organization. Legitimacy of *Jal Samitis* has developed in tandem with the power and position of the *Panchayat*s. In certain cases, when conflicts are not resolved at the level of *Jal Samitis* the village *Panchayat* intervenes to resolve them. Similarly, in any intervention which requires more money than the users have, the village *Panchayat* is requested to share the burden.

Table: 11.2. Strength and weaknesses of *Jal Samitis*

Strengths	Weaknesses
1. Being issue-based organizations, people unite for a single common interest, i.e., safe water.	1. Being a new concept of indigenous organization, people's recognition of *Jal Samitis* is growing only gradually.
2. As support structures to the *Panchayat*s therefore enjoy recognition within the village and gain power to function effectively.	2. Being a voluntary body, organized as supportive to the village *Panchayat*s, the *Jal Samiti* has no formal power and authority.
3. Reduce caste dominance and ensure participation of women and other socially weak groups as active members in their hamlet/locality.	3. Inter-personal conflicts of the households due to caste and class differences also hamper team spirit.
4. With growing heterogeneity in the community, *Jal Samitis* are useful and effective structures of participation and management.	4. Lack of awareness and insensitivity to the issue prevents formation of effective *Jal Samitis*.
5. Are evolving a system of decentralized participation for enhancing cost-sharing and developing a community-based maintenance system.	5. Unsupportive attitude of the implementing agencies operating in a centralized manner restricts growth of such organizations.
6. Provide opportunity for local wisdom and knowledge to be used for developing more effective systems of community management.	6. Prolonged execution and management of development projects by a central organization have lowered confidence of people in themselves which retards development of indigenous organizations.

Jal Samitis function primarily to identify socially acceptable locations, to impart health education and also to evolve a system of maintenance. *Jal Samitis* are also a step forward in the direction of empowering women as a large number of women caretakers have been identified for preventive maintenance and some women have been trained as handpump mechanics. *Jal Samitis* have encouraged rural women to come out of their rigidly defined roles and take up expanded roles in society. Members of *Jal Samitis* find innovative ways of disseminating health education to the villagers, using folk forms of entertainment communication.

Survival of issue-based participatory organizations in the long run may be questioned since, once water delivery and maintenance are stabilized, water cannot remain a pivotal issue for water users. Village *Panchayats*, however, can encourage these organizations to identify other development needs of a community and help fulfil it in support with the *Panchayats*, i.e., the village *Panchayat* can use the structure of *Jal Samitis* for implementing other related development programmes. Non-formal education, sanitation and income generation have shown inter-sectoral links with water and some of the *Jal Samitis* have initiated such programmes. *Jal Samitis* have been able to develop the attitude of cost-sharing among the users, and are gradually changing the mentality of dependence on government assistance.

Conclusion

Participation of village *Panchayats* and creation of *Jal Samitis* in rural water supply are examples of using indigenous organizations and local resources. It has been demonstrated that indigenous knowledge related to drinking-water has been helpful in promoting group decision-making, accepting new technology and inculcating positive practices for better health in a cost-effective and sustainable manner.

The potential knowledge base in sustainable development still remains unexplored in India. There is a need to identify indigenous organizations, understand their strengths and encourage them to adapt science-based technologies. Nevertheless indigenous knowledge is a useful resource-base to be used with a committed team of workers and professionals who will foster indigenous organizations for sustainable development.

Notes

1. The Seventh Plan of the Government of India was for the period of 1985–90.
2. The aims, objectives, functions and project interventions have been given in detail in the PSU publication, 'Participating with the People', 1991.
3. The Review and Support Mission visits the project areas bi-annually and in its report, UP 28, January 1992, the status of handpumps is discussed on page 78.
4. *Pani Panchayats*, or water councils, have been formed in the states of Maharashtra and Gujarat.

References

Beteille, A. (1991), *Caste, Class and Power in Social Stratification*, Dipankar Gupta (ed.), New Delhi: Oxford University Press.
Jain, L.C., Krishnamurti, B.V. and Tripathi, P.M. (1985), *Grass Without Roots: Rural Development under Government Auspices*, New Delhi: Sage Publications.

Srinivas, M.N. (1987), *The Indian Village: Myth and Reality in The Dominant Caste and Other Essays*, Oxford University Press.

UNDP/World Bank (1993), *Human Development Report*, Oxford University Press.

Warren, D.M. (1991), *Using Indigenous Knowledge in Agricultural Development*, World Bank Discussion Paper No. 127.

12 Informal institutions of financial intermediation: Social value of *Vishis*, chit funds and self-help groups

TUSHAAR SHAH AND MICHAEL JOHNSON*

Introduction

IN THE AREA of rural credit, India has long lived with two types of institutions; the formal sector—including banks, co-operatives, and Regional Rural Banks (RRBs)—and the non-formal sector with moneylenders and finance companies. The formal is normally viewed as just and development-oriented but inefficient and remote; the non-formal as efficient and energetic but wicked, exploitative and profit-oriented. The formal has attracted state patronage and the associated operational controls; the non-formal has attracted attempts towards regulation or outright ban. In contrast to the indifferent record of the formal sector (Nayak, 1991), the non-formal sector is replete with robust *swayambhoo*[1] institutions emerging as a result of autonomous local entrepreneurial action. Instead of the organized sector institutions crowding out the non-formal sector, the two have together emerged as strongly complementary systems of rural financial intermediation (for a recent field study, see Datta, n.d.).

Why have the non-formal structures that the state has discouraged produced so much energy and popular participation; and conversely, why have credit co-ops and RRBs created by the state and operating under its patronage so singularly lacked in energy, spontaneity and popular involvement? Perhaps because the institutions in the non-formal sector have been able continuously to adapt their operating rules, structures and systems to fit the needs and priorities of the people better than institutions in the formal sector are able to do. By exploring how exactly non-formal institutions fit the needs of the people better, first, we can clarify the normative positions we—researchers, policymakers and the public—often uncritically adopt about the social value of institutions; and second, we can design superior financial instruments and institutions.

There has been much recent enthusiasm about the potential of self-help credit groups which have been lately co-opted by the National Bank for Agriculture and Rural Development (NABARD) and the Government of India (GOI) as 'informal' members of the formal sector and would therefore qualify for state patronage and associated controls and regulation (NABARD, 1989). Chit funds, on the other hand, which have the same basic configuration as self-help groups have enjoyed notoriety as mystical, exotic, anti-social, exploitative, fly-by-night institutions and have invited strong disapproval from policymakers as well as academics (see, for example, Radhakrishnan *et al.*, 1975). All states except Jammu have banned or heavily regulated the working of chit funds which they view almost as evils of society. Yet all this repression has not been able to liquidate them; if anything, they have multiplied. It is important to understand why.

* Professor Shah is the director, Institute of Rural Management, Anand, Gujarat, India. Mr. Johnson has been involved in Institute projects.

Some 20 per cent of Kerala's household savings go into chit funds (Bouman, 1983: 262–9). A study done by Christ College, Irinjalakuda, showed nearly 10 years ago that in Trichur district alone, 570 registered chit-fund companies mobilized Rs350 crore (crore = 10 million) of capital every year; that for the state of Kerala, capital mobilization by its 1500 registered chit companies in the mid-1980s was around Rs950 crores. The amount of credit made available through chit funds may be twice as high as formal banking institutions provide in the state. This does not include informal chit funds operated by village groups (Christ College, 1987), which are numerous and popular. In the villages of Tamil Nadu, Karnataka, Kerala, Andhra Pradesh, Maharashtra and Gujarat, informal small chit fund groups are an important device people use to cumulate small cash flows into a sizeable amount which can finance a chunky productive investment or family contingency. We found restaurant owners in small towns of Coimbatore using informal chit funds to raise their supply of working capital; in the same district, we found informal chit funds used by farmer groups for mobilizing capital to sink bore wells and by private boring-rig owners to raise money to expand their fleet. We ran across rural women's groups using auction chit funds to cumulate small savings into capital to buy a sewing machine or to pay fees for a college-going son. And we found exactly the same kinds of informal groups using exactly the same kinds of informal auction chit funds to save and mobilize capital in Rajkot and Ahmedabad districts of Gujarat. Popularly known as *'Vishis'* (*'Bishis'* in Maharashtra), Gujarat's informal chit funds typically have 20 members, run for 20 months and involve monthly contributions ranging from Rs10 per member among rural women's groups to Rs10000 per month in the *Vishis* of Ahmedabad's business community.

Regrettably, getting information on the exact scale of informal, self-governing chit fund organizations is well-nigh impossible because of rural people's apprehensions about their legal status. Our analysis is therefore speculative and exploratory in nature. In the first half of the chapter, we describe the features of three basic configurations of chit fund schemes and speculate about what needs each can serve. In the second half, we explore the basis of the prevailing antipathy towards the chit fund as a financial institution and its implications for the design of institutions for rural financial intermediation.

Goals of financial intermediation

The primary task of a financial institution is to provide financial intermediation; it provides a conduit for economic actors to hold their savings for future needs and contingencies; and provides investors with the credit they need to undertake chunky investments that enable them to earn income flows from which to redeem these investments. As savers, people look for safety of capital, attractive rates of return and ease of withdrawal as important services; as investors, they expect affordable capital, a degree of insurance and flexibility as desirable features. *Ceteris paribus*, the economic efficiency of intermediation can be gauged by the spread between the cost of capital to borrowers and the rate of return paid to the savers. We may thus define five motives that govern people's choices of financial institutions and instruments:

○ Safety motive: as a vehicle for 'storing' savings for future use.
○ Convenience motive: for cumulating recurring savings. Here 'convenient' may include informal, accessible and flexible.
○ Return motive: other things remaining the same, economic actors would like to hold their savings in an instrument which offers them a higher rate of return relative to other instruments of that 'risk class'.

○ Insurance motive: often people experience sudden need for large capital for chunky investments; to tide over such needs, economic actors would prefer to hold their savings in forms that they can retrieve as and when they need. Thus a current account balance may serve this need better than a fixed deposit in a bank. This we may call insurance motive.

○ Gambling motive: risk lovers are attracted to instruments which may be low on many other features but offer some probability of securing huge gains.

Different financial institutions and different financial instruments of the same institution offer trade-offs in these various motives. Thus, a high degree of safety may imply a lower return on savings; and a high return may accompany low insurance value. People choose instruments on the basis of their liquidity preference, their attitudes to risk and the available trade-offs that best meet their individual needs.

The concept of a simple lottery chit fund

A chit fund is remarkable as an organization. It is self-creating, self-governing, self-managing, self-enforcing and self-liquidating. It is fully self-financing and completely independent of any external support (often including that of the law of the land to enforce its norms on its members). That the institution has grown and multiplied in spite of a hostile legal environment suggests that it creates value and serves its members' needs and priorities. We first explore the basic configuration of a simple chit fund.

Assume that 10 farmers come together to form a chit fund of Rs10000 per month. At the beginning of every month, each member contributes Rs1000. A lot is drawn; and whoever wins the lottery gets the entire sum. Winners continue to make their mandatory contribution of Rs1000 in subsequent months but no longer participate in the lottery. This is the basic scheme of what we shall call a lottery chit.

What are the gains and costs to the participants of a lottery-chit fund? If we assume that all members face equal opportunity cost of capital at 1 per cent per month, then the decision to join the chit costs the member Rs500 which is the interest foregone on a sum of Rs10000 for five months. The gain from the chit fund is probabilistic; and if the lottery is fair, then at the time of joining the chit, each participating member has equal probability of winning the lottery in each month. But over the months, the probability of a particular member winning the chit will increase as those who have already won drop out from the lottery; in the first month, it is 0.1 but in the sixth month, it will be 0.2 as the number of participating members declines from 10 to five.

A member who wins the lottery in the first month enjoys Rs10000 for the full 10-month period at 1 per cent per month; the total gain is thus Rs1000 and net gain is Rs500. In contrast, a member who wins the lottery in the 10th month loses, in net terms, Rs500. Thus, the primary attraction for participating in a lottery-chit fund lies essentially in winning the lottery in the early months.

For many people, this attraction is unlikely to match the dis-attraction of losses attendant to winning the lottery from the sixth month onwards. We note that as the chit progresses, the subjective assessment of expected losses by remaining members increases rapidly. Thus, having decided to join a lottery chit, a member becomes increasingly unhappy as he loses lottery after lottery.[2] This unhappiness however would not affect the decision of a rational individual to join a new lottery-chit; for before the scheme actually starts, the expected net gain from joining the scheme is zero.

Then why do people join a lottery-chit fund? Primarily because of the service it offers as a mechanism for self-discipline; at the time of joining, members willingly submit themselves to compulsive periodic saving as a device to secure a large sum; saving oneself from one's own strong propensity to consume everything earned by subjecting oneself to an almost coercive mechanism seems to be the primary difference between a lottery-chit fund and a recurring deposit account in a bank.[3]

The attractiveness of a lottery-chit fund would decline as periodic savings required increase in size and as the opportunity cost of capital rises. The progressive unhappiness of lottery losers will increase as the cost of capital increases. Thus, if the cost of capital is 3 per cent per month instead of 1 per cent as we have assumed so far, expected net gain will be three times as large, and compared to the size of the chit, the expected losses in later months will appear far more pronounced. Even so, there will be sufficient disincentive on members' part to default on their monthly contribution since defaulting members would lose their original capital. Indeed, members who are among the last to win the lottery will have greater concern to make monthly contributions to ensure that they regain their principal intact.

This would not be the case with those who win their lottery early. Unless the group is cohesive and has sufficient authority to secure compliance to group norms, early winners may actually lose interest in making regular contributions in subsequent months. Thus one of the principal managerial tasks in running a lottery chit is to ensure payment of periodic dues by early winners of the lottery; group pressure and tough leaders are necessary to minimize default by early winners.

In conclusion, we note that first, the major service that the lottery-chit fund offers is to cumulate small savings (which might otherwise be frittered away on trivia) into a large sum; second, it has poor properties as an investment instrument since it offers neither return on member savings, nor insurance about access to pooled capital when needed; third, it may be somewhat attractive to risk-lovers and housewives, and others, for non-business motives; fourth, its attractiveness as an instrument of intermediation is inversely related to the opportunity cost of capital facing the group members, size of individual contributions and the degree of financial development of the area; and fifth, early winners may have a strong propensity to default which may be the principal managerial problem in managing a lottery-chit fund.

Prize-chit fund

A prize-chit fund is a variation of lottery-chit fund invented primarily to raise cheap capital for the 'foreman' or the 'organizer' of the chit. In this, too, there is a lottery at the end of each period; but the winner gets a prize and stops being a subscriber. Typically, the number of members involved is several times the number of instalments in such a prize-chit fund; non-prize receiving members receive their capital at the end of the scheme with a nominal interest or a gift.

In a slight modification of our earlier example, the organizer enrols 100 members; each contributes Rs1000 every month in a 10-month chit; every month the winner of the lottery gets a fixed prize of Rs10000 and is exempted from future instalments. We assume 1 per cent per month as the general cost of capital but that the organizers can invest money at 2 per cent per month (which is why they organized the chit in the first place). A typical member can either get a prize or the capital at the end of the chit; the real gainers are early winners of the prize; those who win it late or do not win at all may actually lose in net terms. What the non-winners get over and above their capital will depend heavily on the length of the period over which the organizer can use members' money and the rate at which the foreman can invest the members' capital. One reason why the prize-chit fund may fail more frequently is that high return investment opportunities would generally entail higher risk. A compensating factor is that the prize-chit organizer does not have to worry much about getting member contributions since prize winners anyway are to drop out of the race and non-winners will be under strong pressure to contribute regularly: first, to benefit from remaining lotteries; and second, to ensure the recovery of the principal. As a result, the organizer of the prize-chit fund may be willing to make do with lower compensation than the manager of a lottery-chit fund.

In conclusion:

○ Prize chits accentuate the gains to lottery winners by reducing the probability of winning and therefore are more like a gambling device than lottery chits.
○ Prize chits make almost the entire periodic collection of instalments available for use by the organizer who is the principal beneficiary.
○ Since winners are eliminated and losers have a strong incentive to continue contributing, the problem of default is almost entirely eliminated.
○ As a consequence, it would be proper to call the prize-chit fund an organizer's scheme.

Auction-chit fund

Except as a cumulating mechanism, lottery and prize chits are unattractive to members as financial instruments. They do not even serve the purpose of insurance because they do not guarantee that members who commit a certain portion of their cash to chit-fund contributions will get an accumulated fund when needed to tide over a family contingency or exploit attractive investment opportunities when they occur. Thus only the risk-lovers—the potential gamblers—would be attracted to lottery and prize chits as instruments of financial intermediation. Most normal decision-makers are risk averse. 'Auction chit' is the economic mechanism evolved to overcome most of the limitations of the lottery chit. Instead of a lottery, auction chit uses an auction among members to settle which member gets a chit. The member who bids the highest is the winner; members bid higher than others when their felt need is greater or when an investment opportunity is noted with higher pay-offs than other members have. Compared to the lottery, the auction is more responsive to the economic needs of members. In this sense, it is more 'business-like'.

In a simple example, suppose a member facing a major family contingency is willing to accept Rs8500 instead of the full Rs10000 that would be obtained by winning a lottery. In this case, the other nine members split the balance of Rs1500 among them. Two inferences follow: first, the 'reservation auction price', the price that would prevail even if none of the 10 members had any special need for funds, would be low in the first month and rise over later months; second, even those members who do not win the chit will be compensated for their sense of loss. This means that even in normal course, members will be paid at least their full opportunity cost of capital. The 'reservation price' of each month's chit is computed at 1 per cent per month to be the cost of capital. Thus any member who can use the chit at a 1 per cent monthly yield would be willing to buy it at the reservation price. But there will always be members who will spot better-than usual opportunities or have an unusually urgent need for money and therefore bid down the price lower than the reservation price thus ensuring to other members a return on capital higher than its usual opportunity cost.

The auction-chit fund is an attractive instrument for savers; and the return on savings contributed increases as the return available to investor–members of the group rises. This is also true when alternative institutions of intermediation are inefficient, charging high borrowing rates and offering low deposit rates. Consider a group in which members invest their transitory savings in bank deposits yielding 1 per cent per month but have to borrow at 2 per cent per month. This is typically the case with rural communities.

In the *Vishis* popular in Gujarat, auction is the dominant mode for assigning the pool of instalments.[4] There are typically 20 members and the scheme runs for 20 months. An additional feature in Gujarat's *Vishis* is that the group agrees, at the outset, on the base rate of interest (or fixed discount) which dictates the 'reservation price'. The rates typically used are 1 per cent per month and 1.5 per cent per month. In these *Vishis*, the reservation price systematically increases as the scheme progresses. In the first instalment of a Rs5000 monthly *Vishi* with 20 members, the bidding will not be allowed for less than a Rs20000 discount (which is the interest for Rs1 lakh (100000 rupees over 20 months); in the second month, this will reduce to Rs18000; and so on. In these schemes, it is sometimes the case that none of the members is willing to bid; the procedure then is to run a lottery and whoever wins is obliged to accept the pool of funds at the reservation price. This is a restriction that members do not seem to mind, especially because it ensures that even those who do not use *Vishis* as a source of investment funds are assured a fair return on their savings. In a rare opportunity, a business *Vishi* operator in Ahmedabad disclosed to us that the first two collections in a Rs1 lakh *Vishi* were auctioned for Rs45000 and Rs40000 discount implying an interest rate of 25–27 per cent per year; in another *Vishi* of Rs1500000, however, the discount in the second year was Rs80000, that is, an annual interest rate of 33.7 per cent. He assured us that these were far lower than rates charged on short-term business loans by moneylenders; moreover, moneylenders seldom offered the facility of repayment in instalments. Finally, if one takes into account the fact that the member who paid such apparently high discount would also share in the discounts paid by other members (in the form of dividends), the effective cost of borrowing would fall by as much as half of the rates computed above.

The major danger of the auction is that it might degenerate into a monopoly-type market process—with the group as a whole exploiting the neediest member. The Ahmedabad *Vishi* operator we interviewed insisted that this can rarely happen since: first, no group would have fewer than 12–20 members; second, while many *Vishis* permit a member to have more than one share, most do not allow more than 3 per member; third, most members also tend to be members of other *Vishis* so that they can bid on several fronts when they are in dire need of funds; fourth, since all members are uniformly interested in securing the highest possible discounts in *all* periodic auctions, the benefits from shared dividends offset to a great extent the high discount a member might have to pay in times of need.

Here are some conclusions. What makes the 'auction chit' highly attractive to its members is that it ensures that each member gets the opportunity cost of capital; in addition it enables any member readily to acquire a sizeable sum of money at slightly higher than the general opportunity cost of capital—without any questions asked about its use. It ensures insurance and liquidity; at some additional cost, a member can raise money whenever wanted. As with lottery chits, in auction chits, too, those who have won early auctions have a powerful incentive to default on later payments; ensuring regular recovery is the principal managerial function in the smooth running of an auction chit. This function is performed by the 'organizer'.

The role of the organizer

If the crucial task of securing the compliance of all the members to the rules of the chit—essentially of making sure that all make their regular monthly contributions—is left to be performed through informal group processes, it is doubtful if any group would be able to sustain itself. It is highly unlikely that an average group member would either have the stake or the capacity to perform it. Chit funds have found an ingenious solution to this problem: they typically designate one of their members—generally, the strongest and the most respected—as the organizer. In fact, the organizers are not just the managers; they are truly the entrepreneurs for they underwrite the regular payment of each member's contribution. They undertake to make good to the group, from their own resources, the losses from default by any other member. The organizers thus provide the assurance that a potential member needs about protection from default by other members before he or she is willing to join the group.

The compensation typically offered to the informal chit-fund manager for performing this role is the entitlement to the first (or sometimes the second) chit without having to bid for it. Say for example that the chit-fund's manager's remuneration is Rs1 000 paid in the first month; if she had wished, she could have normally bought the first chit for Rs9 000; but because she is the organizer, she gets the full chit of Rs10 000 since the first chit is not auctioned. Organizers of informal village-level chit groups seem happy with this remuneration; but chit-fund companies charge (either in addition to or in place of this) up to 5 per cent of the total instalment as their commission.

Actually, as the entrepreneur, the chit-fund organizer initiates a chit. Other people in the village decide to either join or not to join the scheme on the basis of the reputation of the chit-fund organizer. An organizer whose reputation is doubtful is unlikely to attract members. Since there is enough evidence that organizers are rewarded reasonably well, and since these rewards are critically linked with their reputation for performance, as a class, organizers have a stake in maintaining their reputation of honesty and fair play to well-behaving members and of the group's capacity to secure compliance from recalcitrant members. This latter often proves trying especially if the organizer is not known to be a strong person. Since defaulters in these informal organizations can often not be brought to book through the normal process of law, in many regions, chit-fund organizers evolve their own apparatus, at considerable expense, to secure compliance to the rules of the game by players.

Chit-fund companies

The rise of formal chit-fund companies as important, semi-formal agencies of financial intermediation in many southern states is a logical culmination of these two important features of auction chit: auction as the means to allocate the cumulated group savings, and the designation of the organizer as the rule enforcer/manager/entrepreneur. Chit-fund companies differ from village-chit funds primarily in scale; each company floats several schemes—often hundreds of them—with lives of 1–10 years; and each scheme has several subscribers. Clearly, as 'organizer', such companies cannot bring the same degree of personal touch and informal control that village-level chit-fund organizers can with members. *Prima facie*, chit-fund companies cope with this disadvantage in several ways. First, there appear considerable economies of scale in managing defaults so that companies benefit from them; membership in different schemes of the same company tends to overlap; and there are built-in controls and incentives that discourage wilful default. Second, directors of these primarily private limited companies are chosen for their contacts and influence with existing and potential members; these directors perform two primary functions: of canvassing business and of dealing with defaulting members. Third, large chit-fund companies also maintain specialist staff who also perform the functions of canvassing and recovery. Fourth, most chit schemes combine auction with prize lottery[5] which, as we noted earlier, reduces somewhat the propensity for default by non-prize winning members since the only way a member can hope to win the next lottery is by paying up the instalment; moreover, if a prized subscriber defaults, the bonus accruing is claimed by the organizer as his income (Johnson 1989).[6] Most chit-fund companies obtain a security from members who win the auction to ensure that they continue paying their instalments. Finally, since chit-fund companies run a number of schemes simultaneously, they often use resources pooled from all the schemes to tide over difficulties in problematic ones.

Chit-fund law and property rights of organizers

The popular and even academic discussion on chit funds has been dominated by the implicit belief that chit-fund leaders organize chits primarily to swindle gullible people out of their small savings, and that although people of their own volition enter into these economic contracts, it is the duty of the state to save them. This belief is grounded partly in another belief that there is a high failure rate among chit-fund companies. As far as we have been able to ascertain, no systematic study has shown that the rate of failure for chit funds is significantly higher than in other businesses of comparable type and risk class. This is not to deny the fact of their occasional failure; but private enterprises do fail in all businesses; in some businesses they fail more often than others.

In an old, well-established institution, such as chit funds in south India, people learn fast to assess the risks of doing business with one group rather than another. Thus, only those survive and attract members who have a reputation of solvency and good management. This position is corroborated by the fact that there has not been any major chit-fund failure in Kerala in the last two decades. Moreover, higher perceived risk in a certain class of intermediaries would tend to be offset by the higher return and other desirable properties of services they offer. If this were not the case, it is unlikely that chit funds would be as popular and pervasive as they are in southern states. True, there are gullible people; but it is difficult to imagine that an entire population, especially in a state with as high literacy and awareness levels as Kerala, is being victimized.

Even if it were possible to establish that chit funds have higher than acceptable levels of failure, one would imagine the purpose of regulation to be to reduce failure levels. Instead, almost all legal restrictions on chit funds can be shown to decrease their efficiency of intermediation and increase scope for exploitation of members. The Kerala Chit Funds Act of 1975, for example, stipulates that: no company can float a scheme for a 'sala' exceeding Rs25000; no scheme can run for longer than two years; the maximum auction discount cannot exceed 30 per cent; and the organizer will deposit the bid amount with the Treasury which will pay her savings-account interest. Together, these stipulations dramatically reduced the value of the chit schemes to the organizers as well as potential members.

As a result of the act, chit-fund activities came to a complete halt in Kerala for nearly two years after the passing of the act until many existing and new companies of Kerala began to float schemes first from Bangalore and then from branch offices in Jammu where the act is not yet in force. While the business has been booming in recent years, the schemes floated from Jammu have real limitations. It is difficult and costly for subscribers to travel from Kerala to Jammu to participate in auctions; as a result, they participate through proxy exercised by the agents of the organizer. In effect, thus, the auction is reduced to a tender; moreover, unscrupulous organizers can now have a field day since they conduct the auction all among themselves; and whatever they decide goes.

Michael Johnson's initial explorations in chit-fund schemes run under the Kerala Chit Funds Act suggest that these operate under crippling disadvantages and therefore are seldom fully subscribed. In fact, only some co-operatives and the state's public-sector chit-fund company run chit schemes from Kerala. In many of their schemes, the ceiling of 30 per cent on auction discount ensures that in the early months of a scheme, many members bid the maximum permissible discount. As a result, who gets the '*curie*' has to be decided by a lottery; in the later months of a scheme, there is little or no bidding. In such cases, too, the lottery has to be used to decide who shall accept the *curie*. The auction operates effectively only for a few instalments in the middle of the scheme. This effectively converts an auction-chit fund into a lottery-chit fund with many of the unattractive properties of the latter. Finally, the stipulation that the organizers must deposit a bid amount with the Treasury substantially reduces their net reward. Thus, in order to float new schemes, the organizer would expect a higher commission from members to offset this cost.

There are several other such provisions in most states which are calculated to strongly discourage this enterprise itself rather than to restrict the possible scope for swindling.[7] In spite of all this, the chit-fund activity has grown; and so has people's participation in it. There are only two ways that the extraordinary energy of chit funds can be explained:

○ The risk of failure and of swindling by an unscrupulous organizer is in fact nowhere so high as is implicit in the paternalistic stance adopted by government.

○ Even with their higher riskiness, auction-chit funds offer to people advantages superior to all alternative forms of financial intermediation. All that the law has done is to make it enormously more difficult for organizers and subscribers to enter into economic contracts that meet their needs and enforce them efficiently. As a backlash, there is growing chit-fund activity outside the ambit of the law in the informal sector. Instead of saving the gullible public, in all probability, the new legal framework has achieved exactly the opposite.

In Kerala, a variety of associated informal mechanisms of financial intermediation has emerged and is used to mobilize capital and spend it on uses with high rates of return. Various sorts of arbitrage enhance the range of options open to savers and investors. For example, there are operators who specialize in buying and selling chit-fund 'auctions'. They provide active links between chit funds and informal capital markets. Some organizers also accept deposits. Some early winners can thus deposit their auction amounts with the organizer who then undertakes to pay future instalments on their behalf as interest; at the end of the scheme, the depositors reclaim the full deposit of their original auction amounts. These innovations create an entire menu of financial instruments from which savers and investors can choose depending upon their risk-return, liquidity and safety preferences. In spite of all legal restrictions, chit funds in Kerala have induced financial development which is the backbone of economic growth.

Notes

1. *Swayambhoo*, in Sanskrit, is one who is created by self.
2. Bouman doubts if this is an accurate assessment for, he thinks, poor people join lottery chits as a mechanism for forced savings and therefore often hope they win the lottery later. I doubt if this is true.
3. We note that a member defaulting on contributions in a lottery forfeits the entire capital contributed up to the default. In this sense, the saving mechanism in a lottery scheme is coercive since it imposes a prohibitive cost on defaults. Boumen (1989: 52–66) highlights the service offered by Maharashtras's '*bishis*' in self-discipline in savings.
4. This does not seem to be the case with the '*bishis*' in Maharashtra as Boumen concludes from his studies in Sangli district (Boumen, 1989: 52–66). Boumen noted some discomfort that informal groups experienced with respect to the competitiveness that the auction seems to breed. Most '*bishis*' he saw used the lottery or, more frequently, a combination of a roster system and leadership decision as the dominant mode of assigning loans. He also found a strong tendency for *bishis* to become non-liquidating; a *bishi* thus became a social device to create a lending fund from which anyone (including sometimes non-members) could borrow.
5. Unlike our prize-chit fund discussion earlier, most chit-fund companies require the prized subscriber to pay all the instalments. Thus the prize in this case is the full amount available for the winner's use through the chit period and is therefore identical to what we have described as the lottery chit (see Johnson, 1989). If a prized subscriber defaults on subsequent instalments, the bonus (or discount) is claimed by the organizer as a penalty.
6. In informal chit funds, defaulting appears to be the most important problem. In many areas, organizers have had to be quite tough and even vicious to secure compliance from defaulting members. The tactics they use to recover dues have brought the institution much disrepute.
7. To cite Boumen, from a letter commenting on an earlier draft of this chapter, 'all regulations, restrictions and efforts to control seem counterproductive, rather bothering than helping the poor . . . It is utter hypocrisy to publicly take stance in favour of the poor while in reality smothering every effort [to help them by] bureaucracy and political favouritism.'

References

Boumen, F.J.A. (1983), 'Indigenous Credit and Savings Societies in Developing World', in J.D. Von Pischke, D.W. Adams and G. Donald (eds), *Rural Financial Markets in Developing Countries,* EDI series in Economic Development, Baltimore: Johns Hopkins.

Boumen, F.J.A. (1989), *Small, Short and Unsecured: Informal Rural Finance in India,* Delhi: Oxford University Press.

Christ College (1987), *Economic Relevance of Chits in Trichur District,* Irinjalakuda: Department of Economics.

Datta, S.K. (n.d.), 'Why does informal credit continue to dominate the rural scenario? Lessons from a study of two villages in West Bengal Agro-Economic Research Centre', Vishwa Bharati, Shanti Niketan (typescript).

Johnson, M. (1989), 'Chit Funds Accounting and Auditing', *The Chartered Accountant* 811–15, March.

NABARD (1989), *Studies on Self-Help Groups of the Rural Poor,* Bombay: National Bank for Agriculture and Rural Development.

Nayak, P.R. (1991), 'Cooperative Rural Credit, Continuing Failure of a Concept', *IASSI Quarterly* 9(4), April–June, 1–14.

Radhakrishnan, S. *et al.* (1975), *Chit Funds and Finance Corporations,* Madras: Institute of Financial Management and Research.

13 Taking count of the depth of the ditches: Understanding local organization forms, their problems, and strategic responses

NIDHI SRINIVAS*

WE HAVE FOR over a century been dragged by the prosperous West behind its chariot, choked by the dust, deafened by the noise, humbled by our own helplessness, and overwhelmed by the speed. We agreed to acknowledge that this chariot-drive was progress . . . If we ever ventured to ask 'progress towards what, and progress for whom?', it was considered to be peculiarly and ridiculously oriental . . . Of late, a voice has come to us bidding us to take count not only of the scientific perfection of the chariot but of the depth of the ditches lying across its path.

> Rabindranath Tagore (from Pandey, 1991: 221)

At this stage of history either one of two things is possible. Either the general population will take control of its own destiny and will concern itself with community interests, guided by values of solidarity and sympathy and concern for others; or alternatively there will be no destiny for anyone to control.

> Noam Chomsky (Address to the New York Civil Liberties Union)
> (In Achbar and Wintonick, 1992)

Introduction

The organizational context of the Third World is not well represented within mainstream management research. Reasons for this omission have been given by various authors. Boyacigiller and Adler (1991) have argued that the management field is inherently parochial. Due to the Western origins of the field of management, it is more concerned with Western organizations. Again, Khandwalla (1988) while conceding the important contributions made by Western organizational and behavioural social scientists urged greater concern with wider social and development issues. Even where Third World organizations have been studied, the focus has tended to be on large, profit-making organizations. The Third World is, however, replete with smaller, often informal organizations operating with a blend of profit and social goals. Studies of these, more representative, organizations could benefit the field of management considerably.

For instance such studies would provide a more accurate understanding of organizational success in the Third World. In some developing countries today the official economies are rivalled by the more important black market economy. In Africa, unofficial economies can contribute as much as two-thirds of official GDP figures (MacGaffey, 1991: 15). Focusing on large-scale industrial organizations only can restrict the scope of organization studies to the official economy and distort management needs. Such studies of small, informal organizations

---

* Nidhi Srinivas is a Ph.D. student in the Faculty of Management, McGill University, Montreal, Canada.

indicate more resource-efficient, environment-friendly organizational approaches that may be of relevance to other organization forms. This is because informal organizations often rely on the more accessible local knowledge than the remote and expensive managerial or technical knowledge that may be available. Through their use of such knowledge these organizations are forced to develop ways of working that are culturally sensitive, maintaining a balance with power structures that could otherwise destroy them.

This chapter describes a significant organization form: 'the local organization' (LO). It studies in detail one type of LO, the producer co-operative, its major problems and strategic responses. LOs are organizations started on local initiative, within a community, by an interest group. Here are two examples of successful and relatively large LOs. The Self-employed Women's Union (SEWA) was formed in 1972 to help unorganized women in Ahmedabad, India (Jain, 1980). Today, SEWA has its own bank which administers a credit programme for women. The organization also offers social-security programmes and skill training for members. SEWA's activities have expanded from urban to rural areas, and it has helped members start their own co-operatives (Pandey, 1991). The Kaira District Co-operative Milk Producers' Union Ltd. (popularly known as AMUL), was started in 1946. Resentful of private contractors who were giving them low and fluctuating prices for milk, dairy farmers formed their own milk co-operative. Within a decade, its membership was 26759 farmers in 107 village-level co-operatives. In 1955, AMUL diversified into milk powder and butter, and built a new dairy. Expansions occurred in 1958 and 1960, with cheese and sweetened milk added to its product line (Jain, 1980). From a small regional marketing organization, AMUL grew into a nationwide diversified and multi-product company within three decades (Bellur *et al.*, 1990). While these two examples are of larger LOs, the majority of these organizations tend to be much smaller in size. Even large LOs tend to be federations of smaller organizations.

Types of LOs

When differentiating between LOs by two dimensions—the extent of participation and their predominant organizational goals—four generic types of LOs emerge. Microenterprises, co-operatives, social movements and traditional organizations. Microenterprises, non-participative organizations with an economic role, are owned by a single or set of entrepreneurs and provide services or goods to people of the community. Co-operatives, participative organizations with an economic role, follow participative management and share rewards and losses equally. Social movements, participative organizations with a social role, gen-

Predominant organizational goal	Extent of participation	
	Non-participative	Participative
Economic	Small-scale organizations	Co-operatives
Social	Traditional organizations	Social movements

Figure 13.1: Types of local organizations

erate awareness on various social issues within the community. Finally, traditional organizations, non-participative organizations with a social role, play a crucial role in regulating community resources (see Figure 13.1).

Microenterprises

As the term LOs is understood in this chapter, microenterprises qualify as LOs since these are very small organizations started by local entrepreneurs within a community. The developmental role of microenterprises has, however, been consistently underrated. While they are not usually seen as LOs, they play a vital role in stimulating investment in rural regions and in providing scarce goods and services. For example petty trading, though exploitative of producers, also provides farmers' income and goods that would not be otherwise forthcoming (MacGaffey, 1987). Similarly small-scale hydro power in Nepal meets the needs of villagers (Cromwell, 1992). While the majority of microenterprises remains small, those that grow larger and more profitable can swiftly lose their affinity to the community and cease to be LOs.

Co-operatives

Co-operatives, in return for members' contributions, agree either to buy their produce at a stated price (as in sugar-cane co-operatives) or provide certain services in return (as in credit co-operatives). Each member is entitled to one vote in elections to the management board. Profits are returned to members either as dividends or higher prices for their produce. Co-operatives have a wide variety of goals, such as selling farm produce, providing easy credit or developing irrigation. They are the most representative type of LOs, easily meeting Esman and Uphoff's (1984: 18) criteria of organizations that 'act on behalf of, and are accountable to, their membership and . . . are involved in development activities'.

Social movements

Unlike small-scale organizations and co-operatives, social movements are not primarily involved in economic transactions though such organizations do provide an impetus for members to start economic organizations. A sudden crisis, a cry for help from certain sections of society, demands for collective action, lead to their formation. The Uttarkhand region of the Himalayas has become known for the decentralized ecological Chipko movement. As fuel and food scarcities grew, hills people began to resist the felling of forests for commercial needs. Ultimately villagers stopped commercial felling by preventing tree cutters from doing their job. They did this by hugging the trees, thus inspiring the name of the movement (*chipko* means to hug) (Guha, 1989; Pandey, 1991). Social movements tend to be inspired particularly by charismatic leaders who urge some form of social reform, reflecting an attitude of the 'resourceful taking care of the deprived' (Pandey, 1991: 193). These movements often use religious imagery, forging links between local religious beliefs and the movement's ideology (Tripathi, 1988). For example, the Sarvodaya movement in Sri Lanka evokes Buddhist beliefs in its social work (Korten, 1980).

Traditional organizations

Traditional organizations are an interesting blend of modern purposes and ancient knowledge. Their chief managerial task is to regulate the use of crucial resources. They do this by maintaining their undisputed authority in the community. For instance, Bali's water temples manage the irrigation needs of their farmers through a complex set of rituals that ensure users of canals co-operate with each other. These rituals are conducted by temple priests who also arbitrate disputes (Lansing, 1991). In the deserts of north-west India, religious rules help maintain an intricate system of canals and water tanks that regulate the use of water (Agarwal and Narain, 1989). Some forests in India have been deemed 'sacred ground' by local temples who have preserved them for centuries, creating gene banks and aiding water conservation (Gadgil, 1989). Besides regulating the use of crucial resources, such organizations are also storehouses of ecological knowledge passed down through generations seeking to understand their local ecology (Agarwal and Narain, 1989). Such knowledge, valuable in understanding the ecological history of the region, offers more sustainable alternatives to modern methods. Bali's water temples help enrich the rice-paddy ecosystem, without using chemical fertilizers and pesticides. Agricultural scientists have now begun to study their role in sustaining the paddy ecosystem (Lansing, 1991).

The four types outlined here are very broad and are not sensitive to the differences within the types. Also, these types often overlap with each other. Co-operatives can have the status of social movements since they are initiated not merely to sell certain goods or services but to empower their members to solve social problems. Social movements in turn can spur rural entrepreneurship as SEWA has done by providing support for women who wish to begin businesses or form co-operatives (Jain, 1980). This chapter concentrates on one form of LOs: co-operatives, detailing some of their organizational problems, and the ways that these problems are dealt with.

Problems and strategic responses

The literature on LOs typically lists the various problems these organizations face (see Esman and Uphoff, 1984 for a comprehensive review), providing a useful guide to the NGO worker or interested student on the key areas for intervention (as in Burkey, 1993). But however comprehensive, a listing of LO problems should be linked to the characteristics of the LO, particularly its stage of growth. Further, besides listing organizational problems, the manner in which LOs overcome their problems should be explored. What strategies have LOs learned in order to handle their complex environment, to attain congruence between their goals and that environment?

Co-operatives seem to evolve through three stages: *inception*, when the organization is concerned with surviving, *viability* when it is concerned with growing, and *expansion* when it looks to increase growth. Within each stage LOs face certain problems and develop strategies to minimize these problems. As Korten (1980) points out in the context of development programmes, in each stage the learning tasks differ greatly. In figure 13.2, these tasks are described with specific reference to producer co-operatives.

Inception
During inception, the co-operative's chief task is to meet its stated goals by responding to the needs of its identified target group and learning to be effective (Korten, 1980). Starting any organization is a difficult task, demanding capital, expertise and some luck. Given their limited access to financial support and

The prominent problems in the inception stage	Strategic responses
Board members' relationship: ○ Handling dissent ○ Detached members ○ Corrupt leaders Board—external concerns: ○ Hostile village élites ○ Physical factors	Ethnic identification Incremental learning Use of systems External links
The prominent problems in the growth stage	Strategic responses
Board processing operations: ○ Lack of marketing and technical expertise Board—external concerns: ○ Government interference ○ Capital	 Training Lobbying
The prominent problems in the expansion stage	Strategic responses
Board members' relationship: ○ Alienation and loss of team spirit ○ Loss of ethnic core ○ Leadership overdependence	 Tier structure Dual control

Figure 13.2: The problems and strategic responses of co-operatives in each stage of growth

expertise, the difficulties for co-operatives are compounded. Also, such organizations tend to meet active resistance from community élites fearing challenges to their power. For a co-operative to be effective its founders must identify swiftly those who would be interested in such an organization and find ways of meeting this target group's needs. Thus, the co-operative's immediate concern is to attract and retain members (Shah, 1992b). Specifically, the co-operative's attention is drawn to attracting members to the co-operative and managing relations with powerful external parties. In these tasks, however, the co-operative faces major problems.

Handling dissent. One of the key problems faced by co-operatives is their propensity to suffer incessant and damaging conflicts between members. Since the organization's owners are also its managers (and often its employees), virtually every area of decision-making is open to disagreement. Leadership struggles are common. An Indian weaver co-operative's members took sides on quality control issues, ultimately compromising their sales (Gupta, 1986). While conflict is commonly seen as detrimental to the organization it can also encourage innovation and improve organizational performance (Esman and Uphoff, 1984). In Attwood's (1992) study of co-operatives in western India he found that high factionalism led to a greater emphasis on leaders improving the organization's performance.

Detached members. Co-operatives need a certain number of members to achieve economies of scale. A sugar factory has high fixed costs since it uses heavy machinery. To reduce its unit cost it needs to maintain a high level of capacity utilization through a regular and steady supply of sugar-cane (Attwood, 1992). Again with dairy co-operatives, poor capacity utilization can be a persistent problem (Joshi, 1990). Thus cooperatives need enthusiastic members committed to supporting the LO through their steady contributions to its resources. A co-operative with an optimal level of membership and high commitment from them enjoys lower costs (Shah, 1992a). Many sugar co-operatives in northern India have suffered severe losses due to their members' lack of commitment, leading to the co-operatives being taken over by corrupt and incompetent leaders (Shah, 1992b; Baviskar and Attwood, 1992).

Corrupt leaders. Corruption of leaders is encouraged by the inability of members to understand accounts, making misappropriation hard to trace (Esman and Uphoff, 1984). Leaders once installed can also find various ways of maintaining their power, making it difficult to remove them if they are found corrupt or ineffective.

Hostile village élites. Burkey (1993) describes countless incidents of landed élites suppressing co-operatives. Dominant caste members in the community may threaten a co-operative if it obtains advantages that undermine their caste dominance (Agarwal and Narain, 1989). Besides élites within the community, government bureaucrats can also be a threat, allying themselves with local power structures hostile to the co-operative (Baviskar and Attwood, 1992).

Physical factors. An obvious barrier for co-operatives can be the lack of necessary infrastructure such as roads, electricity and irrigation. Climate may also be a constraint. Drought leads to crop losses and falls in revenue (Attwood, 1992).

Co-operatives develop various strategic responses to cope with these problems.

Ethnic identification strategies. To handle the problems of dissent and detached members, infant co-operatives seek a small and homogeneous membership (Esman and Uphoff, 1984), often looking within an ethnic community. For AMUL, the ethnic affiliation was with Patidars (Patel, 1990), for the Mondragon co-operatives the Basques (Whyte and Whyte, 1991). Shared ethnic identity helps reduce conflicts caused by the divergent views of people of different backgrounds. Attwood (1992) emphasizes the importance of the middle castes in Malegaon, arguing that their homogeneity encouraged co-operation. Member commitment is also enhanced by the sense of belonging and social acceptance that shared ethnic identity provides (Hedlund, 1988). Esman and Uphoff (1984) found ethnic solidarity also effective in coping with hostile local élites.

Incremental learning. Poor prioritization of goals can swiftly cause co-operatives to suffer failures that demoralize their members and lead eventually to closure. Esman and Uphoff (1984) and Paul (1986) suggested that effective co-operatives pursue only one goal or service at first, building a skill base gradually, and learning from experience. Following an incremental approach emboldens members to learn from experience and gradually become more ambitious and demanding in future ventures.

External link. Managing resource dependence is an important aspect of organizational effectiveness, involving the identification of important external parties (notably landed élites, government bureaucrats and village elders) and development of strategies to get their support. Maintaining good relations with these stakeholders is essential (Paul, 1986). Common ground may be found with village élites, particularly in areas of education, health and irrigation where everyone has something to gain (Burkey, 1993). The LO may also comply with certain demands of external parties to ensure or obtain support from one party that helps it resist the demands of another. NGOs are often a good source of expertise and resources that enable the co-operative to resist hostile élites as illustrated by Kumar's (1988) account of a fisherfolk co-operative in Kerala, India. The co-operative decided to distribute its fish on its own without relying on middlemen. The latter responded with price wars and political lobbying. In the ensuing, often violent confrontation, religious and social groups provided an important source of support to the co-operative, enabling it successfully to control the marketing of its produce.

Use of systems. Effective co-operatives develop systems to ensure leadership accountability. The remarkable success of sugar co-operatives in western India is explained partly by their practice of holding regular elections of their managerial committees (Shah, 1992b). These elections compel leaders to ensure the co-operative's good performance lest they be outvoted at the next election (Baviskar and Attwood, 1992). Wade's (1988) study of an irrigation co-operative in south India found measures to ensure the honesty of the managing board, including written records and open meetings. Use of financial systems also reduces some of the hazards of starting a new enterprise. By providing information about costs and revenues, it allows the co-operative better to plan activities and establish task priorities. A knowledge of accounting allows members to check financial records and curb corrupt leaders (Attwood, 1992). Informal finance co-operatives in Karnataka in south India have performed better than formal state-run co-operatives because of their effective use of control procedures that include strict rules of prompt repayment, compulsory attendance at meetings and punitive interest levied on non-repayment (Karanth, 1992).

Conscientization. Burkey (1993: 79) describes the importance of starting a 'process of critical awareness-building among the rural poor. Esman and Uphoff (1984) similarly urge consciousness-raising as a means of shaping consensus on key objectives. Conscientization also involves generating demand for the co-operative's services (Paul, 1986) by discussing the community's needs publicly. Careful management of this process can also reassure village élites, allaying some of the fears caused by misinformation about the co-operative.

Viability

After managing the difficult task of surviving a harsh environment, the co-operative's focus shifts to attaining viability, to strategies that will lead to growth. From the task of learning to be effective it moves to the task of learning to be efficient, 'reducing the input requirements per unit of output', routinizing important activities (Korten, 1980: 500). From a concern with attracting members the co-operative now considers the problem of developing a sufficient resource base. Its concern is drawn to co-ordinating the efficient processing of inputs.

Lack of marketing and technical expertise. As the co-operative becomes viable its members learn skills that enable them to provide their products and services at lower costs. These are technical, financial and managerial skills.

Technical skills include those needed in a sugar factory to operate its machines. Financial skills include an understanding of basic finance and bookkeeping. Managerial skills include the ability to co-ordinate the procurement of raw material and the transport of finished products quickly and cheaply (Shah, 1992b). Learning technical skills may be easier than learning financial and managerial skills. Gupta (1986) cites the difficulty members of a weaver co-operative faced in distinguishing the concept of capital from that of revenue. Another problem faced was in managing distribution channels: the co-operative persisted in using wholesalers that were not interested in selling its products.

Capital. If member contributions are inadequate for its capital needs, the co-operative turns for assistance to formal and informal lending associations. While government-run banks may be preferred for such financing due to their lower interest rates, their stringent requirements of collateral and extensive documentation may encourage the co-operative to turn to local moneylenders (Fuglesang and Chandler, 1986).

Government interference. As the co-operative becomes viable it can attract the unwelcome attention of government bureaucrats and local politicians intent on controlling it for their own purposes (Esman and Uphoff, 1984). Co-operatives unable to resist government control can find their management replaced with bureaucrats not chosen for their expertise but their loyalty to the local ministry; the take-over of the Bugisu Co-operative Union by Ugandan bureaucrats swiftly led to its deterioration since the new managers could not effectively co-ordinate its procurement and transport systems (Bunker, 1988). Thus government interference typically precedes the co-operative's swift demise (Attwood and Baviskar, 1988; Shah, 1992b).

In addition to following the strategies initiated in the inception stage, co-operatives respond to the problems of viability in two broad ways:

Lobbying. Where earlier the co-operative developed linkages within its community, it now explores links with important parties outside the immediate community that can provide valuable resources, expertise or prestige. These include government bureaucrats, powerful politicians, NGOs and social workers. Good rapport with bureaucrats or local politicians can reduce the danger of government take-over. The sugar co-operatives in western India have lobbied successfully for licensing and levy policies that prevent entry of private sugar mills to their markets (Shah, 1992a).

Training. Relevant and affordable facilities for financial, technical and managerial training are often unavailable for co-operatives, though NGOs can represent an important source. Learning may occur through apprenticeship with experienced members or through trial and error. Co-operatives also learn from other co-operatives, imitating the procedures and organizational designs of successful co-operatives. The features of sugar/dairy co-operatives (electoral norms, harvesting and transport controls, allocation of production through shares) have swiftly spread through western India in this fashion (Shah, 1992a).

Expansion

Co-operatives that have reached a suitable level of viability and developed sufficient financial resources may choose to expand. Or, instead of expanding, some co-operatives may choose to merge with other co-operatives with similar goals and create an association that represents their interests. In either case, in this final stage, the key task is learning to manage this dramatic expansion, acquiring the necessary organizational capabilities that enable growth in the range of products and services offered and/or the range of markets served. The expansion of organizational capacity necessarily involves some sacrifice of efficiency and effectiveness though the co-operative seeks to minimize such loss (Korten, 1980).

Co-operatives attract and retain members by providing services specific to their community's needs. Expansion, however, risks conflicting with the co-operative's local focus. It demands considerable organizational change. Further, expansion is not an option available to all co-operatives: the nature of their business and the extent of competition they face can restrict expansion (Shah, 1992a). For instance sugar co-operatives cannot expand beyond one or two communities because the costs of transporting cane would become too high.

By this time, many of the co-operative's earlier problems would have receded in importance due to its success. Village élites have become largely benign. The government and the co-operative have developed links. Reserves have been established by the co-operative for its capital needs. Core competences in marketing and technology have emerged. All these features were evident in AMUL's evolution. In 1958, 11 years after it was started, the dairy began to expand by diversifying into milk products and opening a modern plant (Bellur *et al.*, 1990; Patel, 1990).

In this stage, however, new problems will arise, demanding new responses.

Alienation and loss of team spirit. As the co-operative grows, it employs more people and upgrades its technology. The previously homogeneous, moderately skilled, small work-force starts to change into a larger, highly skilled work-force. The co-operative's homogeneity is threatened, and the family-like work atmosphere the co-operative members had shared is lost. Inevitably, personalized measures of control are replaced with impersonal, routine forms of supervision. The sense of intimacy is lost and a more impersonal culture emerges. Old employees and members find it difficult to adjust to this culture change. As Levin (1988) points out, a co-operative has to strike a careful balance between the use of unbiased impersonal controls on membership behaviour (such as rules and procedures) and the use of personalized measures. As expansion forces impersonal controls to take precedence, the balance is lost. Members and employees feel alienated and conflicts arise. Crises similar to that in the Mondragon network of co-operatives can result. The industrial co-operatives grew exponentially during the 1970s. Soon a need was felt for a more efficient system of job evaluation for the now-large work-force. But worker groups took confrontational positions on the issue with some workers eventually instigating a strike that led to the expulsion of 17 workers (Whyte and Whyte, 1991).

Loss of ethnic power core. The needs of expansion can force the co-operative to open membership to people of other communities and, as it grows even larger, to people of neighbouring regions. The increased membership provides the co-operative with more resources. Again, to obtain access to greater market opportunities, co-operatives may merge and form a federation that links neighbouring communities. Both these actions erode previous power blocks within the co-operative. For example, as AMUL expanded, its Patidar leadership was forced to forge new alliances (Patel, 1990). The shift in alliances, threats to established norms and conflicts that ensued were related problems.

The need to obtain support from other communities leads to alliances between castes and classes and villages. Managing these alliances becomes critical. The Bugisu Co-operative Union was a federation comprising many smaller coffee co-operatives. Those seeking election to the central management committee typically needed to develop alliances with leaders of other communities to get elected. But these alliances became a source of conflict. Co-operatives from north Uganda felt their interests were not being represented in the union and they eventually left to form their own separate co-operative (Bunker, 1988). To reduce the danger of minority members seceding, some co-operatives make efforts to provide token representation (Wade, 1988).

Over-dependence on existing leadership leads most co-operatives to become highly dependent on their founders. A study of co-operatives in the Kolhapur district of western India found an overwhelming pattern of these organizations becoming dependent on their initial leaders despite legislation intended to restrict the leader's term of office. Ways were found to evade the legislation: leaders would field trusted lieutenants in the elections, ceding power superficially while in reality retaining it (Baviskar, 1992). Over-dependence on existing leaders has many difficulties.

Another common one is over-centralization. While small organizations work well with highly centralized structures since they allow fast response and flexibility, as the organization grows it becomes necessary to delegate authority. Delegation tends to be resisted, however, by leaders due to fears that subordinates will challenge their authority (Leonard, 1991). Over-dependence on existing leaders can result in other problems too. The sudden demise of the leader can leave the organization in chaos, unable to locate a successor. Over-centralization can also encourage corruption and the creation of unhealthy power structures that do not represent the co-operative's long-term interests.

To handle these problems, successful co-operatives have found various strategic solutions.

The tier structure. As the co-operative grows, organizational structures are needed that will enable it to expand without drastically losing its local base. One solution is to create tiers: the lowest tier comprises local producer co-operatives which provide the supply; the middle tier collects supplies and processes them; within the top tier the finance, marketing and R&D functions are centralized. Organizations like AMUL have successfully expanded through such a structure (Doornbos and Nair, 1990; Leonard, 1991). Such a structure solves some of the organizational problems faced in this stage. By separating the co-operative into distinct parts, and by limiting the interaction of professionals with members, the intimacy and local focus of the co-operative can be retained to some extent. Also, geographic expansion is enabled since various producer co-operatives can be co-ordinated by the intermediate tier. This structure is very useful for large co-operatives seeking geographic expansion or diversification. But the high costs of managing such a structure make it disadvantageous to smaller co-operatives (George, 1990; Joshi, 1990).

Dual control. To balance the control of professionals and local leaders, a system of dual control accompanies the tier structure. As illustrated by AMUL, the management of the co-operative tends to be controlled by technocrats. Strategic direction is still provided by the co-operative's leaders, but to most members the co-operative is now more like a business enterprise in which they hold shares and their influence on managerial and strategic decisions tends to be quite limited (George, 1990). Dual control is possible only when the co-operative is sufficiently complex to provide decision-making scope for both professionals and co-operative leaders. Further, such a system demands great rapport between professionals and the dominant coalition, otherwise damaging conflicts result. The Bugisu Co-operative Union's severe infighting led to its professionals allying with the Ugandan government, causing swift government take-over and attendant decline (Bunker, 1988). Ironically, dual control can also reduce dissent within the co-operative since the technocracy can buffer the divisive pressures of internal factions since it is non-partisan (Patel, 1990).

Dual control is reflected in different priorities—technocrats are concerned with efficiency in the technical, marketing and financial systems. In contrast, co-operative leaders are more concerned with the basic mission that caused the co-operative to emerge as well as the external parties that need to be managed. Rewards also differ: the technocrat is rewarded by a salary, owners by returns on shares and power held.

It should be noted that the tier structure is largely successful only in stable external environments. Where the co-operative is in an unstable environment it may not want a tier structure, desiring more flexibility. Instead it may decide to terminate the expansion process by splitting the existing organization into smaller co-operatives serving discrete markets or involved in discrete products. This alternative to the tier structure has been adopted by the Mondragon co-operative complex which finds it more flexible, reducing the flaws of excessive bureaucratization (Whyte and Whyte, 1991).

In a sense all these strategies reduce the unique community-oriented identity of the co-operative, gradually replacing it with that of a corporation. They are a compromise. The tier structure still provides members some level of participation in the co-operative. But members now frame the organization's goals and mission in only a highly indirect fashion, through the selection of local leaders who then meet in various committees that represent the co-operative's many agendas.

Debates

The problems that co-operatives face and their responses to these problems seem better understood by identifying the relationship of these problems to their stages of growth. Some of the debates on co-operatives may benefit from identifying how the priorities of co-operatives change at each stage of their growth. In this concluding section two controversial issues regarding co-operatives are discussed.

Context or design? There are two very differing sets of explanations for what factors contribute to the success of co-operatives. One argues that it is the co-operative's external environment; the other argues that it is the specific organizational features of the co-operative. Baviskar and Attwood (1992) argue that the co-operative's social setting is the key factor affecting its success. Certain social settings encourage co-operatives because they embody fewer sources of difference between and within communities. Thus, the success of sugar co-operatives in western India is due to the preponderance in this region of middle castes with relatively equal access to land. This encourages less stratification than for instance in west Bengal where high castes and low castes are dominant with very differing access to land. Maharashtra and Gujarat's less stratified social setting thus encourages co-operation for greater gain. But this explanation for co-operative success seems very deterministic: is there any hope for co-operatives in highly stratified settings at all? Can the success of the co-operative be explained only through its social setting?

Shah (1992a, b) responds with a case for organizational design. He argues that the success of these organizations is due to their following certain organizational structures and systems. In fact, Shah argues, the ultimate test of success for a co-operative is the imitation of its structures and systems by other co-operatives. Other organizations adopt these design elements because they recognize their efficacy. In the sugar co-operatives, such elements were centralized procurement systems, issue of shares linked to cane contributed and open committee elections (1992a). By this argument a suitable design exists for LOs which, once found, can be replicated effectively in various settings. This 'freewill' argument, however, downplays some real constraints: what designs could exist for the highly stratified social setting of west Bengal where people within a village are unable to co-operate on obtaining even essential infrastructure such as irrigation (Bandyopadhyay and Von Eschen, 1992)? Further, while Shah does discuss how co-operatives actively change their environment through their actions, his emphasis is on uncovering design principles; this provides a some-what static picture of organizations, ignoring the dynamic and complex interac-tion between a co-operative's internal elements and its external environment. The design may change due to changes in the external environment. New designs would emerge just as old designs become unsuitable. In Shah's conception, the co-operative tends to be interpreted more in the context of internal elements than the economic and social setting in which it operates.

The question remains: are successful co-operatives the result of a conducive social setting or of good design? A safe answer would be 'both'. Design, when understood as the manner in which the organization configures its technology, task structures, authority and control systems, is an important, albeit largely internal, concern. However, the external context within which the organization operates is also important. Organizations progress by looking both inward at their organizational design (adapting it to attain their needs) and outward at their context (adapting their organization to match it).

The context may diminish in importance, however, as the organization grows. In its earlier stages the social setting is a critical concern of the co-operative. A more homogeneous and less stratified social setting increases the propensity of members to co-operate. While some design principles do help at this stage, more important is the extent to which the co-operative can manage its context, notably obtaining some level of support (or negating the hostility) of external stake-holders. The key is more effectiveness than efficiency. However, as the co-operative survives the stage of inception its design elements become more important. Efficiency is now a concern. Important activities become routi-nized. Ways of doing things become set as standard procedures. These rules, procedures and ways of doing become the basis for a set of design elements. It is these elements, after proving their efficacy, that become models for other, emerging co-operatives. AMUL's structure as Shah rightly points out became known as the Anand pattern after neighbouring co-operatives adopted similar elements of its design. But it is significant that such adoption occurred after the co-operative had been successful for some time, specifically from the mid-1950s onward (Shah, 1992a), much after its inception at a time when its concern had shifted from largely external effectiveness issues to internal efficiency issues.

Exporting the AMUL design. The debate of design and context masks a deeper more controversial debate. The design argument is attractive to those who wish to implement proven organizational structures without expending resources in identifying other equally suitable organizational structures. Thus in India the tiered design of AMUL has been replicated through the National Dairy Devel-opment Board (NDDB) to create a gigantic procurement network that links dairy producers in various parts of India to the country's urban milk market (Doornbos and Nair, 1990). However, while tempting, the use of existing models tends to perpetuate models not always suited for the new context in which they are to be used. The NDDB design, which centralized decisions in bureaucrats and had a very large scale of operations, was not responsive to regional differences in milk production or the needs of participative development. It encouraged a top-down approach to development: unlike in Anand where primary societies had formed processing unions, in the NDDB model it was the other way around (Baviskar and Attwood, 1992; George, 1990). In Saurashtra, the NDDB's milk plant was making constant losses due to high costs caused by the plant's poor capacity utilization. The area could not provide the high milk supply needed for the plant to achieve economies of scale. Poor roads, nomadic herdsmen and competition from private entrepreneurs were some of the factors responsible for this poor supply. The NDDB planners had not considered these factors when deciding the plant's capacity (Joshi, 1990).

The NDDB (three-tier) model would be useful for co-operatives that have reached a certain stage of expansion in a stable environment. Adopting the structure at an earlier time is not only very expensive but reduces the organization's flexibility and responsiveness. Thus the use of the model in Saurashtra prevented development of a structure more suitable to local supply and demand patterns. Blindly replicating a model without considering local needs is neither an effective way of starting organizations nor a suitable means of developing organizations with an intimate link to communities. It is especially ironic that the Anand model, originally hailed as an instance of successful grassroots development in Gujarat, has become characteristic of the fondness of development planners for the top-down imposition of organizational forms in often inappropriate settings.

In a sense the NDDB model indicates AMUL's ultimate success: it has institutionalized an organizational model that provides it with considerable power in allocating resources. However, local organizations, as the term indicates, are local. Imposing these forms of organizations defeats the very purpose for which they are formed, creating a contradiction in terms. Development planners, practitioners and academics should note that the near ubiquity of LOs in most Third World settings is a startling indication of the great need to encourage such grassroots approaches to development problems, rather than co-opting such organizations, replacing them or otherwise destroying them.

References

Achbar, M. and Wintomick, P. (1992), Press list of *Manufacturing Consent: Noàm Chomsky and the media*, Montreal: Necessary Illusions.

Agarwal, A. and Narain, S. (1989), *Towards Green Villages: A Strategy for environmentally-sound and participatory rural development*. New Delhi: Centre for Science and Environment.

Attwood, D.W. (1992), *Raising cane*. Boulder: Westview Press.

Attwood, D.W. and Baviskar, B.S. (1988), 'Introduction', in D.W. Attwood and B.S. Baviskar (eds), *Who shares? Co-operatives and Rural Development*, Delhi: Oxford University Press, 1–200

Bandyopadhyay, S. and Von Eschen, D. (1992), 'Electoral communism and the Destruction of cooperation: The experience of 21 villages in West Bengal', in B.S. Baviskar and D.W. Attwood (eds), *The Political Economy of Cooperation in Rural India*, Report to the International Development Research Centre, Ottawa, 195–235.

Baviskar, B.S. (1992), 'Leadership, democracy and development: Cooperatives in Kolhapur district', in B.S. Baviskar and D.W. Attwood (eds), *The Political Economy of Cooperation in Rural India*, Report to the International Development Research Centre, Ottawa, 12–36.

Baviskar, B.S. and Attwood, D.W. (1992), *The Political economy of cooperation in rural India: Vol. 2*, Report to the International Development Research Centre, Ottawa.

Bellur, V.V., Singh, S.P., Chaganti, R. and Chaganti, R. (1990), 'The white revolution-how Amul brought milk to India', *Long Range Planning* 23(6): 71–9.

Boyacigiller, N. and Adler, N. (1991), 'The parochial dinosaur: The organizational sciences in a global context', *Academy of Management Review*, 16(2): 262–90.

Bunker, S.G. (1988), 'Lineage, District, and nation: Politics in Uganda's Bugisu Cooperative Union', in D.W. Brokensha and P.D. Little (eds), *Anthropology of Development and Change in East Africa*, Boulder and London: Westview Press, 43–57.

Burkey, S. (1993), *People First: A guide to self reliant participatory rural development*, London and New Jersey: Zed Books.

Cromwell, G. (1992), 'What makes technology transfer? Small scale hydropower in Nepal's public and private sectors', *World Development* 20–7: 979–89.

Doornbos, M. and Nair, K.C. (1990), 'The state of Indian dairying: An overview', in M. Doornbos and K. C. Nair (eds), *Resources, Institutions and Strategies: Operation Flood and Indian dairying*, New Delhi: Sage Publications, 9–23.

Esman, M.J. and Uphoff, N.T. (1984), *Local Organizations: Intermediaries in rural development*, Ithaca and London: Cornell University Press.

Fuglesang, A. and Chandler, D. (1986), *Participation as process–what we can learn from Grameen Bank Bangladesh*, Copenhagen: The Danish Centre of Human Rights.

Gadgil, M. (1989), 'Husbanding India's natural resources: The tradition and the prospects', in C.M. Borden (ed.), *Contemporary India: Essays on the uses of tradition*, New York: Oxford University Press, 323–32.

George, S. (1990), 'Operation Flood and centralised dairy development in India', in M. Doornbos and K.C. Nair (eds), *Resources, Institutions and Strategies: Operation flood and Indian dairying*, New Delhi: Sage Publications, 77–93.

Guha, R. (1989), *The Unquiet Woods: Ecological Change and Present Resistance in the Himalaya*, Delhi: Oxford University Press.

Gupta, R. (1986), 'From dependency to self-reliance: The Jawaja experiment', in J.C. Ickis, E. de Jesus and R. Maru (eds), *Beyond Bureaucracy: Strategic management of social development*, West Hartford: Kumarian Press, 37–59.

Hedlund, H. (1988), 'Introduction', in H. Hedlund (ed.), *Cooperatives revisited*, Uppsala: Scandinavian Institute of African Studies, 7–13.

Jain, D. (1980), *Women's Quest for Power: Five Indian case studies*, Sahibabad, Ghaziabad: Vikas Publishing House.

Joshi, V.H. (1990), 'Operation Flood: Constraints and potentialities in Saurashtra', in M. Doornbos and K.C. Nair (eds), *Resources, Institutions and Strategies: Operation Flood and Indian dairying*, New Delhi: Sage Publications, 97–115.

Karanth, G.K. (1992), 'Formal cooperatives and informal cooperation in Karnataka: A micro perspective', in B.S. Baviskar and D.W. Attwood (eds), *The Political Economy of Cooperation in Rural India*, Report to the International Development Research Centre, Ottawa, 263–89.

Khandwalla, P.N. (1988), 'The need for a paradigm shift in organisational and behavioural sciences (OBS)', in P.N. Khandwalla (ed.), *Social Development: A new role for the organizational sciences*, New Delhi: Sage Publications, 13–21.

Korten, D.C. (1980), 'Community organization and rural development: A learning process approach', *Public Administration Review* 40: 480–511.

Kumar, K.G. (1988), 'Organizing fisherfolk cooperatives in Kerala', *Economic and Political Weekly* 23–12: 578–81.

Lansing, J.S. (1991), *Priests and Programmers: Technologies of power in the engineered landscape of Bali*, Princeton: Princeton University Press.

Leonard, D.K. (1991), *African Successes: Four public managers of Kenyan rural development*, Berkeley: University of California Press.

Levin, M.D. (1988), 'Traditional co-operation in Nigeria', in D.W. Attwood and B.S. Baviskar (eds), *Who Shares? Co-operatives and rural development*, Delhi: Oxford University Press, 330–43.

MacGaffey, J. (1987), *Entrepreneurs and Parasites: The struggle for indigenous capitalism in Zaire*, Cambridge: Cambridge University Press.

MacGaffey, J. (1991), *The Real Economy of Zaire: The contribution of smuggling and other unofficial activities to national wealth*, Philadelphia: University of Pennsylvania Press.

Pandey, S.R. (1991), *Community Action for Social Justice: Grassroots organizations in India*, New Delhi: Sage Publications.

Patel, S. (1990), 'The Anand Pattern: A socio-historic analysis of its origin and growth', in M. Doornbos and K.C. Nair (eds), *Resources, Institutions and Strategies: Operation Flood and Indian dairying*: New Delhi: Sage Publications, 27–56.

Paul, S. (1986), 'The strategic management of development programs: Evidence from an International Study', in J.C. Ickis, E. de Jesus and R. Maru (eds), *Beyond Bureaucracy: Strategic management of social development*, West Hartford, Connecticut: Kumarian Press, 7-31.

Shah, T. (1992a), *Design for Democracy: Building energetic farmer organizations*, Discussion paper for Symposium on Management of Rural Co-operatives, Anand: Institute of Rural Management.

Shah, T. (1992b), *Seeking Salience: Governance and management in Indian village co-operatives*, Discussion paper for Symposium on Management of Rural Co-operatives, Anand: Institute of Rural Management.

Tripathi, R.C. (1988), 'Aligning development to values in India', in D. Sinha and H. S. R. Kao (eds), *Social Values and Development: Asian perspectives*, New Delhi: Sage Publications, 315–33.

Wade, R. (1988), *Village Republics: Economic conditions for collective action in south India*, Cambridge: Cambridge University Press.

Whyte, W.F. and Whyte, K.K. (1991), *Making Mondragon: The growth and dynamics of the worker cooperative complex*, Ithaca, ILR Press.

14 Aboriginal agenda or agency agenda? Community-development planning projects in Australia

JACKIE WOLFE-KEDDIE*

Aboriginal community planning in Australia

Government and Aboriginal calls for change
NUMEROUS NATIONAL AND state-level studies, such as *A Chance for the Future* (Standing Committee on Aboriginal Affairs, 1989) and *Our Future Our Selves* (Standing Committee on Aboriginal Affairs, 1990) have documented the failures of government policies and programmes to improve the living conditions and quality of life of the Aboriginal population of Australia. The 1991 *Final Report of the Royal Commission into Aboriginal Deaths in Custody* (Johnston, 1991a: 15) stated unequivocally that:

> Poverty, inadequate living conditions and consequent poor health reduce the ability of Aboriginal people to assert their autonomy and to take control of their own lives . . . Aboriginal people must be involved at all stages and at all levels of the development of strategies to eliminate this disadvantage.
> (Johnston, 1991a: 32)

The report's *Overview and Recommendations* argued forcefully:

> that the elimination of disadvantage requires an end of domination and an empowerment of Aboriginal people; that control of their lives, of their communities must be returned to Aboriginal hands.   (Johnston, 1991a)

Concern for both short- and long-term planning at the community level and for better co-ordination of planning efforts by government agencies providing services to Aboriginal communities had been expressed in many federal reports as a key element in improving living conditions and contributing to greater Aboriginal control over their own lives (Miller Report, 1985: 8, 360, 416–17; Standing Committee on Aboriginal Affairs, 1989: xii, 4–5; Standing Committee on Aboriginal Affairs, 1990: 83; Johnston, 1991a: 76; Johnston, 1991b).

The *Report of the Royal Commission into Aboriginal Deaths in Custody* was by no means the first to recommend community development planning. However, in Recommendation 204, it laid out very clearly the processes and purposes it regarded as critical, saying it:

* Associate Professor, University School of Rural Planning and Development, University of Guelph, Canada, and Research Fellow, North Australia Research Unit, Australian National University, Darwin, with particular responsibility for teaching in public administration, local government, and Aboriginal development and planning.

should be a participative process involving all members of the community and it should draw on the knowledge and expertise of a wide range of professionals as well as upon the views and aspirations of Aboriginal people in the local area. It is critical that the processes by which plans are developed are culturally sensitive, unhurried and holistic in approach and that adequate information . . . is made available to participants.

(Johnston, 1991a: 76)

In the same year a conference was held for all Aboriginal people in the east Kimberley region of Western Australia to participate in identifying current concerns and problems and what strategies should be adopted by local Aboriginal communities and regional indigenous organizations (Kimberley Land Council and Waringarri Resource Centre, 1991). The *Crocodile Hole Report* criticized:

the fragmentation of community services [that] is taking place because the various government departments are disorganised . . . Being disorganised the bureaucracies are able to control and manage in a very unprofessional way but in a very effective way.

(Kimberley Land Council and Waringarri Resource Centre, 1991: 29)

Conference participants agreed that Aboriginal organizations need to be strengthened and need to work together effectively (Recommendation 13), and that:

external control of community development policies be replaced by community control and direction (Recommendation 14).

As this brief review of government and Aboriginal positions illustrates, there is a high level of agreement between Aboriginal people and government that planning of community-level development must be a priority. There are, however, substantial differences between Aboriginal people and government concerning how this should be achieved.

Developing a framework for examining Aboriginal community development planning

The concept of community; the purposes of community development planning; questions of community or agency control; the understanding and operation of participation, consultation and negotiation; and the relationship between participation and Aboriginal empowerment in operational, strategic and normative planning, are all critical elements in community development planning. They are, implicitly or explicitly, posed and answered in any community development planning model, and implementation process. The first part of the chapter discusses each of these as elements of a framework within which particular community development planning initiatives by government and by Aboriginal organizations can be examined.

Government initiatives and Aboriginal initiatives

The chapter then examines two types of initiatives in community development planning under way in Australia in 1991 in response to the criticisms and calls for new and different approaches to planning Aboriginal communities. One initiative was taken by Aboriginal organizations in a remote part of Western Australia; the other was led by the two federal government agencies most involved with providing programmes and services to Aborigines. The second part of the chapter provides some background and introduces the community development planning model adopted by each initiative.

The West Kimberley Aboriginal Community Development and Planning project and several of the joint agencies' community development planning pilot projects are presented as detailed case-studies in order that some lessons can be identified. The case-studies illustrate planning processes that do and do not work, community development skills required and institutional supports which need to be in place if community development planning is to have any chance of being effective.

A framework for examining Aboriginal community development planning

The question of 'community'

Failures in mainstream and conventional approaches to planning for Aboriginal communities have demanded the consideration of new and different approaches. Old ways die hard, though. Physical infrastructure and the whole array of economic development, training, education and other social services continue to be delivered by government sectorally, through centrally designed programmes with, however, some concessions.

One modification which has gained currency in Australia and elsewhere is the adoption of 'community' as the target unit for planning and delivery of services. In most instances, however, the target unit continues to be the village or town, the central place, the residential settlement. The favoured instrument for local-level service delivery and maintenance is some form of elected local government body and its local government staff. The assumption on the part of government agencies which underpins this interpretation of community is that the geographic Aboriginal community, the 'community of locality', as Smith (1989) calls it, is not only coincident with the politically organized community, but is also a cohesive social community. Further, there is an implicit assumption that the community of locality, the community of contemporary politics and administration, and the community of social interaction, is a community of common culture and shared values.[1]

Smith (1989), Ross and Elderton (1991) and Lea and Wolfe (1993) argue that the assumption is misplaced and that many negative consequences flow from it. The Aborigines who now share the space that governments call 'communities' are not bonded communities of social interaction or shared values and culture. Like others before them (Tatz, 1974; Pollard, 1988), they maintain, for example, that elected community councillors may well not be representative of all Aboriginal residents, many of whom came at different times to the contemporary centralized residential settlement from ancestral homelands nearby, and sometimes from quite far away. Elected councillors are likely to be members of prominent or dominant clans or local landholding families, who are bound to promote family interests when they conflict with broader community interests (Gerritsen, 1982). When they are thrust by government agencies into decision-making roles for the community as a whole, their decisions may favour some community members over others—decisions may not be 'democratic' or promote equitable treatment of community members (for further discussion of Aboriginal community representation see Rowse, 1992a).

Furthermore, the groups within the 'community of locality' tend to define themselves more in terms of what separates and distinguishes them from one another, namely their affiliations with their traditional lands and their kinship ties, than in terms of what links them (for a description of the consequences of ignoring Aboriginal constructions of community see Leverage with Lea, 1993, on the Queensland community of Aurukun).

Attempts to undertake any form of 'community-based' planning should, therefore, be aware of, and sensitive to the complex social construction of contemporary Aboriginal communities of locality. Lea and Wolfe (1993: 5) argue that:

> the way forward is to let people define their own communities and for external agencies to recognize that communities may vary greatly in size and that there will be a great variety of organizational structures.

Community development planning: focus on process or on plan production?
Community development is a process whereby a community empowers itself to initiate and sustain its own betterment, and community development planning is one of the tools to achieve this. Community development planning requires both a process and some outcomes or products, one of which may be a written plan. At issue is the appropriate balance between the two. Generally, agencies talk about appropriate process, but place primary emphasis on the production of a document within a specified, and usually short, time-frame (Wolfe, 1993a, b). Appropriate process requires, among other things, establishment of a consistent, sustained and trusting relationship between the intended beneficiaries of the plan and those facilitating the planning process.

Sheldon (1991) responded to distribution by DEET and ATSIC of the draft pilot scheme documents to regional staff and other agencies by arguing that, while agency-driven plan production could, perhaps, be done in a short time-frame, it would take two to three years to develop a truly community-driven plan, saying:

> any meaningful planning process must be preceded by fairly extensive dialogue on development that would be held within communities. These dialogues would not only generate goals and strategies, but would also involve cultivation of critical thinking about what is appropriate and feasible and what should be priorities.
>
> (Sheldon, 1991: 14)

Any community development planning scheme needs, therefore, to resolve the issue of how the community planning process can be supported over an extended time period (Wolfe's 1988 and 1989 critiques of the community-based planning programme of the Canadian federal Department of Indian and Northern Affairs noted the inability of the department to establish appropriate structural and process supports). Between 1990 and 1993 several models were tried in Australia. Government agencies have attempted to provide a planning service to communities using agency staff. Government programmes have provided financial assistance to enable the hiring of planning consultants to develop plans. Some educational institutions have combined provision of a planning service with planning training. And in a few cases Aboriginal organizations have either provided a planning service to communities, or combined the service with planning training (see Wolfe, 1993a, b for details of Australian models).

Agency model or community control
While echoing some of Sheldon's concerns, Elderton (1991) criticized other inconsistencies in the joint agency community development planning pilot. The proposal emphasized that the community should 'own' the process and the plans; at the same time it required that participating communities follow a pre-set agency-designed four-step model within a prescribed time-frame. Instead of a call going out for communities to volunteer as pilot participants, specific communities were nominated by agency staff and by the minister. Elderton was also critical of the notion that there could be one model process or model plan. She argued that differences must be recognized and affirmed so that appropriate community actions would be taken (1991: 10).

The gap between a rhetoric of community control and reality of agency control can be a source of confusion for all those engaged in community development planning. It is also a potential cause of disillusionment on the part of community leaders and members, who are led to believe that this time it will be different. The question of who controls all parts of the planning agenda is critical in community development planning.

Participation, consultation and negotiation
There is a general trend on the part of governmental and non-governmental agencies towards drawing community leaders and members into greater participation in decisions about how services will be delivered in a community. Community consultation has been widely promoted. Government agency staff drop into communities to consult on various aspects of project development and implementation. In the name of community participation, there may be some discussion with members of an elected council, with administrative staff, with some key community leaders, or with anyone who happens to be around at the time.

There is, however, little understanding on the part of government agencies and their staff about what participatory processes are effective in Aboriginal communities and even less sensitivity to the internal politics of Aboriginal communities (see Rowse, 1992b, for a comprehensive review of the literature on the Aboriginal community and political domain).

In such a context, what constitutes adequate or sufficient consultation and participation by the community? What is merely 'perfunctory' consultation? Sanders notes that perfunctory consultation with Aboriginal people on housing, for example, tends to result in a demand for mainstream-style housing. More careful consideration which examines options and pros and cons of options produces different expressions of need by the people concerned (Sanders, 1990).

Dissatisfied with what community consultation has delivered, the report of the House of Representatives Standing Committee on Aboriginal Affairs, *Our Future Our Selves* (1990), called for a shift from consultation to 'negotiation' as the preferred mode of interaction by government agencies with Aboriginal groups. Reflecting this shift, the third step of the DEET–ATSIC community development planning model is termed the negotiation phase. Dale (1991) in a critique of several Aboriginal community-level projects in Queensland, similarly advocated more and better community participation, and more effective bargaining and negotiation by the community.

Meaningful negotiation, however, takes place between parties which are roughly equal in power, or when each party has something the other wants.

Neither applies to most community planning situations in Aboriginal communities, unless one argues that, since agencies have programmes to deliver and funds to distribute, and communities have need for the services, this forms a sufficient basis for useful negotiation. It has not been sufficient in the past.

In some discussions over land and resource use Aboriginal groups do have something which resource development corporations or governments want: in such situations bargaining or negotiating may be possible (Dale, 1991). Though increasing in frequency, these are exceptional cases, and should not be regarded as the normal basis for Aboriginal–non-Aboriginal negotiations (see also Rowse, 1992b: 93–4).

The model of community development planning adopted by the West Kimberley Community Development Units explicitly includes processes for strengthening the capacity of Aboriginal people to bargain and negotiate for implementation of their plans and projects. The model 'attempts to go beyond community development to community empowerment' (Flick, 1992), and is based on the premise that the purpose of community development planning is building the capacity of Aboriginal groups to set and to achieve their own goals.

Aboriginal empowerment and Aboriginal involvement in operational strategic and normative planning decisions

Smith (1982, 1993) has drawn a distinction between what he calls operational, strategic and normative planning, based on what the planning decision is about, and who participates most influentially in making it.

According to Smith (1993: 81–3), operational planning deals with what will be done: the specifics of projects and local delivery of programmes. Most public participation, including the participation of Aborigines, is at this level.

Strategic planning considers the range of options and alternatives, and makes choices between options. With the opening up of planning to greater public participation, citizens have not been content to have a say only on the details of a project; rather, they have insisted that the overall situation be subjected to further analysis, and that decisions about the project or programme already taken by politicians, bureaucrats or specialist advisers be reopened and other options considered. Aborigines are increasingly demanding a voice in these earlier and more significant decisions.

Normative planning involves determining in a more general way what ought to be done, and is driven by social attitudes, values and aspirations. These decisions about policy and direction, which ultimately filter down to the community level in the form of programmes and projects, continue to be made for people 'from above' (Stohr and Frazer Taylor, 1981), by politicians and bureaucrats and business and public-policy élites, with variable degrees of input from the public.

This is especially problematic in cross-cultural situations where the ideals, values and preferences of the dominant society differ from, and prevail over the values and interests and definition of issues of subordinate minorities. Aborigines insist (Johnston, 1991a) that their values, ideals and norms are not identical to those of non-Aboriginal society, and, as a consequence, that they have to have an influential voice in the normative decisions which so insidiously and completely direct their lives.

> Participation in operational and strategic planning produces improvements, but does not substantially change community life as long as the critical decisions continue to be made for people from above.
>
> (Wolfe, 1993b: 17)

Planning which has as its goal substantive betterment of the quality of life of Aborigines, must therefore come to grips with the power relationship between Aboriginal people and the rest of society. It must be concerned for Aboriginal empowerment and the establishment of a strong Aboriginal voice in decision-making at the normative level.

Competing agendas

Elderton (1991) and Wolfe (1993a) have expressed concern over what can be termed 'competing agendas' implicit in schemes for community development planning. One agenda, which tends to dominate government agency thinking and actions, regards community development planning as a way of rationalizing, co-ordinating and delivering services to places, and to people in those places, more efficiently: physical infrastructure, housing, public utilities and roads are particularly important, but an array of economic development and social services can also be planned more cost-effectively with better community participation in their local-level planning. The agenda is largely about management. While this approach can contribute to improvements in material living conditions, it may not improve overall well-being. Nor does it follow that there is any positive improvement in the relationship of Aboriginal people to the rest of Australian society.

A very different agenda sees community development planning as one of many tools Aboriginal people use to increase their ability to control the pace of change and determine the nature of their future for themselves. In this agenda the Aboriginal group determines which priorities are most important to them. It may be housing, or jobs; it may equally be regaining control of land, or being a significant party to land and resource management decisions, or justice and civil rights, or reduction of violence to and within communities. Community development planning, according to this agenda, is a transformational Aboriginal tool for greater self-determination, empowerment and improved quality of life (Wolfe, 1993a: 42).

The two agendas are consistent with different and competing interpretations about the purpose and meaning of development, and the role of government and non-governmental agencies in promoting development. The notion of competing agendas is also consistent with a recent analysis by Fleras and Elliott (1992) of Aboriginal–government relations in Canada, the USA and New Zealand. They concluded their analysis, which unfortunately did not include Australia, by suggesting that we are in a period of transition. Much of the current turmoil reflects a conflict between the conventional relationships of the past and evolving new approaches: between an old and a new paradigm. According to Fleras and Elliott (1992: 230–31) the old paradigm was based on legalism and control: the new paradigm redefines Aboriginal–government relationships around justice, fair and equitable treatment, adaptation and workable inter-group dynamics. Neither paradigm is strong enough to dislodge the other, resulting in a 'paradigm muddle' (Fleras, 1992: 36).

The West Kimberley Community Development Planning and Training Project

Community development planning experience in West Kimberley

Several Aboriginal agencies which provide services to small remote Aboriginal communities in the West Kimberley area of Western Australia, have for some years been developing and applying approaches to community involvement in the process of planning for community identified and driven development. Marra Worra Worra in Fitzroy Crossing and Wanang Ngari in Derby, for example, had evolved a proven and effective participatory community development and planning process (Wolfe, 1993b: 30–32).

The *Community Building Working Framework* (McCauley, 1990) arrays a number of steps in a circle around a central theme of communication skills. The process is not linear. Different parts feed back on themselves. Certain steps are continuous. *Picture Building* requires collection of information particularly on people's perceptions of their situation. *Analysis* involves developing a collective understanding of the community's situation. *Testing the Waters* involves a review of the situation and deciding on which issues to start work. *Getting Started* outlines the first stages of meeting and planning about those issues. *Initial Structure* sets up some sort of a group, committee or other form of local organization to deal with the issues in an ongoing way. The *Initial Plan* is formulated by that group to deal with the nominated issues. *Implement the First Activity* details the way in which the plan will be managed. *Overall Plan* outlines ways to assist the group or community to extend the scope of their activities to a broader based plan. *Review* means carefully checking and evaluating progress (McCauley, 1990).

Aboriginal resource agency staff used this general model for several years with their client communities. The success of their approach stimulated increased demand for their services, and recognition that a new approach was required: one that provided communities with the tools for their own empowerment.

The project

A Steering Committee of members from the three Aboriginal resource agencies, in conjunction with two federal agencies (DEET and ATSIC) and two state agencies (Department of Community Services, DCS, and the Aboriginal Affairs Planning Authority, AAPA) developed a proposal for an expanded planning and training activity to be carried out by the Aboriginal organizations.

The purpose of the proposal was clear and eloquent:

> We do not want any more band-aid courses and solutions. We want to determine and prepare our own plans and development. This is the last chance to start working towards self management and self determination. (West Kimberley Community Development Planning and Training Project, 1990: 1).

Five key objectives define the project:

o The empowerment of Aboriginal communities.
o Placing communities at the centre of planning activities.
o Giving planning, development and management skills to the communities.
o Helping communities to develop the structures necessary to use their new skills and implement plans.
o Improved co-ordination and planning of service delivery.

Empowerment is the primary goal. Empowerment requires expansion of skills, application of skills, development of effective structures within communities and a commitment to co-ordination. The project proposes to combine the activity of community development planning with training in community development planning. As initially conceived, the work plan made the critical link between the communities and the government service delivery agencies, and argued that the government agencies also have to be committed to change both the style and the substance of what they do.

The planning and training proposal called for the establishment of community development units (CDUs) to be established within each of the three resource agencies. Each would be staffed by a team of two experienced community development facilitators and community planners, and four to six Aboriginal community development and planning associate trainees. Staff and trainee selection criteria gave preference to qualified Aborigines for the staff positions and sought a balance between age and youth, men and women.

A co-ordinator would work with all three CDUs, convening workshops, preparing reports and position papers, liaising with the resource agencies and with the federal and state government funding agencies, and also working directly with at least one participating community.

After several years of proposal writing and petitioning, the three Aboriginal resource and support agencies, Mamabulanjin, in Broome, and Wanang Ngari and Marra Worra Worra in 1991 received some state and federal financial support to provide a community development planning and training service for Aboriginal groups in their respective areas.

The importance of having well-established Aboriginal service delivery organizations expand their mandate to deliver both a planning service and planning training was not at issue: rather, the proposal fell between the cracks of government programmes, which were variously directed to job creation, to economic development and to training, with each being funded by a different federal agency. The scope, and the budget, of the project which finally received funding was considerably reduced from earlier proposals.

The CDUs in action

The CDUs understand development as providing a way in which people can establish and realize the goals they set for themselves by acquiring information, knowledge and skills in the process (Flick, 1992). The model makes a clear link between what it regards as three levels of community development: Level One, the 'shopping list'; Level Two, 'intangibles'; and Level Three, 'owning decisions'. The shopping-list level consists of planning for and implementing projects which improve the physical conditions of peoples' daily lives, such as houses, electrification and clean water. Level Two, incorporates the need Aboriginal people express for appropriate and better education and health services, which contribute to their capacity to deal with the external forces that affect their lives. Level Three, owning decisions is the base from which people experience 'empowerment'. The west Kimberley project regards peoples' history, values and culture and intimate connections with their homelands as that empowering base.

The CDU's 'Country, People, Planning and Empowerment Model' for community planning has four major steps: identifying the group vision, setting goals, establishing strategies and taking the steps (Flick, 1992). This suggests that the CDUs are making modifications to the Community Building Framework, and are re-working it to meet their needs better and more closely reflect those of their client communities.

The model also makes a direct link between facilitating community-based planning for community development, and both staff training and training of community members. Training is focused at two levels: training of Aboriginal staff as community development planning facilitators, and training of local community members and organizations. Staff training has immediate priority, and includes training in administration and financial management, and in the use of the modified Community Building Framework.

The CDU staff are now working directly with ongoing and new client communities. Staff training is largely on-the-job, guided and supervised by senior staff, and partly through workshops and specific training modules.

Each CDU is placing different emphasis on the components of the project. The usefulness of having a co-ordinator for CDUs which are several hundred kilometres apart from each other has come into question. Each organization is re-working the community planning model for itself. In many respects, these are the proper and inevitable growing pains of increasingly competent and autonomous organizations.

Commentary

The west Kimberley approach has a mix of elements which are important for effective Aboriginal community development planning (Lea and Wolfe, 1993; Wolfe-Keddie, 1994):

o 'Dedicated' planning units and 'dedicated' staff responsible for the day-to-day work of community planning.
o Continuity and reliability of support to client communities.
o Staffing levels that are sufficiently high for the CDUs to operate as a team, drawing on the skills, knowledge and experience of members.
o CDUs which are housed within existing Aboriginal agencies, thus strengthening, rather than drawing energy from Aboriginal organizations, as many government projects tend to do.
o CDUs which build on the Resource Centres' credibility and acceptance by communities.
o Recruitment of a largely Aboriginal staff with considerable skills and local experience between them.
o Shift in control of the project (with the notable and problematic exception of funding), as well as operation of the project, from governmental agencies to Aboriginal organizations.
o A two-pronged training emphasis which strengthens Aboriginal capacity at several levels.
o Adoption of a successful indigenous model of community development planning.
o Progressive modification of the original model to have full regard for Aboriginal community planning processes. Development of an indigenous Aboriginal model is a critical step for effective community development planning.

However, the future of the West Kimberley CDUs is uncertain. Costs are high, funding has to be applied for annually and is by no means guaranteed. Capital and operating costs of establishing and maintaining a planning service to remote Aboriginal communities are high. Each CDU requires at minimum a four-wheel-drive vehicle, computers, printers and other basic office equipment. Recurrent costs include wages for at least 10 staff and vehicle running and maintenance costs. A conservative estimate is A$275000 (US$1 = A$1.33) for the initial capital cost, and around $500000 in annual recurrent costs (consultants are currently being paid between $30000 and $75000 to prepare community plans).

Security of funding continues to be one of the major constraints on the West Kimberley Community Development Planning Project. The project was initially funded through the ATSIC Community Development Planning Programme. The CDUs now compete with other Aboriginal organizations for funds which are allocated through newly established and locally elected Aboriginal regional councils.

Because of the complexity of the approach (linking training and planning, and linking physical projects, overall service improvement, and empowerment in decision-making), the CDUs are not going to achieve clear, positive, short-term results. Furthermore, Aboriginal client communities, Aboriginal regional councils, external funding agencies and other government departments, and the CDUs and associated Aboriginal service delivery organizations all have their own expectations about what effective CDUs would achieve. The CDUs are not likely to meet these expectations.

The Joint Federal Agency Planning Pilot Scheme

Introduction
The West Kimberley Planning and Training Project was by no means the only Aboriginal community planning initiative in the 1990–92 period. In 1990 a National Workshop on Aboriginal Employment Development Policy (AEDP) held in Alice Springs brought together staff from several federal and state government agencies responsible for delivery of programmes and services to Aboriginal communities to discuss such issues as: What is community development planning? What are its advantages and disadvantages? What is the community planning unit? How can the process be facilitated? What personnel and financial resources are necessary (Chapman, 1990: 43–51)? At the Aboriginal and Torres Strait Islander Commission's December 1990 meeting, commissioners were asked to consider a proposal that the federal Aboriginal and Torres Strait Islander Commission (ATSIC) develop a community planning programme for consideration at a future commission meeting.

Concurrently the notion of a Community Development Planning Pilot Scheme was promoted by the federal Department of Employment, Education and Training (DEET) in late 1990 and early 1991. DEET sought to develop a project which would provide an understanding of what different types of community plans can be produced relatively quickly in a cost-effective manner; develop the community planning process within the communities themselves; produce documents which will form an accountable arrangement between the community and government agencies regarding service delivery arrangements; develop exemplary plans and procedures for the information/guidance of other communities and staff; and identify training requirements for officers.

At its next meeting, in February 1991, the Aboriginal and Torres Strait Islander Commissioners received a joint statement from DEET and ATSIC recommending that six Aboriginal communities be invited to participate in a community development planning scheme to be co-operatively run by DEET and ATSIC regional staff. Commissioners agreed to the pilot scheme.

During 1991 DEET and ATSIC 'trialled' their co-operative scheme and four-step model for community development planning as a preliminary step to establishing an Australia-wide Aboriginal community planning programme. A consulting firm specializing in training was hired to develop the model. DEET and ATSIC held an information and training workshop in Canberra in April 1991 for senior regional staff and officers assigned to the community pilot projects. A DEET and an ATSIC officer from each of the participating regional offices was assigned to each pilot project. These officers participated in a joint agency 'recall workshop' held in Cairns in June, three months after the start-up of the community pilots. Both workshops were facilitated by the consulting firm staff. The pilots were monitored by DEET and ATSIC central offices. Monthly reports were to be submitted, and each pilot was visited by a team from the central offices. The time-frame for completion of the planning steps and production of a community plan was six months.

The four-step model
The model developed by the consultants consisted of four distinct steps (ATSIC, 1991). In Step One, the demographic information and data-base phase, agency staff were to prepare background papers to assist communities identify where they are now. The background papers would identify the training required to enable community members to participate in community development activities; existing economic, educational, health, housing, community infrastructure and social facilities in the community; actual and potential employment activities; other community resources such as CDEP workforce; and government programmes.

In Step Two, the planning phase, communities would identify and write down their social and cultural, economic, employment, education and training, and infrastructure development goals. This would be a community document. If further training was required in its preparation, this would be provided.

Step Three was the negotiation phase in which communities would negotiate a 12-month activity plan with government agencies, establish 12-month objectives and the extent of government support to be provided. This was to be a jointly prepared and very specific document.

Monitoring and review was to be the Step Four. It had two distinct parts. In the first, government agencies would determine what objectives would be addressed by their programmes, and how the performance of field staff would be assessed. The second would review achievements against objectives. This would include the suitability of programme response, level of community support and implementation of the plan and the need for readjustment of the plan.

Six communities were to be nominated for the scheme by agency officers, and would then be invited to participate. Pilot communities should, according to the proposal criteria, have strong community cohesion, effective community organizations, experience in participation in government programmes, potential for further economic development, and an understanding of the need for strategic planning (ATSIC, 1991). The nominees were Yarrabah in the Cairns region and Mornington Island in the Mount Isa region (both in Queensland); Ngukurr in the Katherine region of the NT; three small communities, Mulan, Lamboo-Gunian and Murriwung-Gajerrong, in the Kununurra region (in fact, making eight communities in total); Lightening Ridge in the Walgett/Bourke region, NSW; and Point Pearce in the Adelaide region of south Australia.

The pilot project scheme was launched in a climate of change and uncertainty for both agencies. The ATSIC had only recently been established. Several DEET programmes were under review. Programmes were being shifted from one agency to another, along with staff positions and personnel.

Purpose of the scheme: A model for agency delivery of a community development planning service

Documentary evidence and the results of interviews with staff confirm that the central offices of the two agencies assumed that the planning scheme and community pilots were a demonstration of a model for plan making which would form the basis for a community development planning programme. First, it would demonstrate the value of co-operation between lead agencies for delivery of services to Aborigines, and a method for accomplishing this. Second, it would demonstrate the role and activities of agency staff as direct deliverers of a planning service. Here some fine-tuning could occur. DEET had anticipated that agency officers might need more training. Third, it would confirm the rightness of the four-step model for community development planning. In sum, it was expected to be an efficient and effective method of plan production for Aboriginal communities in Australia.

No formal evaluation was undertaken before ATSIC launched an Australia-wide community planning programme in late 1991, and the regional planning programme in early 1992 (Wolfe, 1993a, b).[2]

The DEET–ATSIC community development planning pilots

Introduction

Four of the initial eight pilot projects are discussed here (for a review of all eight projects see Wolfe, 1993a). They have been selected to illustrate the spectrum of communities involved (large and small, more and less remote) and the different approaches adopted by the joint agencies (direct involvement, use of paid planning facilitators).

Agency plans, consultant facilitation, community realities: the East Kimberley pilot

The East Kimberley project was, initially at least, the most carefully planned of the four northern pilots. Indeed, it started up in advance of the others, before formal announcement of the pilot scheme. DEET and ATSIC staff in Western Australia's remote north-eastern regional centre, Kununurra, had had some experience of trying to work together in the context of the Aboriginal Employment Development Programme (AEDP), and had been attempting to co-ordinate their visits to area communities. It was decided locally that the project would be guided by the DEET and ATSIC managers, the DEET officer, who had been assigned by DEET to the project, and field staff who worked with the chosen communities.

The joint agency project team developed a plan for the pilots. DEET and ATSIC staff responsible for each ATSIC regional council were to attend community workshops. DEET, ATSIC and other agencies, such as the Department of Social Security, were to receive copies of the plans so they could make a commitment to support the goals and projects, and use the plans to guide planning of their programme delivery. Once accepted, the community plan would be presented to each Aboriginal Regional Council, so that council could take local plans into account in regional planning.

DEET and ATSIC officers identified three Aboriginal communities they thought might be willing to participate. One community was suggested from each of the three Aboriginal regional councils administered from Kununurra. Communities were selected to be both traditional and non-traditional, having and not having a work-for-welfare (Community Development Employment Programme, CDEP) project, having different histories and different contemporary social and political structures, and for having some base of community services and enterprises. They were also 'assessed as being capable of meeting the timeframe' (Lane, 1991). The communities were first approached towards the end of January 1991. Community workshops were held in two of the three communities. A joint evaluation meeting, also attended by the WA governments' Aboriginal Affairs Planning Authority, was held in Kununurra after the pilots had been under way for four months. In October, DEET and ATSIC monitors from Canberra met with agency staff, visited the two remaining pilot communities, and made recommendations to staff on what still needed to be done.

Assistance from consultants: Lamboo-Gunian, West Australia
Lamboo-Gunian Aboriginal Corporation is the organization associated with people wishing to return to their lands in and around Lamboo Station. They presently have a lease on Koonjie Park Station, about 20kms west of Halls Creek, where most of the 100 or so people live. The number of people in residence varies considerably with the cattle season. One family plays the major role in community administration. The corporation is having difficulty getting funding for the housing and other infrastructure necessary for the people to live and work on Koonjie Park.

Prior to the planning pilot, Lamboo-Gunian had been involved in training workshops in pastoral management and community management facilitated by a consultant and funded by DEET. They asked that the same consultant be used for the community planning workshops. Two- or three-day workshops were to be held in the community. The chosen consultant was not available for the Lamboo-Gunian workshop, which was facilitated by an alternative less familiar to the community. Attendance at the follow-up workshops was very limited. Community leaders and members had business, and agency staff duties, which demanded their presence elsewhere.

At the key Lamboo-Gunian community meeting the facilitator pushed community people to speak out. 'Agency staff are here, tell them what you want.' The facilitator emphasized housing, asking 'How many houses do you want?' Agency staff were uncomfortable, since they were not in a position to make an immediate response to such demands. They were not convinced that this approach encouraged the community to give careful consideration to their own priorities.

After the official close of the first day's workshop, discussion continued among community members. The following day the people were ready with their priorities. The top priority was land. Then they felt they needed more training for jobs, a homemaker service for the elderly, and some sports and recreation for the young people. As the workshop report noted 'the community had set about a planning activity without the facilitator or agencies'.

The consultant wrote and submitted reports on the workshops. Results from the workshops were presented at a joint agency evaluation meeting in Kununurra. Little more happened until the visit by the central office monitoring team in October. At that meeting regional staff said they did not have the knowledge or skills to do the planning job required of them and that officers needed to be committed full-time to community planning, and not have it as an add-on to other duties. They also believed, based on their experience, that Step One of the model, in which they were to gather data on the community, was not right. They did not, however have any suggestions for alternatives. The monitors were concerned that Step One had not been completed, and demanded that a skills audit and a training needs analysis be done. By that time two of the three pilot communities in the Kununurra region, including Lamboo-Gunian, had dropped out of the scheme.

Commentary

In the early stages, the East Kimberley project was planned. Commitment on the part of senior agency staff was considerable. Parts of staff positions were allocated to the project. The agencies attempted to co-ordinate their support and their community visits. Consultants were hired, and community workshops organized and attended. Follow-up workshops were organized. Reports were filed, and progress and problems identified.

Several of the field officers assigned to the pilots attended the workshops on the pilot planning scheme. They thought that they would have to undertake community development planning directly with the communities, and were concerned that they did not have the array of knowledge and skills required.

Because of high staff turnover and officers being shifted from one position to another within or between agencies there was little continuity of staff making community visits. Indeed, those who visit in a given capacity on one occasion may hold a different position and therefore appear in a different capacity by the next meeting—to the confusion of the Aboriginal council and community members, and of other agency officers.

Somewhat similarly, hiring the same consulting firm does not mean that the same individual will consistently work with the community. Since it takes some time for a constructive working relationship to develop, continuity is desirable, but is difficult to achieve.

Even when a consultant has worked with a community in one capacity and has established a level of trust, that individual may not have the skills needed to take on a different role. One consultant pushed community members to come up with 'wish-list' priority projects and an instant response from agency staff. The consultant did not assist the community to work out its own priorities, or to consider the possible effects on the community if it selected one option over another.

A complex community attempts to plan: the Ngukurr Pilot Project, Northern Territory

Ngukurr is a large, centralized, multi-clan residential settlement located east of the growing Northern Territory (NT) town of Katherine. A Christian mission was established on the homelands of the Ngalakan people in 1901. Other Aboriginal people were encouraged to move from their homelands to the settlement. There are now seven major families or clans in the settlement, and a few minor families. The larger clans have as many as 400 members. Each clan has established a number of small satellite settlements or 'outstations' on their ancestral homelands, and most want to upgrade the facilities of those that already exist and wish to set up more.

The Ngalakan Association, the organization of the traditional owners, is an active body within Ngukurr, although many of its members live in Darwin, Katherine, Alice Springs and elsewhere. The association controls the community store. Members receive royalties from leasing the land and rights to operate the store to a non-Aboriginal operator.

Since the late 1980s Ngukurr has had an elected Community Government Council, Yugul Mangi, established under NT local government legislation. Two members of each of the seven clans are elected to the council. The local government area includes both the central settlement of Ngukurr and the out-stations. Like other elected Aboriginal councils, Yugul Mangi Community Government Council is responsible for local-level delivery of many Territory and Commonwealth government programmes. Control of the policies which produce the programmes lies with each upper-tier government. Consequently the council has to deal with a huge array of government departments and programmes.

A key question for community planning is whether the planning unit for Ngukurr is the central settlement, the settlement and satellite outstations, the grouping of Aboriginal people who spend part of the year at Ngukurr and rely on its facilities, or each of the clans and their homelands. The appropriate composition for community consultations depends on the answer to this question.

The DEET and ATSIC officers assigned to the Northern Territory pilot project were excited by the concept. One wrote 'fantastic idea: the future depends on it'. The project team arranged meetings with the Ngukurr Community Government Council. Council members had little understanding about what formal community planning might achieve or what was involved. Nevertheless there was considerable interest, and a decision taken to form a planning advisory committee.

The council also decided that council and committee members should visit the Laynhapuy Homelands Resource Centre in Nhulunbuy, in far eastern Arnhem Land, which had been successfully doing its own planning for several years. The visit was delayed due to other urgent community and personal priorities. During that time agency officers compiled the basic information as required by the first step of the planning model. The visit to the Laynhapuy Resource Centre opened the eyes of Ngukurr council members to what community development planning could accomplish.

A follow-up workshop with council members and project staff identified community resources, ongoing projects and sources of community income. It also identified some priorities, such as greater community and clan control over all aspects of life at Ngukurr, and improved skills and education.

Early in the community planning process controversy arose over who would be on the planning advisory committee. The Community Government Council had appointed the members. Some parts of the community demanded greater representation of traditional elders and long-standing local landowners on the committee. At that same time some Ngukurr people were attempting to form a breakaway land council, separate from the Northern Land Council.

Ngukurr was also experiencing difficulties with the way in which the CDEP programme was being handled. Much of the business of Ngukurr came to a halt while the CDEP programme was being reviewed. To complicate matters further, the ATSIC officer responsible for the pilot project was seconded by ATSIC to the CDEP review team.

Nevertheless, a planning strategy was decided on. Pilot project officers should meet with each of Ngukurr's clans and do more talking and listening to people. At subsequent planning meetings, the council decided that the best way for Ngukurr to do community planning was for each clan to develop its plan, and then to amalgamate them. A community-wide meeting was held to work out the situation of the community and consider this planning strategy. The officers then began clan consultations. Many groups had already written up vision statements and lists of needs. Others were working on it. The DEET officer discussed these with clan members and facilitated further discussion.

The report of the central office monitoring team was critical of the team for lack of progress and 'no planned approach'. The report also noted that the council president has 'several projects to get off the ground, such as market gardens, fixing up the CDEP. . .'. Reports and materials in regional office files indicate that DEET and ATSIC in Katherine were attempting to follow pilot guidelines which said that the community should own the process and determine its pace. They were also committed to assisting the community with a process of community consultation and discussion that went beyond the agenda of the Community Government Council President. The process was accomplished in seven months by officers and a community with little previous experience of community planning. Given the social and political complexity of Ngukurr and competing community priorities, this represents considerable progress.

At the end of 1991 the Ngukurr CDEP was suspended pending the outcome of the CDEP review. In February 1992 the Katherine ATSIC office announced that resumption of Community Planning would not be possible until CDEP was re-established (not likely until April), even though the Community Government Council had already twice requested that the planning process continue. The Katherine regional manager requested additional funds to enable him to allocate staff to the pilot. Central office did not approve financial support. After running the pilot scheme for a nine-month trial in 1991, the central offices decided that DEET and ATSIC field staff had neither the skills nor the time to provide the sort of planning support that communities were asking for, and decided to provide funds for communities to engage external planning consultants.

Commentary

With its numerous clans and outstations, elected council, local government administration and other powerful organizations, houses, works yards and enterprises, Ngukurr is typical of large Aboriginal settlements in northern Australia. As such it poses particular challenges for community development planning (see Leverage with Lea, 1993).

The DEET/ATSIC team was committed to proceeding carefully and cautiously with the council and the community. They recognized that demonstration is an effective awareness and learning tool, and organized the Laynhapuy Homelands visit and follow-up workshop. They made use of their different skills. The DEET officer had some facilitation skills. He used straightforward language which could be readily translated, as was necessary, into a number of different Aboriginal languages. He talked with people about What, Why, Where, When and How, using this as a basic planning vocabulary. The ATSIC officer compiled the information base. The team provided regular reports as required by central office. For several months they reported slow progress: a realistic assessment of how the pilot was going. In recognition and respect for the complex social and political composition of the Ngukurr community, the officers embarked on a process of consultation with each clan group. Requests from the community council for the planning process to continue indicate that the council felt that community development planning could be of value.

Central office reports reinforce that there were apparently irreconcilable agendas for the Ngukurr pilot: on the one hand a process of careful consideration by diverse and sometimes competing groups of how, collectively or separately, they might achieve their goals, and, on the other, completion of a set of planning steps and production of a document listing projects.

Staff and community roles in a community planning process: the Yarrabah pilot
Yarrabah was invited by the agency central offices to be one of the participating communities. The Yarrabah pilot is instructive not because of what happened, but because of what did not happen and why.

Yarrabah occupies a peninsula south of Cairns in far north Queensland. It is a DOGIT (Deed of Grant in Trust) community under Queensland law, and has an elected town council. It is a large community of several thousand people, with numerous families and factions. While the main town site has the physical infrastructure of water, power and roads, and basic social services are provided, much of what is in place is run-down, inadequate or inappropriate. It is a community which could, according to agency staff, benefit from various sorts of community development planning.

Both of the officers assigned by DEET and ATSIC to the pilot had considerable familiarity with Yarrabah through family connections and through work experience. At the introductory planning workshop in Canberra the officers noted that Yarrabah was experiencing health problems, housing shortages, factional differences, change in leadership and in council membership linked to strong family groups, and alcoholism and violence. It also had a recently established CDEP, and a number of private businesses such as store, petrol, bakery and take-away.

At the meeting the officers, like those involved in the other pilots, drew up an action plan. The proposed plan would involve both joint agency meetings and community meetings. They noted, though, that 'due to current problems associated with the newly elected administration it is envisaged that this process will take at least a few months'. They felt that they were assessing the situation realistically, and that some of the other project action plans were not achievable. As Aboriginal people, they felt they were particularly aware of the difficulties of introducing and doing community development planning with Aboriginal communities.

From the start both officers were concerned by what they regarded as inconsistencies in the model they were instructed to follow. The description of the model emphasized that the community should be directly involved in the whole process, and should determine its pace and direction. They felt it was contradictory for central office to set the timetable for completion of each of the four steps and for completing the whole exercise in six months. Both were concerned about their own lack of knowledge about planning and community development and did not feel that their prior training and experience qualified them for the task. Also, both were conscious that time given to community planning would be time taken from other urgent tasks.

After discussion between the assigned officers, regional managers, and other interested staff, the Cairns office of ATSIC organized a Community Development Planning Workshop for staff and members of the region's Aboriginal community, at which experiences with community-based planning in Kimberley and Canada were presented and the strengths and weaknesses of different approaches discussed by participants. The CEOs of DEET and ATSIC, who were in Cairns for the second of the pilot planning workshops, attended the wrap-up session. The session emphasized the need for skilled facilitators knowledgeable about the processes of community development and planning; the importance of preliminary work not just with the council but with other community leaders, members and organizations; the difference between planning which simply lists a sequence of desirable projects and the community planning developmental of a community's capacity to shape its own future; and the need for performance indicators which measure government agencies' responsiveness to and implementation of community plans.

The pilot proceeded very slowly. In October the joint agency monitoring report expressed frustration over the infrequency of reports from the field and 'lack of understanding and/or appreciation of the importance (especially timeframe) of the pilot project' by regional staff. A meeting between the monitoring team, agency staff and Yarrabah council and shire clerk produced agreement that training for council and agency officers should be organized immediately, a suitable Yarrabah person should be employed to collect community data and act as contact person, and senior regional staff should become more pro-active. Few of these decisions were acted upon.

Commentary
The Yarrabah pilot highlights the limitations of the four-step model and the inconsistencies between the rhetoric of community control and reality of an agency-driven timetable for plan production. The Cairns officers were unable to find a way to deal directly with the problem. Nevertheless, participation in the pilot scheme by the Cairns ATSIC office stimulated considerable debate among some of its staff about the purposes of community development planning and how the agency might most effectively support planning which goes beyond identifying priority projects and actually increases local capacity and local control. Regional staff consider that the Yarrabah pilot continues on, even though the community has still not embarked on a formal process of community development planning. The Cairns ATSIC regional office has established a community and regional planning staff position, to provide support to planning in the region, and has appointed an officer experienced in community development planning to the position.

Planning by the Aboriginal community: the Lightening Ridge pilot
Aborigines living in and around the opal mining town of Lightening Ridge do not have a separately elected local government council: they are included in the local shire. They do, however, have a very active incorporated organization, Barriekneal Housing and Community Ltd (known locally as the Barriekneal Corporation), with an elected board of directors and staff.

As well as constructing, maintaining and administering housing, the

Barriekneal Corporation was already involved in a number of business enterprises, including a shop selling Aboriginal artefacts and T-shirts, and was
seeking to expand its activities to include a local garage and caravan park.
It runs the local CDEP and contracts to carry out construction jobs in the town.

The pilot project was carried out by the Barriekneal Corporation on behalf of
the Aboriginal community, with very little assistance from either DEET or
ATSIC regional staff. The DEET and ATSIC central office monitoring report,
based on a visit to Lightening Ridge in November 1991 eight months into the
pilot project, was initially critical of the project, since virtually no monthly
reports had been submitted. No draft plan had been prepared.

Discussions with Barriekneal directors and staff and with community members at a community workshop made it clear that the elements of a plan were
well understood by the community: it simply had not been written down and
documented. Since DEET and ATSIC insisted on a written plan, the Directors
asked for, and received funds to hire someone local to work on the plan full-time.

The directors saw the pilot planning project as an opportunity to review the
corporation's operations and to develop a plan and strategies for future activities.
A respected community member and voluntary training co-ordinator was hired.
He used the four-step model as a guide, and, working with directors, staff, and
the community, wrote up a plan. Regrettably, the only copy of the plan has gone
missing. Since the Barriekneal group know their own goals, projects and
strategies they are continuing to implement their plan. Without a written plan,
external agencies cannot use the Lightening Ridge Aboriginal community plan
in their own planning of support to the community.

Commentary
The regional agencies do not seem to have been ready for the community
development planning pilot. However, the agencies' hands-off approach
enabled the Lightening Ridge pilot to develop at its own pace, and in its own
way. Agency documents indicate, though, that this was not the result of a
deliberate and planned strategy.

The Barriekneal Corporation in Lightening Ridge has strong and effective
leadership, a respected Board of Directors, and staff with skills and experience.
Once provided with the funds and guidance from the four-step model, it was able
to work with its own capable local facilitator. The ATSIC report took the view
that: 'the nature of the process is not as vital to the success of any community
planning process as the acceptance of the process by the community' (ATSIC,
1992). It could also be argued that the Barriekneal Corporation and Aboriginal
community of Lightening Ridge were 'ready' to make the most of strategic
planning.

Aboriginal agenda or agency agenda?
Aboriginal leaders and the federal and state governments in Australia agree on
the need for community-level planning. There is, however, little consensus on
what it should be aiming to achieve or about how it can be done better. The
purpose of this review has been to learn from some recent experiences.

The first question to pose is: 'What was the impact of the planning projects on
participating communities?' West Kimberley CDU client communities continue
to seek planning support from the CDUs. Staff and community training are

proceeding. If demand is a measure of success, then the CDUs are successful. Insecurity and insufficiency of funding limit what the CDUs can do.

Community response to the DEET–ATSIC pilot projects was variable. Planning has been positive for the Aboriginal people of Lightening Ridge. Yarrabah is no better placed after its participation than before. Lamboo-Gunian and Ngukurr are, arguably, worse off since expectations were raised and not fulfilled. The legacy of the federal community development planning pilots is largely negative. As ATSIC's community and regional planning programmes get under way this should be cause for very careful consideration of how the agency might best support local-level planning by Aboriginal people.

The federal agencies eventually recognized several lessons from their participation in the Aboriginal community-planning pilot scheme. Both DEET and ATSIC were forced to acknowledge that agency staff have neither the skills nor the time to be effective on-the-ground facilitators of community development planning of either type. ATSIC has shifted to a different model of assistance to community planning: one of providing funding to communities to hire consultants to prepare plans. Few consulting firms have the requisite combination of technical expertise in planning, expertise in community development and facilitation, and knowledge and experience of Aboriginal communities. In rare cases, where local educational institutions provide a combined planning and training service, communities are able to gain access to both services (see Dale, 1992, for a review of the Alice Springs Open College programme).

Co-ordination and co-operation between agencies is easy to speak of, and difficult to achieve. Neither DEET nor ATSIC had put in place mechanisms to encourage co-ordination or co-operation, beyond occasional joint workshops and regional office meetings. Although the agencies have abandoned the idea of joint delivery of a planning service the need for agency co-ordination is as urgent as ever. Overlapping and often confused federal–state jurisdiction with respect to services to Aboriginal communities demands Aboriginal, state and federal co-operation. Internal mechanisms which might prove more effective than those currently in place would involve rewards for co-ordination, and negative feedback and disincentives for lack of co-operation. Agencies might consider reviewing and revising individual staff and office performance indicators to provide such incentives.

The DEET–ATSIC pilot project case studies provide ample demonstration of the different positioning of each Aboriginal community: different positioning which affects the ability of the community to make use of more formalized planning. Each, given opportunity, will develop a vision of its future, and goals, which reflects its unique history, political and organizational structure, social composition, and cultures. Despite the recurring desire or expectation within government agencies that there must be a standard model for community development planning, which, if used by people with the required skills, and carefully followed, will be an effective planning process and produce plans usable both by the community and by agencies working with the community, there is a gradually growing recognition that this is not just unrealistic, it is counterproductive.

There is, however, little indication that ATSIC or other agencies are themselves planning how to be responsive and supportive to the community plans which are being produced, beyond accepting the notion of negotiation with the community around proposed projects.

The concept of negotiation remains problematic. The prevalent operational model of Aboriginal community planning by short-term consultants includes broader community participation than was formerly the custom. Nevertheless, it does not provide the consistent long-term support expansion of the knowledge and skills base, sustained training of community members and leaders, and commitment to Aboriginal empowerment that is required for effective Aboriginal negotiation of a community plan.

The West Kimberley project affords one model which addresses some of the limitations of other, government-driven models, because it links overall plan with training, and community participation with Aboriginal empowerment. The CDUs provide the institutional base for long-term support to communities. As indigenous Aboriginal organizations, they are also better positioned than government agencies to be in a relationship of trust with their client communities. There are also indications that they are the leading edge for Aboriginalization of the process of community development planning.

Perhaps the most significant lesson of the two sets of case-studies is the way they illustrate different agendas for community development planning—cost-efficient and effective programme and service delivery, albeit with more community participation, or development of peoples' capacity to get things done and exercise some control and direction over their lives. The different agendas are underpinned by conceptions of an Aboriginal future which are not necessarily compatible. Community development planning is, therefore, set within that paradigm muddle and is part of it.

Putting either conception of Aboriginal community development planning into practice demands sets of skills, processes and institutional supports, few of which are presently in place either in government agencies or in Aboriginal organizations. Establishing viable Aboriginal organizations (that is, organizations which use indigenous models and processes, are directed and staffed by Aborigines, and fulfil Aboriginal agendas) is one challenge. Establishing government systems which enable rather than constrain Aboriginal organizations is another. And finding whether the agendas for community development planning can be functionally linked is a third.

Notes

1. For explorations of the meanings attached to the word 'community' see Toennies (trans. 1957), Hillery (1959, 1968), and Minar and Greer (1969) among many others. Four distinguishable, though related, types of community are: a) the geographic community, or community of locality; b) the community of common bond, people who share something which is inherent, such as Aboriginality or gender; c) the community of common interest, the community of voluntary association around common goals and concerns; and d) the community of formal politics and administration. Perkson's provocative exploration of the notion of 'plastic words' is pertinent (Perkson, 1993). The effects of expert definitions of community may, as Perkson suggests in his theory of 'plastic words', be the removal of the texture of the local, the historic and the personal. Those who have experienced community, who have lived it, may re-evaluate what they regard as community through the eyes of the expert, not through their own. Thus they lose the power of definition. By naming and defining community, scholars, professionals and governments remove it from having meaning in the local idiom, and invest it with multiple, generalized and, to some, increasingly meaningless interpretations (my thanks to USRPD graduate student Tamsyn Rowley for bringing the idea of 'plastic words' to my attention and for her valuable short paper on concepts of community).
2. The Community and Regional Planning Section of ATSIC Canberra Regional Support

Branch now has responsibility for administering the community and regional planning programmes. In June 1992 it began a belated and much-needed review. I was engaged to review the approaches being taken to community and regional planning by selected ATSIC regions and regional offices across northern Australia. I suggested that review of the north Australia pilots should be a component. There was widespread recognition that several of the pilot projects had not gone at all well, though there was much to learn from them. Since the pilots had rapidly been overtaken by ATSIC regional council planning and by the community planning programme, I agreed to base my review on documents, interviews with agency staff and interviews, where possible, with community leaders, rather than engage community members in yet another externally driven agenda of evaluation. Lack of broadly based community input is a limitation of the pilot project component of the consultancy reviews (Wolfe, 1992). In addition to reviewing the government initiatives, I also reviewed a small number of plan-making and planning training programmes, of which the West Kimberley project was one.

References

ATSIC (1991), *Framework for Community Development Planning by Aboriginal and Torres Strait Islander Communities*, Canberra: ATSIC.

ATSIC (1992), *Report on Visit to Bourke Regional Office Concerning Community Development Planning*, Regional and Community Planning Section, Regional Support Branch, Canberra: ATSIC.

Chapman, B. (1990), *Report on Aboriginal and Torres Strait Islander Commission Aboriginal Employment Development Policy*, National Workshop, Alice Springs.

Dale, A. (1991), *Aboriginal Access to Land Management Funding and Services: Case Studies: Kowanyama, Aurukun, Woorabinda and Trelawney*, Division of Environmental Studies, Brisbane: Griffith University.

Dale, A. (1992), *The Northern Territory Open College Community Development Planning Programme: An Independent Evaluation*, Northern Territory: Department of Employment, Education and Training.

Elderton, C. (1991), *Discussion Paper on 'Planning' in Aboriginal Affairs*, North Australia Development Unit (NADU), Darwin: Department of Social Security.

Fleras, A. (1992), *Managing Aboriginality: Canadian Perspectives, International Lessons*, Paper presented at the Canadian Studies Conference, New Zealand.

Fleras, A. and Elliott, J. (1992), *The Nations Within: Aboriginal–State Relations in Canada, the United States and New Zealand*, Oxford: Oxford University Press.

Flick, B. (1992), *Country, People, Planning and Empowerment: A Model of Community Empowerment and Planning*, Broome, W.A.: Mamabulanjin Community Development Unit.

Gerritsen, R. (1982), 'Blackfellas and Whitefellas: The Politics of Service Delivery to Remote Aboriginal Communities in the Katherine Region', in Loveday P (ed.), *Service Delivery to Remote Communities*, Darwin: North Australia Research Unit, Australian National University.

Hillery, G. (1959), 'A Critique of Selected Community Concepts', *Social Forces* (37), 237–42.

Hillery, G. (1968), *Communal Organizations: A Study of Local Societies*, Chicago: University of Chicago Press.

Johnston, E. (1991a), *National Report: Overview and Recommendations, Royal Commission into Aboriginal Deaths in Custody*, Canberra: AGPS.

Johnston, E. (1991b), *Review of the Training for Aboriginals Programme*, Canberra: DEET and ATSIC.

Kimberley Land Council and Waringarri Resource Centre (1991), *The Crocodile Hole Report: Report of the Conference on Resource Development and Kimberley Aboriginal Control*, Derby W.A.: Kimberley Land Council.

Lane, P. (1991), *East Kimberley Community Planning Pilot Project: Report*, July, DEET.

Lea, D. and Wolfe, J. (1993), *Community Development Planning and Aboriginal Control*, Discussion Paper 14, Darwin: North Australia Research Unit, Australian National University.

Leverage, V. with Lea, D. (1993), *Takeback: Planning for Change in Aurukun*, Darwin: North Australia Research Unit.

McCauley, D. (1990), *Community Building Working Framework*, Fitzroy Crossing, W.A.: Marra Worra Worra Aboriginal Resource Centre.

Miller Report (1985), *Report of the Committee of Review of Aboriginal Employment and Training Programmes*, Canberra: AGPS.

Minar, D. and Greer, S. (1969), *The Concept of Community: Readings with Interpretations*, Chicago: Aldine Publishing Company.

Perkson, G. (1993), 'Plastic Words', on *Ideas*, a Canadian Broadcasting Corporation programme, Toronto: CBC.

Pollard, D. (1988), *Give and Take: The Losing Partnerships in Aboriginal Poverty*, Sydney: Hale and Iremonger.

Ross, K. and Elderton, C. (1991), *Remote Area 'Community': Myth, Legend or Convenient Generalization*, North Australia Development Unit, DSS, Darwin, Paper presented at the 2nd Australasian Conference on Rural Social Welfare, Kalgoorlie, WA.

Rowse, T. (1992a), 'The Royal Commission, ATSIC and Self-Determination: A Review of the Royal Commission into Aboriginal Deaths in Custody', *Australian Journal of Social Issues*, 27(1), 153–72.

Rowse, T. (1992b), *Remote Possibilities: The Aboriginal Domain and the Administrative Imagination*, North Australia Research Unit, Darwin: Australian National University.

Sanders, W. (1990), 'Reconstructing Aboriginal Housing Policy for Remote Areas: How Much Room to Manoeuvre', *Australian Journal of Public Administration* 49(1).

Sheldon, B. (1991), *Community Development Planning*, unpublished draft paper, Cairns: ATSIC.

Smith, B. (1989), *The Concept of 'Community' in Aboriginal Policy and Service Delivery*, NADU Occasional Paper No. 1, North Australia Development Unit, DSS, Darwin.

Smith, L. G. (1982), 'Mechanisms for Public Participation in Normative Planning in Canada', *Canadian Public Policy* 8, 561–72.

Smith, L. G. (1993), *Impact Assessment and Sustainable Resource Management*, London: Longman.

Standing Committee on Aboriginal Affairs (1989), *A Chance for the Future: Training Skills for Aboriginal and Torres Strait Islander Community Management and Development*, Canberra: AGPS.

Standing Committee on Aboriginal Affairs (1990), *Our Future Our Selves: Aboriginal and Torres Strait Islander Community Control, Management and Resources*, Canberra: AGPS.

Stohr, W. and Frazer Taylor, D.R. (1981), *Development From Above and Below: The Dialectics of Regional Development Planning*, New York: Wiley.

Tatz, C. (1974), *Aborigines, Political Options and Strategies*, Paper delivered at the Institute of Aboriginal Studies Biennial Conference, 1974.

Toennies, F. (1957), *Community and Society (Gemeinschaft and Gesellschaft)*, trans. Loomis, C.P., East Lansing: Michigan State University Press.

West Kimberley Community Development Planning and Training Project (1990), 'Stop: Listen': *Final Submission from the Project Steering Committee*, West Kimberley Project Steering Committee, Derby.

Wolfe, J. (1988), 'Native Experience with Integrated Community Planning: Promise and Problems', in Dykeman, F. (ed.), *Integrated Rural Planning and Development*, Sackville, N.B.: Mount Allison University.

Wolfe, J. (1989), 'Approaches to Planning in Native Canadian Communities: a Review and Commentary on Settlement Problems and Effectiveness of Planning Practice', *Plan Canada,* 19(2), 63–79.

Wolfe, J. (1992), *Aboriginal Development Planning in Northern Australia: ATSIC District Reports*, prepared for the Community and Regional Planning Unit, Regional Support Branch, Canberra: ATSIC.

Wolfe, J. (1993a), *Whose Planning, Whose Plans? The DEET–ATSIC Aboriginal Community Development Planning Pilot Scheme*, Discussion Paper 15, North Australia Research Unit, Darwin: Australian National University.

Wolfe, J. (1993b), *The ATSIC Aboriginal Community Development Planning Programme in Northern Australia: Approaches and Agendas*, Discussion Paper 16, North Australia Research Unit, Darwin: Australian National University.

Wolfe-Keddie, J. (1994), *Sustaining Aboriginal Community Development Planning: Case Studies of Non-Governmental Approaches*, Discussion Paper, North Australia Research Unit, Darwin: Australian National University.

15 Yolngu *rom*: Indigenous knowledge in north Australia

*IAN HUGHES**

The setting

THE BAWINANGA REGION is part of the oldest unbroken cultural tradition in the world. Economic activity is traced back to the Djanggawul sisters who taught hunting and gathering techniques in the Dreamtime, and archaeologists have dated edge-ground stone axes from the region to 20000 years ago (Isaacs, 1980). It covers about 26000 square kilometres of Aboriginal land on Australia's northern coast. Maningrida, the only town, is at the mouth of the Liverpool River. By air the town is 370 kilometres from Darwin and the four-wheel-drive track is open only during the dry season. The region lies in what has been called 'remote', 'traditional' and 'colonial' Australia (Altman and Nieuwenhuysen, 1979: 22). The indigenous people who live there call themselves 'Yolngu'.

The region has a tropical monsoonal climate. Europeans identify two seasons, the Wet from November to April, and the Dry from May to October. Yolngu recognize six seasons, which influence the annual cycle of economic and social activity (Altman, 1987: 25). The physical environment is varied and rich in fauna and flora. The Arnhem Land Plateau and the coastal plain have different ecosystems. The plateau, generally above 80 metres, has woodlands, savanna grasslands and mixed scrub. The coastal plain is varied, supporting areas of open forest, grassland and scrub, seasonal flood plains, sedge lands and swamps, coastal forest and mangrove scrub. This varied ecosystem provides a wide range of plant and animal species and other resources, which are used by hunter–gatherers.

Yolngu relationship with the land is grounded in a complex spiritual association established in the Dreamtime when the world was created and all became 'one flesh—one spirit—one country—one Dreaming' (Stanner, 1979: 129). Aboriginal people 'move not in a landscape but in a humanized realm saturated with significance' (Stanner, 1979: 131). The story of Yolngu people is written in the land. The land supports and nurtures them as a mother. As they visit each place, they participate in the history, meaning, power and significance of each location.

Yolngu *rom*

The Yolngu word '*rom*' may be translated as indigenous knowledge, and is also the name of a ritual bringing reconciliation after a separation (Wild, 1986). *Rom* does not frame historical experience as progressively unfolding development,

* Ian Hughes is qualified in Social Work and Community Development, and has a Master of Development Studies Degree from Deakin University. He teaches in the Aboriginal Community Development Programme in the Faculty of Health Sciences at the University of Sydney, and is currently engaged in action research in community development in health with indigenous Australians.

but as the working out of an unchanging law known as the Dreaming, which puts opposed or separated elements into mutual interdependence.

Rom emphasizes mutual interdependence and adaptation. Unlike Western notions of individuality, Yolngu knowledge is expressed in terms of complementary pairs which come into interdependent relationships, like the salt water and fresh water which mix at a particular place in the river. What Yolngu know about the salt and fresh water has meaning and reality at two levels, 'the outside view and the inside view. The outside view is the everyday experience . . . this understanding occurs when we actually touch, smell and taste things . . . The inside view . . . is the intellectual and abstract interpretation' (Yunupingu, 1991: 101–2). There are deeper levels of inside knowledge which are arcane or secret. An example of outside knowledge is a stomach ache experienced as pain. The doctor's diagnosis is inside knowledge informed by scientific theory, and the traditional clever man may have inside knowledge of sorcery causing the pain.

A key element in Yolngu *rom* is the mutual dependency of two moieties *Yirritja* and *Dhuwa*. Knowledge of *Yirritja* and *Dhuwa* is difficult to express in words, but is encoded as kinship relationships. *Yirritja* and *Dhuwa* are interdependent classes. Animal and plant species, natural phenomena and some manufactured goods are members of one moiety or the other, and cannot change. Salt-water crocodiles are *Dhuwa*, and fresh-water crocodiles are *Yirritja*, some places are *Dhuwa*, and other natural features are *Yirritja*, *Dhuwa* men marry *Yirritja* women, and so on. The lived experience of kinship is the expression of *rom*, 'like language is to knowledge' (Yunupingu, 1991: 98).

If lived kinship is like language, the land is the library in which it can be read. What Stephen Muecke (Benterrak *et al.*, 1984) has called 'reading the country' is a process of deriving meanings from features of the landscape, which have been inscribed there through discursive practices which are elements of a living cultural tradition. Those who have become literate in this system of symbols are able to re-tell the stories which are inscribed in particular locations. 'The dreaming is not a set of beliefs which is being lost because it is no longer valid, it is rather a way of talking, of seeing, of knowing' (Benterrak *et al.*, 1984: 14). The successful use of land in this system of knowledge depends on proper relationships between interdependent elements, and these relationships are expressed, or coded, in terms of kinship with the land.

Members of two clans, one *Yirritja* and the other *Dhuwa*, are related to each piece of land, and to each other. An *Yirritja* place is 'father country' to members of the *Yirritja* clan, who are called 'owners', and 'mother country' to the *Dhuwa* clan, who are called 'managers', and have responsibilities to look after it. The owners must ensure that the songs, stories and dances which are handed down from the Dreamtime are correctly performed, and instruct the managers in their duties. The managers are owners of another, *Dhuwa*, piece of land on which they control hunting and food-gathering rights. Although they do not own the hunting rights over country which they manage, they are permitted to hunt there. The land has been transformed through the activities of hunter–gatherers. The greatest effects have been produced through the use of fire (Jones, 1969; Lewis, 1982). In Arnhem Land the firing of the bush by managers during the dry seasons is a ritual obligation to the land, a decisive part of the economy, and a key element in caring for country. 'The fires spread rapidly through the tall dry grass to the bases of the trees, and their ecological effects are maintenance of the open parkland appearance and inhibition of the spread and abundance of non fire-resistant species' (Jones, 1969: 226). Firing removes undergrowth for easier travelling, kills snakes, reveals lizards and other species for easier hunting, or drives larger animals towards hunters and regenerates eucalypt leaves, edible ferns, bracken and grasses, making them available for human and animal consumption. After the first rains hunters return to burnt areas for kangaroos and other game attracted by fresh shoots. Repeated firings, in conjunction with practices such as replanting of tubers, increased the quantity of food produced in a given area over the years, leading Jones (1969) to dub the practice 'fire-stick farming'. The tradition of annual burning continued for thousands of years, with little interruption until after the Second World War.

Development

Concepts of development from simple to complex forms are closely related to the Idea of Progress (Nisbet, 1980), a central idea of Western civilization. 'Assumptions about the development of complexity have become a kind of master discourse running through European social theory' (Miller, Rowlands and Tilley, 1989: 18) which has imposed constraints and closures on the analysis of social change. In discussions of Aborigines the assumption of development from an undifferentiated, stateless social formation to participation in the institutions of an advanced capitalist welfare state assumes a 'self-referential and reverential' (Miller, Rowlands, and Tilley, 1989: 18) ideological importance, which has become part of the self-definition of non-indigenous Australians (King and McHoul, 1986; Lattas, 1987). Rowlands has argued that 'the simple to complex meta-narrative served a dominant world order' (Rowlands, 1989: 38) by separating out in time what is experienced as aspects of contemporary reality. Discourse on Aboriginal development conceptually relegates aspects of present cultural diversity to a hypothetical past. This denial of the contemporary relevance of indigenous culture is an act of political dominance. Rowlands (1989) argues that the concept of development is not ideologically or politically neutral, but has the effect of concealing the politics of domination behind a facade of neutral science.

In 1957 the town of Maningrida was established as a government settlement, and grew rapidly to become 'the well manicured showplace for Aboriginal policies' (Stannard, 1975) with a population of 1200 by 1968. The Director of Welfare saw the long-term future of Aborigines as employment in the economic development of the Northern Territory (Giese, 1969).

The Welfare Branch, and later the Department for Aboriginal Affairs, ran a range of development projects with the primary aim of assimilating Aborigines into the capitalist economy and Western society. The largest was a forestry project, with a plantation, sawmill and extensive road works. Others included market gardening; commercial fishing; retailing; housing and service construction; and art and craft marketing (Altman, 1987: 12; Giese, 1969). They were initiated and subsidized by the government 'as a form of training against the time when these communities will be able to be self-supporting' (Giese, 1969: 124). These enterprises shared a number of characteristics (Young, 1988: 183). They were established with government funds; came under close scrutiny and tight regulation; Yolngu participation in deciding to set them up was minimal; and those which were released from direct government control were transferred to Aboriginal corporations with white managers, rather than to individual entrepreneurs or kinship groups.

Controlled annual burning had produced a forest cover dominated by fire-resistant Eucalypt species, with stands of cypress pine (*Callitris Intratropica*) varying from a few trees to two hectares. Building the town of Maningrida created a local demand for sawn timber, and a forestry project initiated in 1961 was to supply timber and provide training for Aborigines in line with the government's assimilation policy. As Aborigines were paid low wages, the economic viability of the scheme seemed assured.

A small sawmill was built and by 1963 over 100 Aboriginal people were employed in track construction and maintenance, logging, fire fighting, propagation and planting cypress pine and removal of eucalypt over-wood. By 1967 about 9000 hectares of forested land was within a road network (Haynes, 1978: 101). Within this area any fires were put out, and as a result large stands of fire sensitive cypress pine were regenerated, as well as some areas of mono-species plantation.

In 1968 a larger sawmill was built and federal legislation mandated the payment of full award wages to Aboriginal people. The number of Aboriginal people employed in forestry and saw milling fell from over 100 to about 40. To supply the new mill the land area under the control of the scheme was expanded, with increased road construction and an annual increase in the area under fire control. This expansion increasingly used machinery requiring skilled operators. The number of non-Aboriginal people employed in administration, supervision and skilled operations increased as Aboriginal training and employment declined.

As Europeans supplanted Yolngu forestry and mill workers, the extent to which local operations were governed by indigenous knowledge and practices declined. Newly arriving Europeans did not know or respect local traditions and custom. Retrenched Aboriginal workers who wished to return to subsistence hunting found the area around Maningrida hunted out, and an expanding region subject to fire controls which decreased productivity for hunting while increasing productivity for timber production. Yolngu resentment increased. Towards the end of the 1968 dry season a series of fires was lit in the protected area. Fuel had accumulated for several years, and an uncontrollable intense blaze lasted for several days. Most regenerated and many mature cypress pine trees were destroyed in about two-thirds of the protected area. Hunting in the following season was the best which had been seen for some years. This loss of timber stock led to further expansion of the fire-protection area, and employment of more Europeans who lacked local knowledge to police fire prohibition. With the loss of employment in town, some Aboriginal family groups returned to live on their clan estates, supporting themselves mainly by hunting. The number of dry-season fires increased as competition developed between traditional and introduced technologies of fire management.

In 1972 a family discovered that a forestry road built over their clan estate without their knowledge passed through and had disturbed an important dreaming site. 'This dreaming place is regarded with such awe that it is unapproachable by all but the proper owner who approaches only from the North West, in winter, burning off the grass as he goes, and singing the song of the dreaming to "make him quiet"' (Haynes, 1978: 103). Considerable resentment was caused, but the modern approach to forestry was unable to accommodate these concerns and two further sacred sites were violated by forestry machinery in the following year. Yolngu were appalled and horrified by these incidents, a situation made worse when fulfilling contracts for timber in Darwin resulted in no timber being available for local needs in 1971 and 1972.

The homeland movement

After a decade of life in town, Yolngu began to reject the hierarchical control, dependency and impersonal relationships of planned development. A trickle of families began leaving Maningrida to resume life on their clan estates about 1969. This became a flood (Department of Aboriginal Affairs, 1980; Meehan, 1979) and the population of Maningrida fell rapidly in the second half of the 1970s. By 1980, 32 permanent homeland communities with populations from five to 100 were officially recognized, as well as a number of seasonal camps. These small self-managing.communities use traditional and modern technologies to attain a standard of living higher than that available in Maningrida. Subsistence production and artefact manufacture which had been almost insignificant in the settlement (Altman, 1987: 5) represent the major economic activity on homelands, with fire-stick farming maintaining productivity. They are supplied from Maningrida with a mobile shop, visiting health workers and teachers, mail delivery and other services. The homeland movement is an assertion of the superiority of the indigenous adaptation to the ecology of this region over Western models of development.

Although the right to own land by native title was not recognized by the Australian High Court until 1992, in the Bawinanga region clans have always maintained customary rights and obligations. In 1972, for example, traditional owners refused access to Forestry Department survey parties. Later that year Prime Minister Gough Whitlam introduced the policy of self-determination 'to restore to the Aboriginal people of Australia their lost power of self-determination in economic, social and political affairs' (cited in Lippman, 1981: 71). With the promise of self-determination, frustration at Maningrida and in the Bawinanga region came to a head. Aboriginal people who had lived in self-governing local communities for thousands of years, and had been subject to internal colonialism since 1957, seized the opportunity to negotiate with the Australian Government. In June 1974 Prime Minister Whitlam with two other ministers attended a town meeting which called for indigenous control of market gardening, commercial fishing and mining exploration, as well as forestry.

The Aboriginal Land Rights Commission (Woodward, 1974) recommended that traditional owners be granted title to their land, but that forestry should only go ahead if a 99-year lease was granted to ensure access to and control of forest resources. Forestry officials did not display skills of negotiation with Aboriginal landowners, and expressed more concern over the two-million-dollars investment in the forestry project than in traditional owners' interests in the land and timber resources on which it depended. Negotiations broke down, and in August 1974 the forestry operation was suspended by Maningrida Council. In the following year a small forestry and milling project commenced, with Aboriginal management. Land-owners and managers undertook conservation work. Controlled annual burning left stands of cypress pine, and increased the food productivity of native forests. During the 1980s customary conservation practices were extended into the Kakadu National Park world heritage area. The use of fire in the traditional way is increasingly accepted in Australia, as a land-care practice which has stood the test of time.

The basis of the movement of Yolngu to clan estates was a reassertion of relationships between people, places, animals and plants which had been disrupted by planned development projects. In their homelands people follow a lifestyle in which some elements of Western culture are incorporated into a traditional structure (Meehan, 1979). This is the reverse of the situation in Maningrida, where elements of traditional culture were incorporated into a Western structure of knowledge and power. The homeland movement is a form of resistance to domination.

Yolngu conflict resolution strategies are well adapted to life on homeland estates. In Maningrida mutually suspicious clans lived under institutional arrangements imposed by an alien culture. Substance abuse and juvenile delinquency are problems out of Yolngu control in town (Alexander, Watson and Fleming, 1987), which are well controlled in the homelands (Downing, 1985; Eastwell, 1979). In town, people from nine language communities live closely together and allegations of sorcery frequently arise (see Reid, 1983). Life on clan estates provides access to ritual power.

The struggle for access to resources is also important in explaining the homeland movement and the revival of practices grounded in indigenous knowledge (Gerritsen, 1982). During the 1960s the Gunavidji-speaking traditional owners of Maningrida felt swamped by European and Aboriginal immigrants. After 1974 they gained a majority on Maningrida Council, which achieved control of the forestry scheme. They also achieved effective control of local political and economic institutions as well as town land and associated ceremony (Bagshaw, 1977). Other language communities took formal (that is, recognized by the government) occupation of clan estates, and looked to the development of villages with a modern infrastructure, as at Jimarda (Bagshaw, 1982), or for minimal levels of servicing with power to exclude modern development, as at Mormega (Altman, 1987).

Most families, living on homelands or in town, have access to cash income from the Australian Department of Social Security. This is distributed through kinship obligations (Altman, 1987) or spent on food which is shared with relatives. Real income is maximized on clan estates where family members enjoy rights to hunt, gather and participate in economic aspects of traditional ceremonies (Altman, 1987). As well as maximizing income, the move to homelands secures control of land and natural resources, enables investment in land through fire-stick farming and ceremonial activity, and assists investment in cultural capital and ritual status.

Conclusion

From 1957 to 1974 a subsidized planned development programme dominated production, distribution and consumption patterns in the Bawinanga region, and placed severe constraints on the hunter–gatherer mode of production. The population of the Bawinanga region has perhaps doubled since contact with European society, and is increasing. Average real per capita incomes may have doubled in the last 40 years, though estimates are unreliable (Altman, 1987). As Maningrida grew, population density quickly depleted food resources near Maningrida (Drysdale and Durack, 1974: 105). Fire-control regulations prohibited fire-stick farming. Meals provided from a communal kitchen tied people to the settlement (Drysdale and Durack, 1974: 115) and cut across kinship obligations of food sharing.

Development projects were imposed by representatives of Western capitalist culture, which was felt to be oppressive. Expert local knowledge of conservation practices, fire-stick farming and other techniques to maintain the ecosystem was ignored by Europeans, and fundamental differences in lifestyle and objectives were not addressed. The expectations of European supervisors cut across Yolngu obligations and responsibilities towards land and family.

The Welfare Branch used the notion of tutelage, the assumption 'that it is by being taught by whites that [Aborigines] will gain the new identity they need in the modern world' (Paine, 1977: xi). Although satisfying long-term employment was not generated for Yolngu, about 200 jobs were created for European administrators, teachers and managers. Those who 'produce, control and administer knowledge and information, that is . . . the new middle class' (Jamrozik, 1991: 19) benefited, while Yolngu found their economic, ritual and family life disrupted by imposed disciplines and techniques (Bagshaw, 1977; Borsboom and Dagmar, 1984).

Development implies change in the direction of realizing potential, but state-controlled development was not potentially present before the European conquest of Australia. Development implies continuity, but economic and political changes which have occurred in the Bawinanga region since the 1950s are discontinuous, and, though explicable after the event, were not predictable as inevitable progress. A notion that Aboriginal self-determination and autonomy have been achieved through a developmental process cannot be sustained, as autonomous Aboriginal communities have been made subject to the state. In short, the key elements of the concept of development—predictable progress, in which later states are potentially present in earlier forms, and change is essentially continuous—are not found in this case. An alternative conceptual model is needed.

In the last quarter century Yolngu have established a contemporary hunter–gatherer lifestyle under traditional leadership. The homeland movement improved the economic welfare, health and social well-being of Yolngu (Department of Aboriginal Affairs, 1980; Eastwell, 1979; Meehan and Jones, 1980; Reid, 1983) and provided a mechanism to escape the contradictions of planned development in the region.

The expression of Yolngu *rom* in the homeland movement is a rejection of imposed discontinuous change, and a successful strategy of resistance by small Yolngu communities to Western domination. The idea of development belongs to Western capitalism. Indigenous peoples have been seen as incapable of development on their own. When faced with these problems in the Bawinanga region Yolngu were able to reject planned development in favour of indigenous models. In this case they produced higher per capita incomes, a reduction in poverty, higher productivity of labour and land, greater autonomy and self-determination, improved health, an increase in cultural capital and ecological benefits. This annual burning by people with the right kinship relationship to the land is a key element, which relies on detailed indigenous knowledge of the land for its success.

References

Alexander, K., Watson, C. and Fleming, J. (1987), *Kava in the North: A Research Report on Current Patterns of Kava in Arnhem Land Aboriginal Communities*, Darwin: Australian National University, North Australian Research Unit.

Altman, J.C. (1987), *Hunter Gatherers Today: An Aboriginal Economy in North Australia*, Canberra: Australian Institute for Aboriginal Studies Press.

Altman, J.C. and Nieuwenhuysen, J. (1979). *The Economic Status of Australian Aborigines*, Cambridge: Cambridge University Press.

Bagshaw, G. (1977), *Analysis of Local Government in a Multi-clan Community.*

B.A.(Honours) Dissertation, Adelaide: Department of Anthropology, The University of Adelaide.

Bagshaw, G. (1982), 'Whose Store at Jimarda?' in P. Loveday (ed.), *Service Delivery to Outstations*, Darwin: Australian National University, North Australian Research Unit, 50–6.

Benterrak, K., Muecke, S. and Roe, P. (1984), *Reading the Country: Introduction to Nomadology*, Fremantle: Fremantle Arts Centre Press.

Borsboom, A.P. and Dagmar, H. (1984), 'Cultural Politics: Two Case Studies of Australian Aboriginal Social Movements', *Bijdragen tot de Tall-, land-en Volkunde* 1(140): 32–56.

Department of Aboriginal Affairs (1980), 'The Outstation Movement', *Aboriginal News* 3(9): 28–31.

Downing, J.H. (1985), 'Petrol Sniffing: Treat the Causes not the Symptoms', *Aboriginal Health Worker* 9(3): 38–43.

Drysdale, I. and Durack, M. (1974), *The End of the Dreaming*, Adelaide: Rigby.

Eastwell, H.W. (1979), 'Petrol Inhalation in Aboriginal Towns, Its Remedy: The Outstation Movement', *Medical Journal of Australia* 2(5): 221–4.

Gerritsen, R. (1982), 'Outstations: Differing Interpretations and Policy Implications', in P. Loveday (ed.), *Service Delivery to Outstations*, Darwin: Australian National University, North Australian Research Unit, 57–69.

Giese, H. (1969), 'Employment and Economic Advancement for Aborigines in the Northern Territory', D.E. Hutchison (ed.), *Aboriginal Progress: A New Era?* Perth: University of Western Australia Press. 108–30.

Haynes. C.D. (1978), 'Land, Trees and Man (*Gunret, Gundulk, dja Bining*)', *Commonwealth Forestry Review* 57(2): 99–106.

Isaacs, J. (1980), *Australian Dreaming: 40,000 Years of Aboriginal History*, Sydney: Lansdowne Press.

Jamrozik, Adam (1991), *Class, Inequality and the State*, Melbourne: Macmillan.

Jones, Rhys (1969), 'Firestick Farming', *Australian Natural History* 16(7): 224–8.

King, D.A. and McHoul, A.W. (1986), 'The Discursive Production of the Queensland Aborigines as Subject: Meston's Proposal', 1895, *Social Analysis* 19: 22–39.

Lattas, A. (1987), 'Savagery and Civilization: Towards a Genealogy of Racism', *Social Analysis* 21: 39–58.

Lewis, H. (1982), 'Fire Technology and Resource Management in Aboriginal North America and Australia', in N. Williams and E. Hunn (eds), *Resource Managers: North American and Australian Hunter-Gatherers*, Boulder: Westview Press, 45–67.

Lippman, L. (1981), *Generations of Resistance: The Aboriginal Struggle for Justice*, Melbourne: Longmans Cheshire.

Meehan, B. (1979), *Australian Aboriginal Outstation Movement: Return to the Past or Preparation for the Future*, Paper presented to 14th Pacific Science Congress, Khabarovsk, USSR.

Meehan, B. and Jones, R. (1980), 'The Outstation Movement and Hints of a White Backlash', in Rhys Jones (ed.), *Northern Australia: Options and Implications*, Canberra: Australian National University, Research School of Pacific Studies.

Miller, D., Rowlands, M. and Tilley, C. (eds) (1989), *Domination and Resistance*, London: Unwin Hyman.

Nisbet, R.A. (1980), *History of the Idea of Progress*, New York: Basic Books.

Paine, R. (ed.) (1977), *The White Arctic: Anthropological Essays on Tutelage and Ethnicity*, Toronto: University of Toronto Press.

Reid, J. (1983), *Sorcerers and Healing Spirits*, Canberra: Australian National University Press.

Rowlands, M. (1989), 'A Question of Complexity', in D. Miller, M. Rowlands and C. Tilley (eds) *Domination and Resistance*, London: Hyman, 29–40.

Stannard, B. (1975), 'The Word Is: Let My People Be', *The Australian*, February 11.

Stanner, W.E.H. (1979), *White Man Got No Dreaming: Essays 1938–1973*, Canberra: Australian National University Press.

Wild, S.A. (ed.) (1986), *Rom: An Aboriginal Ritual of Diplomacy*, Canberra: Australian Institute of Aboriginal Studies.
Woodward, A.E. (1974), *Aboriginal Land Rights Commission Second Report*, Canberra: Australian Government Publishing Service.
Young, E.A. (1988), 'Aboriginal Economic Enterprises: Problems and Progress', in D. Wade-Marshall and P. Loveday (eds) *Contemporary Issues in Development*, Darwin: Australian National University, North Australian Research Unit.
Yunupingu, B. (1991), 'A Plan for Ganma Research', in *Aboriginal Pedagogy: Aboriginal Teachers Speak Out*, Geelong: Deakin University Press.

16 Community development among the New Zealand Maori: The Tainui case

TOON VAN MEIJL*

IN THE EARLY 1970s a power station was erected in the midst of a number of Maori settlements at Huntly in New Zealand. One of these Maori communities is the home of the head of the Maori King Movement and the leadership of the confederation of tribes in the wider region. The local Maori have resided in the area for about three hundred years. Twenty years ago they were still relatively isolated from mainstream life in European-dominated New Zealand. In consequence, they experienced the building of the power station as a tremendous interference with their cultural autonomy. They expressed their anxiety in public and demanded a compensation settlement from the government authorities responsible for the power station.

Initially the government was reluctant to listen to the Maori people, but soon they were forced to enter into negotiations. The relative success of the negotiations for the local Maori communities sparked off an internal review of political, economic and cultural aspirations. The entire confederation of tribes in the area decided to embark on a development course to improve Maori living standards. Tribal organizations were redefined as development agencies in order to manage and implement development autonomously, as well as to re-acquire some of the control which had been lost in the course of colonial history. In this chapter I document the emergence of Maori tribal strategies for development in the course of the 1980s in some detail. This discussion raises all the issues characteristic of the relationship between indigenous peoples and the nation–state. However, I begin with a brief sketch of the historical background of the Maori population of Huntly.

The Maori population of Huntly

Huntly is the centre of a large farming area and serves a wide region of rural villages in the Waikato region. The majority of thc population of Huntly itself, however, is employed in the coal-mines and associated industries. Huntly has been a place of coal-miners ever since it became established as a town for European settlers in the course of the nineteenth century.

In the late 1960s between 40 and 45 per cent of the labour force was employed in the mines or in coal-related industries (Stokes, 1978: 5). The growth of the town's population had, however, stabilized at around 5000 people, and the local economy was also stagnating. Planning for the construction of a power station at Huntly was therefore welcomed by the town's shopkeepers and tradesmen. In 1972 the Power Planning Report recommended the construction of a 1000 megawatt coal gas-fired station at Huntly. Government approval was given in

* Toon van Meijl conducted fieldwork among the Tainui Maori people in New Zealand from October 1982 until August 1983, and from September 1987 until December 1988. Currently he is a postdoctoral research fellow of the Royal Netherlands Academy of Arts and Sciences, and also Academic Secretary of the Centre for Pacific Studies.

August 1973 and site construction works began two months later. In the early 1980s permanent station staff, together with service organization staff and families, added over 2000 to Huntly's population (Ministry of Energy, 1986).

While the Huntly power station has boosted the local economy to some extent, it has also had a significant impact on the natural and socio-cultural environment. The station's cooling water, for example, is drawn from the Waikato River and when discharged back into the river it produces a plume of warmer water which kills all the fish until it cools by mixing with more water two kilometres downstream. In addition, exhaust gases are dispersed through the station's two double-flue chimneys, each 150 metres high. The chimneys can be seen throughout the entire Huntly district, but they utterly dominate, visually and audibly, the Maori communities in the vicinity of the power station. As giants on top of a monstrous building they symbolize the drastic changes in the lives of the Maori people of Te Kauri and Kaitimu, and, above all, Waahi Pa, the principal settlement of all regional tribes.

Waahi Pa is a Maori settlement of special significance. It functions not only as the focus of the community life of the Ngaati Mahuta and its associated sub-tribes of Ngaati Whawhakia and Ngaati Kuiarangi, but also as a nexus for all Tainui tribes and beyond who are associated with the Maori King Movement or *Kingitanga*. Waahi Pa is the home of the 'paramount family' (*kaahui ariki*) of the movement led by the present Maori Queen, Dame Te Arikinui Te Ata-i-rangi-kaahu. The *Kingitanga* was established in opposition to the imminent threat of colonial domination in the late 1850s (see below). At present the movement is primarily supported by the Tainui tribes.[1] Tainui is a loosely structured confederation of tribes whose ancestors reached the land of the 'long white cloud' (*Aotearoa*) on the same canoe from eastern Polynesia between 1000 and 1500 years ago.

Historical records give little indication of when Waahi Pa was actually settled, although the main sub-tribe Ngaati Mahuta does have a long history of attachment to the area. During the early 1800s Ngaati Mahuta emerged as a leading (sub-)tribe of the Waikato tribe(s) as their chief Potatau Te Wherowhero established his reputation as a paramount chief (Kelly, 1949: 428). For that reason, too, Potatau Te Wherowhero was crowned first Maori king in 1858. He became head of the Maori King Movement which was established by various tribes in order to form a political confederation against the increasing pressure to sell land to British settlers during the 1850s. The desire of settlers to acquire the apparently fertile lands in the lush valleys of the Waikato people, from which the local tribes produced most of the food supply for the capital city of Auckland during the 1840s and 1850s, conflicted with the *Kingitanga's* aim to withhold land from the market. Potatau, now, provided a focus for Maori discontent regarding the sale of land and he strengthened the resistance against it. The *Kingitanga* was consequently interpreted by many Europeans as a 'land league' to stop the progress of colonial settlement and the expansion of European society. As a result war broke out in 1860. Following the war 500 000 hectares of Waikato land were confiscated.

After the war the confiscated lands were surveyed and subsequently allocated in farms and town sections to European settlers as Crown Grants, in return for services to the military. Ngaati Mahuta and many other Waikato sub-tribes retreated south of the boundary of confiscated lands to seek refuge with their Ngaati Maniapoto allies. There the *Kingitanga* consolidated in relative isolation from European influence.

Although some 'native reserves' had been set aside in the confiscated lands, it was not until after the Maori Land Court proceedings in 1882–6 that remnants of the tribes who had fled the invading British troops returned to their tribal lands (Mahuta, n.d.: 3). They were resettled on small reserves set aside by their loyalist relatives.

Since the early 1890s Waahi Pa has been established as the main settlement of Ngaati Mahuta and the King Movement at large. King Mahuta, who was raised there, confirmed the status of Waahi as the principal settlement of the *King-itanga*. His successor, Te Rata, who held office from 1912 to 1933, lived there, as well as King Koroki who succeeded Te Rata.

Over the years Waahi Pa has retained its role as the home of the *Kingitanga* 'paramount family', although the present Maori Queen is living publicly at Turangawaewae Marae in Ngaruawahia where she also entertains her most distinguished guests. At the same time, however, she and her family continue to have residence at Waahi, preferring the privacy there. As such Waahi is to Turangawaewae as Windsor is to Buckingham Palace.

As home of the Maori Queen and focus of the Ngaati Mahuta sub-tribe, Waahi Pa is the main *marae* in Huntly. Traditionally a *marae* was the courtyard in front of an ancestral meeting-house used for community assembly. Recently this narrow meaning of *marae* has been distinguished as *marae aatea* or '*marae* proper'. The modern meaning of *marae* is frequently broadened to include the complex around the plaza, such as the meeting-house, a dining-hall, an ablution block and, in the case of Waahi Pa, various dwellings (*cf.* Metge, 1976 [1967]: 227–45; Salmond, 1975: 31–90). *Marae* are usually regarded as the final sanctuary of Maori culture (Walker, 1977 [1975]).

Waahi is not only a special *marae* because it is the home of the paramount family of the *Kingitanga*, but also because, contrary to most other *marae*, a significant community has settled on and around the *marae* site. In the area immediately surrounding the *marae* proper, 10 households, membership of which ranges from one to seven, are located. Just outside the *marae* boundaries, in the adjacent Taniwharua and Miria-te-Kakara streets, another 30 households are domiciled. Altogether approximately 300 people live near Waahi. Scattered about the streets of Huntly West are a further 30 households, while two families live in Huntly East. A small cluster of three households is located at Hukanui, north of Rakaumanga. In total, therefore, Ngaati Mahuta numbers approximately 500 people in Huntly.[2]

Although the Maori community of Waahi Pa, and the affiliated settlements at Te Kauri, Kaitimu and Te Ohaaki, constitute the *tangata whenua*, the 'people of the land' of Huntly, they by no means represent the entire Maori population of the town. Over the past four decades the Maori population of Huntly has increased from 3 per cent in 1951 (Stokes, 1978: 7), to 31.5 per cent in 1986 (Dept. of Statistics, 1986). The increase in the Maori population has been the result of a number of factors, including a high Maori birth-rate, a greater reluctance among Maori than among Europeans to move after the closure of several coal-mines, and, most importantly, an in-migration by Maori families in the 1960s from other tribal areas attracted by employment opportunities in the coal-mines and cheap housing.

In this chapter, however, I am primarily concerned with the Maori communities associated with the local *marae*, Waahi Pa especially, albeit not exclusively. Waahi Pa was closely associated with Te Kauri, Kaitimu and Te Ohaaki, and together they were distinguished from other *marae* in the Huntly region, not only because of closer sub-tribal connections, but also for political reasons.[3] In recent years Waahi Pa, Te Kauri and Kaitimu in particular, have been drawn even closer together by the construction of the power station.

Power-station effects feared

In 1973 the effects of the energy crisis began to be felt. It prompted the government to decide to hasten the start of the construction of the Huntly power station. All sections of the Huntly community expressed their concern at the rate at which the power station construction was pushed ahead. Complaints from the local population focused on two issues: availability of information and public participation in decision-making. Even the local authorities representing the community's interests felt they were not fully informed (Stokes, 1978: 52–4).

The Maori communities of Huntly were particularly angry because there had been no prior consultation with them through their *Marae* Trust or, at the (super-)tribal level, through the Tainui Maaori Trust Board, even though they had to bear the greatest disruption because of their location. The government, however, saw the Huntly Borough Council as the only administrative body with legitimate powers and rejected the Tainui Trust Board as the representative body of the Maori people to discuss their culturally specific concerns. The government's refusal to enter into separate negotiations with Maori communities seemed to be based on a distinct lack of awareness that the needs of Maori people were in any way different from the general population of Huntly.

The announcement of the construction of the power station on a site adjacent to Waahi Pa and close to the communities of Te Kauri and Kaitimu brought about an immediate reaction from the Maori people. The feared effects were outlined by Fookes (1976) and can be summarized as: the removal of Maori households from their land and relocation in Huntly borough; the breaking up of kinship groups; the loss of land and all that this symbolized to Maori people; the undermining of leadership and morale; the loss of quality of life in its social, cultural, economic and spiritual aspects; the resultant community unrest and loss of confidence in the existing social order; and a tremendous social upheaval within the entire confederation of Tainui tribes.

The more specific concerns of the Maori communities followed naturally from the fears expressed in wider terms. Three effects in particular seemed to pervade the fears of the Maori: these concerned their land, the Waikato river, which is considered a mythological ancestor, and their distinct way of life. Confusion arose even prior to the construction of the power project when flood-protection schemes were being constructed in the vicinity of Rakaumanga School, the community school, located immediately north of the site. Maori land had to be purchased for the purpose of the stop-bank and, due to its positioning, some Maori families had to be relocated in Huntly West. In submissions to the Electricity Department and the Ministry of Works (Mahuta, 1973: 6), the Maori community requested that

> where Maori families have to be relocated consideration be given to minimizing the disintegration of kinship groups by subdividing part of the buffer zone, or other Maori-owned land, for residential purposes and allocating sections on the advice of the *marae* trustees or landowners concerned.

However, the stop-bank was built for the Waikato Valley Authority and the Raglan County Council, and, according to the Electricity Department, its construction took place completely independently of the power project site investigations (Meade-Rose 1980: 5). The Maori community viewed this differently and saw all administrative bodies as 'government' and anything associated with it as imposed from outside. They did not consider the different responsibilities of each government department as relevant. Eventually the flood-protection works opposite Rakaumanga School entailed the relocation of eight households. Thus Kaitimu community was broken up physically though with the construction of Kaitimu *marae* in the 1980s a relatively strong sub-tribal identity was still in existence. Some compensation was given to the families which had to move and this was partly invested in the upgrading of the community facilities and the building of an ancestral meeting-house.

When preliminary foundation investigation works started on the proposed power-station site, the commencement of construction had not yet been formally announced. At this point Maori concerns became even more concrete. Fears were expressed that three burial sites (*urupaa*) would be desecrated. These were only allayed after an agreement was reached during protracted negotiations about the lease of land. The power project leased approximately 27 hectares from the Maori Queen during the construction stages for equipment, storage and materials assembly. To the north of the leased land adjacent to the power site was a farm which provided food crops for household use and ceremonial functions of the *Kingitanga*. A Crown offer to purchase the farm was declined by the Queen on the grounds that she did not wish to see further alienation of Maori land (Stokes, 1977:19). However, an important source of agricultural resource was lost and more food had to be bought at local shops. It was also claimed that the land lease caused loss of *mana* for the Queen and the entire movement.

When construction work for the power station began, the Education Board decided to close the Rakaumanga School. Rakaumanga had functioned as a community school since the late 1800s and the Maori people regarded it as 'their' school (ibid.: 18). The school grounds also provided recreational facilities for the community in the form of tennis courts, swimming-pool and playing-field, the latter being used by the Taniwharau Rugby League Football Club as their practice ground. Because of the pressure from the community to keep the school open, it was instead moved from its original site to a new location in Huntly West. During the transition period, classes were held temporarily in the meeting-house at Waahi Pa for several months in 1974. Initially the change in the nature of Rakaumanga School was felt as a great loss. Parents did not feel the same attachment to and responsibility for the new school, which drew pupils from a wider area. However, when the school became officially bilingual in 1984 parental pride and involvement increased again (Harrison, 1987).

The Waikato River and flood-protection schemes

The anxiety about the potential impact of the power station diminished during the course of its construction. At the same time it became clear that the Maori community did not object to the establishment of the power project as such. Only its positioning was seen as a symbolic representation of further intrusion on the Maori way of life by government.

The surrounding *marae* sought involvement on levels as high as the Town and Country Planning Appeal Board. The Maori community lodged an appeal against the granting of water rights to the Electricity Department by the National Soil and Water Conservation Authority in 1973 (Stokes, 1977: 20). Detailed evidence included concern at the effect of hot-water discharges on the movements of eels in the Waikato River and Waahi Creek, and the effect on sources of customary food such as eels, shellfish, fresh-water crayfish, whitebait, catfish, carp, fresh-water mullet and watercress, which Waikato tribes had traditionally obtained from the river. In addition, more general concerns about the disruptive effects of construction were expressed.

The importance, not only of the land, but also the river was summed up in the evidence. The physical as well as spiritual importance of the Waikato River was emphasized. All important visitors to the *marae* used to be landed on the river bank opposite the *marae*. Visiting families landed by canoe up the small Waahi Creek. The river was said to represent their tribal *mana*, their food basket and their living link with their ancestors. Hence the projected use of river water by the power station raised a great deal of resentment among the Maori people. For example, 'Who wants an ancestor that is an open sewer?' (quoted in Stokes 1977: 20).

The conflict about the Waikato river was exemplified in the planning of the flood-protection schemes. The power-station site and Waahi Pa were subject to flooding and a scheme was proposed to prevent inundation. The power-station site was raised in 1973–4 but disagreement followed when the Waikato Valley Authority claimed that this would not stop the flooding of Waahi *marae* (Meade-Rose, 1980: 9). It was decided to build a flood-gated culvert at the entrance of the Waahi Creek to prevent water running up its stream. Along the contours of Waahi Pa a stop-bank was planned to pass right across the *tapu* grounds of the *marae aatea*, the courtyard in front of the ancestral meeting-house Taane-i-te-Pupuke. In designing this, European engineers showed neither knowledge nor consideration for Maori attitudes towards the river. The community did not want to be separated from 'their' river by a stop-bank, particularly because the flood-control works were believed to be only necessary to protect the power station. In order to avoid flooding of the *marae*, the Waahi community wanted to raise the surface instead. Various efforts were made by the *marae* community before action was taken by the government.

Difficulties with communications between local Maori and government did not come to an end until the then-prime minister visited the Coronation celebrations in 1977. In his speech, Robert Muldoon recognized the *Waahi Marae* Trust and the Tainui Maaori Trust Board for the first time as representative organizations of the local Maori communities when he stated that as statutory authorities they were eligible for a share of the development levy. Under New Zealand law, developers engaged in a project costing NZ$100 million or more must contribute 0.5 per cent to a social fund to meet the consequential increased costs of servicing the area and establishing cultural and recreational amenities. Only after this announcement was made did negotiations gather momentum.

Redevelopment of the *marae*

After a period of five years a compensation settlement of an estimated NZ$1.2 million was agreed on and this included flood-protection works, the altering of waterways, the creation of buffer zones and landscaping. The Waahi Creek next to the *marae* was redirected; the *marae* site was lifted; facilities were upgraded. Five houses had to be relocated, four of which were built anew, with trees and shrubs planted around each dwelling. The Maori Queen's house and garden were reconstructed at the expense of the Waikato Valley Authority and the Raglan

County Council (Meade-Rose, 1980: 10). The meeting-house remained intact after it was lifted together with the surface of the *marae* proper. However, a new dining hall and a community lounge were constructed to the design of an architect with the community providing voluntary labour. The savings created by using their own labour allowed the *marae* to build a number of pensioner flats. The Ministry of Energy reimbursed the *marae* NZ$560 000 to cover the cost of refurbishing. An additional NZ$350 000 was obtained by a bank overdraft to complete redevelopment (Mahuta and Egan, 1981a: 13).

Part of the compensation settlement provided for the laying of a football field behind the *marae* and the upgrading of the Taniwharau Football Club rooms. The Taniwharau Rugby League Club was founded by King Te Rata's brother Tonga Mahuta in April 1944 and has remained the focus of sporting interest for the Maori community of Huntly since that time.[4] Compensation for the Taniwharau club rooms was given because the old Rakaumanga School site, where the teams used to practise, had been donated by King Koroki to the Department of Education. While the refurbishing of the *marae* was taking place, the club rooms proved a feasible alternative venue for ceremonial activities that would normally be organized on the *marae*.

All in all there were several positive outcomes of the negotiations, although the efforts of the Waahi *marae* community to persuade the government to re-site the power station were unsuccessful. Apart from the compensation received for any harmful effects as a result of the power station's location, the Waahi community was also drawn closer together. Galvanized by their experiences they realized that they had become more politically active and visible to the bureaucracy. By the same token, government and local authorities became more aware of Maori people and their distinct concerns. It was clear, to some at least, that the construction of the power station constituted a new source of grievance that would worsen unless some further discussions were embarked upon to create some future goodwill. Though the threat of activism was never made, it was Maori solidarity that motivated the development planners to negotiate. Furthermore, the Waahi community responded to the challenge by designing a plan for its own future.

A model for community development

When redevelopment of Waahi Pa was completed, the community had begun to revalue the *marae* and all it stood for as a refuge for their distinct way of life. The communal-based organization of the *marae* came to be appreciated once again and gradually a model for community development began to be formulated. A plan was designed to extend accommodation on the *marae* and increase community facilities around it. In addition, it was planned to start horticulture on the blocks of land still held in communal ownership when existing European leases on them expired. In the long term the community aspired to realize the *Kingitanga* dream of buying back as much as possible of the confiscated lands (Mahuta, 1979). Eventually, it was hoped, a revitalized Maori environment in which people could sustain a living might cause kin who had migrated to urban areas in search of employment to return to their roots.

After the initial stage of development based on the compensation settlement was completed in the early 1980s, the second stage was scheduled in more detail (Mahuta and Egan, 1981a). The construction of eight more family houses, six pensioner flats, four home units and four flats for young people was planned.

Projected community facilities involved two tennis/basketball courts, two squash courts, a swimming-pool, an adventure playground, a rugby league oval and changing sheds, a gymnasium and study libraries for senior students. As part of the economic programme of development, plans were drawn up to embark on commercial horticulture and to construct greenhouses, storage sheds for *kuumara* ('sweet potato'), cooling rooms and a workshop for vehicles and equipment (*ibid.*: 11).

It was envisaged that the costs of development would be borne by the returns from commercial horticulture. Six blocks of land totalling 852 hectares were due to come out of a long-term lease of 42 years (unsuccessful government-sponsored development schemes had been run on the land in the 1930s). The *marae* trustees also initiated other programmes to raise funds. They purchased houses adjacent to the *marae* and in nearby towns in order to mortgage them. A kiln was constructed to make earthenware crockery with Maori designs on it, and the palisades of a model *Paa* were erected. Both projects were to stimulate tourism in the area. Other funds were raised through direct donations from Waikato sub-tribes and through fundraising activities such as 'housie', card games, field days and raffles contributing altogether several hundreds of dollars per week.

A large component of the cost of the community development programme was borne by volunteer labour. In addition, the *marae* successfully used the possibilities offered by the Department of Labour to employ youths on subsidized labour schemes for community purposes over a six-month period. The Project Employment Programmes (PEP) provided the *marae* project with more than 500 temporary workers from 1978 to 1983 (Mahuta, 1983: 4). However, the *marae* never regarded the employment programmes from the viewpoint of labour only. It also offered them the opportunity to re-educate the youngsters in a *marae* environment from which they were mostly alienated. Thus Maori youths were kept off the streets while their cultural identity could be given a more positive meaning on the *marae*.

The *Huakina* model

When development of Waahi Pa was initiated many pressures were placed on the community. The *marae* people had to service debts incurred in (re-)development as well as meet increased demands to make development a success. However, for others aspiring to similar development, Waahi Pa became an exemplar and a model. Thus, a certain ambivalence underlay the feelings of the community towards the power station. On the one hand, there was still resentment against the power station and the change that had been imposed on them, but, on the other hand, there was pride in the new-looking *marae* and its up-to-date facilities.

The Waahi model first inspired a group of *marae* around Manukau Harbour south of Auckland. These *marae* undertook to investigate issues relating to development by the New Zealand Steel Company whose major steel production plant drew its raw materials from the north headland area of the mouth of the Waikato River. Their smelter was at Glenbrook and this steel mill was proposed to be expanded in 1981. The process would involve taking water from the Waikato River, discharging some treated effluent into Manukau Harbour, an increased sewerage output through oxidation ponds at Waiuku, and, finally, the mining of iron sands at Maioro and the railing of the sands to the mill, which could affect Maori land and burial sites.

The immediate response from the Maori communities in the vicinity of the Glenbrook plant was that the spiritual nature of the river and harbour were of prime concern. In the second instance, however, the expansion of the mill was acceptable on the condition that a tribal package of development would not only protect the waterways, but also boost the socio-economic welfare of the local Maori communities. The developments aspired to were all modelled after the project at Waahi Pa, and included employment opportunities, housing, small business development and education.

New Zealand Steel commissioned the Centre for Maori Studies and Research of the University of Waikato to examine the likely impact on *marae* in the area. A survey was conducted and a development programme called *Huakina* ('open the door') resulted (Mahuta and Egan, 1981b). Negotiations followed and New Zealand Steel decided to support a great deal of the package, such as the provision of material to redevelop facilities on some *marae*, the lease of land for a dairying and dry-stock farm to be developed as part of an economic base, the rent of a house serving as an administrative centre, and the employment of a co-ordinator. In addition, *Huakina* was granted a portion of the development levy which was invested in the lease of land for commercial horticulture and other *marae* projects.

The *Huakina* project began operating from the beginning of 1982. Soon after there evolved an organizational structure to meet its administrative needs. The structure consisted of a trust acting as a watchdog over the project, a management committee made up of elected representatives from each of the participating *marae*, and a number of subcommittees to assess needs in a specific area and develop programmes. The organization was supposed to create more effective cohesiveness for policy development and a greater unity for action, while each *marae* was allowed to retain its independence.

The Tainui report

Stimulated by the relative success of the Waahi Pa and *Huakina* projects, Tainui leaders decided to expand development across the Tainui region. At their request the Centre for Maori Studies and Research (CMSR) conducted a needs–resource survey in 1982. The results were published in *The Tainui Report* (1983) written by the director of the CMSR, who is a prominent Tainui leader, and a development consultant. The report contained a comprehensive inventory revealing the poor state of Tainui's human and natural resources. The bulk of natural resources appeared to be marginal lands unsuited to achieve proportional productivity other than through highly skilled management mainly by European personnel. It was argued that the land locked the people into a dependency on the allegedly expert advice from the Department of Maori Affairs that no one wanted. However, because the land was regarded as an asset of great spiritual value, it had to be retained, though it was recognized that 'a solid diet of spiritual value (would) leave one thin to the point of death' (Tainui Maaori Trust Board, 1984: 6). *The Tainui Report* proposed to use the land for tribal development through corporate financial planning, investments, marketing and training.

Education and training were seen as crucial components of any strategy to develop not only the land but the human resources of the tribe as well. A demographic survey showed that 65 per cent of the Tainui population was under the age of 25, and, so it was argued, if nothing were done to re-educate young people in the roots of their culture and develop their skills and potential for the purpose of tribal development, 'a tragedy of national proportion' (*ibid.*: 34) would be inevitable. Research indicated that the socio-economic features of the Tainui population were linked in a vicious circle of underdevelopment: low educational achievement, lower skilled jobs, high unemployment rates, low income, deprived status, low self-esteem, poor health and high crime rates. To achieve socio-economic change and to ensure the survival of a distinct culture a comprehensive crash programme of development was advocated. The ultimate objective was to regain control of their resources in order to manage their own affairs.

Planning of development commenced shortly before *The Tainui Report* was released in 1983. Major *marae* in central areas were visited and at meetings the Tainui community was advised of the results of the survey. The feelings of the people were gauged and they were generally enthusiastic about embarking on a fundamentally new course. Discussions focused on the transformation of 'government structures of organization' into 'tribal structures of organization' with the aim of facilitating tribal planning and development.

It was argued that government structures of organization had been imposed from above to eradicate tribal structures with which the government could not otherwise come to grips. The Department of Maori Affairs, for example, had been in operation since 1840, but it was said still to lack an appreciation of Maori underdevelopment, and to maintain the Maori people in a position of dependency on a complacent bureaucracy. In addition, the New Zealand Maori Council was set up as a national body to express pan-Maori points of view, but it was organized in districts cutting right across tribal boundaries and therefore never accepted by those with an operative tribal organization.

In contrast to government structures organized from the top downwards, it was argued that Maori organizational structures are built up from the bottom. They are based on kinship rather than 'governorship',[5] and they are supposed to allow people at the 'flax roots' level to retain their independence. Sub-tribal groupings, for example, appoint or elect representatives to organizations at the tribal (*iwi*) level, such as *Ngaa Marae Toopu* ('the assembled *marae*'), a platform of all Tainui *marae*, and the Tainui Maaori Trust Board. It was also claimed that all Tainui people are descendants from the crew of the same canoe, and, witness their collective gathering at the annual Coronation Anniversary Celebrations, they are still united in the Maori King Movement.[6]

Management committees and summit conferences

Based on the *Huakina* model it was now proposed to strengthen the traditional network and set up an effective organization to implement development policies. Management committees like *Huakina*, made up of representatives from various sub-tribes, would create more cohesiveness for development and its presentation to private and public sector organizations. Thus it was hoped to enhance Tainui's credibility to negotiate with central and local government about a redirection of what the leadership labelled 'negative funding' for the purpose of social and economic development. The concept of negative funding was based on the argument that hundreds of millions of dollars were spent on education, unemployment benefits, healthcare, prisons and so forth, with little or no positive returns for the Maori people. This 'recipe for disaster', it was contended, would never change the socio-economic condition of the Maori in a fundamental way.

It maintained bonds of dependency which had to be severed in order to strengthen the Maori economic base and create permanent jobs.

Between 1983 and 1988, 11 management committees were set up across the Tainui area. The number of *marae* constituting a management committee varied from one to 29. Some of the management committees were not fully operative but others were engaged in extensive programmes of business development and training, funded with government money distributed through the Tainui Maaori Trust Board.

From the outset the potential success of the Tainui development strategy depended on the goodwill of the New Zealand government to devolve some of its services and funds to the control of the tribes. The expectations, therefore, reached a high level when New Zealand had a change of government in 1984.[7] The new Labour government convened a series of summit conferences aimed both at consulting and informing the community. Following the elections an Economic Development Summit Conference was called as the country's economy had to be brought into order.

There was no doubt that Maori people were suffering the most. A larger percentage of Maori were unemployed, and the social dislocation, compounded with a loss of cultural identity, was consequently greater. Two summit conferences were called by the new government to address Maori concerns and to allow Maori people to put forward their own solution. In October 1984 the Minister of Maori Affairs convened the Maori Economic Development Summit Conference. At this *Hui Taumata* Maori people argued for two basic principles to be accepted: Maori control of Maori resources, and Maori objectives on Maori terms. The summit produced a covenant, *He Kawenata*,[8] which was to set the direction of Maori tribal development for a 10-year period. At the end of the 'decade of development', if funding had been adequate and the accountability criteria suitable for fulfilling Maori aspirations, there should be no need of any further negative funding to bring the social and economic condition of Maori on a par with mainstream New Zealand.

In March 1985 the Maori Employment caucus of *Hui Taumata* was reconvened by the Minister of Employment during the Employment Conference. This second summit further endorsed the call from Maoridom for control of resources and delivery through tribal authorities. The need to address Maori unemployment and achieve parity on all levels was discussed and it was proposed to institute special training programmes and educational incentives to continue into advanced educational institutions. A series of recommendations to this summit came from various tribal authorities which subsequently attempted to implement them in their own areas (Douglas and Dyall, 1985; Tainui Maaori Trust Board, 1985).

Mana enterprises and Maori access

Out of the summit conferences two major initiatives arose. The government introduced a programme called Mana Enterprises aimed at broadening the Maori economic base by the creation of new businesses and the expansion of existing ones. A special pool was created for funding small businesses to provide Maori people with more jobs through the development of viable Maori enterprises. Each tribal authority had the responsibility for vetting applications before they were submitted to the Board of Maori Affairs.[9] To acquire funding, usually at a flat interest rate of 5 per cent, as opposed to commercial interest rates of approximately 25 per cent, proposals had to accord with strict guidelines.

The results of Mana were rather ambivalent. Some businesses failed or did not meet the required standards of accountability for public funds, thus providing grist to the opposition and the media. In spite of all that was against Mana, however, there were also some successes. During the first two years of operation the programme received a total of NZ$26 million in government funds, numbering approximately 200 loans. By the end of 1988 the Tainui Mana Enterprises scheme funded 21 projects of which 16 were meeting financial and employment objectives. Three projects were in financial difficulty due mainly to a dramatic downturn in the economy and the lack of management skills, whereas two projects failed completely. In summary, the total amount on loan was NZ$1.92 million sustaining 52 new jobs (Tainui Maaori Trust Board, 1988: 13–14). Businesses were set up in various sectors ranging from a courier service, a lawn-mowing scheme, a laundrette, a catering service to tourism projects.

After the establishment of the Mana loan scheme the drive by the Maori people to acquire more control over their destiny continued. In 1987 the government offered a further opportunity to extend the aims of *Hui Taumata* and complement Mana objectives. The opportunity was created in job skill training and a scheme called Access was to run in tandem with Mana. Access training programmes were to replace subsidized employment schemes instituted by the previous government. The purpose of Access was to assist people who were at a disadvantage in the labour market to acquire skills to increase their chances of finding employment, thus shifting the emphasis from subsidized work to training for employment.

Access was introduced as a scheme with two delivery systems. The bulk of the budget was distributed through a general system administered by the newly installed Regional Employment and Access Councils. The REACs, as they were commonly referred to, provided a structure where decisions regarding the type and scope of training were determined by representatives of various community groupings in a particular region. Part of the Access pool funds, however, were apportioned to Maori authorities with the legal status of trust boards, incorporated societies or charitable trusts. The training programmes offered under this system were called Maori Access or Maccess.

Maccess funds, too, were made available from a special fund set up under the Board of Maori Affairs (cf. footnote 9). The budget for Maccess training was progressively increased from NZ$3.9 million in 1987 to NZ$40 million in 1988, with a budget of NZ$53 million projected for 1989. Throughout the country 590 training modules were operating with subjects ranging from computers, engineering and fibreglass construction, to sewing, music, video production and even Maori culture and Maori medicines (Earp, 1988). The Tainui Trust Board received a total of NZ$6.6 million over a period of two years. With the funding the board had been able to operate 85 modules. Positions had been offered to 505 trainees in total, 162 of whom were placed in permanent employment.[10]

Non-formal education

From the outset it has been emphasized that the success of the Tainui development strategy depends for a great deal on the education, both formal and non-formal, particularly of its young people. Maori examination successes in the formal education system are few and far between throughout New Zealand. Nationally the proportion of Maori children leaving school without any qualifications was 53.4 per cent in 1986, compared with 21.5 per cent of non-Maori, a ratio of 2.5 to 1 (Benton 1988: 349). In the Tainui area the figures are even more dismal. In Waikato only 17 per cent of Maori pupils left school with some success in the examination system, while Huntly College achieved a mere 11 per cent (Douglas 1982: 30). Employment patterns show a concentration in unskilled work, as well as high and increasing unemployment levels and thus reflect the educational tragedy.

In the Waahi community a long-standing concern about the fate of Maori students at Huntly College tied in with an anxiety about the prospect of future energy developments in the Waikato area. This must be seen against the background of the Huntly power station of which the benefits predicted for the community, such as employment for Maori people in activities associated with the power station, have largely failed to materialize because of the skilled nature of most of the jobs available. When the (then) Ministry of Energy announced further proposed Waikato energy developments in early 1983, the Tainui Maaori Trust Board was determined that involvement of local Maori people should be greater than it had been in the past. It recognized that the key to greater participation in employment of Tainui people lay in education and in training to meet the qualifications and skill requirements of jobs in the high-technology developments proposed.

One recommendation of a report to the Ministry of Energy providing a Maori perspective on the proposed Waikato energy developments was that the ministry should, in conjunction with the Departments of Labour and Education, accept responsibility for training young Maori people so that they benefited from the development process (Mahuta and Nottingham, 1984). The idea of a *marae*-based, affirmative action training programme, to train young Maori people for jobs in the energy development was accepted by the Ministry of Energy. Negotiations for the establishment of such a programme began in June 1985. A Memorandum of Understanding for the Community Training Centre was signed in May 1986. The establishment of the centre was jointly funded by the Ministry of Energy, Department of Education and Department of Labour. Premises for the Community Training Centre were erected at Waahi Pa and the centre commenced operations in November 1986. It was a new project with hitherto unique features, such as its origin, its location on a *marae*, and its philosophy (van Meijl, 1994b).

In the realm of non-formal education Waahi had previously paved new ground with successful negotiations about a preventive health programme on the *marae*. As a result of protracted debates with the Department of Health the Waahi Community Health Centre began operating from the end of 1983.

The health centre was the brainchild of a visiting medical anthropologist. After completing a six-months period of fieldwork Corinne Shear-Wood (1982)[11] concluded that considerable improvements in the health of Maori people could be attained if the strengths and acceptability of Maori forms of social organization were used. She emphasized that the *marae* constituted an invaluable adjunct to health maintenance among Maori people, and that its potential benefits were under-used by health delivery agencies. Therefore, she recommended the establishment of a minimal health facility within a Maori setting to avail of the trust and confidence Maori people experienced in such an atmosphere.

From the very beginning the philosophy of the health centre has been that health is more concerned with habits and beliefs than with disorders and disease. This viewpoint has led to the development of the centre into a place where health is taught rather than sickness treated. The two Community Health Workers attempt to build up an awareness of the importance of health-related matters, thus hoping to create a sense of self-esteem and a more positive self-image, particularly among the younger age groups. In the health awareness programmes offered the emphasis is on the reinforcement of a Maori, or rather Tainui and *Kingitanga* identity. 'Knowing who you are and where you come from' is considered an essential precondition for being healthy.[12]

Bilingual education

In addition to the foundation of non-formal educational programmes, a major objective of the Tainui development strategy concerns the attainment of equal success rates of Maori children in formal educational institutions. Part of the problem Maori pupils encounter in schools is the difference in cultural environment: 'we are brought up one way, but taught another', as one informant put it. Schools generally have a negative impact on the development of a positive sense of identity of Maori children, which is compounded by a loss of Maori language. In 1978 the New Zealand Council for Educational Research calculated that only 56 per cent of the Maori population could speak some Maori, from a few words to fluent speech. It estimated the number of native speakers at that time at 70 000 (Benton, 1979*a*, *b*). However, the general feeling was that Benton's figures were too positive. In 1989 the figure was probably down to 50 000 (Prof. Timoti Karetu, *New Zealand Herald*, 26 May 1989), that is, approximately 12.5 per cent of the Maori population, partly because many of the old people had died. This percentage of native speakers of Maori is clearly too low to maintain the language unaided even in predominantly Maori communities. Only bilingual education can possibly ensure the survival of the Maori language within the classroom (Benton, 1984).

In 1983 the Department of Maori Affairs introduced a salvage programme for the Maori language. The *Te Kohanga Reo* ('birthplace of language') programme was designed to arrest the decline in the number of Maori-speaking people by bridging the gap between the bulk of native speakers over 50 and the new generation aged 0–5 years. Since the generation of parents raising children generally lack an active command of Maori, most Maori children grow up in a predominantly English-speaking environment. Throughout New Zealand, therefore, 500 *Te Kohanga Reo* centres have been set up to offer child-care in a Maori environment where Maori is spoken all the time.

At Waahi, too, a *Te Kohanga Reo* centre was opened in 1983. It could only operate, however, through the enthusiasm of some parents who put their energy into the programme on a voluntary basis. From the outset *Te Kohanga Reo* has been understaffed and undercapitalized, compelled to run on random grants. Tutors do not earn a proper salary and depend heavily on the assistance of parents who themselves are usually far from fluent in Maori. On the other hand, not all parents can afford to send a child to *Te Kohanga Reo*. Hence more middle-class parents, of whom at least one is earning a salary, tend to be interested in sending their child(ren) to *Te Kohanga Reo*. Not infrequently, too, *Te Kohanga Reo* are simply regarded as child-care centres rather than 'language nests'. Still, most centres are completely booked up and parents have to register a long time in advance to obtain a place for their child. In absolute terms 500 centres teaching approximately 9000 children seem like a lot, but only 3 per cent of all New Zealand children have access to *Te Kohanga Reo* (*New Zealand Herald*, 7/12/1987).

More serious problems in *Te Kohanga Reo* concern the manner in which the Maori language is transmitted. In many centres children are taught Maori by rote. They are trained to respond to adult stimulus, and hardly ever to explore the environment themselves. As a consequence, if Maori is never spoken to the children in their home environment, they can only sing a song or say a prayer in Maori after two or three years' attendance. This is due, in part, to the young age of the children who as a result are bound to lose any command of Maori within six to eight weeks after they leave *Te Kohanga Reo*, unless they can move on to a bilingual primary school.[13]

However, in 1988 there were only 10 bilingual primary schools in New Zealand, plus a further dozen schools containing a bilingual unit. One of the bilingual primary schools is the Rakaumanga School in Huntly. Regarded by the Waahi community as 'their' school, particularly after it survived the construction of the power station, Rakaumanga School has become part of the larger effort of the *marae* to establish educational programmes at all levels in order to advance social and economic development of the Tainui tribes. The struggle of the politically mature community for the establishment of Rakaumanga as a bilingual school lasted from the mid-1970s until July 1984 when official approval was given (Harrison, 1987). It was yet another success of the dedicated *marae* to push an official request through political channels and expand the model for community development. And the spiral was far from approaching its end.

To ensure the Maori children of the Waahi community would maintain their command of Maori and their sense of pride in being Maori (nurtured during the years they went to Rakaumanga School), at the time of fieldwork the *marae* and the school co-operated in the deliberations to phase in a bilingual unit at Huntly College. In New Zealand there were only six high schools offering a bilingual programme, and the college at Huntly would add another unit from 1989. The college adopted an approach more sympathetic towards 'things Maori' after a new principal was appointed in 1987. In planning a bilingual unit, however, the principal and the Maori language teacher made the mistake of not consulting the community until preparations had reached an advanced stage. This tended to shatter the novel bond of confidence that was emerging between the college and the *marae*, although both were forced to re-unite in the interests of the children.

The establishment of a homework centre on the *marae* and the involvement of the college principal in running it, ameliorated the early relationship between Huntly College and the Waahi community to some extent. The homework centre was set up to improve the performance of senior college pupils and assist them in preparing for the School Certificate examinations. Students were offered not only facilities to study in a quiet environment away from the more boisterous home situation, but also additional assistance from college teachers in doing their homework. Besides an academic function the homework centre at Waahi Pa accomplished a social function as well. It involved parents in learning and functioned as a meeting ground for parents and teachers. Finally, the homework centre functioned as a place where children could gain more independence. Often pupils lived in the homework centre during examination periods. They not only worked together, but also cooked their own meals together and slept under the same roof to create an atmosphere more favourable to overcoming the unequal pass rate of Maori students in national examinations.[14]

Endowed university colleges

In 1986 the Centre for Maaori Studies and Research published *A Tainui Education Strategy*. Proceeding from this proposal the Tainui Maaori Trust Board designed plans for educational programmes at tertiary levels and proposed, among other things, to establish two autonomous Endowed University Colleges (CMSR, 1987). The idea of endowed colleges arose out of research which revealed that the University of Auckland, from which arose the University of Waikato, and the University of New Zealand before them, had been the beneficiaries of vast tracts of confiscated Maori land. The government had set aside some blocks of confiscated land as reserves, which became university endowments. Thus university education came to be founded on a great wrong, and Tainui argued that they had educated the European majority to the detriment of their own tribal members.

In addition to this, many Maori leaders endowed land to the churches for the specific purposes of establishing schools and churches to benefit their extended family and/or sub-tribe and tribe at large. As these old trust endowments came to light, it was evident that the spirit of these endowments had not been acknowledged. The benefits from these endowments had not accrued to the descendants of the donors. Instead the real beneficiaries had been the European New Zealand community.

To overcome the problem of Maori under-achievement and under-representation in universities, particularly of Tainui children, the Trust Board now proposed the creation of an Endowed College for the University of Waikato and later for the University of Auckland as a critical link in its emerging education strategy. The concept of an Endowed College was based upon the well-worn tradition of the medieval sequestered colleges with their modern counterparts in the Oxford and Cambridge University systems. Each college within the system was said to be a community complete with its own collegial environment and tutorial method of instruction. The concept was not considered to be alien to a Maori environment as the ancient *Whare Waananga* ('House of Learning', Best, 1974 [1923]) of traditional Maori society was believed to share many of the desired characteristics. The objective was to create a collegial, living environment based upon Maori cultural values and adapted to the social, educational and affective needs of Maori students. While the colleges would cater mainly for Maori students they would be open to others willing to live and learn in a bicultural setting.

As part of the broader strategy for tribal development, endowed colleges would be oriented towards human and natural resource development. Management and business skills would be emphasized as well as the skills necessary for resource development and planning, scientific reporting, monitoring and guidance, use of technology and information systems, production rather than service and cultural development rather than welfare (CMSR, 1987: 4).

While the idea for the establishment of an endowed college at Waikato has been endorsed by the University of Waikato, the issue of funding is believed to rest upon the government's willingness to address the question of compensation for lands wrongfully confiscated. Following the changes in the political climate in New Zealand in the 1980s negotiations are taking place between the government and the Tainui people about a compensation package for the confiscations, but this is not expected to be signed before the end of the century.

Future plans

At Waahi Pa there are two more projects in the pipeline, both of which are in the commercial area. On two hectares of the Maori Queen's farmland adjoining the power station a controlled-temperature farm is in the course of construction, intending to use the waste heat from the discharge water of the power station to control temperature in aquacultural development and in a series of greenhouses. The objective is to grow commercial crops and breed fresh-water crayfish (*kooura* or *marron*) for the export market, notably Japan. In the initial feasibility study an array of benefits to the community, to the economy and to the ecology was projected. The ultimate employment capacity was estimated at 400. The economy was argued to benefit from multiplier effects, while the cooled water would benefit the Waikato River ecology (Angus, Flood and Griffiths, 1982).

However, the initial projections of employment may have been somewhat over-optimistic. Compounded by a severe economic depression, the controlled-temperature farm will be commercially viable if only no more than a dozen people are employed, although an ultimate figure of 70 part-time and full-time labourers is still envisaged (Waahi Controlled Environment Farm, 1986: 7). Over the years it has become apparent that the farming planned is not particularly labour intensive.

In addition, the Waahi Marae Trust entered into a Heads of Agreement with Maori International, a financial organization, to undertake a joint venture to construct a 32-unit motor lodge with a 48-guest dining-room along the bank of the Waikato River opposite Waahi Pa.[15] This tourism development would include a landing and boat launching and other access to the river, outdoor dining areas such as *haangi* ('earth-oven') and barbecue, and a swimming-pool. The *marae* facilities would add convention, conference and seminar possibilities. The location of the lodge would also enable the development of a local tour package to use the sights and the recreation potential throughout the Waikato. Some ferry or transport was planned, and tours of the *marae* in the area, tours of the power station and coal-mines, jet-boat trips and water recreation on the river, including fishing, were all considered as possibilities. The local Maori people were expected to make special efforts to welcome guests and provide interest and entertainment (Waahi Holdings and Maori International, 1987).

Concluding remarks

Both the controlled-temperature farm and, in particular, the planning of the tourist lodge exemplify the changes that Waahi Pa has undergone since the construction of the Huntly power station. In the 1970s Waahi was still a community like most other Maori communities in New Zealand. The *marae* facilities were no longer used as an extension to family homes, but only occasionally for ceremonial gatherings at life crises or to entertain guests of the Maori Queen, for example, at the annual 'loyalty gathering' (*poukai*). In 1994, however, Waahi had become the most innovative *marae* in New Zealand. The initial development of Waahi following negotiations with government authorities about compensation for the construction of the power station, caused the construction of a model for community development which, in turn, has sparked off a fundamental review of the social, political, economic and cultural goals of the entire Tainui confederation of tribes. The Waahi model is not only being expanded across the Tainui region, but it has also attracted interest from other tribes, in particular Ngaati Porou, Ngaati Kahungunu and Whanganui.

It is important to point out that the development of the Tainui tribes over the past decade parallels a national revival of Maori culture and the increasing politicization of Maori aspirations throughout New Zealand (*e.g.* Sharp, 1990; Walker, 1990). Maori expectations for fundamental and far-reaching changes were raised when the Labour party was elected in 1984, a turning-point in recent history which also marks an intensification of Maori demands for more political autonomy. In the case of Tainui, the election of the new government enabled the implementation of development through the introduction of the Mana and Maccess schemes, while at the same time it caused the revitalization of the long-standing quest for redress of the confiscations. The latter was made possible by the amendment of legislation regarding historic Maori grievances, which ties in with the government's new policy of devolution of resources from the Department of Maori Affairs to tribal authorities—of this the Mana and Maccess programmes were the first experiments. Ultimately, so it was believed, the change in government policy could enable Tainui to realize the development goal of establishing an economic base in order to become independent of the New Zealand government.

In 1990, and again in 1993, however, the Labour party was defeated in new elections by the conservative National party, which has been the governing party ever since. Initially, it was feared that the election victory of the National party might set Maori aspirations back to square one, but soon it became clear that Maori development had gathered so much momentum in the course of the 1980s that the National party could not possibly obstruct the avenues towards a more independent future that the indigenous peoples of New Zealand had opened for themselves in the 1980s. Thus, following social and political changes at both local and national levels, the aspirations of the Maori people are nowadays still unequivocally focused on community development.[16]

Notes

1. For a brief history of the Maori King Movement and its main ceremonies, see van Meijl (1993b).
2. Outside of Huntly there are, besides the community of Turangawaewae, a significant number of Ngaati Mahuta people at Taharoa in the Kawhia area, and at Mangere *marae* in Auckland. In addition, there are Ngaati Mahuta people living in the cities of Hamilton, Auckland and Wellington, and even in Australia, particularly in Perth, either on a permanent basis or more temporarily in search of employment. Detailed figures on Ngaati Mahuta migrants are not available.
3. In the nineteenth century they were united when other *marae* in the district, such as Maurea and Horahora, were disloyal to the *Kingitanga* and joined the British military forces during the New Zealand wars of the 1860s.
4. Cf. Wiremu Piri Raihe, member of the Tainui Maaori Trust Board, in letter to the Minister of Energy, George F. Gair, *dd.* 16 June 1978.
5. In the Maori version of the Treaty of Waitangi, the term 'sovereignty' was translated with *kawanatanga,* a hitherto unknown transliteration of 'governorship'. It is often argued that if the British concept of sovereign power and authority had been

translated more correctly with the term *mana*, the Maori chiefs would have been reluctant to sign the Treaty (Orange, 1987).

6. For a more extensive elaboration of this argument, see van Meijl (1991: 36–7). It goes without saying, however, that the oppositional representation of 'government structures of organization' concerns chiefly a political stereotype, the theoretical implications of which I have discussed elsewhere (van Meijl, 1994a).

7. For a background to political transformations in New Zealand and its implications for Maori development, see Hopa (1988) and Nottingham (1988).

8. The Maori word *kawenata* is a transliteration of the English 'covenant' (Biggs, 1981: 41), but it evokes Biblical connotations as 'Old' and 'New Testament' have been translated as *Kawenata Tawhito* and *Kawenata Hou* respectively.

9. Initially Mana was administered under the control of the Board of Maori Affairs made up of, among others, six tribal representatives (Dyall, 1984: 39–40). In order to enable the government to resume control of Mana Enterprises the responsibility for the development scheme was transferred to the Department of Maori Affairs in 1988.

10. According to the Tainui Maaori Trust Board (1988: 14–16), this figure of 32 per cent compared favourably with the employment outcome of 19 per cent for General Access schemes.

11. See also Shear-Wood and Gans (1986).

12. For a critical analysis of this perspective on health, see van Meijl (1993a). Shear-Wood (1990) has discussed Maori preventative health programmes within the context of primary healthcare.

13. Douglas and Douglas (1983) and Ritchie and Ritchie (1989: 124).

14. See Stokes (1980) on alternative forms and guidelines for setting up homework centres in Maori communities.

15. For this project a special business was formed, the Waahi Holdings Ltd, which acted as the commercial subsidiary of the Tainui Maaori Trust Board and Maori International Ltd. Waahi Holdings conducted negotiations with various government departments and private-sector organizations to stimulate development in the local area.

16. This article is based on Chapter 1 of my doctoral dissertation (van Meijl, 1991: 13–50).

References

Angus, Flood and Griffiths (1982), *Controlled Temperature Farming*, Report commissioned by the Waahi Marae Trust, Hamilton.

Benton, R.A. (1979a), *Who Speaks Maori in New Zealand?* Paper prepared for the 49th ANZAAS Congress, Wellington: New Zealand Council for Educational Research.

Benton, R.A. (1979b), *The Maori Language in the Nineteen Seventies,* Paper prepared for the 49th ANZAAS Congress, Wellington: New Zealand Council for Educational Research.

Benton, R.A. (1984), 'Bilingual Education and the Survival of the Maori Language', *The Journal of the Polynesian Society* 93(3): 247–66.

Benton, R.A. (1988), 'Fairness in Maaori Education; A Review of Research and Information', in: Royal Commission on Social Policy: *The April Report,* Vol. III, Part Two, *Future Directions (Associated Papers),* Wellington: Government Printer, 285–404.

Best, E. (1974), *The Maori School of Learning* (1923), Dominion Museum Monograph No. 6, Wellington: Government Printer.

Biggs, B. (1981), *The Complete English–Maori Dictionary*, Auckland/Oxford: Auckland University Press/Oxford University Press.

Centre for Maaori Studies and Research (CMSR) (1987), *An Endowed College for the University of Waikato*, Hamilton: University of Waikato.

Department of Statistics (1986), *Maori: Statistical Profile 1961–1986,* Wellington: Department of Statistics, Social Reporting Section.

Douglas, E.M.K. (1982), 'Tainui Population—The Human Resource', in E.M.K. Douglas and Isla Nottingham (eds): *Proceedings of the Tainui Lands Federation Conference*, Hamilton: Centre for Maaori Studies and Research, Occasional Paper No. 18, 27–36.

Douglas, E.M.K. and Douglas, R. (1983), *Nga Kohanga Reo; A Salvage Programme for the Maori Language*, Paper presented to the 53rd ANZAAS Congress, Perth, Western Australia.

Douglas, E.M.K. and Dyall, J. (1985), *Maori Under-development*, Submissions to The Employment Promotion Conference and The Maori Employment Conference.

Dyall, J.R. (1984), *Maori Resource Development: A Handbook on Maori Organizations*, Wellington.

Earp, R. (1988) 'kMaccess: The state of the arts', paper for 'Hui Whahowaa Taumata: Future directions for Maori development', 25 February.

Fookes, T.W. (1976), *Social and Economic Impacts Feared by the Maori Communities at Huntly, 1972–1973*, Hamilton: University of Waikato, School of Social Sciences, Huntly Social and Economic Impact Monitoring Project, Research Memorandum No. 4.

Harrison, B. (1987), *Rakaumanga School; A Study of Issues in Bilingual Education*, Hamilton: Centre for Maaori Studies and Research.

Hopa, N.K. (1988), *The Anthropologist as Tribal Advocate*, Paper presented to American Anthropological Association, Phoenix, Arizona.

Kelly, L.G. (Te Putu) (1949), *Tainui: The Story of Hoturoa and his Descendants*, Wellington: Polynesian Society.

Mahuta, R. (1983), *Unemployment and the Maaori: Report to Government Caucus Employment Committee*, Huntly: Waahi Pa.

Mahuta, R.T. (n.d.), *Waahi: The People and Their History*, Unpublished paper.

Mahuta, R.T. (1973), *Submissions to the Electricity Department and Ministry of Works Concerning the Huntly Coal and Gas Fired Thermal Power Station*, 4 October 1973.

Mahuta, R.T. (1979), 'Kingitanga', in *Kia Mataara*, Proceedings of Seminar on 'The Kingitanga; Where To and How', Waikato-ki-roto-o-Poneke, Wellington.

Mahuta, R.T. and Egan, K. (1981a), *Waahi: A Case Study of Social and Economic Development in a New Zealand Maori Community*, Hamilton: Centre for Maaori Studies and Research, Occasional Paper No. 12.

Mahuta, R.T. and Egan, K. (1981b), *Huakina: Report to New Zealand Steel 1981*, Hamilton: Centre for Maaori Studies and Research, Occasional Paper No. 13.

Mahuta, R.T. and Egan, K. (1983), *The Tainui Report; A Survey of Human and Natural Resources*, Hamilton: Centre for Maaori Studies and Research, Occasional Paper No. 19.

Mahuta, R.T. and Nottingham, I. (eds) (1984), *The Development of Coal-fired Power Stations in the Waikato; A Maaori Perspective*, Hamilton: Centre for Maaori Studies and Research.

Meade-Rose, J. (1980), *The Maori Community and the Huntly Power Project*, Hamilton: University of Waikato, Huntly Monitoring Project, Internal Technical Paper 25.

Meijl, T. van (1991), 'Political Paradoxes and Timeless Traditions; Ideology and Development Among the Tainui Maori, New Zealand', Canberra: Australian National University, Ph.D. thesis (reproduced by the Centre for Pacific Studies, University of Nijmegen, the Netherlands).

Meijl, T. van (1993a), 'A Maori Perspective on Health and its Politicization', *Medical Anthropology*, 15: 283–97.

Meijl, T. van (1993b), 'The Maori King Movement: Unity and Diversity in Past and present', in van der Grijp and T. van Meijl (eds), special issue on 'Politics, Tradition and Change in the Pacific', *Bijdragen tot de taal-, land- en volkenkunde* 149(4): 673–89.

Meijl, T. van (1994a). 'Maori Hierarchy Transformed: The Secularization of Tainui Patterns of Leadership', in M. Jolly, and M. Mosko (eds), special issue on 'Transformations of Hierarchy; Structure: History and Horizon in the Austronesian World', *History and Anthropology*, Vol. 7, Nos. 1–4, 279–305.

Meijl, T. van (1994b), 'Second Chance Education for Maori School 'Dropouts'; A Case-

Study of a Community Training Centre in New Zealand', *International Journal of Educational Development*, 14(4): 371–84.

Metge, J. (1976), *The Maoris of New Zealand: Rautahi* (1967), London: Routledge and Kegan Paul.

Ministry of Energy (1986), *Huntly Power Station*, Wellington: Ministry of Energy, Electricity Division, Information Services.

Nottingham, I. (1988), *Land Economic Development and Cultural Survival: The New Zealand Maaori*, Paper presented to American Anthropological Association, Phoenix, Arizona.

Orange, C. (1987), *The Treaty of Waitangi*, Wellington: Allen & Unwin/Port Nicholson.

Ritchie, J. and Ritchie, J. (1989), 'Socialization and Character Development', in A. Howard and R. Borofsky (eds), *Developments in Polynesian Ethnology*, Honolulu: University of Hawaii Press: 95–135.

Salmond, A. (1975), *Hui: A Study of Maori Ceremonial Gatherings*, Wellington: Reed.

Sharp, A. (1990), *Justice and the Maaori: Maaori Claims in New Zealand Political Argument in the 1980s*, Auckland: Oxford University Press.

Shear-Wood, C. (1982), *Blood Pressure and Related Factors among the Maori and Pakeha Communities of Huntly*, Hamilton: Centre for Maaori Studies and Research, Occasional Paper No. 17.

Shear-Wood, C. (1990), 'Maori Community Health Workers: A Mixed Reception in New Zealand', in J. Coreil and J. Dennis Mull (eds), *Anthropology and Primary Health Care*, Boulder: Westview Press, 123–36.

Shear-Wood, C. and Gans, L.P. (1986), 'Contrasting Patterns of Blood Pressure and Related Factors Within a Maori and European Population in New Zealand', *Social Science Medicine* 23(5): 439–44.

Stokes, E. (1977), *Te Iwi o Waahi: The People of Waahi-Huntly*, Hamilton: Centre for Maaori Studies and Research, Occasional Paper No. 1.

Stokes, E. (1978), *Local Perceptions of the Impact of the Huntly Power Project 1971–1973*, Hamilton: Centre for Maaori Studies and Research, Occasional Paper No. 4

Stokes, E. (1980), *Homework Centres*, Hamilton: Centre for Maaori Studies and Research, Occasional Paper No. 5.

Tainui Maaori Trust Board (1984), *Submissions to Maori Economic Development Summit Conference*.

Tainui Maaori Trust Board (1985), *Whaaia Ngaa Mahi*; *Submission to Employment Promotion Conference*, prepared by J.E. Ritchie, R. Mahuta and L.A. Hura.

Tainui Maaori Trust Board (1988), *Devolution Contracts Package*, November 1988.

Waahi Controlled Environment Farm (1986), *Waahi Controlled Environment Farm Pilot Project*, Mana Enterprise Submission, November 1986.

Waahi Holdings Ltd and Maori International Ltd (1987), *Waahi Te Marae Lodge*, a joint project by Waahi Holdings Ltd and Maori International Ltd.

Walker, R. (1977), 'Marae: A Place to Stand', in M. King (ed.)(1975), *Te Ao Hurihuri (The World Moves On): Aspects of Maoritanga*, Wellington: Hicks Smith/Methuen, 21–30.

Walker, R. (1990), *Ka Whawhai tonu Matou: Struggle Without End*, Auckland/Harmondsworth: Penguin.

17 Indigenous organizations for development in the Canadian north: Native development corporations

LEO PAUL DANA*

Introduction

IN THE INDIVIDUALISTIC societies of the middle and lower latitudes, capitalism, free enterprise, entrepreneurship and competition are concepts which have long been known about. Cantillon (1755/1955) referred to the entrepreneur as the *individual* who took the risk to work for *himself*. Smith's theory (1937) was based on the premise that the *individual's* need for satisfaction leads to wealth.

Yet, for some societies, even today, the unit of economic producer is that of the *collectivity* as opposed to the *individual*. Furthermore, some ethno-cultural groups simply do not value entrepreneurship. Weber (1905–6) argued that culture was the explanatory variable determining a society's propensity towards entrepreneurial activity. Becker (1956) noted that some cultures consider business to be an unholy occupation and, therefore, in those societies, foreigners are required to be the entrepreneurs. Boissevain and Grotenbreg (1987); Enz, Dollinger and Daily (1990); Gadgil (1959); Lasry (1982); Ray, Momjian, McMullan and Ko (1988); Shapero (1984); Shapero and Sokol (1982) and Ward (1987) are among the many who confirmed that different cultures carry different beliefs about the desirability and feasibility of entrepreneurship.

For centuries, the indigenous people of Canada's Arctic lived a nomadic lifestyle, hunting and fishing for food. Team effort was the key to survival. Even if one person could individually harpoon a walrus, the latter, when injured, would struggle to escape, and seldom could a lone individual pull it ashore. Often the mate of a walrus would intertwine its tusks with its partner's in an attempt to free it. The hunter could not succeed without assistance from his group. In turn, all game was shared out among community members.

Life was thus very communal, working collectively and sharing rewards. Somebody who no longer contributed to the well-being of the community was left behind, as were the aged who could no longer earn their keep.

Since the early seventeenth century, traders gradually exposed *some* native groups of the north to mercantilist capitalism, and furs were traded for valued liquor and modern merchandise. The last to encounter white people were the central Inuits (Eskimos) who did so in the twentieth century. During the post-war years, wage economies were introduced to the north. The opening of the North Rankin Nickel Mine brought a wage economy to the District of Keewatin, in 1957.

Although white Canadians brought economic development to the Northwest Territories (NWT), indigenous people, for the most part, generally lacked the skills and values to participate in the new economy. Consequently, during the 1970s, native development corporations (NDCs) were introduced as a means for

* Professor Leo Paul Dana, Faculty of Management, McGill University, Montreal, Quebec, Canada.

a socialist culture to participate in a capitalist economy. Collectively owned by native groups, and creating local jobs, the objective of these NDCs has been to integrate native people into the economy, as proprietors, managers and employees.

Differing structures

Two variations of NDCs exist. The first to have been established in the 1970s was the birthright NDC. Such a corporation is, by definition, jointly owned by *every* member of a specific native group; from the time of birth, each person is a shareholder by virtue of having been born into that group.

During the 1980s, the private NDC came into existence. In contrast to being born a shareholder of a birthright NDC, participation in the equity of a private NDC involves a conscious decision by the investor, and payment for the shares acquired.

Birthright NDCs

During the 1970s, the Metis, the Dene Indian, the Inuvialuit and the Inuit (Eskimos) of the NWT organized themselves politically. The birthright NDC evolved as an outgrowth of this political development.

The Metis Development Corporation (MDC) was incorporated in 1977, by the NWT Metis Association. The president of the association became the single shareholder, holding equity in trust for all the Metis people.

The objective of the MDC was to transform projected land-claim money into economic opportunities for the Metis people. The Nova office building in Yellowknife was leased to the government of the NWT in 1978; the MDC thus was able to obtain financing to purchase it outright.

Being an outgrowth of political development, the MDC had political goals as well as economic ones. In time, this alliance between money and politics created conflict, so in 1979 a new share structure separated the political from economic activities.

In 1981, the MDC built the Frontier Building in Norman Wells, NWT, and leased it to Esso Resources. Also in Norman Wells, during 1983, the MDC obtained a 16 per cent stake in Shetah Drilling. It subsequently acquired interests in a cable television company in Fort Smith, and in three fishing lodges on Great Bear Lake. Further diversification in Yellowknife included equity in the ownership of stationery stores.

More recently, the MDC has been concentrating on supporting smaller Metis enterprises by providing business expertise and, in some cases, equity capital for joint ventures. It is now completely independent of the Metis Nation (formerly the Metis Association).

Another birthright NDC is the Nunasi Development Corporation, established by the Inuit Tapirisat of Canada. Like the MDC, it started out in real estate— thanks to government commitments for long-term leases. Owned by the Inuit people of Nunavut (eastern Arctic), Nunasi began by investing in Iqaluit (formerly Frobisher Bay), and became the largest NDC in the eastern Arctic. In time, Nunasi, like the MDC, also diversified. As well as owning real estate in British Columbia and across northern Canada, since the late 1980s the portfolio of Nunasi has also included the ownership of an enterprise manufacturing sealskin products and an interest in Norterra Holdings (the latter owns the Northern Transportation Company and its subsidiary Grimshaw Trucking).

Among other investments, Nunasi has interests in a travel agency and an optical company, both in Yellowknife.

Unlike the MDC, Nunasi has maintained its political connections. Nunasi operates as the economic arm of the Tungavik Federation of Nunavut, an Inuit group. Among the priorities of the corporation is job creation and the improvement of services to Inuit communities.

An example of a regional birthright NDC is the Qikiqtaaluk Corporation of the Baffin region. Since its creation in 1983, it has been creating jobs for Inuit people. Its activities include initiatives to promote fishing operations as well as efforts to develop new construction techniques. In 1987, it obtained the first licence to harvest shrimp in the NWT. Qikiqtaaluk traded with companies in the south: an opportunity to go shrimp fishing was exchanged for fishing boats and expertise. More recently, the corporation also obtained licences to fish Turbot and Silver Lake. Another of its recent projects is the construction of an office tower in Iqaluit. As is the case with other NDCs, one of the aims of Qikiqtaaluk is to provide benefits for native people. Qikiqtaaluk has provided tool sets to native apprentices of airplane mechanics, and regularly provides tool sets to graduates of the Arctic College co-operative carpentry course in Iqaluit.

Private NDCs

The Rae-Edzo Dene Band Development Corporation is a private NDC which evolved from a birthright NDC. It had been set up by the band in 1979, but it had to sell shares in order to raise sufficient capital for its first project.

Individuals contributed $50 (Canadian) each, and a grant was obtained from the Federal Department of Regional Industrial Expansion (DRIE). This enabled the construction, in 1980, of the Nishi Khon Centre in Fort Rae. Today, the Nishi Khon complex houses government offices, band offices, a coffee shop and a grocery store owned and managed by the corporation.

The Rae-Edzo Dene Band Development Corporation also owns an apartment building and a motel as well as the nursing station in Fort Rae. The corporation has also diversified to have interests in Air Tindi, Bellanca Developments and Polar Vision of Yellowknife.

Thus, the corporation evolved from a birthright into a private NDC. It went public, and by 1993, it had almost 300 shareholders, most of whom are Dogrib Indians from the communities north of Great Slave Lake. Its consistent profitability suggests that private NDCs may be viable instruments of collective entrepreneurship for regional development and job creation in native communities. With the exception of the accountant and the executive director, all the employees of the corporation were born and raised in Fort Rae. Furthermore, the Rae-Edzo Band has a large contingent on the board of directors. It is expected that if and when a Dogrib land claim is settled, then the Rae-Edzo Band would probably buy back the NDC.

The success of the Rae-Edzo Dene Band Development Corporation led to the establishment of others and, since the 1980s, there has been substantial growth of private NDCs. The first private NDC which was established, as such, was the Enokhok Development Corporation, incorporated in 1984. Its activities began when a group of Inuit, obtaining a long-term commitment from the government of the NWT, was able to secure financing to construct the Enokhok Centre in Cambridge Bay. Other successful ventures followed.

The corporation built an office complex in Coppermine, and leased it to the territorial government. Several construction and maintenance contracts assures the further growth of Enokhok. The corporation now owns residential real estate in Baker Lake, Cambridge Bay, Coppermine, Pelly Bay and Spence Bay, as well as the Enokhok Inn in Cambridge Bay and the Kitikmeot Boarding Home in Yellowknife.

Over the years, several private NDCs were established. Across Canada's eastern Arctic, private NDCs have built and leased residential and commercial space. These include Arviat Development Corporation Ltd., Ilagiiktut Ltd., Kangiqliniq Developments Ltd., Katujjijiit Development Corporation Ltd., Piruqsaijit Ltd., Qamanittuaq Development Corporation Ltd., and Tapiriit Developments Ltd.

Due to cultural attitudes, however, the success of a private corporation is not always without political difficulties. In the Nahanni region of the NWT, 33 shareholders started a new venture called Beaver Enterprises. Its success provoked jealousy in the community. Consequently, the Liard Valley Band Development Corporation (LVBDC) was established as a birthright NDC of the Slavey Indians living in the Fort Liard area of Nahanni. The LVBDC then bought out Beaver Enterprises, and now owns Acho Real Estate, Beaver Enterprises Construction, Deh Cho Air Ltd., Liard Fuel Centre, Liard Valley Trucking and Petitot Construction Services, as well as having interest in the Liard Valley General Store and Motel.

Performance

Of all NDCs, the most successful one in terms of economic performance appears to be the Makivik Corporation of the northern Quebec region known as Nunavik. Its early success is largely attributable to heavy government spending in Nunavik. Over the years, Makivik got involved in construction, fisheries, fuel companies and leasing companies.

Since the objective of NDCs is not solely profit-oriented, but also to have a positive impact on native people, social performance is also considered important, and here again Makivik is successful. One subsidiary may be considered entrepreneurial in the Barthian sense. Barth (1963, 1967) described the entrepreneur as an agent of social change, and Seaku Fisheries Inc. caused social change when it increased the number of Inuit fishermen. By 1990, it employed 40 Nunavik Inuit crewmen earning an average of $35 000.

In 1990, Makivik made a significant step in Inuit ownership of northern transport, when it purchased an existing small airline, Air Stol, the parent company of Bradley Air, which operates the regional carrier First Air, with a head office in Carp, Ontario, near the Canadian capital. Makivik is also the owner of Air Inuit, a commuter airline which has created 186 jobs.

Yet not all NDCs are successful. The survival of NDCs is often dependent on government assistance, and even with government funding, the failure rate among NDCs is high. According to an estimate by the Northwest Territories' Assistant Deputy Minister for Business Development, Peter Allen, at least three out of four NDCs fail, mostly due to management problems.

A few years ago, an Inuit group owned Nunasi-Northland Airlines Limited, an airline based in Churchill, Manitoba. Mismanagement led to the demise of the enterprise. Yet its fleet of Douglas DC–3 aircraft was acquired by Air Manitoba, an airline which is now making profits using these airplanes to service the same communities which Nunasi-Northland had served. These include Eskimo Point (population 1189) and Repulse Bay (population 42). In contrast to purchasing fuel in the NWT as Nunasi-Northland had done, the managers of Air Manitoba have found that making all fuel purchases in Manitoba results in substantial savings. The success of Air Manitoba, in general, has in turn allowed native employees to learn managerial skills while on the job.

Nevertheless, NDCs have been experiencing considerable difficulties employing educated native people with entrepreneurial and managerial skills. Dana (1986) emphasized the difference between entrepreneurial and managerial skills; the latter are required for day-to-day business operations, while the former contribute to the innovativeness and competitiveness of a firm.

Due to the shortage of native people with managerial skills, many NDCs are managed by non-indigenous people. Consequently, the training of native people has become a priority of NDCs. Even when managerial skills are learned, however, other difficulties arise. The native culture of the Inuit people lacks the values required in entrepreneurial behaviour, notably the willingness to compete.

Indigenous managers of NDCs are determined to preserve their traditional values and to avoid competition. Whereas in mainstream society competition is the mainstay of capitalism, the indigenous people of Canada prefer to visualize an economic environment in which competition would neither exist nor be necessary, but one where different enterprises would co-operate.

The avoidance of competition is possible in some cases, for example, where potentially competitive corporations have the same shareholders. Often, an individual might have a share in a regional birthright NDC and purchase a share in a private NDC as well. Whenever competition exists from a non-indigenous entity, however, the performance of NDCs may be affected if they remain determined to be non-competitive.

Conclusion

NDCs have emerged in about half of the communities in the NWT. In some communities with mixed cultural groups, there is more than one NDC. In most cases, NDCs have been contributing to regional economic development by serving as major employers in their communities. NDCs have been entrepreneurial corporations. Through the development of a lucrative fishing industry in the Arctic, for example, these corporations have been entrepreneurial, resulting in a major impact on job creation and on the creation of wealth in native communities.

Yet, NDCs differ from corporations or entrepreneurs elsewhere. Unlike the executives and managers of conventional corporations, who try to make their corporations competitive, those in charge of NDCs are determined to stay true to traditional Inuit values and therefore to avoid competition, the mainstay of capitalism. Unlike capitalist entrepreneurs, whom the literature describes as individualists, NDCs were founded to preserve collective values. NDCs are thus a unique socialist version of entrepreneurship in the Canadian north.

References

Barth, F. (ed.) (1963), *The Role of the Entrepreneur in Social Change in Northern Norway*, Bergen: Norwegian Universities Press.

Barth, F. (1967), 'On the Study of Social Change', *American Anthropologist* LXIX (6), December, 661–9.
Becker, H. (1956), *Man in Reciprocity,* New York, NY: Frederick Praeger.
Boissevain, J. and Grotenbreg, H. (1987), 'Ethnic Enterprise in the Netherlands: The Suranimese of Amsterdam', in R. Goffee, and R. Scase (eds), *Entrepreneurship in Europe: The Social Process,* London: Croom Helm, 105–30.
Cantillon, R. (1755), *Essai sur la nature du commerce en général,* London and Paris: R. Gyles; reprinted 1955, Paris: Institute National d'Etudes Demographiques.
Dana, L.P. (1986), 'Towards a Skills Model for Entrepreneurship', in G.A. Pynn (ed.), *Proceedings of the First Canadian Conference on Entrepreneurial Studies,* St. John's, Newfoundland: P.J. Gardiner Institute for Small Business Studies, Memorial University, 77–85; reprinted 1987, *Journal of Small Business and Entrepreneurship* V(1), Summer, 27–31; reprinted 1988, in R.W.Y. Kao, (ed.), *Readings in Entrepreneurship and Small Business Development,* Toronto, Ontario: Ryerson, 164–8.
Enz, C.A., Dollinger, M.J. and Daily, C.M. (1990), 'The Value Orientations of Minority and Non-Minority Small Business Owners', *Entrepreneurship, Theory and Practice* XV(1), Fall, 23–35.
Gadgil, D.R. (1959), *Origins of the Modern Indian Business Class,* New York, NY: Institute of Pacific Relations.
Lasry, J.C. (1982), 'Une diaspora francophone au Quebec: les Juifs sépharades', *Questions de culture,* vol. 2, Quebec, PQ: Institut de Recherche sur la Culture, 113–38.
Ray, D.M., Momjian, A., McMullan, W.E. and Ko, S. (1988), 'Comparison of Immigrant Armenian Entrepreneurs in Los Angeles and Immigrant Chinese Entrepreneurs in Calgary', Calgary, Alberta: University of Calgary, Faculty of Management Research Papers.
Shapero, A. (1984), 'The Entrepreneurial Event', in C.A. Kent, (ed.), *The Environment for Entrepreneurship,* Lexington, MA: D.C. Heath, 21–40.
Shapero, A. and Sokol, L. (1982). 'The Social Dimensions of Entrepreneurship', in C.A. Kent, D.L. Sexton, and K.H. Vesper (eds), *Encyclopedia of Entrepreneurship,* Englewood Cliffs, NJ: Prentice-Hall, 72–90.
Smith, A. (1937), *Wealth of Nations,* New York: Modern Library.
Ward, R. (1987), 'Ethnic Entrepreneurs in Britain and in Europe', in R. Goffee and R. Scase (eds), *Entrepreneurship in Europe: The Social Process,* London: Croom Helm, 83–104.
Weber, M. (1905–6), 'Die protestantische Ethik und der Geist des Kapitalismus', *Archiv fur Sozialwissenschaft und Sozialpolitik* XX–XXI; revised (1920); Trans. T. Parsons, (1930), *The Protestant Ethic and the Spirit of Capitalism,* New York, NY: Scribners.

18 The role of indigenous organizations in the rural development of China: A case-study of a non-farm productive activity

LI XIAOYUN, LI OU AND ZHOU SHENGKUN*

Introduction

INDIGENOUS KNOWLEDGE (IK) refers to the knowledge of indigenous peoples. It is different from the knowledge generated by formal organizations such as universities and institutes. IK includes practical knowledge, and indigenous organizations such as communication systems (here it refers to informal mass communication, e.g. information exchange among larger groups) and the cultural, social or economic organizations conceived and created by indigenous groups. This chapter will discuss the sustainability and the role of indigenous farmer organizations in the rural development of China by means of a case-study approach.

China has a population of more than 1.2 billion, 800 million of whom live in rural areas. Most of the rural labour is engaged in agricultural production, and only a fifth work in diverse rural industries. Among the farm households engaged in agriculture, many conduct non-farm activities part-time to increase their incomes. In these farming and non-farm activities, farmers' indigenous organizations play a very important role in rural development. Through this institutional arrangement, farmers develop and disseminate appropriate technologies, use different resources such as capital, labour, knowledge and expertise in production and marketing to take advantage of the opportunities provided by the market economy. In this way farmers increase their employment opportunities and income, raise their production and marketing capabilities, develop self-confidence and self-help organizations, and accumulate funds for the sustainable development of their own livelihood and the welfare of their communities.

This chapter will show how the local farmers build their indigenous organizations, by examining fur cloth production in a rural area of north China. The purpose of this study is to analyse the sustainability of the indigenous organization and its role in rural development, and to provide the government with recommendations about how to gain support from the indigenous farmer organizations in rural development projects.

The background of the research site and the methodology

This research was conducted in the Raoyangdian Township, Gucheng County, Hebei Province in north China. With a population of more than 30 000, about 8000 farm households and 37 villages in Raoyangdian, the average farm house-

---

* The authors are from the Centre for Integrated Agricultural Development (CIAD), Beijing Agricultural University (BAU), People's Republic of China. Li Xiaoyun is the Director and Associate Professor, Li Ou is Deputy Director and Associate Professor and Zhou Shengkun is a Research Fellow.

hold has about 0.7 ha of arable land for two to four family members. Because it is quite far from any big city, there is not much industrial development and commercial production of fruit, vegetable and animal products has begun only in the last few years. Farmers' income is mainly derived from grain and cotton production. With winter wheat and summer corn cultivated on irrigated land and cotton cultivated on rain fed land as the main cropping systems, Raoyangdian is a typical underdeveloped rural area in north China.

For non-farm enterprises, fur cloth production, inclusive of semi-finished and finished products, is historically an important industry in this area. Located 8 km west of Raoyangdian Township, Daying Town, historically a renowned market in north China for tanned or dyed fur, and semi-finished or finished fur cloth, is famous for its fur products. A large number of goods in the market are purchased and sold by Raoyangdian farmers who are engaged in production. In the 1960s and 1970s, fur cloth production was an important source of income for the communes (now called townships) and brigades (now called villages). But it was run neither individually nor co-operatively, but collectively (fulfilling quotas for the state) at that time. In the 1980s when China began its open-door policy, the commune-brigade system was dismantled and replaced by a new system combining the collective community and farm household responsibility systems. But the community collective organization, such as the village committee, works mainly in the social sphere. Regarding the economic aspect, the collective enterprises, which are organizations conceived by people outside the local community, such as fur cloth production, stopped functioning in Raoyangdian. But the market opportunities were still there. Beside the market-location factor, the farmers have advantages over the urban state factories. The farmers use their surplus labour and time, so that the labour costs are very low in the period when demand is lower. But in the urban factories labour costs remain high throughout the year.

Following the changes, very few of the collective factories remained, but rather evolved into stock-sharing co-operatives, in which the farmers developed their own ideas and made their own institutional arrangements. At the same time many other farmers developed different kinds of indigenous organizations for fur cloth production.

In this study a Farming System Research (FSR) approach was used. Group interviews and key informant interviews were the main tools. Based on the reconnaissance, two villages, Shuidongtun and Shengshulin, were chosen as sample villages. Eight and five key informants, and three and two groups were interviewed in the villages, respectively.

Research results

The forms and development of indigenous organizations

In Raoyangdian Township it was discovered that there are three kinds of indigenous organizations for fur cloth production, i.e. stock-sharing co-operatives, relatively stable organizations and temporary organizations. Two factors contribute to the existence of the different organizations.

First, there are different market demands for fur cloth. One comes from the domestic department stores in large or medium cities, and another from the international border trade between China and Russia, which has developed in the last two years. The domestic market needs guaranteed quality goods and prefers to deal with the state or collective businesses (factories). The contracts between them are relatively long-term and stable, while the latter market consists of small- and large-scale Chinese and Russian dealers. They do not have strict quality requirements and do not care which producers they deal with, whether state collectives or co-operatives or private individuals. The trade contacts are very flexible in terms of partnership and time involved. The requirements of style and types of fur cloth are also diverse.

Secondly, farmer households have different resources enabling them to take advantage of access to the diverse opportunities provided by the market for fur cloth. Resources range from finance, manpower and technology to expertise. Some old technicians are retired from fur cloth factories in big cities such as Beijing, Tianjin and Shanghai. Some young farmers acquired their expertise from their parents or relatives. They know one of several key techniques in fur tanning, dyeing, colour and pattern matching, tailoring and sewing. Some farmers are skilful middlemen or dealers in buying and selling raw materials, semi-finished and finished products. The others simply work as labourers in fur cloth production.

The farmers with techniques or expertise can run a private business to produce semi-finished or finished products employing local farmers, or do business individually. But some of them want to use their different skills and resources by forming an organization to produce different kinds of finished products to meet the diverse demands for fur cloth production and marketing, and gain more profit than they could individually. The main differences between the organizations range from the mechanisms of investment, management, income distribution to the contribution they make to the community.

Stock-sharing co-operatives (former collectives). Stock-sharing co-operatives for fur cloth production, which evolved from former village collective businesses, were found only in Shengshulin Village. There are three such kinds of factories in the village, established in 1984, 1988 and 1990, respectively.

The main products of the factories are fur cloth oriented towards the domestic market, mainly fur-lined jackets. Collective businesses have several advantages, for example in the 1980s it was easier for them than individual businesses to obtain bank loans and trademarks from industrial and commercial management bureaus, and to gain the confidence of and thus procure long-term orders from department stores in the cities. The village then also wanted to set up collective businesses to accumulate funds for community welfare for projects such as drilling wells for irrigation, developing collective fruit orchards, improving buildings and equipment of the village school, etc. In addition they could increase their capacity to receive bank loans and make investments through the village collective, manage production and marketing collectively; both the manager and workers could receive salaries from the collective business. To overcome the shortcomings of the collectives, such as the absence of anyone to represent and protect the interests of the organization, a kind of responsibility system was created in the collective businesses. A group of managers for finance, personnel, technical guidance and quality control, and purchasing and marketing assumed the responsibility for managing these different areas. The group consisted of five, four and two farmer households in the three factories, respectively. They shared the net profit with the village collective 3:7 or 4:6 with the collective taking the larger part. The managers were also responsible for losses. If that happened the collective would get less, but did not pay for the loss. However, the salary and the smaller share of profit were not attractive enough to motivate the managers. And the profit that the factories gained was far less than expected. So some adjustments were made accordingly such as to shift the ratio of profit share to 7:3 or 6:4, with the village collective taking the lower profit share. Eventually all the three factories changed into stock-sharing co-operatives in 1991 or 1992.

Mr Chen Zhenqing, the leader of one of the co-operatives, told us about his organization, consisting of five households—the leader, a manager for money and raw materials, a technician for guidance and quality control and two salesmen. Each household invested 10 000 RMB in the stock shares. New loans from the bank were given under the name of the co-operative leader instead of the village collective. The collective only played the role of guarantor. All the stockholders have a base wage of five RMB (US\$1 = 8.7RMB, 1994) per day. Because sales are the most important factor for making profits, a system of commission was made for the salespeople. They could retain 30–35 per cent of the after-sale 'net profit', as well as all the expenditures they spent in product selling—travelling to and accommodation in the cities, packaging and postage of products, etc. Therefore, if they sell more and save more, they get more income. The technician was also responsible for workers' training and management.

There are 30–40 workers employed in this factory and sometimes more during the busy season for orders, but none in the slack season. The workers receive a salary based on the number of pieces of products they produce, for example, 3–5RMB for sewing one piece of a fur coat. So a girl of 16–18 years could earn 10–15RMB a day, or about 400RMB a month, which equals the net income of farming products from one Chinese mu (0.07 ha) of land in a year (two seasons of winter wheat and summer corn), and 2000–3000RMB a year. In Raoyangdian one farm household can only earn about 3000RMB from crop farming.

The profit (= gross income − cost of production and marketing − taxes − interest on loans) is shared equally among the stockholders. But the profit is not taken away by the stockholders, but accumulated as their own stock. If they need money, they can draw some which is noted in the accounts under their name. In this way the stock-sharing co-operative could be sustained.

The three factories had each turned over 50 000 to 100 000RMB of profit to the village collective before they were changed into co-operatives. Now they share most of the taxes which should be paid by the village. They also provide more than 100 jobs to the farmer households in the village, as well as neighbouring villages. In addition, the co-operatives set up stores in the border market between China and Russia, which could provide market information to the villagers promptly through long-distance calls. The individual or other co-operative producers of the village could also use the trademarks of the stock-sharing co-operatives, which had good reputations and strong competitiveness in the market; the co-operatives carried out quality control for other producers in the village.

Relatively stable organizations. Relatively stable organizations can be found fairly commonly in the village of Shuidongtun. They take two forms, one consists of kinship or relatives, the other is among friends or neighbours in the village. Both socio-cultural factors and economic factors, such as complementary capacities in capital, technology and labour power, contribute to the stability of these organizations. But the socio-cultural factor appears to be a more important factor for the organization between relatives, than for the one among friends. In co-operation among relatives, the distribution of profit does not usually give too much rise to quarrels and suspicion. They also do not care too strictly about the equality of contribution. In the rural regions of China, the idea of the so-called 'great kin' is emphasized. Co-operation among relatives usually requires that better-off families help the poorer ones. The support under this circumstance has the purpose of common prosperity for the extended family.

Co-operation among friends or villages is mainly based on the economic factor—complementary capacities among partners in production and marketing technologies, capital and labour. Personal relationships are also important. This kind of co-operation for making fur cloth is of real importance for production, aiming at expanding production and business, increasing profit, and character-ized by the following points:

o Large scale, with each side bringing a certain amount of money as stock into the co-operative group. In addition, the co-operative group sometimes bor-rows money from other villagers and obtains credit from the bank for its business.
o Relatively distinct division of responsibilities is based on the resources and abilities of the group members. There are people specialized in purchasing and marketing, technical advice and production management, bookkeeping and storage.
o When the co-operative organization was formed, there were verbal or written agreements on group management. Compared with co-operation among rela-tives, this form of organization is more advanced in the economic sense. But it also creates conflicts among the members during production and profit distribution. Although this kind of organization does not contribute money to the community welfare, it does provide villagers with employment.

A case-study of a co-operative organization among relatives:
Mr Han Shukun and his wife, both villagers in Shuidongtun, began fur-cloth production in 1992 with his elder sister and her husband. Han's household is somewhat better-off than his sister's, but he was less skilled in fur-cloth production.

He was in Shijiazhuang, the capital of Hebei Province from 1981 to 1985, doing photography, from which he made a lot of money, and learned about the reform policy. His wife is good in farming and is skilled in sewing fur cloth. So Han's family were the investors in production while Han's sister and her husband did not have enough money to run the enterprise by themselves, but had skills in fur processing. The husband also has business skills. So it can be seen that the co-operation between Han and his sister is based on complementary skills, capital and labour on the one hand and also functions as assistance between relatives on the other hand. In 1992, Han invested 10 000RMB and the co-operative made a profit of 8 000RMB, which was shared equally between the two families. In 1993, as the market of rabbit-fur overcoats was getting better, Han expanded the organization to include his younger brother's family, mainly to provide labour. He collected information and purchased semi-finished products from the local market, and delivered the fur cloth through the post office, while his wife was skilled in sewing. This kind of co-operation has a rough task distribution. The probable difference of contribution did not give rise to conflict, so this co-operation succeeded with a harmonious atmosphere, as well as good profits. In 1993, Han invested 12 000RMB, while the profits reached 24 000RMB and each family received 8 000.

A case-study of a co-operative organization among villagers:
In 1981 the fur processing group of the No. 3 production team in Shuidongtun Village, which was previously a commune, was dismantled. The production equipment was priced and sold to the former team leader Li Baohua, accountant, Xu Kehui, storage technician, Xu Kefeng and another former technician of the group Ma Wenbin. Then the four households formed an organization for fur processing with the equipment they bought as stock. As they were the key people in the former group, they were skilled in production and management. This organization was also based on the skills of the members and performed very well from 1981 to 7. The profit was shared equally among the partners. In 1988 another villager, Zhang Lianzhuang applied to join the group. He had been in the army for three years before he was elected as the deputy director of Shuidongtun Village, so he knew many important people in the township, which allowed him easy access to credit. Although he did not have enough money to provide stocks, he was accepted by the group because he promised to make a profit of 20 000RMB for the group by the end of that year. Finally, he succeeded. However, several months later, Ma Wenbin and Xu Kefeng withdrew their stock-shares because they suspected that Li and Xu Kehui had cheated in the accounting. The remaining three households continued the co-operation until today. This group employs about 10–20 young rural women as workers.
Temporary organizations. Temporary organizations exist during a period of the fur purchasing and selling of raw materials or semi-finished products. Fur cloth production can be divided into three stages in the Raoyangdian area:

○ dyeing the tanned fur (as raw materials) into required colours;
○ matching the colours and pattern of the dyed fur and sewing it into a semi-finished product;
○ tailoring the semi-finished pieces and sewing them into fur cloth.

So producers in this area could also be classified into three kinds of production. The dealers who were involved in the different stages purchase and sell the tanned fur or semi-finished products wholesale at prices favourable to retailers. When individual producers do not have enough money to buy or to sell products wholesale, they will form a temporary group to collect money or gather their products together and negotiate the prices with the dealers, in order to receive favourable prices. This kind of organization would form this flexible partnership only once or a few times, for dealing. Although this institutional arrangement is the primary form of organization based on the common economic interests, it is important also as a means for farmers to learn how to do business.

The role of the indigenous organization in rural development
Compared with the economic role, the social role of the indigenous organization has always been underestimated, and is also very important to rural development. First, the activities of the organization made the farmers aware of the importance of teamwork, and their role in their own enterprise and the community's welfare. The farmers perform as the main actors in rural development and 90 per cent of women in Shuidongtun Village were involved in fur cloth production for a few months in 1993. Some of them were group leaders and they received the same amount of money as their fathers, brothers or husbands which strengthened the women's position within the household and in the community, and promoted women's participation in local development. Second,

a stratum of entrepreneurs has emerged in this area. They understand economics and management through trial and error, and can therefore judge investment risks. The key role they performed in production, marketing and information services benefited thousands of households, and was very important to the formation of a mainstay industry in this area among acute competition, which benefited the farmers and the community.

Economically, the indigenous organization provided considerable employment, and increased farmers' incomes greatly. According to the survey, fur cloth production brought the farmers about 1000RMB profit per capita in Shuidongtun Village in 1993, while the income of the farming and non-farm activities in this village had been just 600–700RMB per capita over the last few years. Most of the farmers spend the increased income first in improving their life—building new houses, purchasing TVs or motor cycles, and even installing telephones at home to get market information promptly. In Shuidongtun a young farmer who was interviewed had bought the first hi-fi music system in the village and planned to send his five-year-old son to the primary school in the county town which offers better education than the one in the village. Additionally, the farmers invest the money in production with higher added value, such as fruit, animal or non-farm enterprises. So clearly the indigenous organization makes an important contribution to rural development in overcoming money shortages.

Implications of the development of indigenous organization
Through the analysis of indigenous organization development, some implications can be found which highlight the sustainability of such indigenous organizations. Compared with the collective factories, the ownership of capital, responsibility in production and marketing and the economic interests are very closely related to individual partners within the indigenous co-operative organization, which is the main factor contributing to the success of indigenous organizations and the failure of most collective factories. According to the survey, most of the collective businesses involving livestock, such as lean swine, broilers and cattle fattening which developed in the Raoyangdian area had lost money for the last few years, while those businesses run by stock-sharing co-operatives or by farm households were profitable.

All the informants considered the three kinds of indigenous organization for fur production sustainable. Although individual households could also run businesses in fur processing and/or cloth production, and some of them can earn even more on average than the partners within the co-operative, the requirements for resources, technology and ability of management and marketing could not be easily met by one household. Complementary capacities are an advantage of the co-operative over the individual household which has fewer resources and fewer people to select from. The increasing requirement for quality goods in the market will favour co-operatives more and more. On the other hand, the assistance among relatives also contributes to the sustainability of indigenous organizations.

Conclusions and recommendations

From this case-study of fur cloth production, some conclusions can be drawn for the sustainability of indigenous farmer organizations and their role in rural development.

○ The sustainability of indigenous farmer organizations is attributed to both external and internal factors. Market demand for various quality goods provided opportunities for individual enterprises, as well as for different types of co-operative organizations. But the complexity of non-farm activities such as fur cloth production in terms of resource requirements, technology, management and marketing favours co-operatives much more. And the increasing requirement for quality will provide more opportunities for the advanced type of co-operative organization.

Economic factors within the organization such as the capacities among partners and economies of scale contribute to the existence of indigenous economic organizations and in addition, the social factor of mutual assistance also plays a role for co-operatives among relatives.

The distinct ownership, responsibility and benefit distribution, which were conceived and arranged by farmers themselves, made the indigenous organization much more sustainable than organizations devised and promoted by outsiders.

○ The development of indigenous farmer organizations in non-farm activities provided a lot of employment and income opportunities, which became increasingly important when agricultural productivity had increased and more and more unemployment or underemployment emerged in rural areas. It also improved farmers' ability to do commercial business, their self-confidence to help themselves and improved the status of rural women. Therefore, the development of indigenous organizations contributes to overcoming the constraints to rural development of capital and qualified labour.

○ To take advantage fully of the benefits of indigenous organizations in rural development, some recommendations should be made:

Owing to the general policy of reform and the important role of indigenous farmer organizations, especially their advantages over collectives in less-developed rural areas, the Chinese government is pursuing a policy favourable to the development of indigenous farmers' organizations. But some concrete measures should still be taken to provide credit and other necessary support to collective and co-operative organizations, as well as to individual enterprises.

In less-developed rural areas, the collective economy at the community level is very weak and the co-operative organizations have no obligation to devote money to the community for its welfare. Therefore it is very difficult for communities, villages or townships to accumulate funds, although the funds are needed for the community projects to benefit farmers. Therefore, the government should carry out projects for rural development, provide financial support to the communities for their service activities, such as training farmers in technologies and enterprise management, and offer them support services such as market information.

19 Using indigenous organizations from West Kalimantan

CAROL J. PIERCE COLFER, REED L. WADLEY AND ENIS WIDJANARTI*

Introduction

IN 1992, A conservation project began in West Kalimantan,[1] designed to manage the major wetland area which comprises and surrounds the Kapuas Lakes. This area, officially designated as the Danau Sentarum Wildlife Reserve, was selected because of its unique flora and fauna, and because of the presence of numerous endangered animal species. One of the assumptions on which the project was founded was that co-operation with the population who lived in and around the reserve would be essential for successful management and protection of the area.

In this chapter, we discuss the approach that we have taken to working co-operatively with local people. Although the project is only one year old, we have been surprised and pleased with local co-operation with, and interest in, project activities and goals. We have found many concerns which are shared by local people and by outsiders concerned about conservation. We think the approach we have taken would be useful elsewhere, and therefore want to report it here.

Setting: geographic and ethnic

The Danau Sentarum Wildlife Reserve (DSWR) is remote, located in the province of West Kalimantan, near the Malaysian border, about 700km inland from the provincial capital, Pontianak. The trip to DSWR from Pontianak normally takes two days, including nine hours by car to Sintang, and another six hours by speedboat up the Kapuas River. DSWR is an area of seasonal lakes and seasonally flooded tropical forests. Its watershed consists of lowland tropical rain forest on hilly lands, much of which has been or is being logged by commercial timber companies.

Altitude is roughly 30–35m, and latitude is 0° 50'N; daytime temperatures are normally 30°C; and rainfall ranges between 3000 and 3500mm (according to Soemarna and Giesen, 1993) or around 4000mm per year (according to Dove, 1988). Soemarna and Giesen report the population within the reserve to be roughly 3000. If the surrounding hills and the Kapuas River communities are also included, the relevant population soars to 7000. Although the population has grown since Giesen's study (1987), the rise is not yet dramatic. But the population in the area surrounding the reserve is likely to increase significantly in the future, due to the expanding road network which is part of Indonesia's efforts to open up this isolated area (see Wadley, 1992).

---

* Carol J. Pierce Colfer is an anthropologist who has served as a Natural Resource Specialist on the Conservation Project discussed here. Reed L. Wadley of Arizona State University is an anthropologist who has collaborated with the project while conducting doctoral research among the Iban in the Batang Lupar district of West Kalimantan. Enis Widjanarti, a biologist specializing in fauna at the Asian Wetland Bureau in Bogor, has conducted fisheries research in the project area and helped co-ordinate meetings among local fishermen.

Within the reserve, most of the people are poor, Muslim, Melayu fisherfolk who catch fish to eat and to sell to buy rice and other necessities. Small communities of 50–200 people, with close kin and political connections to one or other of the larger Kapuas villages, dot the reserve. These people's residence within a wildlife reserve is illegal, according to Indonesian law; but the idea that they should be moved (as has happened in many other areas of Indonesia) is not now under serious consideration. The traditionally very productive fisheries that the Kapuas Lakes comprise may be one reason. There has been a dramatic decline in fish production during the past few years, as well as the near extinction of several wild species (most notably the *arwana, Sclerophagus formosus*, a fish which is considered good luck by the Chinese, and in the past brought prices in the thousands of US dollars). This decline has in fact represented an opportunity for the project to work more closely with local people than might otherwise have been possible, since they too are concerned about the sustainability of their fisheries.

The surrounding hills are populated by Christian Iban, Banuaka' (Maloh/ Embaloh) and Kantu' swidden rice cultivators. The Iban are the most numerous in the area immediately surrounding the reserve. These Dayaks' subsistence is based on a complex agro-forestry system which includes rice, fruits, vegetables, cash crops, and timber and non-timber forest products, significantly supplemented by hunting, fishing and visits by the men to nearby Malaysia for wage labour. Like the Melayu, many Dayaks have significant environmental concerns. They report reductions in hunting success which they attribute partially to habitat destruction, both by swidden cultivation and, probably more significantly, by logging activities. They blame timber companies for soil erosion and chemicals which pollute their drinking-water and reduce fish populations; and they are concerned by what they consider destructive and unsustainable timber harvesting which will leave few construction materials and other non-timber forest products for their children and grandchildren.

Both ethnic groups engage in activities which represent environmental threats. Some swidden (rice/rubber) cultivation by Melayu occurs within the reserve; some Iban communities have large tracts of *Imperata cylindrica* (an invader grass), which may indicate insufficient swidden fallow periods due to local population increases on small longhouse territories with generally poor soil; both groups kill endangered species, use destructive or unsustainable methods to catch fish and cut timber illegally.

The conservation project: goals, assumptions, and strategies

As with most complex projects, different parties have had different priorities. Even within the team (of ever-changing composition) there has been considerable variation, with the team leader most drawn to reserve management and fisheries issues; Colfer, focusing on beneficially involving local people in reserve management; personnel from the Asian Wetlands Bureau (AWB, the implementing agency) emphasizing research needs; and Indonesian staff from the Office for Conservation of Natural Resources (SBKSDA) concerned to build up infrastructure and enforcement capabilities. Throughout the year, however, there have been recurrent threads. We knew we wanted:

○ to assess fisheries and how they could be managed more sustainably;
○ to assess the effects (present and future) of logging, plantations, roads and

other large-scale development activities in the area on the reserve and on local people;

o to determine what local people know and do, and how that can and should affect the reserve and its management.

Below we focus on this last topic.

There was general agreement, in theory, among all parties that local people's co-operation would be essential if the unique environment of DSWR was to be preserved. The Indonesian government does not have sufficient funds or trained personnel to police remote areas like DSWR in an effective way. We also all recognized that local people must perceive some benefit to themselves if they were going to be actively involved in reserve management on a sustained basis. We knew we could not simply tell the Iban that they should not hunt endangered species, if (as they are) these species were a significant part of their subsistence diet. Nor could we simply urge poor fishing people not to catch the outstandingly valuable *arwana*, with any hope of success. We would have to work on developing some alternative income sources for local people as well as addressing the more conventional conservation issues.

Our general strategy was to begin with research, in order to understand the locale and the people in it. We hoped fairly quickly, as our understanding grew, to shift over into a more collaborative mode, where we actually began managing the reserve with local people. We also planned, as time went by, to distribute appropriate, 'bottom-up' awareness materials—targeted to problems identified both locally and internationally—to communities in and around the reserve.

In search of collaborative opportunities

In determining what people know and do, and how they could contribute to reserve management, we began with three topics of enquiry. First, we initiated several studies to document people's existing patterns of behaviour. How were they using their resources now? We instituted two spot-check, time-allocation studies (cf. Johnson, 1975; see also Colfer, 1981, Sigman *et al.*, 1989), one in Nanga Pengembung (a Melayu community) and one in Wong Garai[2] (an Iban community, being studied fully by Wadley).[3]

We designed daily record keeping studies in the same communities. A sample (eight–13 families from the same two communities) was selected to record information every day on what they got from the rivers and lakes, from the forests, from agricultural endeavours and from wage or contract labour. They also recorded what they ate every day. Each sample family kept these records for one full month in (roughly) September and December 1992, and March and June 1993.

Colfer also did part-time participant observation in three Melayu communities and one Iban community, and collaborated with Wadley. Ian Hood (a wildlife student), Wadley and Colfer designed a hunting study, which Wadley is implementing in Wong Garai, to begin to quantify the importance of hunting for the Iban and the hunting pressure on different species. This past year we have conducted nine small, community studies focused on specific human actions related to reserve management.

Second, we tried to determine areas in which local people had significant indigenous knowledge that could be useful in reserve management. Our method was simply to follow up on areas identified in our studies and in informal conversation. We learned, for instance, that the Melayu set out concave wooden troughs where honeybees come to make their nests. This honey is then harvested during December/January, and generates significant funds for many families. We used one of our local speedboat drivers (An) who was interested in this topic and an experienced honey collector himself, to do a small, focused study on honey production. This information can now be used by ecologists interested in the flowers that draw the bees, by entomologists interested in the bees themselves, and by people interested in developing honey as a business in this area (see recommendations by Dixon *et al.*, 1991, for honey production in Borneo).

At Wong Garai we found that the community had forbidden logging companies from cutting the old-growth forest within their territory in order to preserve the watershed and hunting area. This kind of indigenous management has been highlighted in the project, to serve as a potent example to other communities.

Other areas where we have discovered significant local knowledge include fisheries, floating horticulture, animal/bird identification and behaviour, timber and non-timber forest products, constantly changing aquatic pathways through the lakes and streams, hydrology, agro-forestry in the hills. All of these, and undoubtedly more, can be used in reserve management and in further environmental research in the area.

Besides the practical wish to make use of existing knowledge within the conservation project, we felt that use and publication of indigenous knowledge could serve an empowering function. If outsiders began to realize that indigenous people were not simply 'poor, dumb villagers', this could give them a greater voice in their own destiny. We also suspected that the respect *we* showed them, by recognizing their knowledge of this environment that scientists too were trying to understand, would make them more receptive to our conservation efforts, more confident in their own ability to conserve and protect the environment, and more interested in preserving the valuable indigenous knowledge they possess about it.

Partly to facilitate the sharing of indigenous knowledge and resource management strategies and partly to increase conservation awareness in the DSWR, we began publishing a newsheet every month. The *Suara Bakakak,* which means 'The Voice of the Stork-billed Kingfisher', is usually only two pages of short articles. Our idea again is to empower local people and to encourage co-operation in conservation. We avoid preaching or threatening, and we tie every article to local interests or local people. In our eight publications to date, we have had articles on topics such as the following:

○ *Local management practices.* We have reported, for instance, on traditional protected forest areas and fisheries regulations.
○ *Indigenous knowledge.* We interviewed a retired crocodile hunter and showed how his knowledge of their habits could be used by scientists specializing in crocodiles.
○ *Project news.* We thank local people who are helping the project, and inform them of planned studies/activities.
○ *Awareness/co-operation efforts.* We recently sponsored a contest to draw a Stork-billed Kingfisher (*bakakak*, featured in a well-known Melayu story) for a logo for the project, and the Rhinoceros Hornbill (*kenyalang*, important to the Iban) to be used as a symbol.
○ *Development ideas.* We suggest ways to improve the area to make it more attractive to tourists, or feature local handicrafts that could be sold.

Our third topic of investigation was indigenous management and organization. We knew that people tend to group together and organize themselves, that they tend to have traditional methods for meshing their environment with their human needs. We wanted to know what those were, hoping we would be able to build on them. Again, we looked into this on an *ad hoc* basis.

We tried to identify potential avenues by looking for titled positions, by seeing how people grouped together, by listening for named groups. We were not only looking for indigenous organizations (although we had a sense that they might be most effective for reserve management, in the long run); we have been looking for any grouping through which we might encourage conservation. Among the official grouping mechanisms which we expect to use are the schools, the mosques, the churches, the health centres, the village heads and the county and village governments. These will be useful in spreading information from the conservation project or sharing it among communities.

Indigenous grouping mechanisms among the Melayu include households, fisherwomen who farm small plots together near the villages and the fishing group (a head fisherman and the fisherfolk who fish within the village's area).[4] Although Colfer's participant observation skills were useful in identifying these groups, the fishing group was the obvious one for us to begin working with. Fishing groups typically have a leader, a second in command and a secretary; they develop and enforce (with differing degrees of success) their own regulations on fisheries and other natural resources; they have methods for dividing up scarce resources and for dealing with offenders; and they have a defined area with borders. We discuss our progress to date working with them in the next section.

Among the Iban and Kantu', there are fewer formal organizations;[5] among the Banuaka' (Maloh) there was a traditional ranking system similar to that among the Kayan and other central Borneo groups (see King, 1985) with aristocrats, commoners and slaves. This ranking, however, is no longer viable. Instead the Banuaka' have adopted the Iban system of regional leadership with the *temenggung* as the district leader of customary law (*adat*) and his deputies called *patih*. These elders are called upon to deal with disputes and traditional matters such as marriages and funerals. Their positions are recognized and promoted by the Indonesian government. These men have tended to be older and largely uneducated. There is, however, a growing awareness that future *adat* leaders should be educated in both Iban customary law and in Indonesian national law. Literacy is becoming more important, in order to deal better with the outside influences that are expected to come.

The most enduring local Dayak organization is the longhouse, consisting of several separate family apartments; each family, however, is an independent unit of production and consumption (see Freeman, 1970). Iban longhouses in West Kalimantan range in size from only six families to over 60 in some cases; most range between 15 and 25 families. Longhouses themselves have traditionally been independent of each other, being led in a very democratic fashion by a headman and group of elders. Since the mid–1980s, however, longhouses have been grouped by the government into a formal village system with generally five longhouses under one government-appointed leader. Because of the current governmental literacy requirement such leaders are often young, inexperienced and without traditional authority; given Iban values on independence, they have very little authority in other longhouses within their jurisdiction.

Other indigenous organizations among the Iban are more fluid in leadership and membership, being largely specific to particular needs at certain times. These include groups of men who hunt together or travel to Malaysia for wage work, and agricultural work parties consisting mainly of women.

Given the different needs and interests of the Iban and other Dayaks in the area surrounding the reserve and because of difficulties of transport to the hills where they tend to live, we have developed, though not yet implemented, an alternative strategy for work with the Dayaks which we discuss in the section entitled 'Planned Collaboration with the Dayaks'.

Collaborating with an indigenous organization among the Melayu

The fishing groups seemed like the organization with the most potential for enforcing appropriate fishing regulations. It was already clear that the government's fisheries department had inadequate funding even to visit the DSWR fishing communities, let alone provide extension services or enforce their regulations. Individual communities already had regulations for their own community members that were similar to typical fisheries regulations enforced by governmental organizations. The fishing people understood the necessity to protect particular species at particular times or against over-effective fishing gear. But there has been no co-ordination among communities. And the fish, like most fish, know no human boundaries. They swim all over the lakes.

We felt that a first step should be to bring fishing groups from several communities in the same ecological area together to discuss existing regulations, and to learn what the fishing people thought might be appropriate future regulations. Our thinking was that common regulations, agreed on by fishing people, could be enforced primarily by the communities, with some minor support from other governmental agencies (Fisheries, SBKSDA, the police).

Our team met to discuss how these meetings should be arranged. For this purpose we decided to focus on the Melayu, as the major fishing peoples. We would deal with the problem of seasonal Iban poisoning (*tuba*) of fish in another context. We decided that the overall reserve area could be divided into five major areas, largely determined by rivers. Communities were grouped as follows:

○ along the upper Tawang River, to the west;
○ along the lower Tawang and Tengkidap Rivers, to the south-west;
○ from Sekulat down the Belitung River, to the south-east;
○ from Nanga Leboyan up the Leboyan River, in the east;
○ from Pulau Majang towards Lanjak, in the north.

Our first meeting was in May 1993, to which we invited representatives from five communities from the upper Tawang River (nearest to our field centre at Bukit Tekenang and one of the areas we know the best). We invited the head fisherman (*Ketua Nelayan*) and his assistant (*wakil*) from each community. Recognizing the involvement of women in fishing, we requested that at least one woman come from each community as well. Although women are less well represented in the formal structure than are the men, they are nearly as actively involved in making the family's living, along with their more typical household responsibilities.

In our invitation, we emphasized the purpose of the meeting as an opportunity for fishing people to discuss their own problems and possible solutions. We asked them to bring copies of their existing regulations and simple maps showing the borders of the areas managed by their respective communities.

The project's field centre, at Bukit Tekenang, was arranged with local mats made by local people on the floor so that the fisherfolk would be at ease. Project boats picked up the fishing people and brought them to and from the meeting, where they also received lunch. Project staff were briefed on the importance of letting the community members take the lead in discussions. The fishing people selected their own leader, with only introductory remarks and occasional technical input by project staff.

We recognized the difficulty of getting Melayu women to speak out in public fora such as this, so we gave them the alternative of meeting separately, though they did not do so. We are still not satisfied with the level of female participation, but we continue to feel it is important because of the interface between regulation of the fisheries and population control within the reserve. Although few people want to move the existing population out, there is general agreement that resources could be sorely strained by any significant population increase.

Part-time fishing families who come into the reserve during the dry season, when fish are concentrated in the few remaining rivers and are therefore caught in great numbers, represent another environmental threat. We were curious if the people understood that these visiting families represented competition for increasingly scarce resources, and whether they would entertain the idea of limiting access by outsiders to their areas.[6] The issue is complicated by the close ties between fishing communities within the reserve and their 'mother' communities on the Kapuas. A majority of these ties appear to be through women.

We were anxious to bring up this issue early on, because we feared that if the project were successful in efforts at income generation for local people, this could draw still more people into the reserve—an almost certain guarantee of failure of the overall conservation project goals.

Although the meeting was held only recently, we are encouraged. The fisherfolk suggested banning the raising of *toman (Channa microlepis)* in cages, a business in which many of them are already involved. They fear that the species is being over-fished as *toman* fingerlings are taken from the wild; and that since *toman* are carnivorous, large amounts of other species are caught simply to provide food for the caged *toman*, many of whom die in their cages.

The discussions which occurred seemed to us an excellent first step in trying to develop the best approach to protect and manage the environment here. One of the fisherfolk's suggestions was to limit the catch of *toman* fingerlings, by closing the season during spawning and/or allowing people to catch *toman* fingerlings only once a year. One outcome of the discussions was a request (subsequently printed in the *Suara Bakakak* newsletter) that outsiders discuss their plans to use local natural resources with the appropriate head fisherman before harvesting anything. One remaining problem is the differing schedule of fishery closures in different villages. It is not now possible—though perhaps also not necessary—to make a single regulation that will fit all villages.

Besides this, the use of the *jermal*, a large net which effectively blocks off a river mouth and collects all the fish which come out of that river, was discussed. In this case there were some differences of opinion about the allowable mesh size and open and closed seasons for the *jermal* in the different communities. Some communities are overtly hostile to the use of *jermals*, particularly nets with very small meshes. While the use of this gear is allocated by lottery in each community, only people with the right to fish can win the lottery. Not all the communities which attended this first meeting use this gear, because its use depends on the location and water conditions in the vicinity.

There were also a few people present who did not agree with the suggestion for a closed *toman* season in this area, arguing that their only source of income was from fishing for *toman*. They only fish for other kinds of fish in order to feed them to their captive *toman*. In general, though, most agreed that regulations which limit the catch on these fish are needed for sustainability of the fishery in the short run and, even more importantly, for use by future generations. One result of the cage-culture activities discussed above, for example, is the rarity with which certain species of fish, such as *ketutung* and *pacil*, are now encountered in this area. These are probably fish that are often used to feed the caged *toman*.

There are already existing regulations from the Kapuas Hulu Fisheries Department about size and quantities of *toman* which can be caught, size of gear used, etc.; but these regulations are not effectively enforced. The Fisheries Department has given authority to local communities to make additional local regulations which are consistent with their needs relating to size and kind of fish which can be caught, work areas, regulations about outsiders coming into the area, and other things which fit with the formal rules. The degree to which these rules are followed varies considerably and whether they effectively protect the local natural resources has not yet been established. What is clear is that no regulations will work without the active involvement of local communities.

That *jermals* have a significant, and negative, impact on local fisheries is fairly well established (see also Giesen, 1987), as are the concerns of many local fishing people about them. Existing regulations will have to be strengthened and supported both within local communities and from governmental agencies.

In pursuit of this goal, the project will continue meeting with the other four clusters of fishing communities. This facilitates interaction among communities and provides both the conservation project and local Fisheries Department officials with a better understanding of what the fishing people can and want to do about the sustainability of their fishery. The opportunity to air their views itself seems to serve an empowering function as well.

Planned collaboration with the Dayaks

As mentioned above, hunting among the Dayaks is a sticky and central problem. Some Melayu hunt animals for sale in Malaysia, others catch a few in their fishing nets by accident. But the Iban constitute a much more serious hunting population. They have few religious restrictions on what they eat,[7] their diet has traditionally included bushmeat as an integral component, their boys are taught to hunt as a significant part of becoming adult. Hunting is consistent with their traditional forest lifestyle and with their concern to protect the essential rice and vegetable crops from animals such as pig and deer. Many of the animals they hunt are endangered species, such as sambar deer (*Cervus unicolor*), barking deer (*Muntiacus muntjac* and *M. atherodes*), and mousedeer (*Tragulus javanicus* and *T. napu*); and particularly in the area immediately surrounding the reserve, they may be killing reserve animals which flee to dry ground when the waters rise.

The fact that the Dayaks perceive a reduction in the populations of at least some animals in recent years represents one possible entry point for collaboration with the conservation project. Deer particularly have been mentioned as in decline; conversely, there are many examples globally of successful management of deer populations. We are trying to learn about existing Iban wildlife management strategies, which we suspect are intimately intertwined with their agro-forestry system.

Since some habitat problems for animals can be linked to timber harvesting, the Iban, for instance, may be interested in helping to monitor the timber companies' compliance with governmental regulations. Currently timber companies have almost free rein to harvest as much as they like without supervision. These Iban communities are well placed to serve a monitoring function if they see it in their interest to do so.

These efforts, however, may be complicated by the logging companies' practice of giving fees to village headmen for having logged within their village's official territories, whether or not logging was done within the headman's own home longhouse area.[8] The *adat* leaders as well receive fees for dealing with relations between the companies and local Iban communities affected by the logging. And at least one *temenggung* is a co-holder of a logging concession on the lower Leboyan River which is on the border with the reserve. All of this creates divided loyalties and split obligations, making the local leaders less than independent of the companies' interests. Because of the scarcity of local jobs to obtain cash, leaders would find it hard to turn down such fees unless there were viable alternatives.

The complexity of and interconnections among these issues, combined with inter-ethnic and logistical problems of transport in this place with few roads, prompted us to consider developing a conservation cadre of Iban youth. There are increasing numbers of unemployed, high-school educated young people in this area. We suspect that the opportunity to get training in conservation, in community development and in research techniques would be welcome to many of them.

We would like to select perhaps 10 individuals, from different communities, who would be interested in working on these problems. Again we are concerned about empowerment of local communities. We would like to bring these people to the project's field centre for two weeks of training, during which we could expose them to the 'bottom-up' approach of the project and exchange ideas about important conservation and human issues in the area. We would also train them in interview and participant observation methods which would allow them to learn to codify their communities' wildlife management strategies, including patterns of wildlife harvesting, habitat enrichment, and any other efforts which might support wildlife in the area.

These young people would then return to the field centre for one to two weeks to write up and share their findings with each other and with conservation project staff. Together with project staff, they would develop several scenarios for wildlife management that would be consistent with local interests and practices, as well as protecting endangered wildlife and enhancing wildlife habitats and reproduction. These they would bring back to their communities for discussion.

Their final visit to the field centre would be to prepare for one or more meetings, composed of the official village leaders, the *adat* leaders, and respected elders from selected Dayak communities. Several such meetings may be necessary, based on geographical considerations, differences in wildlife or hunting patterns and linguistic differences. The purpose of this final meeting would be to come to some agreement on wildlife management in the area which would be enforceable largely by local communities.

We would anticipate that part of such a management plan would involve the development of core reserve zones where no hunting was allowed, and buffer zone areas where management was designed to protect the endangered populations and manage those species which could continue to be hunted. Taming the timber companies will probably be an important part of successful reserve and buffer-zone management; and these Dayak communities could play an important part. An important side benefit would be the training of the young people on conservation and development, as well as the airing of key conservation issues in a variety of fora around the reserve. Since these issues bear directly on many aspects of Dayak life, and focus on some of their concerns as well as more global conservation concerns, we think this approach could activate these communities effectively.

Conclusions

Although this conservation project is still young, we feel that the approach we have taken is the right one. Contrary to the experience of many conservation projects, we have had excellent co-operation from local people to date. We have been pleasantly surprised with their interest in conservation, and their awareness of many of the factors that contribute to habitat destruction. Indeed, we would argue that the significant hindrances to involving local people in reserve management to date have come from bureaucratic and logistical constraints, rather than from any antagonism or lack of capability of local people.

Notes

1. This project was funded by the Indonesian Government and the British Overseas Development Administration (ODA), as part of a larger project called the Indonesian Tropical Forestry Management Project, implemented co-operatively by a Scottish consulting firm (IFSC) and the Indonesian Forest Protection and Nature Conservation Agency (PHPA) within the Indonesian Department of Forestry. The Asian Wetland Bureau (AWB) and Worldwide Fund for Nature (WWF) formed an association which held a subcontract for the conservation component of this larger project. In this chapter, we will concern ourselves only with this subcontract, referred to simply as the conservation project. Wadley's research is funded by the National Science Foundation (Grant No. BNS–9114652), Wenner-Gren Foundation, Sigma Xi, and Arizona State University; it is sponsored by the Balai Kajian Sejarah dan Nilai Tradisional, Departemen Pendidikan dan Kebudayaan, Pontianak, West Kalimantan.
2. This is a pseudonym selected by Wadley, a doctoral student at Arizona State University.
3. We had actually planned to institute these studies in four communities (two from each ethnic group, scattered around and in DSWR). However, most of the proposed team members could not join us, so we had to scale down our plans.
4. These Melayu are unusual in the degree to which women are involved in fishing. Both sexes and all ages fish, using a variety of methods. Although women are less involved than men in managing the fishery within the context of these fishing groups, there are several who hold formal positions.
5. Besides our own experience, we have been fortunate to have access to relevant literature on people in or near this area, especially Padoch (1983) who worked just across the border in Malaysia among the Iban; and Dove (1988) who worked with the Kantu', up the Empanang River not far from this area. We are also grateful for our opportunity to collaborate with Pak Ir. Jacobus Frans (an educated Banuaka' from Ukit Ukit in the Lanjak area) and Beben (our field centre administrator, also from Ukit Ukit).

6. We later learned from local people that the head of the Regency (Bupati) had decreed some years ago that outsiders *had* to be accepted and allowed to fish throughout the lakes area. We have written to the Bupati to ask that this be altered officially.
7. Some Dayaks have a specific restriction (for example, they cannot eat orangutan because one of their ancestors became one when he died), but most plants and animals are considered edible by most Dayaks.
8. The administrative unit, the village, consists now of several longhouses, which were not traditionally affiliated.

References

Colfer, C.J.P. (1981), 'Women, Men and Time in the Forests of Kalimantan', *Borneo Research Bulletin* 13(2), 75–85.

Dixon, A., Roditi, H., and Silverman, L. (1991), *From Forest to Market: A Feasibility Study of the Development of Selected Non-Timber Forest Products from Borneo for the U.S. Market*, Cambridge, Massachusetts: Project Borneo.

Dove, M. (1988), 'The Kantu' System of Land Tenure: The Evolution of Tribal Land Rights in Borneo', in Fortmann and Bruce (eds), *Whose Trees? Proprietary Dimensions of Forestry*, Boulder, Colorado: Westview Press, 86–95.

Freeman, J.D. (1970), *Report on the Iban*, Oxford: Oxford University Press.

Giesen, W. (1987), 'Danau Sentarum Wildlife Reserve: Inventory, Ecology and Management Guidelines'. Bogor: WWF and PHPA.

Johnson, A.W. (1975), 'Time allocation in Machiguenga', *Ethnology* 14: 310–21.

King, V.T. (1985), *The Maloh of West Kalimantan*, Dordrecht: Foris.

Padoch, C. (1983), *Migration and its Alternatives among the Iban of Sarawak*, Koninklijk Instituut voor Land, Taal, en Volkendunde, Leiden, The Netherlands.

Sigman, V., Colfer, C.J.P., Yost, R. and Wilson, K. (1989), 'Farm-Based Research in the Tropsoils Project, Sitiung', *Working Together: Gender Analysis in Agriculture*, Vols. I,II (Feldstein and Poats, eds), West Hartford: Kumarian Press.

Soemarna, K. and Giesen, W. (1993), 'Developing a Model to Combine Exploitation and Conservation: Danau Sentarum Wildlife Reserve, West Kalimantan, Indonesia', Paper presented in Japan.

Wadley, R.L. (1992), 'Jalan Lintas Utara: The Road to Change in Kapuas Hulu', Unpublished manuscript.

20 Personal networks and agricultural extension in the Philippines[1]

RICARDO C. ARMONIA*

Introduction

IN THE PHILIPPINES, the government has the most extensive agricultural extension network in terms of geographical coverage, relative to any other organization in the country. It does not, however, have enough resources to reach out to every individual. Therefore, unless people from remote communities take the initiative to reach out, their presence and their needs are unlikely to be recognized.

From the above perspective, an ethnographic action- and research-oriented study conducted in 1991 in a remote Philippine coastal village investigated how the concept of a farm-family initiated extension may be evolved and if it is appropriate at all. In the process, the investigation led to the furtherance of the relationship-based network concept relative to extension work. This chapter was therefore intended to address two related topics: farm-family initiated extension in general terms, and relationship-based networks in more specific terms, the latter underpinning the former.

In the study, farm-family extension has been used to refer to the effort wherein each family member, singly or in groups, effortlessly assumes roles to reach out to support systems. This approach is to give particular consideration to non-joiners of formal village organizations who are most likely to be left out, as the development trend now is to support formally organized groups. To create this environment of 'effortlessly assuming roles' means to seek out the creation of a system within existing approaches that is based on personal ties. It is a system which takes advantage of the various social roles that each member of the family assumes other than occupational roles. That is, agricultural extension should not be focusing on the farmer alone but on the family as a whole. This is to treat the family as a corporate unit as Paolucci *et al.* (1977) appropriately puts it: 'where family members act interdependently or independently of each other but guided by values formed through family interaction'.

Relationship-based networks are those interactions founded on personal ties such as kinship, friendship and patronage ties. Development-oriented institutions have too often overlooked the fact that friendship and patronage ties are forms of social networks and kinship a form of social organization because of the emphasis on 'organizations' as formalized and legalized groups or associations. In other words, social organization has been forgotten in the emphasis on 'organizations'.

Developing a system around such informal networks (particularly emphasizing the positive attributes of kinship and friendship) *vis-à-vis* formal social structures may encourage the non-joiners of formally organized groups to reach out more actively. By formal social structures reference is made to groups like associations and co-operatives that have a set of officers and members guided by fixed roles based on rules and regulations (constitutions and by-laws). They are

* Programme Researcher in the Office of the Vice President for Programme of the International Institute of Rural Reconstruction (IIRR) Silang, Philippines.

often formed on the initiatives of outside groups—usually development agencies both from government and non-governmental organizations. These formal groups have (or are working towards achieving) legal status to enable them to deal with support systems which are often structured in a similar fashion.

In summary, this chapter talks of two interrelated themes: the potential of personalizing extension and the expansion of its network base using informal and personal links to the formal structures.

Personalizing extension

The setting

The study was conducted in Barangay Alimsog, Municipality of Sto. Domingo, Province of Albay, the Philippines. Access to the village was through the facilitation of the Alimsog Development Co-operative, Inc. (ALIMDECO) and the International Institute of Rural Reconstruction (IIRR). The IIRR assists the village as part of the Local Resources Management (LRM) Project commissioned to it by the National Development and Economic Authority of the Philippine Government. The LRM was aimed at ensuring the genuine participation of the poor in the development process along with the strengthening local government capabilities (IIRR, 1988). Barangay Alimsog is a fishing and farming village with six *sitios* (sub-villages): Sadit na Alimsog, Iraya, Alimsog Proper or Sentro, Inabuyan, Banago, and Balete. The major livelihood activities of the people in the village are fishing, farming and burlap weaving. Existing formal groups are the village council and ALIMDECO. Alimsog is more than 500 kilometres south of Manila and can be reached (from Manila) by a combination of various modes of transport—plane, bus, the public utility *jeepney*, motorized *banca* (boat), paddled *banca,* and by walking along the coastline and/or the 35-kilometre earth-fill mountain trail. The village is 23 kilometres from the provincial capital of Albay Province (Legazpi City) and 13 kilometres from the town proper of Sto. Domingo—the municipality to which Alimsog belongs. Though the *barangay* is only 13 kilometres away from the town proper it takes about an hour to negotiate the distance by motorized *banca* (excluding waiting time), and more than an hour if one is to take a combination of *jeepney* ride and walking or paddling the *banca*. But in spite of this, the villagers are rarely late for their appointments in Sto. Domingo.

It is important to bear in mind that mobility and information flow in Alimsog are not facilitated by high technology gadgetry, as the village has yet to be reached by electricity, although there are battery-operated transistor radios and combustion engines for a few boats. But the remoteness of Alimsog is not the only limiting factor here. It is just one link in the chain of interwoven concerns. Of equal concern should be the family's cash security in a money-oriented economy, the people's views and attitudes toward personal and community development, their socio-cultural behaviour and their current thinking on the ecological environment. It is not enough to assume that making more cash and farming/ fishing equipment available will spur economic growth, that community welfare and aspirations equate to personal welfare and aspirations, that emancipation from patronage ties is a step toward a self-reliant community, and that people are simply resisting changes and are unaware and insensitive to the deterioration of their environment. In essence, agricultural extension is not just about the development and use of appropriate agricultural knowledge but also of understanding people and communities in their totality. These are not constraints. They are the challenges awaiting extension practitioners.

Three extension models

Following the analysis of Bawden (1989) and Woog (1988), three extension models are identified that have evolved through decades of agricultural development. These are the production, productivity and sustainability models. Variations and combinations of the concepts of these models may be evident in various extension strategies and approaches that existed and continue to be adapted to the present. In brief, the production and productivity models put emphasis on change (knowledge adoption, particularly of science and technology) while the sustainability model looks at extension (and agricultural development in general) as a human activity system in interaction with the environment.

In the production model, change is directed at agricultural practices and technology which would lead to increased production. Application of technology is the focus and the farmer is one of the limiting variables to be manipulated to achieve change. Approaches that fall under this model are the contract-growing scheme and the Training-and-Visit System.

The productivity model looks not at maximizing the rate of technology adoption but at making choices between alternatives and at putting together a combination of innovations and practices. The viability of the farmer as well as the farm is the focus. The farming systems approach falls under this model.

The sustainability model concerns itself with the consequences of technological change more than with failure to accept the changes. It looks beyond the individual economic rationale as a basis for desirable change by considering the impact of progress (and of the action of the farmer) on the larger socio-ecological environment. It therefore works toward the concept of sustainable agriculture. In the Philippine context, sustainability has an added angle: that is, the sustainability of the extension process itself for the promotion of a sustainable agriculture given the country's very limited resources for extension work. The participatory technology development concept of Jiggins and de Zeeuw (1990), the farmer-to-farmer extension of IIRR (Ibus, 1991), and the farmer-back-to-farmer concept of Rhoades (1984) are examples of approaches that use this model.

Interestingly in the Philippines, one does not only see a happy mix of these three models but also that, in terms of reaching the intended beneficiaries, there has been a major shifting from diffusion theory to that of the 'target categorization' approach described by Roling (1988). The former places emphasis on the progressive farmers/early adopters who are expected to pass on the information/technology to other farmers as a natural consequence. The latter zeroes in its interventions directly to the resource-poor farmers who need extension services the most. The only problem with the target categorization approach, however, is that it has been equated with forming active constituencies (mostly referring to formally organized groups) which have systematically, though unintentionally, kept the non-joiners of formal organizations in their usual marginalized position.

Personal ties

If extension is ever to achieve a wider base of participation, it has to go beyond the agent–client relationship that characterizes so much extension work. The agent–client relationship is relevant but so far it has failed to recognize the value of informal resources systems (Heraud, 1979) to extension practice. The relationship has too often been equated with a professional imparting advice/information to a client. In the Philippines, the cash-poor farmers are not confident enough to mix or rub elbows with the professionals. Thus, they often seek 'non-professional advice' in a personalized setting, mostly from friends and kin. The emerging interest in integrating indigenous knowledge and information systems within the framework of participatory approaches to extension and rural development is an encouraging trend to correct this situation.

Inasmuch as this chapter argues for integrating personal networks into the Philippine extension system, it will be necessary to describe briefly kinship systems and the other forms of social relationships particular to the Philippines.

Jocano (1982: 105) defines kinship as involving 'a network of interpersonal relationships which is reckoned by blood, by affinity, or by performance of rituals associated with baptism, confirmation and marriage'. This definition essentially describes two types of kinship—real and fictive. Real kinship ties are ties contracted either by descent or by being relatives by blood (Fox, 1967), or by marriage. Fictive kinship ties are formed for reasons other than kinship but are given the strength and permanence of real kinship (Taylor, 1973). The various types of fictive kinship found in different societies are adoption, institutionalized friendship, and the *compadrinazgo* (Taylor, 1973; Hart, 1977).

Some attributes of fictive kinship in the Philippine context as described by Hart (1977), Morais (1981), and Jocano (1982) are:

○ It is used to intensify existing relationships, particularly those of the same sex.
○ It is a mechanism for creating formal social contact to extend one's connections.
○ The tie is extended beyond the principals (godparents, parent, parents and godchild) or to the principal's kinsmen.
○ Ritual kinship ties are also extended even to non-sponsor friends of the ritual kin to solidify social relationships within a neighbourhood.

The relative ease with which a network of ritual bonds can be developed has led to some politically-active Filipinos using it to their advantage in mobilizing people to their cause.

The other forms of social relationships in Philippine culture which, like kinship, have high affective content are friendship, market-exchange partnership, patron–client bonds and relationships born out of special debts of gratitude (Morais, 1981). The notion of friendship is based on mutual trust and reciprocity, (Goody, 1973) but unlike kinship is a matter of choice. Respect is based on equality and not on seniority.

The special market-exchange partnership in the Philippines is commonly termed the *suki* system (Hart, 1977; Morais, 1981). *Suki* literally means a regular customer who gets discounts without haggling; extending credit may be part of the relationship but is not necessary (Szanton, 1970; Jocano, 1982). In this relationship, two individuals agree implicitly regularly to exchange goods or services in the commercial context. It is face-to-face personalized contact (making public relations personal) couched in friendliness that results in mutual trust with the exchange of gossip as a common feature (Morais, 1981: 46, 54–5).

On patron–client relationships, Scott offers this definition:

A special case of dyadic ties involving a largely instrumental friendship in which an individual of higher socioeconomic status (patron) uses his own influence and resources to provide protection or benefits, or both, for a person of lower status (client) who, for his part, reciprocates by offering general support and assistance, including personal services, to the patron (Scott, 1977: 125).

In Alimsog, patron–client bonds exist not only between landlord and tenants but also between farmers and farm workers. And since such a relationship is usually merged with friendship and kinship ties, development practitioners should be cautious in attempting summarily to dismantle patron–client ties.

Patron–client ties are strengthened by one additional form of social relationship in the Philippine context—the debt of gratitude (*utang na loob* in local terminology). It is a 'feeling of indebtedness which is incurred when one receives a favour, service or good and, of a deep sense of obligation to reciprocate when the appropriate moment comes' (Quisumbing, 1990: 152). Some community development and extension workers get accepted and establish healthy work relations in communities assigned to them in this manner, for example, after doing a favour to some community member to impress on them that s/he can be trusted.

Overall, what the above attributes of the different forms of social relationships are conveying is the potential role of a network such as an interactive mechanism, for creating and intensifying social contact, especially among the poor, enabling them to be reached by extension services.

As soon as the personal bond between field staff and the people becomes 'institutionalized' as did the 'extended families', research, extension and other support systems (including the local village associations) find they fit better in an 'extended network'. An extended network based on a sincere personal bond is the best way to make extension accessible. Such a system may encourage people to reach out.

Enhancing the participation and network base: an extension agenda

Participation and non-participation

A contextual analysis of sets of information culled from field notes and various documents relating to Alimsog showed that a distinction has to be made between participating in the process of development (as a goal) and participation in organizations (as a means). Furthermore, the analysis revealed that the general view of participation is associated mostly with joining groups involved in projects/ programmes. However, there was no clear mention of non-participation. Either people participated more or they participated less.

A good starting-point to pick up from, therefore, is to accept the fact that some people participate more actively and others less actively. If participation is really central to project implementation, there is a need to orient those projects to take more advantage of the quality of participation, whether it be less or more active participation, rather than to wish for full participation by most people. One should not be so much bothered that people are participating less actively but that people are not giving their best whenever they do participate.

Some of the information analysed suggests that many among the poor are not ready for long-term commitments to projects and activities (of growing complexity) outside the immediate family agenda. This becomes more problematic for families in which some household members are ready for longer-term commitments while others are not, thereby threatening the smooth interpersonal relations in the family. This is exemplified in one of the situations analysed below.

Years ago, Millet used to quarrel with her husband, Pons (who is very active in the village co-operative—ALIMDECO), because, at times, even the little money they have for buying rice is spent during the performance of his duties. But she gradually understood the importance of the co-operative when she got a job as day-care teacher for the day-care school project of ALIMDECO. To be accepted as a teacher, she had had, reluctantly, to apply for membership and through time had become as active as her husband in the organization.

The above situation illustrates one of the 'growing pains' that an organization has to overcome. These are the crucible tests that help enrich organizations which are able to respond positively to them. Such predicaments strain not only the relationship of the member with the organization but the relationships within the family as well. It is under such pressures as strained relationships that an active member drops out of the association, or at the least, decides to be inactive for some time.

People like Millet who are 'overtly against' are actually active participants in the development process, only that they are outside the organization/project. They should not be dismissed as people who are simply not prepared to commit themselves to the co-operative cause. They should be treated as people who are pointing out deficiencies in the organization that need to be addressed. In professional circles, they are called 'critics'.

To join or not to join

People know when to draw the line between friendship/personal relationships and business once they have 'crossed the bridge'. Once there, they are able to cope well. One impression is that the concern of many residents in Alimsog is first to 'get across the bridge' in terms of getting assistance. What usually gives them the confidence to cross the bridge is having relatives or friends who have reached the other end (or more ideally, who already belong at the other end. In this way, they put to good use a system which is termed a relationship-based network. In using such a network, the desired assistance is obtained through an interconnected series of actions, plans, and decisions. Subconsciously, they observe a concept of sequential decision-making (Rosenhead, 1989: 197–8) or the theory of performance (Chambers *et al.*, 1989) wherein they try to keep their options open despite the very limited choices. Why their choice becomes relationship-based and one of sequential decision-making is illustrated below based on a story related by a resident.

If one village resident who is not a member of any of the village organizations decides to go into burlap (mat made from *abaca* fibre; *abaca* is a local plant similar to a banana plant) production, the first thing she will do is to make an inventory of the family's resources. Can her husband gather the *abaca* stalks? Can the children help in the stripping and in the drying of *abaca*, in making the twines and weaving? Will she have enough time to make burlap on top of her regular household activities? If she answers 'yes' to these questions, she then commits those resources to the planned activity. That is the first decision.

She then goes to a close friend or neighbour whom she thinks will provide her with the *abaca* stalks on credit. But because this person needs immediate cash for the stalks (otherwise his own family makes the burlap themselves), she is then accompanied to a middleman-friend in the village who can give her a loan to buy the stalks (or even provide her with the *abaca* on credit) but has to sell her burlap to this middleman for an agreed flexible price (depending on how much the middleman is able to sell the burlap to his buyers). She agrees to the arrangement, and that is decision two.

Later, in a time of emergency (for example, illness in the family), she discovers she can also borrow money from the middleman not only for purchase of *abaca* stalks but also for other domestic needs. So, she borrows extra money with the commitment that she will produce more burlap for the middleman. In the process, she actually commits more of her time and her family's resources to burlap production. That is decision three.

After several years, she hears of the launching of a burlap project by the village co-operative of which she is not a member. The project reportedly buys burlap at a better price. She approaches her friend again, who is a member of the co-operative, and explores the possibility of being involved in the project. After several conversations, she agrees to commit her burlap to the co-operative. Decision four.

Weeks later, she realizes she has cut off relations, but not friendship, with the middleman and now is unable to borrow money for emergencies or for purchase of *abaca* stalks. She cannot sell burlap to the co-operative because she does not have the raw materials. Unfortunately, she cannot get a loan from the co-operative because she is not a member. She is aware, though, that if she becomes a member, she could get the loan plus a greater possibility of being involved in other livelihood projects of the co-operative with support from development programmes of government organizations (GOs) and non-governmental organizations (NGOs). However, neither she nor her husband can commit any of their time to attend regular meetings of the co-operative once either of them becomes a member. Their eldest child is only 12 years old and is not in a position to join the organization. In short, she decides not to join the co-operative and resumes her business relations with the middleman. Decision five.

From there, the situation will be changing from time to time and, each time, the woman will make new decisions as a consequence of the situations and resources at hand. She is constantly pursuing her long-term plans as she lives by the day. Her friends and neighbours (who may not be in a position to tilt situations or policies in her favour) however, will always be instrumental in getting her involved in the new situations as a direct line of communication has been created between them.

The above case speaks clearly of the ensuing sequentiality of decisions in a relationship-based network. The other implication is that subsistence farmers resist innovations because accepting one means departing from a system that is efficient in minimizing the risk of a catastrophe for one that significantly increases this risk. For the co-operative, membership means a greater chance to earn more in an equitable set-up. The burlap weaver, however, sees membership as less time for weaving in order to attend to co-operative affairs and, therefore, a likely decrease in income. Her fifth decision conforms to Scott's (1976) subsistence ethic implying her action is based more on how the alternative can complicate or ease her problem of staying above the subsistence-level crisis.

Relationship-based networks

For a family (particularly the non-joiner in formal organizations) in Alimsog, there are three types of immediate relations through which outside contact is effected. These are the non-member relations, the member relations and relations outside the village. When membership or non-membership is mentioned, it is relative to ALIMDECO which is the most visible formally organized group in the village other than the *barangay* council.

The most frequently used relationship is that with people in the most immediate vicinity—whether these are neighbours, close relatives or close friends. In Alimsog, the closest neighbour is also likely to be a close relative and friend rolled into one. At the time of doing this field research, contact between and among non-member relations is most notable in *sitios* Inabuyan and Balete. This is for the simple reason that only one household each in Inabuyan and Balete had membership to ALIMDECO. The non-member relations prove very helpful when it comes to seeking immediate help for non-monetary needs like borrowing a non-motorized boat, *abaca* twines for burlap making or milled rice to be replaced later, and so on. However, when it comes to higher-order needs (for example, looking for markets for products or credit for farming needs), the non-member relations who have been approached are likely to do either of these two things. One, because they do not have the necessary contacts with people who may be of help, they will simply offer a listening and sympathetic ear, then some minor advice, without actually improving the situation; or, two, they take the issue to one of their close relations who may have membership of a formal group that can help. This would usually trigger a series of relationships that eventually lead to the support system. The support system can be either be a GO programme or NGO programme.

Non-member relations

One of the most common types of non-member relation contact in Alimsog is with the middlemen. These are residents or non-residents to whom the caught fish, the woven burlap (local matting material), the dried *copra*, and/or the dried *palay* (unhusked rice) are sold. There is a very special sort of friendship based on a business trust between the middlemen and the residents. The relationship is strengthened further by the fact that the middlemen are highly approachable and accessible in time of immediate monetary need. They provide credit without collateral but a verbal agreement that the borrower will sell his/her produce to them. The one drawback about contacting the middlemen in Alimsog is that, because transactions with them are very direct, one usually gets either a 'yes' or 'no' answer immediately, so chances of making further contacts are almost nil. One does not get into any network outside the village.

Admittedly, there are many middlemen charging usurious rates. There are also, however, good middlemen with whom the *suki* system is operational rather than the ill-famed patron–client ties. Though the debates on this sensitive issue are all still raging, there is one big concern that ALIMDECO has to address. That is, while the very existence of the co-operative is effectively marginalizing the middlemen/moneylenders, it is at the same time marginalizing the fisherfolk and farm workers' groups, if membership of ALIMDECO is any indication. In 1990, ALIMDECO had 29 associate and fully pledged members—none of whom belonged to the farm labourer category and only one to the fisherman category

(IIRR Albay Field Office, 1990). About the same year, there were more than 60 fisherfolk, 21 hired labourers and 126 people involved in services-related occupations in Alimsog (Cabria, 1991). These are the people who would be most attracted to the middlemen and to patron–client relationships.

Member relations and outside parties

In Alimsog, for higher-order and future needs (particularly of a monetary nature), a non-joiner of organizations is most likely to approach a close relation who is a member of an organized group in the village for help and advice. Usually, non-joiners expect that they will be referred to the organization or to the GO/NGO field staff collaborating with the organization, with the close relation acting on their behalf. This way, non-joiners get access to services (projects/programmes) of the organization and/or of the GO/NGO, which are normally open to all interested residents.

There is still a third kind of relation within the network that residents in Alimsog hold dear on which a lot of expectations are sometimes built. These relations are with people living outside Alimsog; they could be relatives, friends, patrons, researchers, students and/or simply strangers and visitors to the village who exude a friendly aura. Except for with relatives, contacts with these outside parties are usually by chance and once-in-a-while occurrences. Often, there is no fixed commitment or promise of assistance with this type of relation. Nevertheless, there is the encouraging thought that somehow, in the distant future, these relations may be of help to them. If not, it can be consolation enough that these people are sympathetic and neutral parties with whom they can air their concerns. Still, on occasions, these outsiders become instrumental in elevating the concerns of unspoken residents to the village association/council or to the outside support system to which they have ties.

Formal structure-based relationships

The village council, the village co-operative, GOs and NGOs are key points in the formal structures. Government-based support systems generally reach the resource-poor rural families through the village councils or through NGOs working in villages and engaged in community mobilization and organization. To date, government extension policies are geared towards planned co-operation with community-based organizations (Serrano, 1988). Because of this heavy emphasis on village associations as conduits for development programmes, the communication flow from the support system down to the village is likely to be limited to the active participants of the village association/council. Although the initiatives of the support systems are also expected to filter out even to the non-joiners because of personal ties, this will depend much on, first, the types of initiatives (projects/information/services) being passed on, and second, the strength of the relationship between the member and non-member families.

Social and infrastructure projects always affect the non-members because there are more than enough capital resources budgeted in them for member families and the existing manpower (membership) of the village association is not usually enough to complete the task within a specified period. This is in addition to the argument that such projects are to benefit the whole community.

The strength and openness of personal ties also largely determine how much of the support system assistance can filter out to non-members. Two instances in Alimsog illustrate this. In one case, an active member never tires of informing his non-member neighbour of the activities of the co-operative from which the neighbour may benefit whether or not she is a member—even if he is aware she is not terribly interested. In the second case, a non-member interested in obtaining a crop production loan from the co-operative got information from his relative (a member) that he could obtain the same loan by becoming an 'associate member'. He was given a copy of the notice testifying to this and he was supposed to post it in his neighbourhood. He did not post it, saying it was his copy and that his non-member neighbours would not be interested in it anyway.

There have been government agricultural credit programmes in the past which took into consideration the informal social structures in the villages. They have largely failed because they overlooked the fact that the intra-group relationship would change once it was brought into a legal or contractual framework— putting it on the level of purely an economic transaction.

Members of associations have, in general, a shorter path to the support systems relative to the non-joiners. On the one hand, people with a shorter path to the support system may see it as a means of getting the benefits or information first. And for a few with selfish motives, they can actually block the benefits or information from further filtering behind them. On the other hand, those farthest from the support systems may see the intervening ties as a shield to ward them off bureaucratic procedures and requirements without necessarily making them worse off. With these two views existing at the same time in the same place, it is no wonder that patron–client relationships have survived.

Towards expanding relationship-based networks

Because of resource limitations, it is absurd to think of the support systems giving equal emphasis and privileges to both joiners and non-joiners of formal organizations. To do so would not only be incompatible with current thinking about community organizing, but would also undermine the strength of this work. Strategically, there are two overlapping courses of action by which this dilemma might be handled. The first is to strengthen and expand personal networks beyond the village set-up. The second is the localization of information generation and dissemination by taking advantage of existing social settings and institutions. The second has more to do with the grounding of information within local experiences conveyed through informal social settings people are generally comfortable with—relative to the different roles they assume in the family and in the community.

Six proposals
Within the context of Alimsog, here are a few proposals that may help put on track the two courses of action suggested above. The proposals are endorsed from the perspective of a farm-family initiated extension wherein each family member, singly or in a group, effortlessly assumes roles in order to reach out to the support systems. These are also partly in recognition of the concepts of, first, the family as a corporate unit where family members act in concert and/or independently, with their actions continually being re-defined as members grow old (Paolucci *et al.*, 1977); and second, of looking at individual households as belonging to other corporate groupings (neighbourhood, kinship, church) which

carry with them patterns of access to resources (Feldstein and Poates, 1989). Here are six proposals.

○ Holding 'Sunday Clinics' by field staff in the market site on market days (Sundays) inasmuch as it is the best day and the best place to catch up with as many types of people as possible. The Sunday Clinic may be likened to establishing a *suki* type of relationship between the people and the extension service where the exchange is not in terms of merchandise and gossip but of agricultural services and information.

○ Complementing the planned 'Reading Centre' in Alimsog with letter-writing activities to information sources. This assumes that the Reading Centre will have many up-to-date newsletters and journals from both local and national development-oriented institutions. The reading community should then be encouraged to write letters of enquiry directly to the sources of information on topics that interest them. However, since many in Alimsog have not yet developed the habit of letter writing for such purposes because they think that they would not get a response anyway (plus the cost of mailing), the local organization may be of assistance. The ALIMDECO or the *barangay* council or the Sunday Clinic may receive the enquiries/letters for mailing. These groups can allocate a small budget for mailing expenses so they may be able to post the enquiries on behalf of the individual readers. People should also be ready to receive negative responses without feeling rejected. Otherwise, the letter-writing alternative faces a dead end. This continued personal contact, at least through letters, is important if ties of mutual exchange and friendship are to be established.

○ Orienting school assignments toward village concerns and involving students in links with the support systems. This may require special assignments or projects in history, science and mathematics. Even mathematics problems can be designed to make use of situations in the village, like calculation of kilograms of fish caught in a day or kilograms of *palay* (unhusked rice) harvested in two successive croppings, and so on. To keep up contact with those who send information materials to the Alimsog Reading Centre, older students may be encouraged to write to them using the English and Filipino language lessons on letter-writing.

○ Photographs can establish the 'symbolic connectedness' of villagers to other people, places and events. One resentment that some residents of Alimsog have for outsiders who take their pictures is that they never get to see the photographs. This is not that they demand to see the pictures but, like anyone else, they hope to know how they looked in them. Their having a copy of the photographs can symbolize their 'connectedness' to other people, places and events. Pictures can remind them of people and institutions that they may have access to for certain needs.

○ Getting people (including children) involved and interested in radio broadcasting and listening activities. Inasmuch as the most popularly used form of media in Alimsog is the radio, there must be a way in which it may be better utilized to bridge the gap between the village and the support systems. The suggestion of Fraser (1982) to encourage existing groups (co-operatives, village associations, women's and youth groups, and even children's groups or a combination of sectoral groups) to meet and discuss a regular broadcast put out specially for them can be one effective means of transferring information and building up relationships within the listening group. Local villagers, especially children, may even be made regular guest artists on the radio programmes (if someone can draft the appropriate scripts for them) to make it more attractive to local listeners. The occasional presence of extension workers, friends and/or guests from outside the village in the collective listening group may lead to more meaningful future collaboration.

o Encouraging more people from the support systems (particularly from the academic community and research stations) to attend major social functions in the villages. It may prove beneficial for Alimsog in the long run if the village can regularly invite or be introduced to students, researchers and others in their area whenever possible. Village fairs, *fiestas* (feasts of the patron saint) and other yearly social functions or special village events provide such opportunities as well as the renewal and reinforcing of ties of kinship and friendship (Simmons, 1974). On the part of the support systems, the notion that attendance of fieldworkers at village social functions, especially the *fiestas*, is purely a personal concern and not in any way part of official duties has to be re-thought. These social functions are good opportunity for the fieldworker to introduce colleagues in development work in a more relaxed setting while at the same time giving his colleagues the chance to see in a broader context how much of their efforts have been successful. The more contacts villagers have met personally, the more likely the possibility of them being reached by development programmes and the more confident they will feel to reach out.

All six proposals arise from a common conviction: extension work aimed at poor rural families needs to be personalized before it can achieve an acceptable and effective formalized set-up.

En route to 'kinship extension'

This chapter is not an argument against formal structures and organizations that have evolved through the years within the agricultural extension service. The suggested emphasis on working around individuals within groups, instead of working around groups to create opportunities for the 'deprived sector' to reach out, is not to discredit the contributions of and need for formal organizations. It is to recognize the unique contributions and needs of individuals in organizations. There will always be a need for formal organizations. There is also, however, a need for 'traditional structures' if deprived groups are to gain entry into the formal structures. It is in this respect that the complementary value to extension services of a relationship-based network can be developed.

Fictive kinship and friendship ties present themselves as options to meeting a major and recurring concern in extension—strengthening links and communication between and among the rural poor and the various support systems. This, however, differs from 'means to effective extension' in that the relationship these ties offer is an end in itself.

The potential value of kinship and friendship attributes in strengthening links relative to extension is evident in the relationship-based network systems that often exist in poor rural communities. It is a highly supportive and interactive system based on family, kinship and friendship ties cast more in moral, rather than legal, terms. This moral nature of the relationship puts communication among kin and friends on a highly interpersonal basis. This makes kinship-tie attributes the more relevant as many agricultural extension people are now proclaiming the need for improved interpersonal communication with their clients.

Improved interpersonal communication may only be achieved if the relationship between the people and extension staff becomes an end in itself rather than simply being a means to implement programmes. Some extension projects have failed in this respect by forcing the issue of formalizing village organizations, or, in taking advantage of indigenous/peer groupings have inadvertently over-emphasized legal obligations at the expense of moral obligations (which have the higher value in Philippine rural communities). There has been too much emphasis on how formalized social organizations can positively affect the development of the poor using successful formal organizations as models. Little, however, has been done to analyse critically how these successful formal organizations came into being. Replication of the success stories is more a result of the resultant structures than of the adaptive process that led to the structures. For example, one has yet to hear in community organizing work an acknowledgement pointing to real and fictive kinship ties as a strong base for a successful formal organization despite its having a membership comprised essentially of kin. As such, many cash-poor villagers view formal organizations/ (extension projects) as largely a 'means' to alleviate their economic plight and likewise base their decisions to join/participate in them on that perspective. Those who decide not to join see the relationship as rewarding only at the initial stage when their economic needs can be met (usually through credit and hand-outs). They see the relationship as unpleasant in later stages, with the prospect of regular meetings they have not conditioned themselves to attend, or with the possibility of not being able to repay loans. This usually results in non-joiners of formal organizations being marginalized and unreached by extension programmes that emphasize organized constituencies.

With a complementary system based on kinship and friendship attributes, however, such drawbacks may be minimized. This is because friendship and kinship organizations are both means and ends. They are generally rewarding relationships throughout one's life, not only for being the means to gain access to minor services and small-scale needs but more so for their interpersonal and supportive moral nature. But inasmuch as the resources in these ties are very limited among poor communities, such ties may need to be strongly complemented by formal organizations which can bring the people's needs to the organized bureaucracy for administrative expediency. Each family member and support system has a role to play, and activities to undertake, in developing and maintaining this type of link. The six proposals endorsed earlier form an initial list of possible family-focused initiatives towards this end. Still, the support system should be able to devise schemes wherein strong personal groups or networks may be recognized and be given some of the privileges available to formal organizations. Associate membership as practised by some associations is a step in this direction. 'Organizational sponsorship' is another possible option. Organizational sponsorship means a formal organization acts as a guarantor or sponsor for a strong informal group (for example, a kin group/ network) that wishes to negotiate with the support system or other formal institutions on a legitimate basis. This, in a way, is a variation of the *padrino* system in the Philippines (blamed for acts of corruption and nepotism). In the *padrino* system, a person in authority extends favour to an individual or group (often friends and kin) over a possibly more qualified individual group by ignoring or circumventing policies. Proposing organizational sponsorship, however, is not to seek preferential rights that have unjust implications but simply an endorsement that can either be accepted or rejected based on merits of the endorsed party. It is more a strengthening of the formal and informal groups interface.

Friendship and kinship are not new to extension work. They may even be as old as extension practice itself but have been kept aside because of the fear of 'breeding nepotism'. People everywhere are now aware of this danger—thanks to the past decades of political history in the Philippines which have been tainted with many examples of nepotism. In this new decade, people can more readily apply the only sanction inherent in friendship/kinship ties—the withdrawal of ties—if one party abuses or exploits the implied reciprocity in the relationship. Friendship and kinship ties within extension programmes can now do more good than harm for the cash-poor farm families. If the current extension programmes are sincere in treating people as equals, co-learners and partners in the development process, then why not develop the relationship through development-focused friendship and kinship ties?

Other than the initial six proposals, this chapter has not endorsed any framework or model in establishing relationship-based networks relevant to extension practice. The proposals imply the need for a conscious recognition of the value of friendship and kinship ties and their attributes to extension through a gradual and iterative process. It will be counter-productive at this stage to assume that 'relationship-based extension' can be structured to fit a general extension framework and adapted to specific situations later on. It will be counter-productive because personal ties are particular moral relationships that need to be treated as an end in themselves and not a means for the convenience of extension and technology adoption. Extension practice and personal ties, therefore, have to be treated as two separate but complementing goals. One is not merely a means to achieve the other; both are means and ends in themselves for a professionally and personally fulfilling life. The building up of relationship-based networks is, therefore, a call not necessarily for the encouragement of peoples' participation in extension programmes, but for the participation of extension in people's life-long activities.

Note

1. Condensed version of an M. Sc. Thesis submitted in December 1992 to the School of Agriculture and Rural Development, University of Western Sydney–Hawkesbury, Richmond, NSW, Australia (The author wishes to acknowledge the support and critique given by Dr Robert J. Fisher in the development of this chapter).

References

Bawden, R. (1989), *Towards Action Research Systems*, Richmond, NSW, Australia: UWS–Hawkesbury.

Cabria, R. (1991), Compilation of unpublished socio-economic reports on *Barangay Alimsog*, Sto. Domingo Municipal Hall, Albay, Philippines.

Chambers, R. *et al.* (eds) (1989), *Farmer First: Farmer Innovation and Agricultural Research*, London: Intermediate Technology Publications.

Feldstein, H. and Poates, S.V. (eds) (1989), *Working Together (Gender Analysis in Agriculture)*, Connecticut: Kumarian Press.

Fox, R. (1967), *Kinship and Marriage: An Anthropological Perspective*, London: Penguin Books Ltd.

Fraser, C. (1982), 'Radio Listening Clubs: the Pros and Cons', in *RRDC Bulletin No. 16*, December 1982, London: University of Reading, 13–15.

Goody, J. (ed.) (1973), *The Character of Kinship*, Cambridge: Cambridge University Press.

Hart, D.V. (1977), *Compadrinazgo: Ritual Kinship in the Philippines*, Illinois: Northern Illinois University Press.

Heraud, B. (1979), *Sociology in the Professions*, London: Open Books Publishing Ltd.

Ibus. A. (1991), 'Farmers As Good Managers and Cautious Gamblers', in *ILEIA Newsletter* 1 & 2/91, special issue, 55–6.

IIRR (1988), LRM Project Beneficiary Participation Component, Nov. 1986–June 1988, IIRR: Philippines.

IIRR–Albay Field Office (1990), 'Household Participation in PO's', *Quarterly Project Reports*, Philippines: IIRR.

Jiggins, J. and de Zeeuw, H. (1990), 'Participatory Technology Development for Sustainable Agriculture', draft chapter for *Farming for the Future: Indicating a Path to Low External Input and Sustainable Agriculture*, Leusden: ILEIA.

Jocano, F. (1982), *The Ilocanos: An Ethnography of Family and Community Life in the Ilocos Region*, Philippines: Asian Center, University of the Philippines.

Morais, R.S. (1981), *Social Relations in a Philippine Town*, Illinois: Center for Southeast Asian Studies, University of Northern Illinois.

Quisumbing, L.R. (1990), 'Philippine Cultural Values and Development', in C.D. Ortigas, *Group Process and the Inductive Method*, Philippines: Ateneo de Manila University Press, 148–54.

Rhoades, R. (1984), *Breaking New Ground (Agricultural Anthropology)*, Peru: International Potato Center.

Roling, N. (1988), *Extension Science (Information Systems in Agricultural Development)*, Cambridge: Cambridge University Press.

Rosenhead, J. (ed.) (1989), *Rational Analysis for a Problematic World (Problem Structuring Methods for Complexity, Uncertainty and Conflict)*, England: John Wiley & Sons.

Scott, J.C. (1976), *The Moral Economy of the Peasants*, Connecticut: Yale University Press.

Scott, J.C. (1977), 'Patron-Client Politics in Southeast Asia', in *Friends, Followers and Factions: A Reader in Political Clientelism*, University of California Press, 123–46; reprinted from *American Political Science Review* 66 (1972): 91–113.

Serrano, S.C. (1988), *Extension Policies, Methodologies and Applied Development Support Communication*, Philippines: Agricultural Training Institute.

Simmons, R.A. (1974), *Palca and Pucara: A Study of the Effects of Revolution on Two Bolivian Haciendas*, California: University of California Press.

Szanton, Ma. C.B. (1970), *A Right to Survive: Subsistence Marketing in a Lowland Philippine Town*, Pennsylvania: Pennsylvania State University Press.

Taylor, R.B. (1973), *Introduction to Cultural Anthropology*, Needham, MA.: Allyn and Bacon Inc.

Woog, R.A. (1988), *The Evolution of Extension in Australia from a Theoretical Context*, in *Improving Agricultural Extension in Australia*, AgPack No. ex112, Hawkesbury: University of Western Sydney, 22–8.